Created and Directed by Hans Höfer

INSIGHT GUIDES
FRANCE

Executive Editor: Andrew Eames
Project Editor: Anne Roston
Photography by Catherine Karnow and others
Editorial Director: Brian Bell

HOUGHTON MIFFLIN COMPANY

APA PUBLICATIONS

France

Second Edition
© **1994 APA PUBLICATIONS (HK) LTD**
All Rights Reserved
Printed in Singapore by Höfer Press Pte Ltd

Distributed in the United States by:	Distributed in Canada by:	Distributed in the UK & Ireland by:	Worldwide distribution enquiries:
Houghton Mifflin Company	**Thomas Allen & Son**	**GeoCenter International UK Ltd**	**Höfer Communications Pte Ltd**
222 Berkeley Street	390 Steelcase Road East	The Viables Center, Harrow Way	38 Joo Koon Road
Boston, Massachusetts 02116-3764	Markham, Ontario L3R 1G2	Basingstoke, Hampshire RG22 4BJ	Singapore 2262
ISBN: 0-395-68233-9	ISBN: 0-395-68233-9	ISBN: 9-62421-037-3	ISBN: 9-62421-037-3

ABOUT THIS BOOK

With an excess of ambition, perhaps, this book attempts to encapsulate the nation about which everyone has a different opinion. Consider, for example, just a few *bons mots* delivered by its neighbours across the English Channel. "France is the most civilised country in the world and doesn't care who knows it," said writer John Gunther. But Shakespeare described it as a "dog-hole", Joseph Addison accused it of having "infected all the Nations of Europe with its Levity" and Tobias Smollett declared that "they have not even the implements of cleanliness in this country." From America, Mark Twain added: "France has neither winter, summer, nor morals – apart from these drawbacks, it is a fine country."

The dirt that the world's critics like to fling at France just doesn't seem to stick, however, because it remains Europe's biggest tourist attraction – big both in terms of its size as Europe's largest country and in terms of the number of annual visitors, which, at 56 million, falls just a million short of equalling the total French population.

The reasons for such popularity are plain to see from a quick perusal of this book: France's diversity of landscape is overwhelming, from swamps to deserts, from glacier-covered Alps to Mediterranean plains; its monuments are among the most famous in the world; its arts are of the top quality, and its cuisine is unsurpassable. What's more, the country's cultural influence is universal.

All these facts made France an essential addition to the collection of travel titles created by Apa Publications, a truly international publishing operation which combines its own proven expertise in producing world-beating guidebooks with the first-hand knowledge of local authors and photographers. Not surprisingly, *Insight Guide: France* has become one of the best-sellers in the 180-strong series.

Nowhere stands still, of course, and, to keep abreast of France's changing face, this edition has been treated to a top-to-toe revision, with new text, new photographs and a fresh, new approach. This has been provided by a panoply of contributors, some British, some American, some living in France, some realists and some committed Francophiles.

Coping with Change

This book builds on the original *Insight Guide: France*, edited under the expert guidance of editor **Anne Roston**, at the time a resident of France. Now back in New York where she works as an editor and newspaper contributor, Roston has lived all over the US as well as in Greece, Mexico and Finland. She also edited *Insight Guide: Provence*.

Roston asked **Catherine Karnow** to handle the majority of the photography. Born and raised largely in the Orient, Karnow, now an *Insight Guides* regular, has worked in Scandinavia, Great Britain and the European continent, Japan, the Caribbean and the United States. Jobs held with *Paris Match*, *Le Point* and Magnum Photos helped give her a special understanding of France.

The history section was written by **Ted Widmer**, an American of French parentage who has a Harvard degree in French history. His chapter on the French has been supplemented by **Mary Deschamps**, a French journalist who writes in English.

Grace Coston, an American who now has a translation agency in Paris, contributed

   Coston

Roston   Karnow   Widmer   Coston   Morley

extensively to the Places section with chapters on Paris, Île de France, and the Loire region. Similarly prolific in this section was **Marguerite Morley**, like Coston an American married to a Frenchman and living in Paris. In this book she wrote about the eastern areas of Champagne, Lorraine, Alsace, Burgundy and the Rhône, as well as Bordeaux, Limousin and the Auvergne.

John Wain, the British poet and novelist, wrote about northern France. **John Smith**, a Texan who now lives in Paris, wrote about the Côte d'Azur and Corsica. **François Dunoyer de Segonzac**, a Franco-American who lives in southern France and leads kayak trips and skiing expeditions, penned the section on the southwest, while **Rodger Goodson**, a freelance author living in Geneva, put together the chapter on the Alps.

The New Recruits

Considerable new expertise was brought to bear on the original edition of this book under the direction of **Andrew Eames**, Insight Guides' London-based executive editor, aided by **Rosemary Bailey**, the editor of several regional French *Insight Guides*. Bailey helped restructure the contents and updated coverage of the southwest and the Côte d'Azur.

Among the new contributors are **Diana Geddes**, a British journalist who has lived in Paris for more than a decade and writes in this book about France's fascination with technology; **Susan Bell**, who works in the Paris editorial office of the London *Times*, added much new material to the arts chapter as well as a new box on cleaning up Paris. She also revised the Île de France section.

Philip and **Mary Hyman**, consumer writers of some repute living in Paris, wrote the new chapter on wine and reworked the coverage of Poitou Charentes and Burgundy. **Jim Keeble**, a recent Oxford university graduate who launched himself into travel publishing with his own book on Provence, tackled the new chapter on EuroDisney with enthusiasm, as well as reworking the Paris and Provence chapters.

Peter Graham, an Auvergne-based prize-winning food writer and veteran of several regional French *Insight Guides*, produced a new chapter on cuisine as well as updating the Auvergne coverage. **Jill Adam**, who also worked on several of the regional guides, combined her expertise and experience to put together a new Travel Tips section.

Very valuable time and expertise was brought to bear on reworking the various regional chapters as follows: in France **Rex Grizell**, author of several of his own books on France, tackled the Rhône and the Alps; **John Ardagh**, best known for his book *France Today*, checked the eastern wine chapters. In the UK, **Martin Symington**, author of a book on the Loire Valley, updated the information on that region, and **Nigel Tisdall**, a British travel writer and regular *Insight Guide* contributor, made appropriate changes to this book's coverage of northern France.

New photography for this edition came from two other regulars, **Bill Wassman** and **Lyle Lawson**. The new whole was proofread and indexed by **Carole Mansur**, while production was supervised by **Jill Anderson**.

Eames   *Bell*   *Keeble*   *Graham*   *Adam*

E. MOTSCH
42 Av. L'ALMA
et
68 Rue François
PARIS

History & Features

Places

Maps

TRAVEL TIPS

Compiled by Jill Adam

**For detailed information
see page 321**

EUROPE'S OLDEST NATION

Neatly symmetrical – almost hexagonal – in shape, France, the world's fourth richest country, is Western Europe's largest nation, although it would fit quite easily into the state of Texas. It is a rural country, with the population of 57 million thinly spread through the land, at an average of 104 people per square kilometre (the UK averages 240 per sq. km). Some 56 percent of the land is farmed and 25 percent under forest. The nation's largest industry is the business of food production.

There's one huge and famous urban area: almost 9 million people live in and around Paris, one of the world's finest and favourite destinations, but the second and third French cities – Lyon and Marseille – are very much smaller, with populations of 1.2 and 1.1 million respectively.

France is also Europe's oldest nation, existing in its present form since the 15th century. The nation's boundaries are largely natural ones, with the English Channel to the north, the Atlantic to the west, the Pyrenees and the Mediterranean to the south, and the Alps, the Jura mountains and the Rhine to the east. These all contrive to make the nation almost insular, and the overwhelmingly-Catholic French are not perhaps as cosmopolitan as other European countries which have more openly shared borders. And yet this nation has immense cultural influence on the rest of the world, and the existence of several minority languages within France – Breton, Basque, Catalan, Elsassdutch and Italian – suggest something of the extraordinary variety that is to be found within its borders.

Despite its insularity, France has 56 million visitors a years, making it the most popular tourist destination in Europe. These visitors are attracted by its superb landscape and historic cities, its unsurpassable food and wine, its unique culture and elegant shopping. And yet the French have a reputation for lack of interest in tourists. This seeming indifference stems from a sense of pride in their own national identity, which they perceive as under assault from the cultural invasion that comes hand in hand with tourism. But don't misinterpret this pride as hostility: indeed, in a recent survey, 82 percent of the nation said they would be happy to act as a guide for tourists, and 54 percent said they would be happy to have tourists to lunch.

Whether you are one of the fortunate 82 percent, or the even luckier 54 percent, you are sure to enjoy France. The nation that gave us the word "elite" is very, very special.

Preceding pages: Spring ploughing in the Vaucluse; café society on the Côte d'Azur; picking grapes in Bordeaux; skiing in the Alps. **Left**, the face of an elegant nation.

Considering the English Channel, Atlantic, Pyrenees, Mediterranean, Alps and Rhine as preordained natural boundaries, the French often compare their plot of earth to a divinely shaped hexagon that absorbs and unites all the different parts of Europe. Indeed, France is at once a northern and southern European country, connecting the cold Atlantic Ocean with the warm Mediterranean Sea, and the empyreal Pyrenees with Flemish flatlands. A detailed map of France, using different colours to describe regional characteristics, would bear a striking resemblance to an Impressionist painting.

The French tend to lose themselves in praise of their country's proportional symmetry. Recognising disparate attributes and uniting them in a way that makes such good sense, they see in the shape of their country a national character that may be quirky and erratic, but is nonetheless supremely ordered.

At 550,980 sq. km (212,741 sq. miles), France is the 37th largest country in the world. It escaped the gouging glaciers of the Ice Age. Its landscape, therefore, is generally mellow and pastoral with gentle hills and plateaus, carved by deep river valleys. Imposing mountains lie only along the eastern and southern frontiers. It is a remarkably rural nation, with the population spread thinly over huge areas, which is perhaps why French farmers have such political power.

The rock and its rolling: Later geophysical development in the large southeastern Garonne region left profound impressions between younger and older hills, providing the perfect conditions for the formation of valuable minerals as well as oil and natural gas. To add to France's fortune, the existence of an extensive network of rivers, like the Garonne, promises an eternal fertility unmatched by other countries; in fact, France possesses the highest percentage of arable land in Western Europe.

To the northwest lie Brittany and Normandy, each with independent peoples and traditions dating back millennia. The thatched

huts, bent apple trees and locally produced cheeses and ciders of Normandy contribute to its popularity as a place to visit. Many painters, understandably, have been drawn to the gentle green countryside, dotted by black and white cows under a dramatic and often stormy sky. Further west, the craggy coastline and harsh landscape of Brittany still conjure up the druidical presence of its original Celtic population, although today's descendants are relatively unwarlike fishermen. Particularly intriguing are the mysteri-

ous fields of megaliths and the pink granite rocks of the Corniche Bretonne.

To the northeast are the old provinces of Alsace and Lorraine. The Rhineland is the least well-defined of the six borders of the Hexagon, and the result has been an unending series of nasty disputes between France and Germany ever since these two countries first came into existence. Alsace is especially valuable because its mines have turned France into the world's third largest producer of iron ore. The city of Strasbourg, which houses the European Parliament, resembles a German town with its architecture and taste for beer and sauerkraut, but is nonetheless defiantly

Preceding pages: Spring in Gascony. Left, the Atlantic coast at the Pointe du Raz. Right, Aquitaine agriculture.

French. Indeed, the paragon of French patriotism, Joan of Arc, hailed from neighbouring Lorraine, although she was martyred by the English in Rouen.

Not far south rise the gentle Jura mountains and below that the French Alps, which stretch all the way down to the Alpes Maritimes and Côte d'Azur. The icy white peak of Mont Blanc, at 4,810 metres (15,780 ft), is the highest mountain in Europe.

The subdued Loire valley, dug out by France's longest river (980 km/609 miles), is one of the country's chief tourist attractions. The splendid châteaus and gardens of Touraine still boast the glory of the *Ancien Régime* and its aristocratic pleasures. Di-

rectly south is the enormous Massif Central, which lies in the heart of the country and supplies France with much of its grain. The strange *puys* of Auvergne (steep conical hills, caused by volcanic eruption during the earth's formation) contrast pleasantly with the rolling hills, plateaus and deep river valleys of neighbouring Périgord and Limousin, just to its west.

That the particularly lush Dordogne river valley, in Périgord, has been alluring mankind for thousands upon thousands of years is evidenced by the prehistoric cave paintings found in its grottoes, particularly the Lascaux cave complex.

Further south still is the sunny Midi. The landscape here, with its reds, yellows and browns, is very different again, with sun-baked clay buildings and a slower pace of life. Not that even the south is visually uniform. The wide, yellow fields that seem to stretch forever, the even rows of plane trees and charming red towns of Languedoc meld into the impossibly verdant Pyrenean mountain range towards the Spanish border, or the Cévennes and Ardèche national parks away to the east.

There is an indefinable languor about all the old southern cities like Montpellier, Toulouse, Nîmes and Perpignan. The exceptions are the bustling seaport of Marseille, the jet-set towns of the Côte d'Azur and, of course, the cosmopolitan principality of Monaco.

The Mediterranean island of Corsica not only *seems* like a separate country to the northerner, it would even become one if the independence movement had its way. Its barren landscape, steep cliffs and mountains make it a difficult destination but an interesting one for the traveller.

Many French towns and provinces are most famous for the splendid wines that bear their name. Yet that delightfully bubbly stuff is only one of Champagne's patriotic offerings; the entire northeast is a major industrial region producing coal, oats and sugar beet. Similarly, the long river valley running parallel to the eastern frontier and connecting the Saône with the Rhône river, not only cradles the vineyards of Burgundy and towns like Beaujolais, it also aids communication between the north and south.

Eye of the hurricane: Paris has been called everything from a whore by Henry Miller, to "one of the most noble ornaments of the world" by Montaigne. It is certainly the centre of everything French and the nexus of French transport (all distances are measured from the square in front of Notre Dame Cathedral). It is the world's fashion capital; it is revolutionary in its grand arts and architectural projects, its museums and galleries, but it also has one of the best preserved city centres in Europe. It also has a distinctive population – stylish, intellectual and difficult – and very different to the rural French. But more of that later.

Left, heading up into the Alps. **Right**, reflections in the Dordogne.

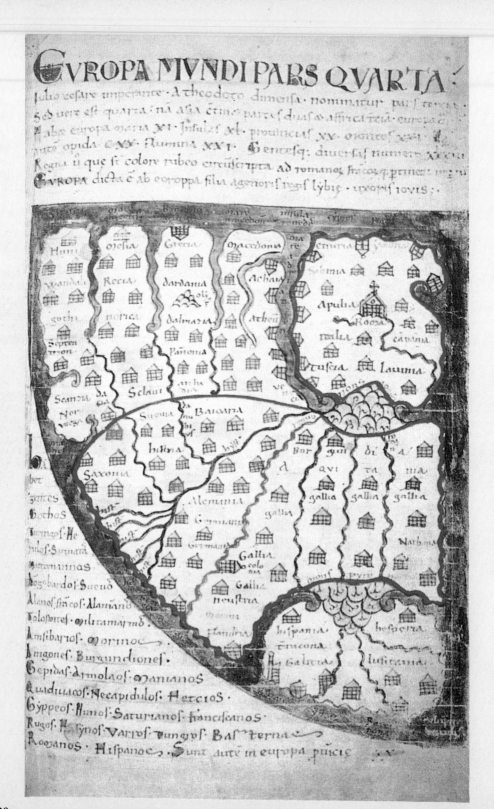

FROM THE EARLIEST MAN TO JOAN OF ARC

There is much evidence that France has been inhabited for many millennia. Anthropologists have discovered in the southern part of the country human fossils that date back at least 35,000 years. The splendid Lascaux cave drawings of the Dordogne region suggest that these earliest tenants of early France even had a strong propensity to create art.

After the glaciers receded from Europe, around 450 BC, France was populated from the east by a large influx of Celtic peoples. These were the legendary Gauls, or Galli, celebrated in every French language classroom from Paris to Martinique as *nos ancêtres les Gaulois* (our ancestors the Gauls). Renowned for long hair and fighting naked in battle – and for cartoon heroes Asterix and Obelix – the Gauls were a strong and independent people who left an indelible stamp on the French character. To this day, if nowhere else, their savage spirit is commemorated by the throat-burning and omnipresent cigarettes, Gauloises, that bear their name.

The southern part of the country, meanwhile, received the attention of the classical civilisations. The coast was hellenised by Greek merchants who founded the flourishing port of Massilia (Marseille) around 600 BC. In 121 BC the Roman Senate assumed a protectorate over the region, expanding its influence into Provence. Then in 58 BC, the Gallic tribes were invaded by an ambitious Roman proconsul seeking prestige through conquest, Julius Caesar. Ostensibly, he aimed to protect the lucrative land route between Spain and Italy for the purpose of trade. The war dragged on a bit, and the Gauls, under the famed Vercingetorix, put up a brave fight, but in the end Caesar triumphed.

The Roman occupation of Gaul brought such refinements as roads, architecture and urbanisation, especially in the southern Midi, Nîmes and Arles. Lyon became a capital of sorts, and the French language began to develop from Celtic and Latin. On the Seine sprung up a small town called Lutetia ("Mudville" in Latin), that would someday grow to be the great metropolis of Paris.

Preceding pages: Lascaux cave paintings. **Left,** Medieval map puts Burgundy at Europe's centre.

Attracted by its relative peace and prosperity, many "barbarian" peoples migrated to Roman Gaul from the 3rd to 5th centuries. Among these were the Franks (whence France derived its name), the Burgundians, the Goths (Visi and Ostro), the badly behaved Vandals, and the Alan. In 451, the growing town of Lutetia narrowly escaped total destruction by Attila the Hun, through the intervention of its patron saint, Genevieve. In the 5th and 6th centuries Britons from Cornwall and Wales emigrated, giving the peninsula of Brittany its name.

The incoming barbarian presence began to undermine flagging Roman authority and, in 486, a Frankish king, Clovis, attacked and defeated the Gallo-Romans at Soissons. He consolidated his power by defeating the Alemanni at Tolbiac in 496 and the Visigoths near Poitiers in 507. Converting to Christianity and moving his capital to Paris (507), Clovis was an important precursor of the French state, which he called "Francia". His descendants, however, were weak leaders, and when Charles Martel led the French troops to victory over the invading Muslims at Poitiers (732), the groundwork was laid for a new dynasty. His son, Pepin the Short (whose wife was called Big-footed Bertha), crowned himself King of the Franks, officially beginning the Carolingian succession.

Emperor Charlemagne: Pepin's offspring was the famous Charlemagne, whose papal coronation at Rome in 800 created the Holy Roman Empire. Charlemagne shrewdly doubled his domain to include what later became Germany, by fighting the pagans of western Europe in the name of Christianity. He is also known for unifying the Franks and Gallo-Romans under his leadership and encouraging education in his court at Aix-la-Chapelle. One result of the latter was the *Chanson de Roland*, an epic description of a brave knight's death in the Pyrenees after the battle of Roncevaux. This work traditionally marks the conception of both French literature and the chivalrous ideal of a *douce France* worthy of self-sacrifice.

The problem of succession plagued Charlemagne as it had Clovis, and in 843 the Treaty of Verdun divided the empire into three, with the French portion going to his grandson Charles the Bald. The dynasty lost further prestige when, in 877, it allowed a king by the name of Louis the Stammerer to reign. Matters worsened in 911 when King Charles the Simple was forced to give Normandy and his daughter to Rollo and the invading Vikings from the north.

From this central weakness evolved a complicated feudal system of local authority that essentially reduced the king's jurisdiction to the Île-de-France region encircling Paris. In 987, after Louis the Sluggard died from falling off his horse, the Count of Paris Hugh Capet ended this ill-starred succession by declaring himself king. Eight hundred and

six years later, his descendant Louis XVI was addressed as "Citizen Louis Capet" before his execution.

Religious fervour inspired the erection of some of France's most impressive monuments. The Romanesque church at Mont-St-Michel was built from 1024 to 1144. France accommodated the rise of monasticism with two of the greatest orders: the Benedictines at Cluny and the Cistercians at Cîteaux. Although it was destroyed during the French Revolution, the abbey church at Cluny was the largest of its kind until the construction of St Peter's in Rome.

French participation in the Crusades (1096–

1291) bolstered nationalism (*Gloria Dei per Francos*, or the Glory of God through the French, was the motto of French crusaders) and worldliness, and the Romanesque style was strongly influenced by Eastern architecture. The 1066 invasion of England also expanded French influence and marks the last time England was occupied, although strictly speaking this was more the result of of Norman than French foreign policy.

French fortune was checked, however, by the 1152 marriage of Eleanor of Aquitaine to England's Henry II, and his consequent possession of this huge chunk of France. The accession of Philip II (Augustus) to the throne in 1180 greatly strengthened the monarchy, and his victory at Bouvines in 1214 helped win back from England some of its French possessions (including parts of Normandy, Poitou, Anjou and Touraine) as well as some sense of a national identity. It is said that this victory caused seven days and nights of dancing in Paris. Philip greatly improved the status of his capital by advancing the construction of the Notre Dame cathedral (1163–1320), the University of Paris (founded in 1120), and the Louvre fortress.

In 1253 Robert de Sorbon established the Sorbonne. The growth of cities and universities was complementary, and signalled a shift away from the dominance of monasteries and feudalism. New rational thinkers like Pierre Abélard emerged, although the castration he received for tutoring his student Héloïse a bit too affectionately shows the precariousness of the urban intellectual's position. Nevertheless, his example also proves the zeal with which the French pursued scholarship and romance. Concomitant with the growth of cities was the construction of majestic Gothic cathedrals from the 12th century on. Those at Chartres (1194–1260), Rouen, Reims and Amiens are among the most impressive buildings in the world.

The monarchy and kingdom grew stronger under forceful leaders such as Louis IX (St Louis, 1226–70), who established the Parliament, built Sainte-Chapelle and fought the infidel; and Philip IV (the Fair, 1285–1314). Yet France remained a confusing hodgepodge of independent duchies for some time. The southern region of Languedoc suffered vigorous repression at the hands of northerners angered by the Albigensian and Waldensian heresies. Languedoc was so-called because the word for yes in the Provençal language was "oc" as opposed to the "oïl" (forerunner of the modern French oui) used in the northern "Languedoil". *Langue de*, of course, means tongue of. Interestingly, Provençal has survived to this day.

The Hundred Years' War: This war actually lasted from 1337 to 1453, but the 116 Years' War has a harsher ring. It was a long and protracted struggle to remove the English presence in France. Supported by the truculent Burgundians, the English tried to get a continental foothold, and it was not until 1558 that they were finally kicked out of Calais. Indeed, it was not until 1802 that the British sovereigns relinquished the title "King

Battle of Agincourt: In 1415, the English army under Henry V, composed largely of archers and light infantry, routed the more numerous but less mobile French at Agincourt. Seven years later, when Charles VI died, the French crown was awarded to his grandson, the English King Henry VI, rather than the French Dauphin. The tide of French affairs seemed at its lowest ebb when a peasant girl from Lorraine appeared on the scene, Joan of Arc. Inspired by an angelic vision, she led the French troops to raise the siege of Orleans and crown the Dauphin king at Reims in 1429. She was captured by the English and burned at Rouen in 1431, but Joan's defiant patriotism illustrated the peo-

of France and England". Internal matters were complicated by the decimating Black Death (1337–50) and by the so-called Babylonian Captivity (1309–78) when the papal seat was transferred to Avignon to escape the petty intrigues of Rome. Then, to worsen matters, Charles VI (son of Charles the Wise) began to go insane in 1392. Instead of being able to temper the growing conflict between the dukes of Burgundy and the dukes of Orléans, in his idiocy he only increased their bitterness.

ple's growing sense of national identity. The words spoken at her trial, *Dieu enverra victoire aux Français* (God will send victory to the French), inspired the nation. The end of the war in 1453 essentially marks the end of the medieval period.

The reign of shrewd Louis XI (1461–83) prepared the way for the French Renaissance, eliminating much of the opposition to royal authority and adding Maine, Provence and Burgundy to the realm. With this, most of present-day France was united, apart from the duchy of Brittany – and its annexation was soon enabled by the 1491 marriage of Anne of Brittany to Charles VIII.

Left, Héloïse and Abélard. **Above**, Joan of Arc, the Iron Maiden martyred by the English.

LUDOV. XIV. D. G. FRANC. ET NAVAR. REX CHRISTIANISS.

Ludovico Magno

The 16th century brought important changes to France in almost every area. The discovery and absorption of the Italian Renaissance inspired great artistic activity at the courts of Francis I (1515–47) and Henry II (1547–59). Leonardo da Vinci himself spent his final years at the royal château of Amboise in the Loire valley, and writers such as the poet Ronsard, the essayist Montaigne and the bawdy comedian Rabelais all contributed to the growth of French literature. Explorer Jacques Cartier (and later Samuel de Champlain) carried the fleur-de-lis (symbol of France) into the North American wilderness. The reformed teachings of Martin Luther and John Calvin took hold, especially in the south of France. Even more important was the general rise in knowledge, particularly outside the aristocracy and church.

The latter part of the 16th century was marred by fierce religious wars between the Protestants, called Huguenots, and the Catholics, culminating in the St Bartholomew's Day massacre (1572), when thousands of Protestants were slaughtered by royal troops as they prayed. The blame for this has been laid on Catherine de Medicis, the scheming Florentine who exerted power through her husband Henry II and her sons, Francis II, Charles IX and Henry III.

A strange sequence of deaths and assassinations among Catholic rivals to the throne actually brought the crown to the Protestant Henry of Navarre (Henry IV), destined to be one of France's greatest kings. To appease the worried citizenry, he converted to Catholicism with the memorable declaration that "Paris is worth a mass." The womanising Henry, whose tongue had been sprinkled with wine and garlic at baptism to give him proper spirit, endeared himself to France with his leadership and boisterous behaviour. He declared there should be a chicken in every pot, and improved the religious climate with the Edict of Nantes (1598), granting some tolerance to the Protestants. All France mourned when he was stabbed to death in 1610 by the fanatic Ravaillac.

Left, Louis XIV, the Sun King. **Right**, Cardinal Richelieu, man of God and money.

The rigorous Richelieu: The tender age at succession of Louis XIII (1610–43) made his reign vulnerable to the wily machinations of interlopers such as Cardinal Richelieu, a humourlessly strong-minded man who got his daily exercise jumping over the furniture of his apartments. Richelieu, nonetheless, did much to strengthen the central authority of the monarchy. Indeed, the combination of royal power and longevity that characterised the 17th and 18th centuries led this period to be known as the Age of Absolutism.

As Grand Master of Navigation and Commerce, Richelieu also bolstered France's mercantile status, expanded its American holdings and founded the Académie Française (1653). At the same time, the wars and intrigues pursued by Richelieu caused great misery among the people. The Thirty Years' War (1618–48) was expensive and inconclusive, and Richelieu ended the tolerance of Henry IV with the seige of the Huguenot city of La Rochelle.

The death of Louis XIII left his five-year-old son Louis XIV on the throne. Destined to rule longer than any king of France, his reign began somewhat inauspiciously with a regency presided over by his mother, Anne of Austria and Richelieu's successor, Cardinal Mazarin. The nobility sought to regain its former power during the rebellion of the Fronde (1648–53), but was ultimately subdued. Yet, in spite of these difficulties, the reign of the *Roi-Soleil* (Sun King) marks the apogee of the French monarchy, and stories of the luxury surrounding Louis are legion.

The Sun King: Determined to escape the complications of Paris, which was becoming so important a city as to be independent of all authority, Louis decided to build a royal court so magnificent that it would require the presence and consequent submission of the aristocracy. The construction of the palace at

Louis judiciously chose his ministers from the bourgeoisie and petty nobility to keep the nobles in their place. He gave France the largest army in Europe. He was indeed the state, as he boasted. Yet under him the "state" also grew somewhat distant from the people. The bourgeoisie became envious of the opulence of Versailles, while workers and peasants grew jealous of the bourgeoisie. The revocation of the Edict of Nantes (1685) renewed hostility toward the Protestants, many of whom left the country for good (including 200,000 artisans France could scarcely afford to lose). There was a renewal of hostilities between the sects in the Cévennes to the south (1702–05), and a brief

Versailles accomplished this very well.

The splendour of architecture and rigidity of etiquette at the new court reduced the nobility to mere courtesans whose most important responsibility might be to hand the king his undershirt at the *Lever de Roi* ("Kingrise" – as opposed to sunrise) or kneel and salute his dinner, crying out "The king's meat!" as it passed from the royal kitchen to the dining room. Five hundred cooks prepared Louis's food, and he commanded 4,000 servants. When the smell of outhouses became a problem at the palace, he simply ordered that an enormous garden of orange trees be planted.

peasant uprising in Brittany was crushed. The famines of 1662 and 1693 underscored societal differences.

In spite of these ethnic problems, the age of Louis XIV witnessed a great revival of popular interest in classical learning and art. The theatre of Corneille and Racine, the fables of La Fontaine, the comedies of Molière, the oratory of Bossuet, and the brilliant thought of Pascal and Descartes all brought to French literature a refinement that it had not known before.

The Enlightenment: Louis's death in 1715 left his five-year-old great-grandson Louis XV on the throne, who in turn reigned until

1774. Despite Louis XV's personal mediocrity, France's reputation as the most sophisticated nation on earth grew steadily. The Enlightenment spawned unprecedented cultural activity, and Paris justifiably felt itself to be a beacon illuminating the rest of Western civilisation.

The fight for intellectual progress took place along a number of fronts. Montesquieu argued for representative law and political reform. Diderot and d'Alembert directed the mammoth *Encyclopédie* from 1750 to 1780. Buffon studied natural history, and the Montgolfier brothers recorded the first balloon flight in 1783. Jean-Jacques Rousseau suggested sweeping changes in society and

possessions to England after the Seven Years' War (1756–63). The French did, however, later gain a sort of revenge by aiding the American rebels in their subsequent War of Independence. French support of the Americans was vital, and the United States officially came into being with the 1783 signing of the Treaty of Versailles.

Discontent brewing: The philosophical import of this revolution was not lost on the French, who associated American idealism with their own Enlightenment. Men like Benjamin Franklin and Thomas Jefferson, who served as ambassadors to Paris, and the young Marquis de Lafayette were widely acclaimed for their espousal of republican

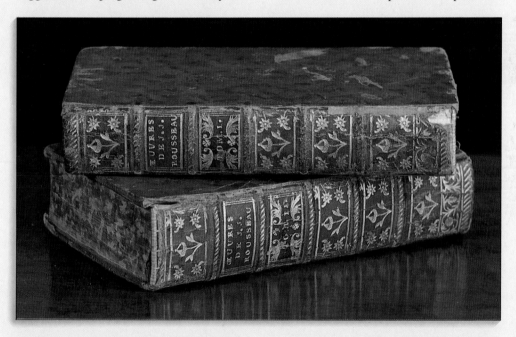

education, and composed an exceptionally candid autobiography. Voltaire, perhaps the brightest light of all, virulently satirised oppression and intolerance wherever he saw it. The presence in France of these gifted writers and thinkers not only reflected but promoted a growing literacy and rationality, especially among the bourgeoisie.

The acquisition of knowledge apparently did not quite extend to military matters, however, for France lost its North American

Left, the Gallery of Mirrors at Versailles. **Above**, significant and weighty tomes from Jean-Jacques Rousseau.

precepts. An amusing diary of the period registers Abigail Adam's dismay at the licentious behaviour that Paris seemed to elicit from Franklin.

The success of the relationship between France and America was offset somewhat by the enormous expense that France had sustained during the war. The taxation proposed by Louis XVI's (1774–93) ministers Turgot and Necker grated on a populace that had become less tolerant of inequality. Discontent was fuelled by bad harvests of the 1780s, and for reasons that remain murky even today, France plunged headlong into a revolution that changed the course of history.

PASSAGE DU MONT S^T. BERNARD.

40

PASSAGE DU MONT ST. BERNARD.

What we refer to as the French Revolution began in 1789, but it actually consisted of several different power struggles that overlapped and fed off one another. To settle the fiscal crisis, Louis XVI convened an assembly of deputies elected by the nobility, clergy and Third Estate (everybody else). The bourgeoisie seized the occasion to create an assembly charged with electing a new constitutional government.

On 14 July 1789 a Parisian mob stormed the Bastille prison, long a symbol of royal power. Inspired by this audacity, peasants organised across the country and the bourgeois National Assembly abolished the privileges of the nobility and clergy. The Declaration of the Rights of Man and the Citizen, signed on 26 August, was the culmination of a century of enlightened thought.

In this spirit of reform, France was reorganised into a constitutional monarchy and its ancient provinces converted into 83 smaller departments. The republican *tricolore* replaced the royal fleur-de-lis as the national flag. Meanwhile, however, Queen Marie-Antoinette had secretly requested intervention from her brother, the Emperor of Austria, and so war was declared. Counter-revolutionary activity in Brittany, the Vendée and Lyon confused matters further.

A new assembly, called the Convention, angrily abolished all royal authority, instituted the metric system, adopted the "Marseillaise" as the national anthem, and declared 1793 to be Year One of the Republic. With a new system of months and dates to replace the Julian calendar, not even time was held sacred by the zealous insurgents. Louis and his family were arrested trying to flee, and on 21 January 1793 the King of France was guillotined by his people in the Place de la Concorde.

Napoleon Bonaparte: To maintain control, the Convention, under the direction of Robespierre, assumed draconian powers and executed any who challenged its authority

Preceding pages: *Liberty Leading the People* by Delacroix. **Left**, Napoleon crossing the Alps. **Right**, Robespierre beheading the executioner after having beheaded everyone else.

(the final death toll was around 40,000). This period, known as the Terror, ended only after the execution of Robespierre himself (1794).

A young Corsican general who had distinguished himself in battle – one Napoleon Bonaparte – took advantage of the climate of confusion by seizing power in 1799. He quickly consolidated his power by enacting a sweeping body of civil legislation known as the Code Napoleon. This code remains the backbone of the French legal system even today. In addition, Napoleon reformed the

French educational and monetary systems, founded the Bank of France, appeased French Catholics frightened by the revolution and reunited the divided country. His popularity enabled him to crown himself emperor in 1804. He also sold a large chunk of middle America to Thomas Jefferson in 1803.

Unfortunately, these early successes led Napoleon to believe he was capable of creating an empire on the order of Charlemagne's, and, although he almost succeeded, France became embroiled in an unending succession of wars that culminated in the disastrous expedition into Russia in 1812. Defeated and exiled to Elba, Bonaparte escaped and made a dramatic return during the short-lived "Hundred Days", but the alarmed European powers defeated him once and for all at Waterloo (1815). Napoleon's wars had reduced France to poverty.

The Bourbon kings were placed back on the throne by the victors and initiated a period of great interest in palatial repair, which is why their reign is known as the Restoration. The bourgeoisie, however, were unhappy to serve a fat king again after the great expansion of their importance under the Revolution and Napoleon. When Charles X (1824–30) unwisely curtailed the freedom of the press in July 1830, students and workers erected barricades in Paris and began three days of rioting in protest. The King was forced to flee, and his cousin Louis-Philippe, who claimed to support republican principles, was appointed to replace him and was publicly embraced by the ageing Marquis de Lafayette before the Hôtel de Ville. France became a constitutional monarchy again.

The emotions that precipitated the "July Days" of 1830 were in many ways the legacy of the unfinished Revolution. The desire for individual expression and modernity was also translated into an exciting new body of literature that defied classical rules.

Romanticism: Feeling restless with the complacency of the Restoration, a new generation of writers sparked rejuvenated interest in literature and sought to stage an intellectual revolution to parallel the political ones that had taken place. Led by the young Victor Hugo, these writers emphasised the power of the imagination in distinct contrast to the rationality of the 18th-century *philosophes*.

The most important literary form of the romantic period was that best equipped to describe and appeal to the now-powerful bourgeoisie: the *roman* (the French word for novel, which of course corresponds closely to the French word *romantisme*). Allowing free expression, the novel was well-suited both to paint exotic pictures of foreign lands and less flattering ones of a progressively industrial and aggressive French society. Authors such as Stendhal and Honoré de Balzac disparagingly exposed the rapacity and snobbery of their fellow citizens, and subjected them to minute analyses of character and appearance.

The reign of Louis-Philippe, referred to as the "July Monarchy" after its 1830 origins,

accelerated these social changes in spite of its relatively moderate character. Technological innovation and urban growth consolidated the dominance of the bourgeoisie and fostered the development of a large, urban working-class. Photography was invented by Joseph Niepce in 1816 and advanced by Louis Daguerre in the 1830s. The railways (1832) revolutionised transportation in France as they enhanced the capital city. Paris became the capital not only of Europe, but of the 19th century.

Aware of the changes taking place, complicated class doctrines were advocated by philosophers such as Saint-Simon, Auguste Comte, E.P. Fournier and Pierre Proudhon

VICTOR HUGO par FAUSTIN

that were later to serve as an inspiration to Karl Marx. History writing, as exemplified by Jules Michelet, Alexis de Tocqueville and François Guizot became a newly respected mode of expression. The caricatures of cartoonist Auguste Daumier also reflected the changing nature of the times.

In spite of 17 assassination attempts in 18 years and several serious urban riots (Paris, 1831 and 1834; Lyon, 1831), opposition from extremists of the left and right, and growing class tension, the July Monarchy was at least able to avoid foreign conflict. Moreover, the government, led by Louis-Philippe's minister Guizot, presided over a steady economic growth. Responding once to a complaint that his government favoured the rich, Guizot earned a measure of notoriety by responding to the plaintiff, "Then make yourself rich!"

The Second Republic: The downfall of Louis-Philippe remains as difficult to explain as the previous revolutions. Again, one of the issues at stake was the unhappiness of those who felt strangled by society. The 1847 fiscal crisis and unfair voting laws combined to remind workers of their inferior status. In February 1848, Guizot forbade an anti-government banquet to be held in Paris and provoked public rioting and barricades similar to those of 1830. The National Guard

ricades again went up in Paris, but this time the insurrectionists were crushed and 4,000 of them killed. A presidential election conferred power upon the surprisingly popular nephew of Napoleon, Louis Napoleon Bonaparte. A man without the dynamism that his name suggested, Bonaparte declared himself emperor and arrested his opponents in a coup on 2 December 1851. The idealistic republic ended where it had started, with yet another monarchy.

The Second Empire continued much of the expansion, both industrial and intellectual, that had taken place under Louis-Philippe. France acquired Savoy and Nice from Italy in 1860, the importance of which should be

supported the demonstrators, and suddenly Louis-Philippe had to flee the country as unceremoniously as his predecessor.

The poet Lamartine proclaimed the founding of the Second Republic, and a provisional government was formed that shortened the working day, declared universal male suffrage and abolished slavery. After initial elections were won by moderate republicans, workers of the far left rioted during the so-called "June Days" of 1848. Bar-

fully realised by the many topless sunbathers on the Côte d'Azur today. The Crimean War against Russia (1854–55) was inconclusive, but France began to extend its influence into other regions, including China, Mexico and northern Africa.

Having learned the importance of street barricades in overturning governments, Louis Napoleon entrusted the Baron Haussmann with the beautification of Paris. Haussmann changed the face of the city by widening its avenues, eliminating its congested areas and creating large public parks like the Bois de Boulogne. The result was a truly grand, international metropolis that also happened

Left, caricature of Victor Hugo by Faustin. **Above**, Daumier believed that incarceration did not always produce the best results.

to be a much harder place to stage a good riot.

Novel criticism: The retrenchment of the monied bourgeoisie under Louis Napoleon gave added fodder to the novelists and government critics who had thrived under the July Monarchy. Indeed, the republican Victor Hugo was forced to live in exile on the English Channel Islands of Jersey and Guernsey. The description of social mores received further refinement at the hands of Gustave Flaubert, whose *Madame Bovary* and *The Sentimental Education* shocked readers by their graphic accounts of adultery and avarice. The poet Charles Baudelaire, too, excited indignation by his celebration of sensuality and morbid attraction to death.

The status of the Second Empire ended abruptly in 1870. Tricked into a precipitous declaration of war against Prussia by the insulting Ems Telegram, which allegedly made sport of his moustache, an overconfident Bonaparte established his lack of military ability once and for all by leading his troops to a cataclysmic defeat at Sedan.

Following this debacle, the entire superstructure of the Second Empire promptly collapsed, and a provisional republican government was formed that tried in vain to perpetuate the war against the better-equipped Prussians. Although this attempt failed, wounded French pride was assuaged somewhat by leader Léon Gambetta's escape from besieged Paris in a balloon. Victory for Bismarck's army was inevitable, however, and the French were forced to cede the eastern province of Alsace and Lorraine.

The Commune: In Paris, a feeling of patriotic indignation, combined with resentment towards the extreme hardship that had been inflicted upon the capital during the Prussian war, created a climate of bitter discontent. When the provincial government, temporarily seated at Bordeaux, surrendered to the Prussian demands, exasperated Parisians declared the formation of an independent workers' commune. With the support of its National Guard, the Commune refused to comply with orders to surrender to the French Army based at Versailles. The result was a bloody two-month civil war in which Paris was again besieged and which only ended after 20,000 *communards* gave up their lives to protect their city from their fellow countrymen. The northeast wall of the Père Lachaise cemetery, where the last insurgents were gunned down, has since become a pilgrimage site for members of the left.

In spite of the disastrous conditions which spawned it, the Third Republic continued for 70 years and escorted France confidently into the 20th century. In the aftermath of the violent Commune, the republicans chose to concentrate on stability both at home and abroad. Basing its power among the enormous petty bourgeoisie, the Republic nevertheless made important concessions to workers such as allowing unions in 1884. The Ferry Laws (1880–81), moreover, granted free public education across France. The Republic also managed to atone somewhat for the loss of Alsace and Lorraine by

developing an enormous colonial empire in Africa and Asia. At its greatest extent, the French network of overseas possessions was second only to that of Britain.

Measured against the industrial and military standards of Germany, Britain and the United States, France's worldwide importance diminished somewhat during this period. There are many other indices of a nation's greatness, however, and during the *belle époque* the French inspired the envy of the world with their *joie de vivre*. The late 19th century witnessed an artistic flowering that foreshadowed the cultural preeminence Paris would enjoy for the next half-century.

Impressionism: Bored by realistic representation, a group of innovative painters abandoned the confines of traditional styles to found the school of Impressionism. The work of Manet, Monet, Renoir, Degas and Pissarro at first scandalised the public with their show at the Salon des Refusés. Supported by the literary community, however, the Impressionists gradually grew into favour and produced dazzling works that redefined the depiction of light.

Monet transformed the innocent water lily into one of the most famous botanical species of the art world. Even today, visitors flock to his home in Giverny, just outside Paris, to see the lovely plants float calmly by.

into a painstakingly descriptive, naturalistic style of his own. The poetry of Paul Verlaine and his occasional pistol target Arthur Rimbaud described the world with much of the same subjectivity that the Impressionists were trying to convey. The mad ravings of Lautréamont, as difficult as they are to align with any movement, were memorable for their fantastic images and intensity.

Absinthe and opium: It was about at this time that Paris began to cultivate the racy, *risqué* image that it has never ceased to enjoy or worked especially hard to dispel. Attributable in part to the excitement generated by its artistic and literary communities, in part to the prodigious amounts of *absinthe* and opium

With his unique use of light and perspective, Degas created dancers that seemed to spill forth from the canvas into the onlooker's arms. Their success inspired successors such as Gauguin, Seurat and Cézanne, and Paris attracted the foreign palettes of Van Gogh, Whistler and Sisley.

At the same time, and for many of the same reasons, French writers were applying new brush strokes of their own. Art patron Émile Zola, a great champion of the new aesthetic, adapted the realism of Flaubert and shaped it

consumed by them, in part to the many nightclubs open to connoisseurs of the *demi-monde*, stories of "Gay Paree" titillated listeners around the world.

Although the stability of the Third Republic was conducive to this sort of activity, it would be misleading to ascribe the cultural ascendancy of Paris to any particular government. The true genius of French culture seems to lie in its ability to weather political hurricanes without losing equilibrium. At any rate, Paris reminded the world of its importance with Universal Expositions in 1855, 1867 and 1889. The chief attraction of the latter was the then newly completed

<u>Left</u>, *The line for rat meat,* Cham's cartoon on the Commune. <u>Above</u>, *Four Dancers* by Degas.

Eiffel Tower, with its 1,792 steps painfully reminding visitors of the weight of their history. Criticised by many for its ugliness, the Tower was also hailed as a sign of the energy with which France faced the future.

The Dreyfus affair: The atmosphere of modernity did not, however, disrupt the cherished French tradition of political divisions. A minor tremor occurred in the late 1880s when General Boulanger excited great patriotic fervour and seemed capable of upsetting the political balance. This only served as a prelude, however, to the Dreyfus affair.

Suspected of assisting German spies, and convicted in part because of his Jewish background, Captain Alfred Dreyfus became the focal point of an outbreak of national paranoia that severely rocked the French Army, Republic and standing order. Defended by the ever-volatile intelligentsia, summoned to the cause by Émile Zola's incendiary letter entitled "J'Accuse!", the Dreyfus affair was somewhat similar to the American experience with McCarthyism and the Rosenberg Trial in that it aroused vehement emotions that greatly transcended the importance of the specific case.

The struggles between right and left, the military and the intellectuals, ceased altogether with the inevitable, yet unexpected outbreak of World War I (1914) and the chance for revenge upon the hated Germans. Opening the floodgates of patriotism, the war proved to be as shattering to the French as it was to all the other parties involved.

Quick German penetration of France was stopped by the Allies at the Marne. Protracted trench warfare followed, with tremendous losses sustained by both sides. Abortive campaigns in Champagne and Artois were followed by the costly victory of Verdun, in which there were 700,000 casualties. Ironically, Verdun was also the site of the partition of the Carolingian empire that had originally created France and Germany.

While most of the war was a bloody stalemate, the harsh terms imposed upon Germany by President Georges Clemenceau in the Treaty of Versailles (1919) allowed the French to perceive it as a glorious victory in the grand tradition of Vercingetorix, Roland, Joan of Arc and Napoleon. Besides claiming enough reparations to gild the Eiffel Tower, the French were able to reunite Alsace and Lorraine under the *tricolore*. The heavy price of the victory, however, may still be seen in the lengthy list of names inscribed on memorials in every French village.

The *années folles*: Paris emerged from the catastrophe with characteristic élan. The 1920s proved to be one of the most lively decades in the city's history, partly because of the large expatriate colony whose attention had been called to France by the war. Hemingway, Fitzgerald, Gertrude Stein, James Joyce and Henry Miller all spent considerable time imbibing French culture. France's notoriety soared along with Charles Lindbergh and the *Spirit of St Louis*, which landed at the Le Bourget airfield in 1927.

French writers, too, were well-represented during the interbellum. The novel profited from the craftsmanship of old masters like Marcel Proust and André Gide, while André Malraux injected it with adventure.

Paris also continued to be the undisputed capital of the art world. The pre-war appearance of talents such as Pablo Picasso (naturalised French) and Henri Matisse had augured a new era of creativity. The daring of Cubism and Fauvism, however, positively paled in comparison to the excesses of the Dada movement. Shocked by the absurdity of the war, artists such as Henri Magritte, Marcel Duchamp and Bushmiller de Nancy deliberately cultivated nonsense to establish their independence. The surrealists, led by writer André Breton, were less extreme, but also flirted with meaninglessness and the limits of language to create new images.

Unfortunately, the ebullience of the 1920s, known in France as the *années folles* (crazy years) did not serve as an accurate barometer of the rough weather ahead. The depression of the 1930s hit France hard. The collapse of the European money order, accelerated by the unstable cycle of reparation payments following the war, wreaked havoc on the French economy and political structure.

The left, reorganised as the Front Populaire in 1932, made great strides in popularity, culminating in the short-lived socialist government of Léon Blum in 1936. However, the most lasting achievement of the Front Populaire was undoubtedly the 1936 law that required holidays with pay, which today accounts for the lemming-like race from Paris to the sea during the month of August.

Right, Matisse's 20th-century *Venus*.

The military buildup in Germany and Italy under Hitler and Mussolini not only threatened the European balance, but resulted in the humiliating German repossession of the Rhineland in 1936. The Spanish Civil War greatly aroused the ire of French intellectuals, but they were powerless to lift a finger to dispel the rising storm. In 1938, France joined England in the capitulation to Hitler at Munich, and, after Poland was invaded on 3 September 1939, World War II was declared.

Much of the fault behind this sequence of events lay in the irrational certainty with which the French believed their country to be impregnable. The Maginot Line, a fortified wall stretching across Alsace and Lorraine, was so confidently believed inviolable that today it has come to be synonymous with the idiocy of relying too heavily upon only one line of defence.

Indeed, when a similar plan of defence was suggested to Napoleon Bonaparte 100 years earlier by one of his military counsellors, the Corsican general reportedly sneered in response, "What do you think we are trying to do? Stop smuggling?" Unfortunately for the French, and particularly those living in northeastern France, this scathing remark was either forgotten or ignored.

All military historians know what happened; after eight months of the "Phony War," during which neither France nor Germany dared to attack the other, the German *blitzkrieg* penetrated deeply into France from Belgium and rendered the vaunted Maginot Line useless by encircling and capturing it. Apparently its guns only faced Germany and, of course, due to the strategy of spreading their men thinly across the entire border rather than concentrating them in substantial groups, penetration by the enemy was swift. Only a few days beforehand, Winston Churchill had appeased the House of Commons with the words, "Thank God for the French Army!"

The armistice signed on 22 June 1940 created a German occupation zone in the north and a nominally autonomous region in the south with its capital at Vichy. The famous World War I general Marshal Henri-Philippe Pétain was given full leadership powers in

this region, and the constitution of the Third Republic was abrogated. At the same time, General Charles de Gaulle, the Undersecretary of State for the National Defence, had fled to London to organise the Free French in their resistance effort. The British were forced to scuttle the French fleet moored in Algeria, although this action produced painful hostility between the former allies.

Under General de Gaulle's leadership, the Resistance grew steadily throughout the war, and the troops of the Free French were in-

strumental in the North African and other campaigns. It would be inaccurate, however, to suggest that the Resistance enjoyed widespread support from its inception. The beloved Marshal Pétain was one of France's most respected men and appealed to the country's strong traditions of agriculture, family and Catholicism. The collaboration (a word avoided today) with the Nazis was believed to be the least painful method of coexistence, even if it implied a lamentable deportation of Jews and other French citizens. This question still has ramifications of almost unbearable delicacy for the French conscience, and it has been agonisingly debated.

The question of allegiance was solved, of course, by the successful invasion of France by the Allied troops in 1944. Although the D-Day assault on Normandy (6 June 1944) was the most dramatic moment of the invasion, there was a slow, arduous penetration from Provence in the south as well. The liberation of Paris on 25 August 1944 was one of the craziest and happiest days in the city's chequered past, partly because Eisenhower diplomatically allowed the French troops, under the leadership of General Leclerc, to be the first to enter the city. Needless to say, French participation in the invasion of Germany was sweet revenge.

In spite of this happy conclusion to the a world in which the United States and the Soviet Union were the Big Cheeses.

After a brief period of intense self-analysis, during which thousands of suspected collaborators were executed, France began the long road to recovery. Massive projects toward urban rehabilitation were undertaken. It is a credit to the supreme aesthetic sensibility of the French that despite financial hardships, most construction was carried out with good taste.

The laws and government also experienced a massive rehabilitation. Women were accorded the vote in 1945, and in 1946 the Fourth Republic was formed. Charles de Gaulle now turned his attention to the resto-

most tragic chapter of French history since Californian wine was invented, the nation's position in the world of 1945 was more precarious than it had been in centuries. First, its cities and most precious architectural treasures had been mercilessly razed by the German and Allied invaders. Second, and more important, the all-too-easily wounded national ego had been shattered by defeat and collaboration, and now looked out upon

ration of French *grandeur*. He was disgusted by the reluctance of the government to give him sweeping presidential powers, however, and withdrew from the political arena.

The instability of the Fourth Republic was proven by the succession of 24 ministries from 1945 to 1958, during which French Indochina was lost to the Viet Minh at the battle of Dien Bien Phu (1954) and the Algerian independence movement grew out of hand. It was this latter fiasco that prompted the imperial return of de Gaulle, who summoned up all of his prestige and six feet four inches to bulldoze the National Assembly into passing a new constitution, creating the

Preceding pages: World War II cemetery at Normandy's Omaha Beach. <u>Left</u>, General Charles de Gaulle in office. <u>Above</u>, General de Gaulle and Winston Churchill in time of war.

Fifth Republic and giving him the authority he desired.

In typically French fashion, General de Gaulle's reign of power offered several salient contradictions. In spite of his militaristic appeal, he presided over a gradual withdrawal from Algeria (completed in 1962). In spite of his vigorous nationalism, he supervised the dismantling of the widespread French colonial apparatus. And in spite of his wartime allegiances, he vehemently rejected the leadership of the United States and Great Britain, kicking NATO out of Paris (1967), vetoing England's admission into the European Economic Community (1963) and organising a rapprochement with Ger-

history hastily teaches us to abandon the confines of rationality. In the month of May, a general feeling of malaise and spring fever erupted into aggressive demonstrations against the Vietnam War, government control of the media and the stagnant values of the adult generation. The tension increased when the students dug up the stones of the Latin quarter streets, constructed barricades in the finest French revolutionary tradition and occupied the Sorbonne. Joined by the workers of the left and citizens across France who disagreed with de Gaulle for various reasons, the student demonstrations escalated into a profound national crisis.

Shaken badly by these events and by his

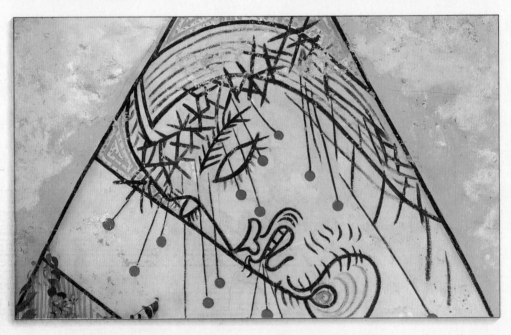

many to reassert European independence.

During the postwar period French culture underwent its usual renaissance. The existentialist philosophy of Jean-Paul Sartre and Albert Camus electrified the world with its chic pessimism. The *nouveau roman, nouvelle cuisine* and *nouvelle vague* all brought important innovations. Inspired largely by the French cinema, the world again looked to Paris as its hippest city, populated only by young people wearing black turtle-necks, sunglasses and berets and emanating that certain *je ne sais quoi.*

The year 1968 should not have been as chaotic as it was, but the study of French

failing foreign and economic policy, de Gaulle relinquished power to his former Prime Minister Georges Pompidou in 1969. Now known chiefly for the cultural centre at Beaubourg bearing his name, Pompidou died after a long illness in 1974.

The ensuing presidential election saw the Gaullist Valéry Giscard d'Estaing win against Socialist François Mitterrand. Despite his rightist nature, Giscard's seven-year presidency incorporated some of the reforms which were desired by the left: less restrictive divorce laws, legalised abortion and widely available contraception, and an 18-year-old voting age.

In 1981, the tables were turned when Mitterrand defeated Giscard, bringing the left to power for the first time under the Fifth Republic. Like Giscard, Mitterrand surprised those unfamiliar with the vagaries of French politics by maintaining close ties with the United States and advocating only a limited nationalisation of French industry. And he has clung to power for two presidential terms, despite uneasy periods of "co-habitation" with a right-wing government.

Despite the enormous differences between General de Gaulle, Pompidou, Giscard and Mitterrand, France continued to function in very much the same way along a number of fronts. The government continued to de-

est train (the TGV – *Train à Grande Vitesse*) French technology has made advances in weapons (the Exocet missile), satellite communications (the Ariane rocket) nuclear energy and computer technology, all of which are profiled in the chapter *Futuristic France* later in this book.

In 1989 France celebrated the bicentennial of the French Revolution, an event which led to an orgy of self-congratulation and analysis. And the early 1990s saw the completion of several grand projects, such as the new Louvre and La Défense in Paris.

If it is difficult at times to see a clear and linear progression in all of this ridiculous French history, it is largely because the na-

velop its independent *force de frappe* rather than cower beneath the NATO nuclear umbrella; today it continues to maintain close ties with the Third World, particularly those parts of Africa which were originally French territories; and it continues loudly to express its opinion.

In the 1980s and 1990s François Mitterrand has presided over a country that prides itself on the gloried remembrance of things past, but is deeply resolved to keep pace with modernity. Besides boasting the world's fast-

tion itself has always been such a patchwork of different regional identities and conflicting intentions. Yet for better or worse, the history of France has been central to the wider history of Western civilisation, and indeed of the world itself. France has illuminated and taught both by her brilliance and her incomprehensible absurdity. No matter what, she has always commanded attention. And through all the turbulence of the last few millennia, the genius of France, her ill-defined national character, has somehow triumphed over all of these tawdry political events to emerge essentially intact. That in itself is no small accomplishment.

Left, modern art from Jean Cocteau. **Above**, Socialist President François Mitterrand.

My dear friend, one cannot suddenly unite a country that claims 265 different kinds of cheese.

— Charles de Gaulle

France is the 13th most populous nation in the world, with over 53.5 million inhabitants. Moreover, commensurate with its geographical diversity, these citizens come in an astonishing variety of shapes, sizes, regional personalities and odours.

Some French villages may seem indistinguishable from neighbouring towns in Spain, Italy or Germany. Other French villages seem to bear no similarity to any other place on earth. Yet each French village has an identical SNCF *gare*, proudly flies the *tricolore* before the local *mairie*, and has its own statue of Marianne, the female figure who represents the French Republic and all of its civilised virtues. Originally, Brigitte Bardot herself posed for the highly revered bust, but Mariannes are now being remodelled after Catherine Deneuve.

The sharpest contrasts belong to France's most eccentric (in the sense of farthest from the centre) provinces. The Breton civilisation has been jealously preserved since the days when ancient Brittany was known as Armorica. Like Wales in Great Britain, whence many of its settlers emigrated, Brittany's westernmost position vis-à-vis invaders established it as a final retreat from the successive waves of newcomers to France. The region enjoyed independence well into the 16th century, and even today a wealth of Celtic customs have prevailed. The Breton language has survived a long decline in use and is currently experiencing a renaissance of interest among scholars. Many local rites are still in use, including the wearing of bizarre white pillbox hats by Bretonne women on festival days.

Like Brittany, the southern regions of Languedoc and Provence considered themselves separate from France for centuries and developed their own language, Provençal,

Preceding pages: the village *boules* team; cheerful scyther in Auvergne. **Left,** fisherman in Marseille. **Right,** Parisian nightclubber.

in which medieval love ballads were composed by the troubadours. Religious heresies were periodically wiped out by domineering northerners, but the region never surrendered its independent spirit. Even today, the people, like the landscape, seem to be made of a different stuff from the more active and cosmopolitan Parisians. Frankly, the southerner is perceived to be rather less sophisticated than his northern brother. At the same time, he evokes widespread affection from all. Preferring the simple but good things in

life – midday naps, sumptuous meals, fine wine, idle conversation – to the more elusive pleasures of big city life, the southerner occupies an important place in the French personality.

Independent languages and customs are perhaps most prevalent in the Basque region of the Pyrenees and on the island of Corsica. Unfortunately, the 1980s saw advocates of local autonomy become rather dangerously overzealous. It is strange to think that it was Corsica's famous son, Napoleon Bonaparte, who did the most to unite France into a strong collective body. Napoleon is still revered as a national hero on the island.

Serving as the standard by which all of these "deviations" are measured is, of course, the Parisian himself. Paris has always been the lodestar of all that is French, and the Parisian acts as the model for most of the traditional French stereotypes. According to his mood, he is brilliant, vainglorious, rude or irresistibly engaging. From the pinstripe-suited banker to the blue-uniformed worker, the Parisian never hesitates to declare that he lives in the world's great metropolis.

But despite the differences between the regions, most Frenchmen have the same concerns: passing the baccalaureate, following the *Tour de France*, planning the next August vacation, picking up the daily newspa-

and Vietnamese are the most numerous.

Lightning speeds: Besides containing these diverse ingredients, France is host to a number of apparent contradictions that may at first confuse the visitor. Foremost among these is the contradiction between stereotype and reality. Although the clichés do have their accuracies (alcoholism, big noses and an abundance of moustaches), not all French men look like Jacques Cousteau, Maurice Chevalier or Inspector Clouseau. While the French are indeed the inheritors of all their ancestors have done, they are also forging new paths toward the future.

There is a big difference between the historic France of textbooks and the modern

per and *baguette*, breaking the sound barrier on a moped. Most are also remarkably articulate, and display a philosophical bent at every level of society. It is fair to say that every Frenchman is capable of being both a poet and a politician.

France also has many communities of foreign extraction, partly due to its physically (and politically) central position in Europe, and partly due to its former imperial possessions. The population, therefore, includes a plethora of Africans, Iberians, Southern Europeans, Eastern Europeans, Arabs and Asians – not to mention "expatriate" anglophiles. Algerians, West Africans, Poles

nation that exists today. France is both an old-fashioned agricultural land and a new-fangled industrial power that is the world's fourth largest producer of automobiles. While you may not notice it on your tour, the French have to grapple with the same ugly late 20th century as everybody else. They have succeeded pretty well in some areas (nuclear energy, transport, weapons technology) but the economy remains sluggish, and unemployment is a perennial problem.

French cities do have charming old quarters and big cathedrals, but they also have problems with housing, pollution and some of the ugliest modern architecture on the face of the planet. But while embracing the new, they do also hang on to well-tested designs. One example is the Citröen *Deux-Chevaux* automobile. Its powerful two-horsepower engine ought to be about right for a medium-size lawnmower, yet somehow the French coax it into lightning speeds, especially in small back alleys with large groups of foreign pedestrians. Rather appropriately, it looks funny, sounds like tin cans rattled together, performs pretty well, and is impossible to imagine anywhere else.

Morals and mistresses: If France has the reputation of being a country of lax morals it most certainly goes back to the mistress system, also called *le cinq à sept*, that time of day

government and to have a mistress is still accepted practice.

"One can only dress well in a country where one undresses a lot," couturier Jeanne Lanvin is reputed to have said. French women do certainly change their clothes often during a day and the Paris fashion industry has always been synonymous with feminine elegance and daring innovation.

French women have kept pace with the industry's changes; those that can afford to do so buy their clothes with labels, the others do their own sewing or use a seamstress to copy the latest novelty from designers such as Christian Dior or Yves Saint-Laurent. "That does not mean that French women are in the major-

– between leaving the office and having to report home – when lovers meet.

For a long time, thanks to their mistress system, the French had one of the lowest divorce rates in the Western world. (Divorces have doubled in France since 1960 and today one out of three marriages in Paris ends in divorce.) The divorce laws of 1975 were to inspire equal responsibilities between men and women, and to provide legal measures of protection for women. To be prominent in

<u>Far left</u>, north African restaurateur in Dijon; <u>left</u>, young bloods on vacation in Provence. <u>Above</u>, mime artists at St-Germain-des-Prés.

ity fashion-conscious," says Theodore Zeldin, author of *The French*. "It means first that France has a successful and long-established fashion industry, but also secondly that French women generally think they are above the average in beauty."

French women have long been kept out of public life. Married women were deemed legally incapable until 1942. And it was not until 1944 that French women were granted the right to vote by General de Gaulle. As recently as 1965, husbands were the "official" heads of the family and could legally prevent their wives from having a professional activity. Before then, wives could not have their own bank account nor handle their own money. And it is only in 1970 that parental authority has been shared by mother and father.

But the impression that this gives is actually rather deceptive. "Though legally women occupy a much inferior status to men," wrote an English visitor at the beginning of this century, "in practice they constitute the superior sex. They are the power behind the throne, and both in the family and in business relations undoubtedly enjoy greater consideration than English women."

Before the world wars, women worked predominantly in agricultural occupations or menial office jobs. The wars saw male confidence and strength dented, and today women

compete with men for executive positions. However, the percentage of working women (39 percent) has not changed since 1909. As in other democratic countries, there are many rules ensuring women equal pay. Yet national statistics show that, on the average, there remains a 33 percent discrepancy between men's and women's salaries.

Today's Frenchwoman has inherited the charm and power of her ancestors, royal courtesans and *demi-mondaines*. She continues to use that charm in her daily life, confirming Simone de Beauvoir's opening line of *The Second Sex*: "One is not born a woman, one becomes one."

A time of change: The French are changing along with their architecture and their lifestyles. The development of large businesses, chain stores and the widespread pursuit of leisure have led to what is generally called, to the distress of this *fier* nation, as an "Americanisation" of French society. Shrinking are the old conservative traditions of family businesses and enclosed social circles. Pushed by the young, a growing number of the French are increasingly content to watch television for their information, shop at supermarkets and eat fast food (although they shall always insist on buying fresh bread). There is presently a superabundance of American-style burger joints in Paris, with no sign that the trend is abating. Beside drinking beer at McDonald's, the youth of France can play pool, go bowling and watch *Dynastie* on the *télé*.

Yet French culture remains formidable and the French continue to pay greater tribute to their artists and writers than other nations. To this day there remains something stylish about the very word "French", even when placed before the dullest of items: toast, bread, cigarettes and water.

The final contradiction worthy of note is that between the alleged rudeness of the French towards foreign visitors and their actual hospitality. It is undeniable that there exists a time-honoured Gallic tradition of impoliteness that had been honed and perfected over the centuries of foreign fascination with France. It is also true, however, that the French will rapidly respond to any genuine attempt to appreciate their culture for what it is worth. Too many tourists allow themselves to be blinded by petty inconveniences and as a result, they miss the whole *bateau*. As Henry Miller said: "That's the first thing that strikes an American woman about Europe – that it's unsanitary. Impossible for them to conceive of a paradise without modern plumbing."

The French love their country with good reason, and they naturally do not like to see it misunderstood, or even praised without understanding. But if you make even a marginal attempt to savour the *délices* of France with the right attitude, your efforts will not go unnoticed or unrewarded.

Left, Parisian self-confidence. **Right**, contemporary poet with imperial connections.

For the French, eating is more a way of life than of keeping alive. Food and wine, from the humblest cheese or *vin de pays* to foie gras or vintage claret, are the subject of constant interest, assessment and discussion. The French are also gastronomic chauvinists – but then they have good reason to be. True, there have been alarming developments in recent years: the advent of the perfidious microwave and of pre-prepared chilled products has been a boon to lazy restaurateurs; and those who forecast that fast food would never catch on in France have had to eat their words, particularly in Paris. Even so, French standards of cooking, both in restaurants and in the home, are still comfortably ahead of those in most countries.

The French nation's love of good food is only natural, for France offers an enormous variety of produce. It is able to do so because it is a land of great climatic and agricultural diversity. And its coastline is washed by both the Atlantic Ocean and the Mediterranean, which together offer a temptingly wide variety of seafood.

Regional strengths: Each region has its specialities, both animal and vegetable. With its high concentration of restaurants and demand for fine produce, Paris is surrounded by a belt of top-quality market gardens. They provide the capital with many early vegetables, from tender green peas and infant carrots to crisp spinach and new potatoes.

The Loire valley, site of many of France's most famous châteaux, offers fresh salmon from its river, cultivated mushrooms from the caves around Saumur, and a rich variety of game and wild mushrooms from the lake-studded woods of Sologne, in addition to a host of fruit and vegetables – plump asparagus, cherries, plums – as befits a region called "the garden of France". The full-flavoured specialities of the Southwest include foie gras (goose liver pâté) from Gascony, truffles from Périgord, raw ham from Bayonne and cured anchovies from Collioure, while Provence is the home of fragrant Cavaillon melons, sun-gorged tomatoes and

fragrant basil, which gives *pistou* soup its distinctive flavour.

One of the delights of visiting small restaurants and bistros all over France is tracking down unusual regional specialities found only rarely in Paris, let alone the rest of the world. In the Pyrenean town of Castelnou, you may find a dish called *cargolada*, a grill of local snails, sausages and lamb chops cooked successively over a fire of vine cuttings and eaten in the open air. Some restaurants in Nice still feature *estocaficada*,

a pungent dish of stockfish (dried cod), tomatoes, peppers, potatoes and black olives. *Baeckeoffe*, an unusual stew of mixed meats (beef, lamb and pork) and potatoes, can still be found in the local country inns of Alsace, washed down with fine wine.

The French calculate freshness in hours, not days, which is why French markets are such good sources for local specialities. This also shows in dishes such as *plateau de fruits de mer*, a sumptuous platter of raw shellfish and cooked crustaceans that brings with it the tang of the sea. If you eat at restaurants in seaside resorts like Deauville in Normandy and Bouzigues or Cassis on the Mediterra-

Preceding pages: fresh local produce. **Left**, chef Paul Bocuse. **Right**, *baguette* by bicycle.

nean, you are quite likely to see fishermen wandering in with buckets of fresh seafood for the chef.

It is always a good idea, when sizing up a strange restaurant from the menu posted outside, to see if any attempt has been made by the chef to give his dishes a regional touch: pride in one's origins can often stimulate that extra bit of care and effort.

Famous names: Nowadays even France's grandest restaurants – Georges Blanc in the Burgundy village of Vonnas, Troisgros in Roanne, Paul Bocuse outside Lyon and L'Oustau de Baumanière in Les Baux-de-Provence, to mention but four – will provide their own versions of regional fare alongside

of the place where it originated – Camembert, Roquefort and Munster, for example. The highly-prized *belon* oyster is called after the Belon river in Brittany. Cognac is a town as well as a world-famous brandy, Calvados an administrative department as well as a prized applejack. And of course many a fine wine, from Chablis to Château-Chalon, reveals its place of origin in its name.

Anyone driving through France cannot fail to be struck by the overwhelming importance of food in daily life. Whenever they can, the French prefer not to stock up at a supermarket for the week, but to shop carefully for the next meal or two. Outdoor markets selling anything from fruit and veg-

the more sophisticated *haute cuisine* their customers expect.

Blanc's menu regularly features snails from the Burgundy vineyards and frog's legs from the nearby Dombes lakes, while Bocuse offers France's finest (and most expensive) poultry, chicken from Bresse, in various guises. The famed local Alpilles lamb at L'Oustau de Baumanière is accompanied by vegetables and herbs full of Provençal scents and flavours.

More perhaps than in any other country, French specialities of food and drink are named after the towns and villages that produce them. Many a cheese carries the name

etables to meat, fish and cheese are regular weekly events in towns both large and small. They are also social occasions which give people a chance to catch up on the latest gossip, discuss the latest developments on the political scene and talk about the weather (which the French do just as much as the British). Such exchanges usually take place in the packed neighbourhood or village café, over a glass of pastis or wine.

Food merchants take a loving interest in their wares. The fishmonger does not merely sell fish – he may offer a recipe for, say, grilling bright fresh sardines in tender vine leaves. The fruit and vegetable merchant knows which potato variety is best for a gratin, and if you ask whether the peaches are ripe he will often let you taste one, free of charge, so you can decide for yourself.

Seasonal fare: A common sight along major roads are the roadside stands that sell just-picked peaches, apples and plums, homemade preserves, home-cured olives, or honey from local hives. There are also large signs pointing enticingly to nearby farms, where eggs, poultry, goat's cheese or homemade foie gras and *confits* are available. Some filling stations even offer customers a selection of surplus vegetables (lettuces, tomatoes, young white onions, shallots) from the owner's garden. And of course wine estates and cider

June, you may find the road blocked by a herd of cows or a flock of sheep with clanging bells round their necks. They are being led up to their summer pastures in the mountains, where they will feast on sweet grasses and wild flowers. In Savoie, the milk of Tarine cows is best for the finest cheese of the region, mountain Beaufort, which is made into huge wheels like Gruyère. At local markets, merchants discuss the age of a Beaufort just as seriously as wine buffs compare vintages. As a Beaufort matures (over a period of anything up to eight months), its flavour gets better, nuttier and more profound.

By July, towns and villages come alive with the first of the harvest festivals. The

producers also put up signs to make their presence known to the passing motorist.

Each food has its season. When asparagus from the Loire valley appears in the shops you can be certain that spring is in the air. The charming Pyrenean village of Céret produces the first-of-the-season cherries in mid-April. Come May, juicy new garlic comes on the market (garlic lovers like to roast the cloves, then spread them like butter on freshly toasted bread).

If driving through France in the month of

peach is celebrated in the Roussillon village of Ille-sur-Têt. In August the entire spa town of Digne, in the Alpes-de-Haute-Provence, turns out for a lavender festival, while in November the inhabitants of the Normandy village of Beuvron-en-Auge gather to sample the new crop of apple cider.

Even wine has its season. On the third Thursday of November, in wine bars, cafés and restaurants and at private tables all over France, the first wine of the season, Beaujolais Nouveau, is eagerly tasted. Ready to drink only about six weeks after the grape harvest, this wine cries out to be drunk young. At its best it is a light, fruity, uncomplicated

Left, seasonal offerings on the streets of Paris.
Right, sausage for sale.

tipple, ideal for washing down an improvised meal of dry pork sausage and buttered country bread with friends.

The daily diet: The French spend about 20 percent of their income on food and wine. In such a culturally varied nation as France there is no absolutely typical meal, though there are typical local eating patterns. The biggest dividing line is between city and country. Most French begin the day with a large bowl or mug of white coffee and a *tartine* (a slice of bread or a rusk spread with butter and jam). Farmers and other country-dwellers who get up early and do manual work will usually follow this up with a *casse-croûte* (snack) of bread (often half-rye) and sausage or pâté at about 9.30am. A substantial three- or four-course lunch comes next, often beginning with soup based on a homemade vegetable or chicken broth, and almost always comprising a meat course. Supper is often a light meal, with more soup, maybe some leftovers, and cheese.

Many office workers lunch in company canteens, which are usually a cut above such establishments in other countries. The food on offer is generally designed to cater for the weight-conscious as well as those who do not need or want to care about their figures. Some office workers make do with just a sandwich (usually ham or cheese, or both, in a buttered *baguette*) and a glass of wine. With more and more working mothers, the evening meal will often consist of something simple like *bifteck frites*, which has almost become a national dish in recent years, or frozen fish (sold complete with its sauce), followed by cheese or a fruit yoghurt. As in many countries, Sunday lunch provides an opportunity to let rip with a big meal. But even then the fare is likely to be straightforward and traditional – roast beef or leg of lamb, often with a tart or cake bought from the local *pâtisserie* for dessert.

It should come as no surprise to learn that the French are big eaters and drinkers. They get through 109 kilos (240 lbs) of meat per person per year (only slightly less than the Americans), 22 kilos (48 lbs) of cheese, 62 kilos (137 lbs) of bread and about 80 litres (21 gallons) of wine, which is itself a world record. But more of that in the next chapter.

<u>Right</u>, dining out is one of the greatest pleasures for locals and for visitors alike.

If wines were no longer produced on this earth, a void would be created affecting both the health and mind of man. That void would be much worse than any damage that wine drinking is said to cause. Is it not true that those who never drink wine, thoughtlessly or deliberately, are either idiots or hypocrites? … A man who drinks only water is a man with something to hide.

– Charles Baudelaire (1821–67).

Wine is not a drink in France. It may quench thirst and intoxicate but, for those who enjoy it, wine is the source of a civilising pleasure comparable to listening to music, studying a work of art or eating fine food. It is *more* than a drink. Fine wines speak to the palate and to the mind. Wine, like bread, is inseparable from life.

One cannot visit France without gaining a profound respect for wine. It is omnipresent. It fills shop windows, is served at every meal and is offered as a gift. Vineyards line the roads, not only in Burgundy and Bordeaux but along the Mediterranean coast, the length of the Loire, near the German border, and can be found even in Paris itself. Visitors to France are struck not only by the vast amounts of land devoted to grape growing but to the quality and diversity of the wines produced. The purpose of this short chapter is to introduce the reader to the wines of France via a brief look at the nation's topography, then to discuss what makes French wine special and, lastly, to evoke how French wines are best tasted and served.

Vines and vineyards: A map of France showing the grape-growing regions looks as if someone had spilled a glass of wine on it. A large ring-shaped stain covers roughly two-thirds of the country. The ring starts just below Paris, extends westward to the Atlantic, curves inland along the Mediterranean then swings up north again to where it began. Being a stain, it is far from regular. Indeed, portions are very thick, particularly towards the top and western half of the ring, and numerous dribbles seep out along the lower

rim covering most of the Mediterranean coast. A large drop just east of Paris (Champagne) and a streak in the far east near the German border (Alsace) are clearly visible.

This spill does not touch the Brittany peninsula, nor any of the area along the English Channel. Indeed, most of the Belgian border is stain-free, as is the very centre of the ring roughly equidistant from La Rochelle in the west and Grenoble in the east. At the time, the spill was clearly a dramatic one since even Corsica was dampened, especially in the north, but large patches are prominent both on the southeast coast and inland from Ajaccio as well as on the extreme southern tip near Bonifacio. In all, very few regions were spared and regardless of where you are in France, you will never be more than 160 km (100 miles) from an area in which wine is being made.

The range and density of vineyards account for the extraordinary variety of French wines. There is no one wine-making region – virtually the entire country makes wine – and, given the diversity of climates and soils, it is not surprising that France produces wines with "personalities" as different as those of the people who tend the vines. The fruit of an Alsatian Riesling is as different from that of a white Graves as the red-faced Alsatian peasant is from an austere château-owner in Bordeaux.

This said, similarities exist on occasion and though one can quickly learn to recognise wines with very strong personalities, only those who have participated in countless wine tastings can distinguish one Bordeaux from another or pin a name on a glass of fine Burgundy. Luckily, most French wine drinkers don't bother themselves with such gustatory gymnastics and are no more interested in taking wine courses than in learning to cook… an innate confidence permits most of them to feel capable of fully appreciating a bottle of Château Latour even if their daily fare is Loire valley red.

Wine is so much a part of French life that people in France could no more imagine studying wine than studying how bread is made – both products are so readily available and so frequently consumed, they believe

Preceding pages: grape-picking in Santenay, Burgundy. **Left,** ending the day with a glass.

that through the sheer extent of their exposure they know how to evaluate both. The general consensus is that those who drink poor wine, or repeatedly purchase a rubbery *baguette*, essentially deserve their fate.

Insofar as quality goes, one can confidently purchase wine in France and generally expect it to be fairly decent, without much knowledge of how it is made or even precisely from where it comes. Fortunately, you can't go far wrong because wine is quite good throughout the country. This said, one should not conclude that all French wines are fine wines – not by any means. Within such famous regions as Burgundy and Bordeaux the truly fine wines form only a small per-

Loire valley, Provence, the Languedoc-Roussillon, the Southwest and the Franche-Comté. Though the first four may be known throughout the world, the remaining seven enjoy varying degrees of notoriety and some have an extremely limited audience even within France itself. What makes each of these regions special? And what is one to do when faced with the hundreds of bottles bearing similar names, some even purporting to be the very same wine? This is what we will tackle next.

Grapes and wines: Though grape varieties are thought by many to be the key to understanding and identifying wines, many fine French wines are made by blending varieties

centage of the total production. Indeed, most French wine comes from neither of these regions (production is most heavily concentrated along the western half of the Mediterranean), and part of the pleasure of exploring France is discovering the many "obscure" wines that are rarely exported and often have remarkably specific tastes. Anyone, for instance, who has not sampled the sherry-like whites of the Jura are in for a surprise. As a general rule, wines are always best savoured in or near the vineyards where they are made.

France possesses 11 major wine-producing regions: Bordeaux, Champagne, Burgundy, Beaujolais, Alsace, the Rhone valley, the

to temper their individual tastes (this is systematically the case in Bordeaux). Even in regions were only one grape variety is employed, results can vary enormously from vineyard to vineyard. France is a country of microclimates and this, combined with strong Gallic personalities, means that neighbours often produce wines bearing similar labels but with strikingly different flavours.

This is particularly evident in Burgundy. The Clos de Vougeot vineyard, for example, is archetypical in that it counts over 100 owners. Like almost every other vineyard in Burgundy, it has been divided and subdivided so many times that, every year, there are potentially a hundred different Clos de Vougeot wines to choose from! In reality, some of the plots are so small that their owners simply sell the grapes to a shipper (*négociant*) who combines them with others from the same property to make a Clos de Vougeot under his own label. Hence, unlike Bordeaux where each famous growth belongs to an individual owner, and one bottle of 1982 Château Latour is like another, in Burgundy the quality of a bottle of Clos de Vougeot depends on which of the many individual owners or shippers made it. Within a given *appellation*, some plots of land are better than others and some wine-makers are more talented than others. In short, in Bur-

grape varieties where quality wines are involved and wines made, for instance, with the Gamay grape (such as the wines of Beaujolais) rarely attain the finesse of those made with Pinot Noir.

Though "noble" grape varieties flourish in France (Cabernet Sauvignon, Pinot Noir, and Chardonnay to name but the "top three") they cannot be grown successfully everywhere and, indeed, very strict wine legislation governs the better French wines and even forbids the use of these noble grape varieties in certain *appellation contrôlée* wines in regions where other grape varieties have traditionally been grown. One might go so far as to say that the French emphasis is

gundy, the name of the wine-maker is as important as the name of the wine.

The contrast is even greater when the same grape variety is used in different regions of France. The same Pinot Noir grape, for example, used in all the finest red Burgundies, is also used to make the still red wines of Champagne and Alsace. Though the former can produce sublime bottles, the latter two regions make simply pleasant red wines which are as much curiosities as anything else. Nonetheless one can never discount

Left, wines such as these Burgundies can be the product of several local vineyard owners (**above**).

not necessarily on producing the highest quality wine in every region but a distinctive wine in every region. This, for the most part, is certainly the case today.

Despite such an emphasis on tradition, French wines have evolved and continue to change (generally for the better) even today. Champagne, for instance, was actually one of the great red wines of France until the 18th century when the method for making sparkling wines was perfected and then eclipsed the reds. And in the 17th century, the *clairet* (claret) wines of Bordeaux were not ruby red but pale, almost rosé.

In recent years, the greatest changes seem

to have occurred in the far South where the wines of the Languedoc-Roussillon (a vast area extending from the Spanish border all the way to Montpellier) have attained "name wine" status. This has occurred thanks to the proliferation of new *appellations contrôlées* (wine legislation controlling the way in which wines with specific place names are made). Until 30 years ago, most of these wines were cheap table wines sold under brand names rather than their own. Today's *Côtes de Roussillon, Minervois, Fitou* or *Corbières* may not bring tears of joy to your eyes but many are excellent value and all will be highly appreciated when served with the local food.

to telephone before dropping in), but don't consider such a visit a simple occasion for a free drink. Serious tasters don't even swallow the wine they are offered but politely spit it out onto the gravel floor of the cellar or into the spittoon which is frequently provided for the purpose. Wine cellars are for *tasting* not drinking and, if language is not a barrier, listening as well.

Owners and growers will invariably taste their wines with you and you may get the impression that they are discovering it anew with each sip. Wine, they will tell you, is a living thing and the glass one sips today will not be identical to the glass one sips tomorrow. However, even if one becomes aware of

Tasting wine: Throughout the country, French vineyards are planted not only with grapes but with signs inviting travellers to stop and sample their wine. Accepting such invitations is the best way to learn what French wines are all about but both tact and caution are required. A French proverb warns *À bon vin, pas d'enseigne*, translates as "Good wine, No sign". In other words, wines of high quality don't need to advertise. Indeed, many of the best growers (particularly in Burgundy) live in unpretentious homes with little or no indication that their wine is for sale. Despite such discretion, most will receive visitors (though it is highly advisable

the respect that wine merits and receives in the depths of these French *caves*, it is only at table that wines blossom into the taste experiences that make bottles memorable.

Wine and food: It is a truism in France to say that local wines are at their best with local food. The idea of drinking an Alsatian Riesling with a *bouillabaisse* in Marseille would not even occur to a normally constituted French brain. A Burgundian shivers at the thought that the most potently aromatic cheese of his region (Époisses) could be served up with a glass of Bordeaux. When travelling in France, the golden rule – "local wines with local food" – must be rigorously observed – or else expect your waiter not only to frown but shown signs of consternation and despair. Given this, some surprising regional food associations have evolved. For instance, in Alsace, the local dry white wines are served with pork and sauerkraut and no one seems to notice that this breaks yet another cardinal rule: white wine with fish, red with meat... no matter, Alsatian whites are perfect with pork (and even better with the local Munster cheese).

What if there are no local specialities on the menu? This is frequently the case in the finest restaurants that pride themselves on serving creative dishes and little, or no, local fare. In this case, two other golden rules

difficulty is always which wine to choose?

The elegant choice, regardless of the region you are in, is Champagne (the drier the better) as an apéritif; the more realistic choice will be a local white wine, probably of a recent vintage. Afterwards, best drink the local wines anyway even if the food takes a creative turn. Nevertheless, if your budget permits, remember that the finest white wines come from Burgundy (*Meursault, Pouligny Montrachet*), the best red Rhone wines (*Hermitage, Côte Rôtie*) can be excellent value; sweet wines such as *Sauternes, Jurançon,* or *Monbazillac* are not fashionable but outshine the reds with *foie gras*; the great red Bordeaux *are* the great red Bordeaux, and

should help you make your choice: white wines are served before red and the best wine is always served last. Reflect for a minute on the implications. Both rules suggest that in a well orchestrated meal at least two different wines will be served. The allusion to both white and red hints that both a fish and a meat course will be presented and, lastly, if the very best wine is served last it is not because it is served with dessert but because it will accompany cheese – in short, a three- to four-course meal is in the making. Now, the

Left, a glass of wine is an essential ingredient in every social gathering. **Above**, château tasting.

late-vintage (*vendange tardive*) wines are a must in Alsace or anywhere else they might be proposed.

Lastly, grower-bottled (*propriétaire*) wines should always be preferred to shipper-bottled (*négociant*) wines and, in better restaurants, don't hesitate to engage your *sommelier* (wine steward) in intense discussion ("Was that a good year in Loire?"). Remember, wine is not just a drink – otherwise it would suffice to order "red" or "white". Each sip includes a drop of French culture and each glass potentially contains sensorial memories that will live on long after it has been emptied and the bottle has disappeared.

France has long been considered synonymous with art and culture; with a government that spends 30 times more per capita on arts than the US, this reputation is not surprising. It is a reputation which has drawn many a talent to France: Van Gogh was Dutch by origin, Picasso Spanish, Chagall Russian… but the fact remains they chose to live and die in the *beau pays*. Even the Italian master, Leonardo da Vinci, spent his last years on French soil.

Similarly, although France might never surpass Germany's musical genius, when the

cism, Fauvism, Cubism, Symbolism, Existentialism, Dadaism…) more often than not led by a French citizen. And, perhaps more significantly, art has always been a major discussion point in any political agenda.

And although each new movement meets with relentless public criticism – consider the condemnation of Rodin as an improprietous pseudo-sculptor reputed to use casts of naked bodies to create his sensuous forms, not to mention the banning of Baudelaire's volume of "obscene" poetry – the French seem to

Polish composer Frederick Chopin moved to Paris in 1831, he was delighted to find "the best musicians in the world" already there. Among these were such talented French artists as Massenet and Berlioz, but also the Belgian (naturalised French) Franck, the Hungarian Liszt and the Italians Rossini and Donizetti.

What is it about this nation, that has attracted artistic talent for so long? The warm reception of individualism, dissension and experimentation has not only encouraged scores of talented French artists to pursue their callings, but has continually attracted a large expatriate artistic community and produced new cultural movements (Romanti-

thrive on cultural controversy. The same breath that whispers with reverential horror to its neighbour, stoutly defends with nationalistic pride any artistic infamies. Take the new pyramid outside the Louvre, for example. It was derided in many French newspapers, but now seems to be shown off with pride as a symbol of the nation's creativity. The pride the French take in their artistic communities – be they vaunted or taunted – is never daunted.

That *esprit*, which delights in the daring and the free-spirited, goes hand-in-hand with an element of laissez-faire that readily enables each citizen of the *tricolore* not only to ridicule, criticise or applaud what goes on around them, but also to ignore it. One can imagine Sartre or Oscar Wilde's landladies shrugging at their tenants' controversial attitudes, despite the good gossip it provided them, with the view that, after all, for an *écrivain*, what is normal? In their own ways they too are adamant advocates of live and let live.

Nonetheless, although no good French citizen will ever admit it, things have changed since World War II. The people aren't any less supportive of their country's cultural tradition, but a good number of French musicians, dancers and painters, in particular, seem to be packing their bags for the overseas trip to New York. Due in part to a difficult post-war economy Paris can no longer claim artistic

can industries remain the largest and many critically acclaimed films come out of smaller places like Italy and Japan, the French can be said to have been the true modern revolutionisers of the moving picture – just as they have been with so many other art forms before.

In 1956, a young producer named Raoul Levy teamed up with an even younger actor-turned-journalist named Roger Vadim, to make what was to set off a whole new approach to film. The result of their work was the very steamy (for those days) *Et Dieu créa la femme*, starring the very beautiful and very bare Brigitte Bardot. The film differed from its predecessors by taking on a real-life subject (the amorality of the young set at St-Tropez) and de-

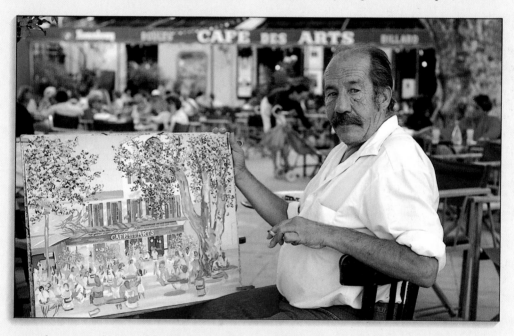

precedence over the rest of the Western world.

The New Wave: However, things are far from grim. As ever, the French have turned their talents towards new horizons. Cinema, for example, has emerged as a real *tour de force* in the latter half of the 20th century, particularly on the back of the energetic star Gérard Depardieu. The French, of course, were the original pioneers of cinematography back in the 1890s. And, while the Indian and Ameri-

picting it in a direct and personal fashion. This kicked off the enthusiasm of a group of state-funded documentary-makers, who were more than happy to turn their talents towards shooting features. One of the indisputably greatest films of all time, *Hiroshima mon amour*, by Alain Resnais in 1959, was the result.

At the same time, some young critics for the magazine *Cahiers du cinéma* began attempting their own short features. Among their number were such later-to-be-premier directors as François Truffaut, Jean-Luc Godard, Claude Chabrol and Eric Rohmer. With a very small amount of capital – a generous system of state aid, flexible trade union regulations and

<u>Preceding pages</u>: spray-painting, as on this bunker in the Landes, has become a state-sponsored art form. <u>Left</u>, Van Gogh on wheels. <u>Above</u>, reflections of the Café des Arts, St-Tropez.

an open-market system of production/distribution have made France particularly hospitable for film-makers – they skipped all the normal rungs of apprenticeship to introduce a whole new kind of cinema. The magazine *L'Express* was quick to dub their innovative style the *nouvelle vague*, or "new wave".

Nowadays the *nouvelle vague* is no longer new or even in fashion, but its impact back then was enormous and still endures. No longer did the screenwriter or even actor seem to influence the creation of a film; the director alone was responsible. The result was an intensely individualistic cinema where each director's hand was immediately identifiable. Truffaut was the first to call this the *film*

1941 and possessing a Renoir-style humanism and strong social conscience, doesn't fit in the new wave group at all. This is the beginning of what became called "kitchen sink" drama, and which later developed into television soap-operas: the depiction of daily life.

A noble prize: The French have always been willing to appreciate the cinema as a legitimate art form, and fine writers like Cocteau showed an eagerness early on to work within the medium. More recent decades have seen literary stars such as Sartre, Robbe-Grillet and Marguerite Duras (who wrote the above-mentioned *Hiroshima mon amour*) trying their hands at film. Some critics, indeed, of the French literary and theatrical scenes have

d'auteur or "author's film".

In 1982 Truffaut renounced auteurism, stating his support for the more recent vogue of "collaboration". And it is true that while most of the great directors of the *nouvelle vague* are still making films, both their popularity and ingenuity have tapered off substantially. The new breed of cinema coming out of France continues to be straightforward in subject and intimate in style, but much more varied and much less selfconscious.

Probably the most highly esteemed director of the 1980s and 1990s has been Bertrand Tavernier, who believes in the "minor heroism of daily life" but, having been born as late as

blamed the widely popular and certainly more lucrative cinema for the decreasing awareness of other artistic disciplines. Cinema, they claim, stole the nation's talents and its interest.

These same critics cheered up when the first Nobel Prize in literature to be offered to a French writer in more than 20 years (Sartre turned down the award in 1964) was given to Claude Simon in 1985. Ironically, Simon is a French novelist of the *nouveau roman* tradition, but, the *nouveau roman*, or new novel, which Robbe-Grillet and Michel Butor championed in the mid-1950s to late 1960s, has long passed from favour – to the relief of most readers and writers alike.

The new novel emphasised stylistic technique and form, discarded classic plot lines and supported *choisisme*; the rejection of metaphorical personification. A long time ago, Ruskin defended *choisisme* with the explanation, "Around us, defying the onslaught of our animist adjectives, things are there." It became up to the reader to decide what a character would or would not do – and sometimes to even rearrange the order of the chapters. Needless to say, the highly intellectualised *nouveau roman* was extremely difficult to read.

As with the *nouvelle vague* in cinema, no real school has replaced the new novel. Françoise Verny, a well-respected French editor, said in 1986, "There was a moment when

community is far from dead. It is simply evolving; from the stereotype of the closeknit café society to a mutually respectful but disorganised breed of modern writers. Instead of in smoke-filled bars, they, the editors and the publishers now only gather two or three times a year at functional "happenings" like the annual *Salon de Livre*. Held in Paris beneath the enormous glass dome of the Grand Palais, this grand book fair runs for a week in March. Twelve hundred publishers put up stands, and it is one of those few chances for anyone to get involved. The *Salon de Livre* also epitomises France's determination to liven up the literati.

And, in testament, an exciting new crop of novelists has emerged – literary critics Yann

the French lived under the dictatorship of the new novel, but...for some time now, there has been a return to adventure, to immediacy, to a greater pluralism, and independence. There are no schools these days, no currents, no dominant gathering places or literary reviews. We're in a period of individual ferment."

Perhaps the French have brought their belief in individualism so far as to exclude the possibility of any artistic clubbing. There really don't seem to be "schools" in any of the arts these days, although the ideal of the literary

Left, publicity for the **Cannes Film Festival**. **Above**, **Brigitte Bardot** in *Et Dieu créa la femme*.

Queffelec and Michel Brandeau, sometime playwright Elisabeth Huppet, biographers Jean Lacouture and Annie Cohen-Solal, to name a few – each strikingly different, yet similar in their emphasis upon the personal approach to narrative. Here again, one finds the influence of individualism and, perhaps, a left-over or two from the intimacy of the cinematic new wave. In a strange way, individualism – or not belonging to a school – seems itself to be the central school since the 1970s.

Art and the State: In France, the old adage that "love and marriage go together like a horse and carriage" might equally well be applied to politics and the arts. The two are so intimately entwined that they often appear inseparable, enjoying a symbiotic relationship rarely seen elsewhere. Today, French culture is nurtured and protected by state sponsorship, while political careers flourish as the country's leaders bask in the approval generated by their benevolent patronage.

Historically, France's leaders have repeatedly used patronage of the arts as a means to glorify themselves and the state. One does not have to search very hard to find examples: Louis XIV and Napoleons I and III were hardly wallflowers when it came to vaunting their power and prestige, through palaces, paintings, furnishing styles, etc.

One of the most compelling examples of

in Europe, perhaps in the world today," said Nobel prize-winning author Elie Wiesel.

The figures alone are staggering. Not only did Lang head up an extraordinary cultural machine with a staff of 12,500 in his direct employ, he also controlled the immense arts budget. Under Mitterrand's presidency, spending on the arts in France more than doubled in real terms between 1981 and 1993, when the proportion of the state budget allocated to the arts topped 1 percent at 13 billion francs ($2.3 billion).

Compare these figures with the $176 million allocated to the National Endowment for the Arts in the US or the British Arts Council's $225 million. Consider that the

the unique relationship between the state and the arts in France is not to be found buried in the history books, but alive and well at the end of the 20th century: that of the latter-day sun king, President François Mitterrand and a man who was once the most powerful cultural politician in the world, Jack Lang, his charismatic and flamboyant minister of arts and culture who dominated the French arts scene throughout the 1980s and early '90s – so much so that they were informally dubbed "l'époch Lang" by the left-wing daily *Libération*, considered by many to be France's cultural bible. "Jack Lang has made the French state the greatest patron of the arts

US government spends $1.43 on culture per capita compared with nearly $41 in France.

Dream team: This is in no small part due to Mitterrand's personal love for art, literature and architecture. But if Mitterrand and Lang were often seen as a sort of cultural dream team, pumping in energy, creativity and billions of francs to preserve French culture, detractors claim that their motives were more to do with personal ego than a simple love for the arts. The accusation of self-interest, which has plagued France's leaders down the centuries, contains more than a grain of truth.

The *grands travaux* provide the easiest targets for the critics. Located mostly in

Paris and virtually all instigated at the behest of the president, cynics point out that these vast architectural projects serve primarily as monuments to the glory of Mitterrand.

It is true that the *grands travaux* have received uneven reviews, from universal acclaim for I.M. Pei's glass pyramids at the Louvre to derision for Daniel Buren's black and white striped pillars in the elegant courtyard of the Palais Royal, home of the culture ministry, to controversy over designs for the still-unfinished Grand Bibliothèque (the new National Library). The Grande Arche at La Défense (a modern Arc de Triomphe) remains largely unoccupied and the glittering new opera house at the Bastille has been

dubbed "the white rhinoceros" by design critics. Yet, these projects remain remarkable achievements and there can be no doubt that Mitterrand and Lang have between them presided over the greatest changes in the Parisian landscape since Haussmann cut through the medieval sprawl to lay out the tree-lined "grands boulevards" in the 1860s.

Outside Paris: But Lang's and Mitterrand's cultural legacy does not stop there. A badly needed decentralisation programme was put into effect in the early 1980s to give the

Left, State involvement has produced the Pompidou Centre; and subsidised theatre (**above**).

provinces a fairer helping of the cultural feast. In a decade, more than 300 museums have been built or restored, and the country has been enriched with new libraries, festivals and theatres. State support was provided for regional orchestras, theatre groups and dance troupes. Always receptive to the new and hip, Lang succeeded in extending the notion of culture to embrace circus, rap music, strip cartoons, fashion and cuisine.

As surveys revealed the disturbing statistic that the average Frenchman reads barely one book a year, Lang launched *La Fureur de Lire* (The Reading Craze), an annual book festival.

A National Photography School opened in Arles, a National Centre for Circus Arts in Châlons-sur-Marne and an Urban Archaeology Centre in Tours. Even decidedly untrendy places like Dunkerque and Villeneuve-d'Asq were provided with museums of modern art.

Not all French cultural institutions are in such robust health, however. The Paris Opera struggles from crisis to crisis despite an annual budget of 8,000 million francs, two-thirds of which comes from the government.

French television is in a fragile financial state which culminated in the 1992 collapse of La Cinq, the entertainment station. While heartened by the success of the new Franco-German culture channel, Arte, the cultural élite bemoan the preponderance of American-style sit-coms and game shows which have invaded French television. The government has drawn charges of protectionism and "cultural imperialism" for its insistence that television use a large proportion of French or European-made programmes.

Some of Lang's projects made him an easy target for those who accused him of being a self-publicist, a gimmicky creature of the media age. His invitation to a French rap group to play at an official reception brought scornful laughter, and a state-sponsored spray-painting contest led opponents to accuse him of encouraging vandalism.

But few would seriously dispute Mitterrand's and Lang's achievements in making the arts more accessible. After the Socialists' crushing defeat in the 1993 elections, Lang's successors face a daunting task in trying to match their cultural legacy and the outstanding record of a man whose patronage Italian film-maker Frederico Fellini compared to that of "Renaissance princes and popes".

"We protest against this column of iron sheets bolted together, this ridiculous vertiginous chimney glorifying the vandalism of industrial enterprise," cried 300 of France's most illustrious literary and artistic figures in a petition against the construction of the 984-ft (300-metre) tall Eiffel Tower just over a century ago. Among the signatories were Alexandre Dumas, Guy de Maupassant Leconte de Lisle, and Charles Gounod, the composer. Other were no more flattering about Gustave Eiffel's engineering masterpiece, seeing it as a "solitary suppository" desecrating the capital's skyline.

But their outcry was to no avail, for Gustave Eiffel had official backing for his startlingly ambitious project, chosen from among 700 others, to commemorate the 100th anniversary of the French Revolution. Had not the prime minister himself asked for "something sensational, the like of which has never been done before?" Well, he got it, and on 31 March 1889, Gustave Eiffel, followed by a panting band of government and city officials, climbed the 1,792 steps to the top of what was then the world's tallest tower and hoisted the French flag to the patriotic strains of the "*Marseillaise*". Instead of later being pulled down, as its detractors had hoped, France's "Iron Lady" has lived on to become the nation's most popular public monument.

Controversial change: No one much liked the Pompidou Centre either, when it was first erected in the Marais district of Paris in 1974. Its extraordinary inside-out jumble of multi-coloured pipes and steel scaffolding reminded people more of an oil refinery than an art museum. But now, 20 years on, it has become an accepted, if still not always entirely beloved, part of the Paris cityscape.

President Mitterrand's decision to slap a startingly modern, 21-metre (70-ft) glass pyramid in front of the Louvre's classical facade provoked a similar outcry. The *Figaro* newspaper called it "a mournful tomb… soulless, cold and absurd". But the purity of I.M. Pei's – the Chinese-American architect's – geometrical lines and his brilliant manipulation of light and space have long since won most Frenchmen over. It may take them a bit longer to accept Mr Mitterrand's dashing decision to break the capital's unique vista – running from the Carousel arch at the Louvre, through the obelisk at the Place de la Concorde, up the Champ-Élysées to the Arc de Triomphe – by placing, deliberately off-centre, a massive, hollowed-out, white-marble cube at La Défense, the capital's ultra-modern business and commercial centre be-

yond the Arc de Triomphe. The 105-metre (344-ft) Arche de la Défense now dominates the city's western skyline.

French kings, emperors and presidents have always liked to leave a three-dimensional mark behind them for posterity. But with the possible exception of Louis XIV and Napoleon, François Mitterrand has outdone them all. He has personally initiated or completed no fewer than nine monumental works in Paris: the Grand Louvre (including the pyramid), both the Cité des Sciences and the new music centre at the Parc de la Villette, the Musée d'Orsay, the Opera de la Bastille, the Arche de la Défense, the Institut du Monde

Preceding pages: La Défense, now complete. **Left**, the Futuroscope, a science park in Poitiers. **Right**, the Louvre pyramid.

Arabe, the Finance Ministry at Bercy, the new international conference centre near the Eiffel Tower, and the much-contested four-towered National Library near the Gare d'Austerlitz. No expense has been spared. The total cost to the taxpayer is estimated at over 30 billion francs. Like them or loathe them, Mr Mitterrand's *grands travaux* certainly make a bold and exciting addition to what the French claim to be the most beautiful city in the world.

The French are a proud, fiercely patriotic people, with an eye for beauty and design. They love to make a splash, to attract attention, to be in the avant-garde. They take a personal pride in their nation's innovative

to carry them out. The ordinary Frenchman does not usually stop to count the cost. For him, anything which is seen to aid the country's greatness is justification enough.

In the past, France has often been in the forefront of scientific invention. It has produced leading pioneers in many fields, including radiology, pasteurisation, aeronautics, photography, and nuclear physics. But it has only really been in recent decades, under the impetus of Presidents Giscard d'Estaing and Mitterrand, that it has moved into the era of advanced technology.

Take nuclear power. In 1978, at the time of the first oil shock, nuclear power accounted for less than two percent of France's basic

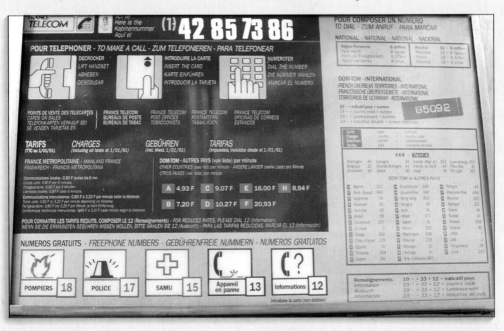

achievements whether in the field of architecture, haute couture, or advanced technology – particularly if such projects are carried out on a grand scale. The Suez Canal, the Concorde supersonic aircraft, the Channel Tunnel, the Ariane space rocket, the TGV (*Train à Grande Vitesse*) – these are the kind of projects at which the French excel. France has the advantage of having both a powerful, highly-centralised state with the means and vision required to back such projects, and an élite corps of engineers trained at the nation's most prestigious universities (the *grandes écoles* founded under the Revolution) with the imagination and skills required

energy needs. Today, France has become the most "nuclearised" nation in the world, with three-quarters of its electricity and over a third of its total energy being supplied by nuclear power. Or take biotechnology. A decade ago, France was so far behind in this highly competitive, fast-moving field, that it looked as if it had missed out on the race altogether. Now, thanks to a massive injection of government cash, it has become one of the world's front-runners.

Telecommunications provides another example of the successful partnership between state direction and native French technological flair. In the early 1970s, France had one of the most backward telecommunications systems in Europe, with fewer telephone lines per capita even than Greece. Today, thanks again to massive investment, it has one of the most efficient and advanced systems in the world. Of particular note is the success of its home viewdata system, Minitel, launched in 1984. With more than five million subscribers (the terminals are provided free of charge), it has become the biggest videotex system in the world, providing access to over 16,000 database services ranging from train timetables to advice on where to get the best fresh foie gras and a chance to participate in erotic, multi-party, screen conversations (the famous *messageries roses*).

have often been slashed by half or more. Once the tunnel opens, the journey between Paris and London will take just three hours. It would have taken half an hour less if the British had built a high-speed link between London and Dover... A high-speed Paris bypass linking the northern TGV line directly with the south, including stops at Charles de Gaulle airport and the Euro Disney leisure park, is under way. Further TGV extensions to Marseille and Montpellier are expected to be completed in 1998.

In aeronautics, France has long been a pace-setter. The first man to fly the Channel was a Frenchman, Henri Blériot, in 1909. France has been the driving force behind the

Getting there fast: In transport technology, France is again one of the world's acknowledged leaders. As well as holding the world rail speed (with a top speed of 514 kph or 320 mph), its TGV train is a model of comfort and efficiency. Opened on specially-constructed track between Paris and Lyon in 1981, the TGV service has since been extended westward to Tours and Le Mans and northward to Calais to link up with the Channel Tunnel. With an average cruising speed of 300 kph (186 mph) on the new lines, journey times

Right, advanced telecommunications. **Above**, the Géode at La Villette, Paris's science museum.

highly successful, wide-bodied Airbus commercial aircraft, produced by a six-nation European consortium (including Britain). Although, by contrast, the Franco-British supersonic aircraft, Concorde, has proved a commercial flop, it nevertheless marked up another triumph for French aviation technology. France has also been the prime mover behind the European space effort, providing the bulk of both the funds and technology for the Ariane space rocket (around 80 commercial satellites successfully launched in nearly 60 flights and for the planned Hermes manned space shuttle (now indefinitely postponed for want of money). Four Frenchmen have already been into space (on American and Russian flights) and France's first woman astronaut will go into orbit in 1996.

With 26,000 employees, France's Centre National pour la Récherche Scientifique (CNRS) is one of the biggest and finest centrally-financed research bodies devoted to pure science in the world. Thanks to the state-financed *grandes écoles*, France also has one of the best teams of engineers and applied scientists in the world. Yet, the two have traditionally remained woefully isolated from one another. Over the last couple of decades, there has been a big effort to remedy this failing, notably by setting up *technopoles* to bring academic research sci-

entists and industrialists together. Based on the university-centred science parks in the US and Britain, the first French *technopole* was set up in Grenoble in the late 1980s. The idea caught on like wild-fire. Today, there are 40 such centres ranging from the three-hectare Helioparc at Pô to the huge 2,600-hectare research park cum new-town of Sofia-Antiopolis on the Côte d'Azur. No French city now considers itself complete without its own *technopole*.

The political decentralisation of the 1980s helped to accelerate this trend. The result was a veritable orgy of spending as towns vied with one another in the splendour of

their new opera houses, pedestrian zones, museums, sports stadiums, new-age public transport systems and high-tech research facilities. The extent of regional renewal over the past decade has been impressive. The legendary sleepy, backward, French provincial towns are now largely a thing of the past.

Accessible science: The enormous success of Paris's new "hands-on" science museum, the Cité des Sciences et de l'Industrie in Parc de la Villette, bears witness to the ordinary Frenchman's fascination with technological and scientific marvels. Commissioned by President Giscard d'Estaing and completed by Mitterrand in 1988, the 4.6 billion franc museum has already become one of the three most popular tourist sites in Paris, attracting more than 6 million visitors a year, three-quarters of them French. With over one million square feet of exhibition space, it claims to be the biggest and most innovative centre of its kind in the world. It likes to describe itself as a "city of activities" with the emphasis placed on making science fun.

A similar approach to the understanding of science through personal discovery has been adopted in the government-funded "centres of science, technology and industry", which have been set up for young people throughout the country over the past decade. The scheme has attracted enormous interest and some 20 such centres are now in operation. The government has even started taking a caravan of fun scientific activities around French holiday sites in its effort make science accessible and attractive to all.

France spends over 50 billion francs a year on government-sponsored civil research. As a proportion of GNP – 2.4 percent – this is less than Japan (2.9 percent), the US (2.8 percent), and Germany (2.8 percent), and exactly the same as Britain. Yet more than most countries, France somehow gives the impression that it is rushing joyously headlong into the 21st century. It looks into the future and plans for it. Its massive investments in high-tech projects do not always pay off. But the French, with their glorification of intellect, have never been very business-minded. They have always had their heads in the air, which is part of their charm, and may also be the path to genius.

Left, Sofia-Antiopolis, technology centre on the Côte d'Azur. **Right**, innovation everywhere.

The architecture of France can be confusing in its variety. Here is an abbreviated guide to some of its major categories, along with the appropriate catchwords.

The Paleolithic period is associated with the cave dwellings that served as homes to the talented artists of about 15,000 years ago. It is noted for its lack of excess ornamentation and its dampness.

Found primarily, but not exclusively, in the south of France, Roman architecture dates from about the 1st century BC and consists

churches, with their elevated naves and complicated masonry, constitute the first monuments of native French architecture.

The Gothic style, so called by Renaissance critics who found it disorderly and barbarian, was actually remarkably sophisticated, having slowly evolved from the Romanesque in the Île-de-France. The great urban cathedrals of France date from this period, and are notable for their vertical lines, sculptural ornamentation and increasing emphasis on design rather than function. The flying

largely of civil improvements such as roads, viaducts, triumphal arches and arenas. It is remembered for its durability and engineering. The towns of Nîmes, Avignon, Arles and Orange offer especially good examples.

In spite of its name, Romanesque architecture (10th–12th centuries) borrowed as much from the Orient and the barbarians as it did from classical antiquity. It focused entirely on ecclesiastical structures, including the monasteries at Cîteaux and Cluny and the church at Mont-St-Michel. Although the thick walls, heavy buttresses, groined vaults and small windows seem primitive in comparison with later styles, the Romanesque

buttress, ribbed vault and pointed arch were the technological innovations that allowed the Gothic architects to attain these new heights, and improved weight distribution allowed thinner walls and magnificent stained-glass interpretations of scripture.

The cathedral at Chartres illustrates perfectly the transition from Romanesque to Gothic, endowed as it is with a tower from each mode. The contrast between the sturdy bulk of the Romanesque tower and the craftsmanship of its Gothic twin (with gargoyles ingeniously combining structural balance with didactic purpose) shows the progression of French architectural taste.

The Renaissance of the 16th century brought from Italy a new interest in secular architecture and classical order. As the monarchy strengthened, the construction of royal palaces accelerated, including Fontainebleau and many of the Loire châteaux. In fact, today these styles are known best by the names of the monarchs who approved them. By far the most splendid court in Europe, Louis XIV's Versailles represented the apotheosis of classical symmetry and the idea of state construction.

Following Louis's death in 1715, interest grew in the decoration of private apartments and salons. The straight lines and angles of classical influence were rejected in favour of

leon favoured grand imperial structures. The Arc de Triomphe, the Vendôme column and the austere La Madeleine are all based on neoclassical models.

The 19th century revived a number of past styles, but is best remembered for the ornate buildings of the Second Empire period (mid-to late-19th century). Charles Garnier's Opera House, the Hôtel de Ville, the Grand Palais and Paris's stone apartment buildings all evoke this era of grandeur.

Although they were at first considered proper only for engineers, the new materials of glass, metal and concrete slowly gained acceptance towards the end of the century, especially in functional buildings such as

gentler curves, floral forms and delicate shell motifs. The name of this decorative style, rococo, is derived from the French word for rockwork (*rocaille*). It was an extension of the baroque style, also somewhat elaborate, that dominated in Italy but never really took hold in France.

The Revolution diverted architectural attention from royal to civic construction. Like the Romans whom he so respected, Napo-

train stations and department stores. The Eiffel Tower went up in 1889.

The 20th century rebelled against 19th-century eclecticism in favour of simpler expression. The streamlined Art Nouveau style may still be seen in Metro entrances and cafés around France. The Art Deco Palais de Chaillot almost suggests the German Fascist tastes of the 1930s.

Finally, modern architecture brought to France the work of Le Corbusier and the post-war rehabilitation of many cities. The Centre Pompidou, the Tour Montparnasse, and the Louvre pyramid are all examples of additions to the panoply of French styles.

Preceding pages: Gothic style in Le Mans Cathedral. **Far left**, Pont du Gard, Roman legacy in Provence; **left**, guardian of a medieval church. **Right**, Corbusier's Notre Dame at Ronchamp.

France is divided into 22 regions, each of which has its own distinctive landscape and which break down into a total of 96 *départements*. The country is laced with 806,000 km (500,000) of roads, 7,000 km (4,500 miles) of autoroute or motorway and 50,000 km (31,000 miles) of long-distance path; it has 5,000 km (3,100 miles) of coastline, ranging from the wild and rocky Breton coast in the north to the sandy beaches that bask on the Mediterranean coast in the south. Its longest river is the Loire, at 980 km (609 miles), with some 300 glorious châteaux spread out along its lazy length. Mont Blanc in the French Alps is the highest mountain in Europe at 4,800 metres (15,780 ft).

And yet despite these nationwide statistics, France is essentially a local country. Each area has its own individual characteristics, perhaps best exemplified by French food, which is a particular source of pride and the nation's principal export: every town has its own market, reflecting the fresh produce of the surrounding land, and its own butchers, bakers and regional cuisine. Nationwide food chains are anathema to the French; indeed, nationwide anything is relatively unimportant compared to other European countries.

Therein lies the nation's charm for the traveller, and the following pages attempt to do justice to the character of each region. The chapters are grouped into eight sections which reflect particular areas of touristic interest: Paris, the city of lovers and of the birthplace of elegance; the Loire, the river valley that became the seat of kings, with its glorious châteaux; the North, rugged, remote and charismatic; the Eastern Wine Region, lands of verdant vineyards and peaceful villages; Central France, with its rivers, rolling hills and Massif; the Southwest, with the steep Pyrenees and white Basque beaches; the Alps, with high resorts and lakes; and the Southeast, lavender land in Provence and Europe's sumptuous playground on the Côte d'Azur. And finally there's a brief introduction to Corsica, France's island in the Mediterranean.

It would take an enthusiast a lifetime to get to know the length and breadth of France. For those who don't have a lifetime to spare, this book provides a full-colour tour of the nation. Choose what you want, and go.

Preceding pages: Wild surf north of Biarritz; equestrian outing at Arnac-Pompadour; a calm moment at Gissey-sur-l'Ouche in Burgundy; the Pyrenees. **Left:** the walls of St Malo.

France

75 miles/ 120 km

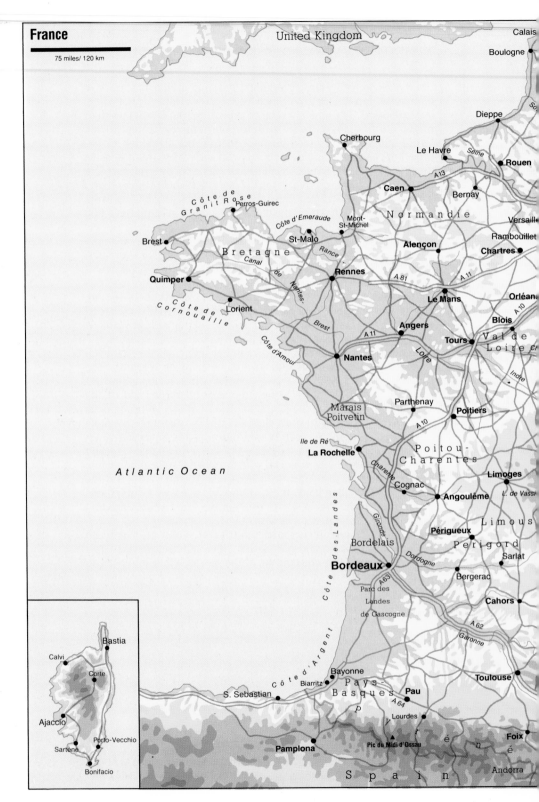

United Kingdom

Calais
Boulogne

Dieppe
Cherbourg
Le Havre
Seine
Rouen
Caen
A13
Bernay
N o r m a n d i e
Versaill
Côte de
Granit Rose
Perros-Guirec
Côte d'Emeraude
Mont-St-Michel
St-Malo
Rance
Alençon
Rambouillet
Chartres
Brest
B r e t a g n e
Canal
Rennes
A 81
A 11
de
Le Mans
Orléan
A 10
Quimper
Côte de
C o r n o u a i l l e
Lorient
Brest
A 11
Angers
Blois
V a l d e
L o i r e
Tours
Loire
Côte d'Amou
Nantes
Indre
Marais
Poitevin
Parthenay
A 10
Poitiers
P o i t o u -
C h a r e n t e s
Ile de Ré
La Rochelle
Charente
Limoges
Cognac
L. de Vassi
Angoulême
Atlantic Ocean
L i m o u s
Gironde
Périgueux
P e r i g o r d
Bordelais
Dordogne
Sarlat
Côte des Landes
Bordeaux
A 63
Bergerac
Parc des
Landes
de Gascogne
Cahors
A 62
Garonne
Côte d'Argent
Bayonne
Biarritz
P a y s -
B a s q u e s
Pau
A 64
Toulouse
S. Sebastian
P
y
r
Lourdes
é
n
Foix
Pic du Midi d'Ossau
é
Pamplona
Andorra
S p a i n

Bastia
Calvi
Corte
Ajaccio
Porto-Vecchio
Sartène
Bonifacio

110

PARIS AND SURROUNDINGS

Topographically central to the nation and with an urban area second in Europe in terms of size (only London is larger), Paris is very much in the driving seat of French administration, politics and cultural life. Chic capital of the world, it is so unlike much of the rest of its own country that it has been described as almost a city-state in its own right. Largely undamaged by two world wars, its centre dates back to the days of Napoleon, with grand boulevards and elegant city mansions in remarkable uniformity. Its street corners reek of history, its monuments and museums are loved by the world, and its people are an endless source of controversy. In Paris, every pavement is a theatre of daily life.

Perfectly preserved though it is, this is also the city of planners and the city which is unafraid of change. The pyramid in front of the Louvre and the massive development out at La Défense are evidence of that. But there are regrets in this continual process of change: this is the city where poets and intellectuals used to gather over strong coffee, and where Voltaire was reputed to drink 40 cups of coffee a day at Le Procope – but the café culture is threatened by the fast food invasion, and the number of Parisian cafés has drastically fallen from 12,000 at the beginning of the 1980s to 5,000 in the early 1990s.

This is also the city of lovers and the city of arts par excellence. There's endless entertainment here for the observant, who will learn more about Paris and the Parisians from walking the streets than from visiting the great museums. The chapter that follows takes you to the most celebrated sites of the city, but it also points out the items of street furniture that make Paris so distinctive.

One of the beauties of Paris is a superb public transport system, and it is thanks to the RER and SNCF that the region surrounding the city is so easily accessible. Day trips to such essential sights as Chartres cathedral, Monet's house at Giverny and the palace at Versailles are described in the Île de France chapter. And one of the area's newest and controversial attractions, Euro Disney, is also profiled in its own section.

Preceding pages: view from the Arc de Triomphe down the Champs-Élysées to the Louvre. **Left:** young *Parisienne*.

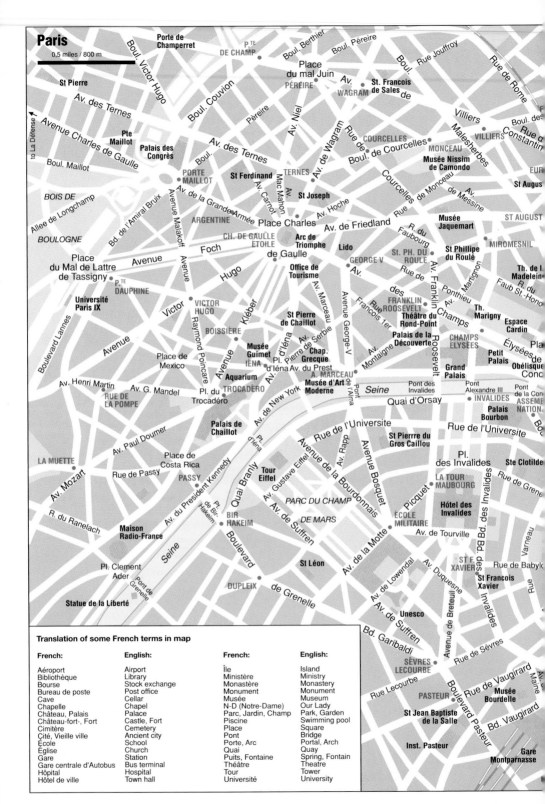

Paris

0,5 miles / 800 m

CIMITIÈRE MONTMARTRE
Av. de Clichy
Rue Caulaincourt
Rue Lepic
St Pierre
R. Lamarck
Rue Curtain
Rue de Clignancourt
BARBES ROCHECHOUART
LA CHAPELLE
Rue de Flandre

PL. DE CHY
 gnolles
Moulin Rouge
Pl. Blanche
Place de Parvis du Sacré Coeur
St Jean de Montmartre
Théâtre de l'Atelier
Boulevard de la Chapelle
Théâtre des Bouffes du Nord
Place de STALINGRAD
Stalingrad

BLANCHE
PIGALLE
Boul. de Rochechouart
ANVERS
Gare du Nord
la Villette
JAURES

Rue de Fontaine
Rue Pigalle
Av. Trudaine
Boulevard de Magenta
GARE DU NORD
Rue du Faubourg St Denis
Rue du Faubourg St Martin
St Georges

Th. de Paris
Casino de Paris
Rue Moncey
Rue la Bruyère
R. de Dunkerque
Rue Lafayette
Place du Colonel Fabien
COLONEL FABIEN

Rue de Londres
Rue Clichy
ST GEORGES
Ste. Trinité
Rue des Martyrs
Rue de Rochechouart
POISSONNIÈRE
Pl. Franz Liszt
Pl. de Valenciennes
R. du 8 Mai 1945
Gare de l'Est
Av. Claude Vélefaux
Boul. de la Vilette

Gare St-Lazare
TRINITÉ
Rue de Châteaudun
N.-D. de Lorette
CADET
Rue Bleue
GARE DE L'EST

T-LAZARE
Galeries Lafayette
LE PELETIER
Rue Lafayette
Folies Bergère
Rue de Paradis
St Laurent

ulevard Haussmann
Rue Laffitte
Musée Grévin
RUE MONTMARTRE
St Eugène
Boulevard de Strasb.
Boulevard de Magenta
JACQUES BONSERGENT
GONCOURT

Th. Athénée
Olympia
Th. Edouard VII
OPÉRA
Opéra
CHAUSSÉE D'ANTIN
Bd. Montmartre
Th. des Nouveautés
Bd. Poissonnière
Porte St Denis
Th. Antoine
St Martin
Rue de Faubourg du Temple
St Joseph

ADELEINE
deleine
Opéra
Av. de l'Opéra
Quatre-Septembre
du BOURSE
BONNE NOUVELLE
Pte. St-Martin
Th. de la Porte St Martin
RÉPUBLIQUE
Av. Parmentier

R. St Honoré
ORDE
de Paume
QUATRE SEPTEMBRE
Bourse
Bibliothèque Nationale
N.-D. des Victoires
STRASBOURG
Th. de la Renaissance
Conserv. Nat. des Arts et Métiers
TEMPLE
Place de la République
Av. de la République

ngerie
ie
ny
JARDIN
DES TUILERIES
Place Vendôme
PYRAMIDES
Palais Royal
R. Étienne Marcel
Rue Réaumur
RÉAUMUR SÉBASTOPOL
ARTS ET MÉTIERS
R. de Bretagne
Bd. du Temple
Boulevard
OBERKAMPF

Rue de Rivoli
Comédie Française
PALAIS ROYAL
Rue de Rivoli
R. des Petits Champs
St Eustache
É. MARCEL
LES HALLES
Rue de Turbigo
Boul. de Sébastopol
St Nicolas des Champs
St Leu
RAMBUTEAU
FILLES DU CALVAIRE
ST AMBROISE
St Ambroise

Musée du Louvre
Palais du Louvre
Bourse
LOUVRE
Centre Nation. d'Art et de Culture G. Pompidou
Rue Beaubourg
Archives Nationales
Rue Vieille du Temple
Bd. Denys du St Sacrement
Boulevard Richard Lenoir
Voltaire

sée d'Orsay
Pont Royal
Quai du Louvre
Pont du Carrousel
Palais du Louvre l'Auxerrois
St Germain
Th. du Châtelet
PONT NEUF
St Merri
HÔTEL DE VILLE
N.-D. des Blancs Manteaux
Musée Carnavalet
Boulevard Beaumarchais
BRÉGUET SABIN

St Thomas d'Aquin
École Nationale Supérieure des Beaux-Arts
Pont des Arts
Institut de France
Pont Neuf
Conciergerie
CHÂTELET
Hôtel de Ville
Cité Int. des Arts
R. des Francs Bourgeois
ST PAUL
BASTILLE

Germain
Rue Jacob
Rue de Seine
Palais de Justice
Ste Chapelle
Bd. du Palais
Q. aux Fleurs
Q. d. l'Hotel de Ville
St Paul
Place de la Bastille
Colonne de Juillet

RUE DU BAC
St Germain des Prés
Boulevard St. Germain
R. St. André Arts
ST MICHEL
Pl. St-Michel
CITÉ
Notre-Dame
Pl. L.Phillipe
PONT MARIE
Temple Ste Marie
Centre d'Exposition

SÈVRES BABYLONE
R. d. Sèvres
Rennes
ODÉON
St Séverin
Pl. St. Louis
St-Louise en l'Île
Bd. Henri IV
Bibliothèque de l'Arsenal

Boulevard Raspail
Théâtre Nat. de l'Odéon
CLUNY LA S.
St Julien le Pauvre
Pt. de la Tournelle
St-Louis en l'Île
SULLY MORLAND
Quai Henri IV
Rue du Faubourg

ENNES
ST-SULPICE
St-Sulpice
Vaugirard
Musée de Cluny
St Nicolas du Chardonnet
M. MUTUALITE
Quai
Bd. de la Bastille
Av. Ledru-Rollin

res
Petit Luxembourg
Sorbonne
Rue des Écoles
St Étienne du Mont
JUSSIEU
Univ. Paris VI et VII
Saint Bernard
QUAI DE LA RAPÉE
Bd. Diderot

ST PLACIDE
de
Palais du Luxembourg
Sénat
JARDIN DU LUXEMBOURG
Jacques
St
Rue du Cardinal
CARDINAL LEMOINE
Arènes de Lutèce
Rue Jussieu
JARDIN DES PLANTES
Pont d'Austerlitz
GARE D'AUSTERLITZ

N.-D. DES CHAMPS
Th. du Lucernaire
Rue Monge
Panthéon
Monge
MONGE
Musée Nationale d'Histoire Naturelle
Gare de Lyon

Boul. du Montparnasse
N.-D. des Champs
Rue d'Assas
St Jacques du Ht Pas
École Normale Supérieure
Rue Lussac
Institut Musulman et Mosquée
Rue Buffon
GARE D'AUSTERLITZ
Quai d'Austerlitz

arnasse
Edgar Quinet
Bd.
ntparnasse
Pl. E. Denis
l'Observatoire
Avenue de
RASPAIL
Institut National Agronomique
St Médard
Bd. de l'Hôpital
Gare d'Austerlitz
Seine

CIMITÈRE DU NTPARNASSE
Boulevard de Port Royal
Bd. Saint-Marcel
St Marcel

117

PARIS

Paris is the hub of Europe, and its most densely populated capital. One fifth of France's 57 million people live in and around the city, along with immigrants, students, artists, teachers, business people and political refugees from around the world. The expatriate community is active; theatre, cinema, arts and news publications abound in various languages, including English. So many of the people living in the cosmopolitan region come from foreign lands and the provinces of France that the native *parisien* has become a rare beast indeed.

The first to arrive in this enchanted spot were the Parisii, a tribe of Gaulish fishermen and boatmen. The appearance of the Roman Empire brought about the strange mixture of Latin and northern civilisation that makes France unique. Though the Romans imposed their tongue, their official name for the city, Lutetia, disappeared from use over the years. Since then the number of emperors, philosophers, ambassadors, adventurers and outcasts who have arrived in this city is as uncountable as the lights bedecking it by night.

One question all newcomers and visitors face is: *Why are the Parisians so rude?* The legendary brusqueness of shopkeepers, waiters and drivers is the epitome of impertinence, an expression of independence and a test of mettle. Besides, the dark rainy winters and the high cost of living are enough to make anyone a little crabby. The fractious are easily disarmed by a little sincerity.

Strollers' city: Lovers know the city best. Silent green courtyards, the river's edge, the misty air are all accomplices to seduction. Some visitors never see the inside of a museum or monument, yet they know and love Paris deeply.

"There is never any ending to Paris," Hemingway wrote in *A Moveable Feast.* Actually, Paris isn't that big, tucked inside a 34-km (21-mile) perimeter. It is divided into 20 *arrondissements*, or districts. Everything is accessible by public transport, though the elderly and those in wheel-chairs will encounter difficulties. Free maps are widely available, but they won't show you the lanes of Montmartre or the key outer districts such as La Défense or La Villette.

Begin at the beginning: Paris was founded on the **Île de la Cité**, the primitive cradle of the city. Some of the ancient soul remains in the island's celebrated monuments. **Notre Dame Cathedral** was built during the 12th and 13th centuries, and extensively restored in the 19th. The original Lady of the Cathedral was a "black virgin", a popular ancient fertility figure. This dark, hooded lady was already credited with several miracles before disappearing during the Revolution. A 14th-century statue of unknown origin stands in the same place (to the right of the choir) and is venerated still.

The building is a masterpiece of Gothic art. The tall central spire (82 metres/270 ft) is flanked by two square towers. Visitors may climb all the way up during daylight hours and see the **Bourdon**, the 16-ton brass bell that the

Left, Paris rooftops.
Right, permanently perched on Notre Dame.

hunchback Quasimodo rang in Victor Hugo's novel, *Notre Dame de Paris*. The view from the top, alongside the devilish stone gargoyles, is a heavenly reward after the long climb up the spiralling stone staircase.

Between the towers stretches a long gallery, and below this the central **Rose Window** has a diameter of 9 metres (31 ft), forming a halo above a statue of the Virgin Mary. The window surmounts the **Galerie des Rois**, 28 modern statues of the kings of Judah and Israel. The statues were all decapitated during the Revolution. Only recently were the heads discovered in a nearby construction site; they are now on display at the Cluny Museum. On a level with the *parvis*, the paved terrace in front of the cathedral, the three doorways of Notre Dame are, left to right, the **Virgin's Portal**, the **Judgment** and **St-Anne's Portal**. Each one is covered with intricate carvings that relate biblical tales and the lives of the saints.

A number of events from French history took place both on the *parvis* and inside the cathedral. In 1430, the young Henry VI of England was crowned king of France in the middle of the Hundred Years' War. French King Henry IV arrived at the cathedral after abjuring Calvinism to receive the coveted crown. His cynical remarks caused the population to doubt the sincerity of his belated conversion. Nevertheless Henry le Grand rode fearlessly to the altar, surrounded by troops in full battle dress.

The coronation of Napoleon I in 1804 was certainly the most grandiose ceremony witnessed here. The gilded imperial coach materialised out of the snow. The gathered crowd saw nothing more than the curtained windows – Josephine and Napoleon drove to the back of the building to don their coronation robes in the wings. In the rear of the cathedral nave, they mounted the specially constructed double staircase to their thrones. The privileged guests, ladies bursting out of their low-cut gowns, gentlemen in uniform and high black boots, were accommodated on tiers of seats. Pope Pius VII agreed, for diplomatic reasons,

Notre Dame in the spring.

to be present at the three-hour ceremony, but balked at performing the actual crowning. In fact, after the Pope's blessing, Napoleon simply crowned himself as the crowd cried *"Vive l'Empéreur!"*

More recently, on the liberation of Paris in 1944, Charles de Gaulle came to give thanks at Notre Dame, while the Bourdon bell tolled joyously and sniper shots rang out in celebration.

Twenty-nine chapels line the walls of the cathedral. The large main altar represents the **Offering of Louis XIII.** It commemorates the birth of the king's heir. To the left and right of the Nicolas Coustou Pietà are statues of Louis XIV (who completed the memorial) and Louis XIII.

The *Trésor* is open daily, except Sundays and religious holidays, and contains richly ornamented robes and chalices. The catacombs are also open to visitors. On Sunday evenings, the organ master gives a free recital for the public. Check the press for details.

In Memoriam: Behind the cathedral on the eastern tip of the Île de la Cité, a small park was inaugurated in 1962. It harbours a monument by Pingusson honouring the 200,000 French martyrs who died in concentration camps in World War II. The **Mémorial de la Déportation**, moving in its simplicity, marks the grave of an unknown victim.

The western end of the island is almost entirely occupied by the **Palais de Justice**, a huge Gothic structure (much restored and rebuilt) where the first 12 Capetian kings lived. At the corner of the Quai de l'Horloge, the **Tour de l'Horloge** dates from the 15th century and is echoed on the northern facade by three round towers which mark the entrance to the **Conciergerie.** Many a death sentence was pronounced in the shadows of this infamous prison of the French Revolution. In one dark room the prisoners ate (the more fortunate had dinners sent in) and slept, struggled to keep warm and clean in the general squalor, and sometimes died of fear before reaching the guillotine. One of the last to go was Fouquier-Tinville, president of the Revolutionary Tribu-

Sainte-Chapelle, jewel of Gothic art.

nal, who sent 2,278 men and women to the chopping block before him.

Queen Marie-Antoinette was held here, in a cell now open to visitors and replete with royal relics of her last days. She left the Conciergerie, hair shorn and wrists bound, in a dirty cart, sitting with her back to the horse so that the crowd might insult her to her face.

On the Boulevard du Palais, an ornate 18th-century gate opens onto the **Cours de Mai**, with the **Sainte-Chapelle**, a glittering jewel of Gothic art, rising up amid the stark walls of the high court. The church was constructed in 1246 by Saint Louis to hold the Crown of Thorns. The lower chapel was frequented by the palace servants and the upper by the royal household. Above, 15 great stained-glass windows fill the room with the precious coloured light that has given the chapel its renown. The walls soar up 31 metres (102 ft) and seem to be made of sparkling glass held by the scantiest skeleton of ornately carved stone.

Île de la Cité connects with the **Île Saint-Louis** by the Pont St-Louis. The iron bridge leads to the smaller of the two Seine islands, soaked in 17th-century calm. Along the quiet streets the visitor will discover small art galleries, some intimate restaurants and tea rooms, and **Berthillon**, home of what is reputed to be the best ice-cream in Paris, which is just at the end of the bridge.

Across the river: Several bridges link the two islands to the south ("left") and north ("right") banks. From the **Pont de la Tournelle** on the Île St Louis, the view onto the left bank is dominated by the glass and steel edifice of the Institut du Monde Arabe, an avant-garde, curved construction celebrating French ties with the Orient. The top floor of this museum, library and conference centre is a terrace café, offering exceptional views of the Seine and Notre Dame. Next door is the famous restaurant **La Tour d'Argent**, with three Michelin stars and the same view as the Arab Institute.

Closer to Notre Dame, the **Petit Pont** links Cité to the *rive gauche*. The shortest bridge in town has the longest history, reaching back to the origins of

Painter on the Pont des Arts.

Roman Lutetia. Originally a wooden bridge, it was burned down many times in the course of numerous battles. In 1718, the bridge and its surroundings blazed up once more, under strange circumstances. A custom of the times was to seek the repose of a loved one's soul by casting a bowl containing bread and a candle into the river. The mother of a drowned child did so, setting a barge packed with straw afire, and the bridge, packed with wooden houses, blazed out of control. This tragedy led to a law banning all buildings on bridges, which changed the face of the city.

Facing the Petit Pont on the Square Viviani is the bookstore Shakespeare and Company. Sylvia Beach founded it as a lending library in the 1920s. Many great and near-great authors have walked through the doors since; some of their pictures adorn the walls of the shop. Poetry readings are held in the upstairs sanctum, often by candlelight, and the atmosphere probably hasn't changed much since James Joyce's day.

The **Pont Neuf** ("New Bridge") at the eastern end of the Cité is, despite its name, the oldest bridge standing in Paris, completed in 1607. It was the first bridge to be built entirely in stone, the widest, and the only one to be equipped with raised pedestrian walkways. These qualities, plus its central location, made the Pont Neuf a popular meeting place for peddlers, acrobats, tooth-pullers, musicians, pick-pockets and prostitutes. From the lower *quai* or aboard a *bateau mouche* tour boat, notice the 900 faces carved along the sides of the bridge, each one unique, and some of them particularly expressive.

Latin love: The heart of the *rive gauche*, that is the left bank, is the **Quartier Latin**, an area made up of the 5th and 6th *arrondissements*. In the early Christian era, the Roman city of Lutetia could no longer be contained by the protective confines of the small islands and spread to this southern hillside.

Here in the 13th century a number of schools opened their doors, most notably the **Université de Paris**, which still draws students to the quarter, though

George Whitman, owner of Shakespeare & Company.

they no longer speak scholarly Latin. The main boulevards are **Saint-Michel** and **Saint-Germain**, both lined with shops and cafés and packed with people. The labyrinth of smaller streets winding around them is full of activity. Students and young people wander in and out of the bookshops and cafés all day long. At night, they head for Greek, Chinese and Italian restaurants, cinemas and nightclubs. On **Rue de la Huchette** a tiny theatre has been playing Ionesco's *La Leçon* and *La Cantatrice Chauve* for 40 consecutive years. The smell of couscous and the jangle of oriental music have become a permanent part of the production. Classical music sometimes wafts out of the **Église St-Séverin.**

At the corner of St-Michel and St-Germain is the **Musée de Cluny**, housing the ruins of the Roman Lutetia, including the **Roman Baths**. The *hôtel* (residence) itself is one of the few medieval mansions remaining in Paris and contains artifacts from castle and church life, such as the exquisite tapestries of *The Lady and The Unicorn.*

A few blocks down the Boulevard St-Germain to the right, the austere facade of the **Sorbonne** welcomes the curious. Cardinal Richelieu is buried here along with his hat suspended above, which will fall, so legend has it, when he is released from hell. Further along St-Jacques, to the left, the **Panthéon** sits at the top of the Rue Sufflot. This 18th-century monument marks the top of **Mont St-Geneviève**, the outer limits of the Roman city. The Panthéon is where illustrious Frenchmen are put to rest, and these include Victor Hugo, Voltaire, Rousseau, Zola and Resistance leader Jean Moulin.

Life is less serious on the **Place Contrescarpe** and the **Rue Mouffetard.** Gaily lit at night and full of song and the pervasive odour of Greek restaurants, the long winding street and quaint square seem to have only recently entered the 20th century.

The only other Roman vestige in Paris proper (besides the Baths at Cluny), near the Place Contrescarpe, is the **Arènes de Lutèce**, the ancient arena.

Arriving for mint tea at the Paris Mosque.

Tough Roman combatants have been replaced by peaceful *boulistes*, playing France's most popular game. *Pétanque* is a good spectator sport too, and the Arènes is a lovely park to have a rest in.

Nearby, the **Jardin des Plantes** is a good place for a stroll, with a slightly mangy zoo, a small labyrinth, and a natural history museum. Near the labyrinth exit, down the Rue Quatrefages, is the **Paris Mosque**. You can enjoy a wonderful glass of hot mint tea and sweet honey cakes in the mosaic tea room. The adventurous can relax in the cavernous marble steam baths (alternate days for men and women).

Intellectual outings: The 6th *arrondissement* lies on the opposite side of the Boulevard St-Michel from the area described above. It has a more formal atmosphere, beginning with the **Jardin du Luxembourg**. The palace, constructed in the 17th century for Marie de Medicis, today houses the French Senate. In the park, children are more in evidence than politicians, sailing boats on the carp-filled pond. Beware lest the enchanted surroundings carry you away – the gates are locked at nightfall.

"Lost Generation" readers will wander wistfully down the **Rue de Fleurus** to stop at No. 27, Gertrude Stein's home of many years; and **Notre Dame des Champs**, where Hemingway lived in a flat above a sawmill in the 1920s. His favourite café, the **Closerie des Lilas**, is still operating to the south at 171 Boulevard Montparnasse and serves excellent meals inside or on the terrace.

The crossroads at **Saint Germain-des-Prés** is another gathering place, the most chic in the Latin Quarter. The cafés **Flore** and **Deux Magots**, favoured by well-dressed intellectuals, face the **Brasserie Lipp**, where (rumour has it) only the most famous authors are invited to sit by the windows. There are a number of fine dress and shoe shops here. Behind the 11th–12th century Abbey of St-Germain, on the delightful Rue Furstenberg, the **Musée Delacroix** shows that painter's work in his *atelier*.

Sacré Parnasse: The southern end of the Latin Quarter is dominated by the

Café de Flore.

Tour Montparnasse, a shiny black skyscraper shooting up above the Montparnasse train station. The 58-floor complex, completed in 1973, certainly changed the artists' haunt of the 1920s, and Picasso, Boris Vian and F. Scott Fitzgerald might say for the worse. But what the quarter lost in old-fashioned charm it has regained in dynamism. Today, Montparnasse is a nocturnal hot spot still favoured by artists.

Above the underground station, a shopping mall boasts small boutiques and department stores. In the tower, an elevator will whisk you to the top floor in 40 seconds. There you may enjoy the panorama of all Paris from the terrace or inside the rooftop restaurant and lounge.

For night owls: On the street, Montparnasse is ringed with cinemas and several good restaurants. Down **Rue de la Gaité**, a number of small theatres, *boîtes de nuit* (discos) and bars attract local night owls. A short walk down the bright and busy Boulevard Montparnasse brings you to **La Coupole**, a spacious, popular café-restaurant with a low-key dance hall. Singles beware (or be brave): La Coupole is possibly the biggest pickup joint in town. The scene goes on until 2am, often animated by heated debates between colourful regulars. The nearby **Select** and the **Dôme** have similar atmospheres, but the Coupole remains the king of cafés.

Just a block down, on the Rue Vavin, Rue Chaplain and the neighbouring streets, there are several all-night bars and clubs with naughty floor-shows. In **Jockey's,** author and feminist Simone de Beauvoir had her first taste of gin fizz, and bid *adieu* to the "dutiful daughter" she had previously been. Stop in for a late nightcap, and you too may leave your past behind.

Elsewhere in Montparnasse the controversial Rodin **Statue of Balzac** stands at the crossroads of Boulevard Montparnasse and Avenue Raspail, and the **Montparnasse Cemetery** accommodates Sartre and Baudelaire. Under the lion at Place Denfert-Rochereau stretch the **Catacombs**, miles of underground tunnels containing six million skele-

Dinner at La Coupole.

tons, stacked against the walls. The Catacombs are open daily; bring a torch, and someone to hold your hand.

The Emperor's tomb: The Boulevard Montparnasse divides the Latin Quarter from the 14th to 15th *arrondissements* and turns northeast to the Boulevard des Invalides. Though most people who visit the **Hôtel des Invalides** approach this impressive monument from the north side, facing the river, a less sterile and imposing first view offers itself from the perspective of the **Avenue de Breteuil**. This avenue, laid out in 1680, rolls forth like a long green carpet to the **Place Vauban**. As one nears the dome, its vast proportions become evident.

Louis XIV ordered the construction of the Hôtel des Invalides in 1671, to serve as a home for disabled soldiers. In fact, it functioned as a clearing house for veterans, many of whom, despite their infirmities, were sent to guard fortified places all over France. The regimen was fairly strict: those who arrived late for meals sat at isolated tables in the middle of the refectory, drinking only water.

The graceful dome, topped by a spire reaching 102 metres (336 ft), originally capped the Royal Church. Today, the building has the tombs of French military heroes, including Napoleon I, Vauban, Turenne and Foch, and contains the **Musée de l'Armée**, the world's largest military museum. In the former dining hall, now the **Salle des Armures**, magnificent suits of armour are displayed, and in the same wing is a fine collection of early arms and battle dress. The facing wing is dedicated to the world wars, and includes some of the famous Marne Valley taxis – cabs which were mobilised in World War I and contributed to the key victories in the valley. Also in the museum are the bed where Napoleon died, a number of personal artifacts and Far Eastern exhibits.

But the Invalides is probably most widely known as the **Tomb of Napoleon I**. In 1840, King Louis-Philippe gave permission to bring the emperor's remains back to Paris. A roaring crowd greeted the funeral chariot on 15 December. According to Victor Hugo, it

Below left, **Les Invalides**; **right**, smiling *gendarme*.

resembled a "mountain of gold". Decorated with eagles, golden bees and 14 statues of victory carrying the symbolic coffin, the gilded creation weighed 11,818 kg (26,000 lbs). The coffin was then set in the Church of the Dôme for 10 days as admirers filed through. The present sarcophagus in red porphyry was designed shortly afterwards by Visconti and has since been directly under the dome.

Eve in the garden: A more peaceful spot is the nearby **Musée Rodin** on Rue de Varenne in the Hôtel Biron, where the sculptor lived and worked. The setting is sublime, and visitors can admire a number of Rodin's most celebrated works (*The Thinker, The Gates of Hell, Eve, The Burghers of Calais*) in the charming garden of roses, trees and ponds. Inside, the various models for his statue of Balzac, which shocked the city officials, are alongside the collection of drawings, etchings and studies. Early critics accused the artist of making plaster-casts of real bodies and pouring his bronze into them. The museum is a magical place to savour the master's work, especially in the late afternoon, when the guard with his long black cloak circles the garden ringing his bell.

A short walk away is Paris's most famous monument: **La Tour Eiffel**. Recently tons and tons of rust have been scraped off her and "Eiffie" looks better than ever. She won her fame the hard way, however. Erected for the Universal Exhibition of 1889, the 300-metre (985-ft) tower designed by Gustave Eiffel was snubbed and disdained by the stylish and intellectual crowd. But ordinary people grew fond of the tower as it rose up slowly over two years, and cheered when Eiffel himself climbed up to plant a French flag on the top. The stormy aesthetic debate raged on for years. Ultimately, the telegraphic communication saved the Eiffel Tower, which became a relay station and is still used for radio today.

There is a choice of eating places in the tower, one very expensive. You can visit the elevator machinery, and a small museum on the first floor shows films of the tower. The view is dynamite, whether you stand at the bottom and watch the iron framework whooshing up, or look down at Paris from above. The best citygazing is about an hour before sunset.

The rectangular park at the foot of the tower is the **Champs de Mars.** The large field has been used for popular celebrations (the first Bastille Day commemoration was held here on 14 July 1790) and military exercise. Indeed, the park runs from the Seine to the **École Militaire**, an 18th-century edifice designed by Jacques-Ange Gabriel.

Trocadéro: As you stand at the foot of the Eiffel Tower, your eye is carried across the river by the elegant span of the Pont d'Iéna. The buildings and terraces spread along the riverside on the far side of the bridge are known as the **Trocadéro.** The site was a wooded hill when Catherine de Medicis built a palace there, and Napoleon planned to build an imperial city, "a Kremlin a hundred times more beautiful than that of Moscow", on the spot. In 1827, Charles X had a fantastic stage-set installed where the reenactment of the battle of Fort Trocadéro in Cadiz was played out. The name remained when the site was prepared for the Universal Exhibition. The present buildings of the **Palais de Chaillot** crowning the hilltop date from the 1930s. One wing holds the **Théâtre National de Chaillot**, devoted to monumental productions of both classical and modern plays, and the **Musée du Cinéma**, whose exhibits trace the development of film from early photos and flip cards through to the present day. In the other wing are the **Musée de l'Homme** (anthropology) and the **Musée des Monuments**.

Whether you cross the Seine by foot on the Iéna bridge, or take the elevated Métro at Bir Hakim you will find yourself in the ultra-chic 16th *arrondissement:* The 16th is home to the *grande bourgeoisie* of Paris, as a quick look around at the sumptuous apartment buildings, expensive boutiques and exotic food markets will confirm. The area has been an enclave of wealth for over a century. When it was incorporated into the city of Paris, the area was given arrondissement number 13. But the in-

The Eiffel Tower from the Palais de Chaillot.

fluential residents made short work of obtaining a more desirable number for their address. Visitors will find the Trocadéro a bustling spot, alive with tourists and kids on roller skates. But at night-time, the residential nature of the 16th makes it quite a bore.

The **Paris Museum of Modern Art**, rather sparsely frequented since the opening of the Pompidou Centre, is inside the **Palais de Tokyo** (another vestige of the 1937 Exposition). In the **Jardins du Trocadéro**, an **aquarium** has been cut into the hillside.

The wine museum: Also cut into the hillside, though at a much earlier date (13th century), are the *caves à vin* located near the Passy Métro station on Square Charles Dickens. Today the ancient cellars are home to the **Musée du Vin** (Wine Museum), where visitors can study the tools of wine-making and the evolution of different bottles and glasses. The walls are covered with engravings, posters, sketches and watercolours, some of them quite funny. There is a shop with mouthwatering merchandise, and you can taste wines and have a light meal at the **Caveau des Échansons**.

On the top of the Passy hillside, **Balzac's House** has been converted into a museum where visitors can see mementos and manuscripts of the famous writer. The house was ideally suited for the ever-indebted author; while creditors knocked at the main entrance on Rue Raynouard, he slipped out the back on to Rue Berton.

In the woods: One reason the wealthy prefer to live in the 16th is its proximity to the **Bois de Boulogne**, a lovely 872-hectare (2,500-acre) park on the western edge of Paris. The several lakes and the many paths through the woods as well as the **Longchamps Racetrack** are all popular with city dwellers. Especially beautiful is the **Pré Catalan** with its outdoor theatre, the **Jardin Shakespeare**. In this enchanted spot, gardeners have tried to plant every type of tree, bush and flower that the Bard spoke of in his plays. There are plays and concerts in the Pré in the summer season, in an unforgettable setting.

The fountains of Trocadéro.

The **Bagatelle Gardens** are bewitching in the rose season, when every species blooms along the fragrant paths. This corner of the park has long been the city's frivolous Lovers' Lane, and *faire la bagatelle* means what lovers do together. There are a few high-class restaurants in the park, but unless you're headed for one it's wise not to venture into the woods after dark. Prostitution and concomitant crime are rampant.

On the edge of the park, on Rue Louis Boillu, the **Musée Marmottan** holds more than 130 works by Impressionist painter Claude Monet. About 30 of the pictures represent his house at Giverny and the water lilies that inspired him. Quite a few paintings from the series on Rouen Cathedral are hung here, too, a startling revelation of Monet's advanced colour technique. Of particular interest is the painting *Impression,* which gave the whole movement its name.

Further west beyond the Périphérique sprawls the space-age city of **La Défense**. Europe's largest business centre and a testimony to the French inclination to innovate, the district found its focus with the opening in 1989 of **La Grande Arche de la Défense**, one of Mitterrand's *grands travaux* which mirrors the Arc de Triomphe. Glass elevators whisk you to its summit, from where there is a dramatic view back to central Paris. The **Esplanade de la Défense** is crowded with business people during the week and tourists at weekends, when the **Sculpture Park**, **Automobile Museum** and **Imax Dome** (the world's largest wrap-around cinema screen) come into their own.

Famous promenade: North of the museum, the Avenue Foch leads from the Bois straight down to the **Champs-Élysées**, the famed promenade crowned by the **Arc de Triomphe**, in the centre of **Place Charles de Gaulle-Étoile**.

The Arc de Triomphe was completed in 1836, and commemorates the victories of the Napoleonic Empire. In 1920, an unknown soldier was buried beneath the arch and a flame marks his grave. If you want to climb to the top for the view and the museum, do take the under-

Below left, the Arc de Triomphe; right, la Grande Arche de la Défense.

ground passage to the arch – the roundabout is notorious for angry traffic.

Stroll down the prestigious avenue or sit on a terrace in the sun. The Champs-Élysées is one of the world's best people-watching places. The window shopping is grand too, and a number of covered galleries and arcades make it a pleasure in any weather. About halfway down, you will find the elegant **Hôtel Georges V** (on the avenue of the same name) a dignified luxury hotel with beautiful sitting rooms and a fine courtyard restaurant. Some of the city's most exclusive eateries are found on side streets off the Champs, but the over-priced fast food bistros on the avenue are mostly pretty awful.

The lower half of the avenue runs through majestic chestnut trees. Several fine theatres and restaurants are set among the trees, including the **Théâtre du Rond Point**, where the legendary couple Jean-Louis Barrault and Madelaine Renaud are still performing. The **Grand Palais** and the **Petit Palais**, two distinctive glass- and steel-domed museums have changing shows and 19th- and 20th-century painting.

Continue walking and you will emerge onto the frantic **Place de la Concorde**. The central **Obelisk**, which graced the tomb of Ramses II at Luxor 3,000 years ago, was erected on this spot in 1836. The great drama of the *place* was on 17 January 1793 when King Louis XVI was guillotined here. At 10am, the king arrived in a cart with his confessor and two gendarmes. He took off his coat and tie and mounted the scaffold. As the terrible roar of soldiers' drums filled the air, the king cried out "*je suis perdu!*" (I am lost!) His severed head was then held up for the crowd's inspection.

The Louvre: The arcaded pavements of the **Rue de Rivoli** are always busy. Facing the arcades, the **Jardin des Tuileries** stretches down to the Louvre. At the Concorde end of the gardens, the small **Jeu de Paume** has temporary exhibitions, and opposite, the **Orangerie** contains Monet's "Waterlilies" series, as well as Cézannes and Renoirs. The

Left, **Place de la Concorde.**

Tuileries were designed by landscape artist Le Nôtre, who also conceived Versailles and other royal gardens. The wide paths and small lawns in the midst of trees are dotted with stately stone statues. Between the palace wings at the bottom of the garden, the **Arc de Triomphe du Carrousel** completes one of the longest architectural vistas in the world, stretching all the way from this small arch past the obelisk and Concorde, through the Arc de Triomphe to the Grand Arche at La Défense, ghost-like in the distance.

There is an obelisk at Concorde, so why not a pyramid at the **Louvre**? Conceived by the American I.M. Pei, the Louvre Pyramid was inaugurated in 1989. Whether loved or despised, the design ingeniously disperses daylight round the ancient courtyard around it and the foyer below, as well as providing multiple entrances to the Louvre's mighty galleries. The original 13th-century palace was a royal residence until 1793, when it was turned into the world's largest museum. The collections are seemingly infinite, from Roman, Greek, and Egyptian artifacts (the latter in the refurbished Richelieu wing), to Renaissance painting, and without a floor-plan it is easy to get lost. The old favourites, however, are well signposted – *Mona Lisa* ("La Joconde" in French), *Winged Victory* and *Venus de Milo*.

The medieval city which succeeded the ancient Roman Lutetia huddled close about the walls of the Louvre. The maze of lanes and dead-end streets was so confusing that Queen Marie-Antoinette, preparing to flee Paris, wandered lost for two hours before discovering the royal coach waiting on the Rue de l'Échelle. Bonaparte was the victim of a terrorist bomb as he rode down the streets on his way to the opera. He made the clearing up of the area around the Louvre an important part of his vast urban programme.

At the Ritz: The **Place Vendôme**, two blocks off the Rue de Rivoli, is a 17th-century marvel of harmony. Under the stone arches, the **Ritz Hôtel** is well suited to its surroundings. Its opulence created the word "ritzy". Hemingway

was such a regular that they have named the old bar after him, and it's a great place for cocktails. The public rooms are richly decorated, and the long corridor from the entrance to the bar is lined with cases showing off France's finest products: silks, crystals, fashions and curious *objets d'art*.

Further along the Rue de Rivoli, the **Palais Royal** also escaped destruction. Cardinal Richelieu built it in the 17th century and willed it to the king at his death. Anne of Austria moved here with her son, the future Louis XIV, because she so much preferred it to the gloomy Louvre. The garden behind the palace is a bright and sunny park. In the shaded gallery at the north end is the **Grand Véfour** restaurant, perhaps the most beautiful in Paris. The 18th-century décor is listed, and its food merits two Michelin stars.

At the far end of the park, you can cross the street and enter two unusual *galleries*, covered streets lined with shops. The **Galleries Colbert** and **Vivienne**, spacious and quiet, covered with

Escape artist in front of the Pompidou Centre.

high glass roofs, are an oasis in the crush of midtown. Tea or lunch at **A Priori Thé** in the Vivienne Gallery is guaranteed to soothe the most jangled nerves.

Just a few blocks down from the 17th century lies the future, in the form of the **Forum des Halles**. This super-modern, glass and steel commercial centre is on the site of the old Paris market. Despite the high-tech building, some of the atmosphere of the old quarter is seeping back. A few notable restaurants, like the **Pied de Cochon** (Rue Coquillière), still serve meals and hot onion soup night and day, as they did when the market kept the quarter lively around the clock.

Across the mall, the **Square des Innocents** occupies the site of the city's oldest cemetery, dating from the Gallo-Roman period. A ghastly spot surrounded by charnel houses, the cemetery absorbed some 2 million corpses before it was emptied in 1786. Today it has come full circle: now it's the preferred hang-out of stylish youths and street musicians. The most outrageous costumes in Paris are on parade here.

New silhouette at the Louvre.

Perhaps the Euro-tramps in motley attire who soak their feet in the fountain don't look so very different from the area's 15th-century wanderers.

Contemporary culture: There's always a colourful crowd around the **Pompidou Centre**, known locally as *Beaubourg*. Designed by an Italian-British team of architects (Piano and Rogers), the building presents a glass facade supported totally by an external skeleton. The skeleton as well as the practical housings are painted bright blue, yellow and red. Though some Parisians claim to detest it, the inside-out museum has become the most visited attraction in town.

There are lots of off-beat exhibits here, and the **Contemporary Art Collection** has recently improved its exhibit space. Dance, music, cinema, theatre and poetry all have a place on the museum's varied programme.

Escalators run up the side of the building in clear tubes. From the top, there is a view towards Notre Dame from the terrace of the cafeteria (the most affordable rooftop in the city), and down on to

SCOOPING THE POOP

Since 1977, when opinion polls revealed that the cleanliness of the streets came top among Parisian concerns, the newly-elected mayor, the proud and energetic Jacques Chirac, made it a priority to overhaul Paris's entire waste disposal and street cleaning system. The distinctive green uniform and vehicles were introduced in 1980. An *école de la propreté* has been added to teach new recruits the finer elements of street cleaning, and today the green, gnashing wagons have become a symbol of the city.

Paris boasts one of the world's most efficient clean-up services, employing 4,525 men and four women to collect 3,500 tonnes of rubbish daily at an annual cost of 2 billion francs, about 10 percent of the city's annual budget. And the green gnashers have gone international: over 230 foreign delegations, including officials from Tokyo and New York, have travelled to Paris anxious to learn the secrets of efficient waste disposal.

The fact is that Paris faces a singularly challenging obstacle to maintaining the cleanliness of its streets: *déjections canines*, of which no less than 20 sticky tonnes are vacuumed off the streets daily by M. Chirac's team of mobile pooper-scoopers. The annual bill amounts to 42 million francs; spread amongst the city's 200,000 dog population, that's 210 francs per dog.

Paris's unusually large canine population can perhaps be explained by the fact that the Parisian pooch is not merely man's best friend; he is also an essential fashion accessory. Just as residents of Los Angeles define themselves by their cars and Italians by their wardrobe, so Parisians tend to express their personalities through their dogs.

From the toy poodle prancing along the Faubourg Saint-Honoré in a tartan raincoat and matching hair ribbon, to the muzzled German shepherd dozing on the Métro after a hard night's guard duty, the capital's dogs are as diverse and eclectic a breed as the city's human inhabitants. In fact, the distinction between animal and human often seems blurred in a city where it is not uncommon to see dogs seated at café tables.

Indeed, far from being banned from shops and restaurants in France, almost every boutique or eating establishment worth its salt has its resident canine character, whose acquaintance it is advisable to make if you plan on becoming a regular customer.

Needless to say, this indulgence towards their pets does not translate well when it comes to teaching *frou-frou* the *toutou* (bow-wow) to use the gutter.

The discovery that the curious elongated sausage dogs with accompanying arrow which appear at regular intervals on the capital's pavements were not yielding satisfactory results, recently inspired M. Chirac to introduce a system of hefty fines. The new law is enforced by an undercover 50-strong cleanliness squad, the plainclothes *agents de propreté*, who patrol the streets and are instructed to swoop on sight – presumably watching where they put their feet.

But despite their valiant efforts, Paris remains a city where canny pedestrians keep a wary eye on the pavement. An estimated two serious falls a day are the result of what the French call *le chocolat*. If, during an unguarded moment, you too find yourself thus inconvenienced, take comfort: Parisians believe it brings good fortune. ∎

Praise for the pooper.

the sloping terrace alive with fire-eaters, pavement artists, mimes and musicians. From the northern end, there is a view over the Marais.

Old Paris: The **Marais** (literally, "swamp"), was *the* place for nobles to live in the 16th and 17th century. The charming streets were then neglected for 300 years, and the grand residences crumbled. Since 1962, the quarter has been renovated, and is now a mixture of rough charm and refined elegance.

The ornate Gothic style **Hôtel de Ville** (City Hall) on the Rue de Rivoli, is the most monumental reminder of the neighbourhood's heyday. The original 16th-century structure was burned to the ground on 24 May 1871 by angry *Communards*. One year later, architect Viollet-le-Duc directed a scrupulous restoration. Recently scrubbed clean and beautified by a fountained esplanade, the Hôtel de Ville has added a visitor's centre with documentation and exhibits on the city.

Behind the Hôtel de Ville and off the Rue de Rivoli, the **Rue Vieille du Tem-** ple wanders into the oldest section of the Marais. The street takes its name from the Knights Templar, an ancient secret order of powerful princes of finance. The Knights went underground in 1312, but their temple, until it was destroyed in 1811, was a sort of safe house where police did not penetrate. The young son of Louis XVI was held there when his parents were tried – prisoner or guest? – and mysteriously disappeared. Likewise, the fabulous treasure they were supposed to have amassed over the years, including the Holy Grail, has never been found.

The **Rue des Rosiers** is the heart of the Jewish quarter. The kosher restaurants and shops sell products from Eastern Europe and North Africa.

To discover even more about the neighbourhood, drop in the **Musée Carnavalet**, Rue de Sévigné, the historical museum of Paris, which also has information about local activities; the Marais has retained a strong cultural identity and is the site of many special festivities. The house itself once belonged to

Singing for her supper at the Place des Vosges.

Mme de Sévigné, 17th-century authoress and vicious gossip, whose *Letters* revealed the intricacies of aristocratic life at court.

Nearby, at Place Thorigny, a new **Picasso Museum** occupies the restored **Hôtel Salé**, built by a wealthy tax collector. Picasso's family donated a large collection of his works to the state, in lieu of huge inheritance tax payments due after the painter's death. The well-organised collection is displayed in this beautiful Renaissance setting.

Behind the *hôtel*, down the Rue Birague is the charming **Place des Vosges**, named after the first region to pay taxes to the new Republic. The rectangular *place*, the oldest in Paris, is where Victor Hugo lived. You can visit his house at number 6, and see not only manuscripts and notes, but also his drawings and handmade furniture. The view of the square from his windows probably hasn't changed much since Hugo gazed out seeking inspiration.

Paris populaire: The limits of the Marais are marked by the **Place de la Bastille**.

This was the site of the dreaded prison constructed in the 14th century, whose walls were about 11 metres (30–40 ft) thick in some places, protected by high battlements and heavy artillery. Despite the apparently impregnable walls, the Bastille fell before the onslaught of the furious population on 14 July 1789. "Is it a revolt?" asked Louis XVI. "No sire," he was told, "a revolution."

The hated jail was completely destroyed and in its place was erected, in 1840, the towering **Colonne de Juillet** commemorating the victims of the Revolution.

Dominating the Place de la Bastille is the new **Opéra de la Bastille**, another monument to glass and concrete, opened in 1989. The "opera of the people" has been dogged by scandal and criticism, but has led to a gentrification of the Bastille quarter (to the consternation of some of its more colourful residents). This is the upwardly trendy corner of Paris – the place to watch, and be watched in your Saturday night best.

From the **Port de l'Arsenal**, the city's

Fast food, Paris-style.

marina on the south side of the Place de la Bastille, you can catch a canal boat northwards underground to **Place de la République**. The canal emerges there and continues through several locks to Port de la Villette. Here, the old slaughterhouses have been transformed into one of the capitals' most enjoyable high-tech parks, Parc de la Villette. The **Géode**, a 37-metres (120-ft) diameter geodesic dome covered with polished steel mirror surfaces, houses a hemispheric cinema screen which takes you on a journey from the galaxies to the depths of the oceans, whilst next door the **Cinaxe** is a giant flight simulator, not for the easily sick. The **Cité des Sciences et de l'Industrie** is a futuristic museum, celebrating man's ingenuity with numerous interactive exhibits. In contrast, the solidly 19th-century **Grande Halle** on the other side of the canal seems a relic from the age of iron.

Rowboats and orchids: The canal boat is a slow and unusual way to arrive at La Villette. But you will have to use more prosaic transportation to arrive at the **Bois de Vincennes** on the eastern edge of the city. The largest Parisian park, Vincennes covers 907 hectares (2,241 acres). Part of it is devoted to the spacious **Zoo** and the **Botanical Gardens** *(Parc Floral)* famed for its annual Orchid Show. Bikes and boats are for rent by the big lake, and after your exercise, you can try some delightful French treats at a snack stand: *gauffres* (waffles piled high with whipped cream or chocolate), *crêpes, glaces* and, in the autumn, hot roasted chestnuts. Alternative worship is found at the Buddhist Temple, rising incongruously from the trees, built for the Marseille Exhibition of 1906.

Though the park is now open to the public, it was long a private hunting ground for kings. Charles V built the fortified **Château de Vincennes** in 1373. Under restoration for over a century, the château now contains a video display of its history, housed in the dungeons.

Père Lachaise: Memories of the past are preserved with more reverence at the **Père Lachaise Cemetery**, beyond the Marais. This graveyard with its

Père Lachaise Cemetery.

streets and boulevards, above-ground monuments and regular visitors feeding the wild cats, is like a miniature city. You can buy a map of some of the most famous grave-sites. These include the tombs of Rossini, Chopin, Edith Piaf, Gertrude Stein, Molière, Oscar Wilde and *Doors* leader Jim Morrison.

The French who visit the cemetery usually come to see the **Mur des Fédérés**. In 1871, the last of the insurgents from the *Commune de Paris* took a stand among the sepulchres of the hilly cemetery. They were trapped and executed against the wall, which still bears the marks of the fatal muskets. Rumour was that some of the *Communards* had escaped detection and were living in Père Lachaise secretly. Even today, there are rumours of strange and unwholesome goings-on after nightfall.

In fact, the area around the cemetery, the 20th *arrondissement*, is a popular residential zone. The pavements of the 20th were the first stage for Edith Piaf, who hit the streets singing aged 12. Her forceful, emotional style won many admirers. Popular slang uses her name – *piaf* – to mean a singing bird. About the only other trace of her is a tiny *place*, east of the cemetery, recently rebaptised in her honour. Another famous singer, Maurice Chevalier, wandered through the quarter as a youngster. He sang, *"Oh, les rues de Ménilmontant, sont-elles toujours montantes?"* – in reference to the steep hill that starts up from the Belleville district to peak at that most Parisian hilltop, **Montmartre**.

This particular *mont* is dominated by the distinctive white domes of the **Sacré Coeur Basilica**, which was built in 1876 on the site of the bloodily vanquished *Commune de Paris*. Few Parisians are very fond of the monument, perhaps by association with the repression of the popular uprising. It certainly occupies a choice spot: the highest in the city, on its northern rim.

A Picasso party: Upper Montmartre residents long considered themselves a village apart from the rest of the town. Painters Toulouse-Lautrec and Utrillo,

Left, on the steps of Sacré Coeur.

and later Picasso, Matisse, poet Guillaume Apollinaire and pianist Erik Satie enjoyed the image of the free-thinking hilltop and made it the happiest place in Paris for artists to live.

If the Commune was the greatest political expression of the Montmartre temperament, the *banquet Rousseau* must sum up her artistic glory. Picasso decided to give a banquet in his studio to honour naive painter Henri Rousseau. The young Spaniard was full of admiration for the older painter's work, but the dinner party grew into an event to celebrate an epoch, not just one man. Amongst the guests were Apollinaire (who escorted the guest of honour), Gertrude and Leo Stein, Alice B. Toklas, Max Jacob, Georges Braque, Maurice de Vlaminck and Marie Laurencin. The guests met beforehand and were feeling very festive by the time they left the bar. The evening progressed (despite the caterer's failure to deliver the food, and perhaps because of the quantities of wine served), through a number of songs, poems and dances performed in honour of Rousseau, who sat on a high platform playing his violin tearfully. One of the guests fell into the pastries, another ate a lady's hat, and no one was surprised when a donkey wandered in for a drink.

The innocent drunkenness of the time is still lingering in the atmosphere of the **Lapin Agile**, a Montmartre cabaret on Rue des Saules. The Lapin is one of the last places in Paris you can hear a complete repertoire of popular French music. Guests sit elbow to elbow at rough wooden tables. Everyone is served a *cerises à l'eau de vie*. One by one, the singers, actors and comics come in off the street to do their gigs, then hurry off to another cabaret or restaurant. The piano player and the boss keep things rolling between acts. It opens late and fills up quickly – latecomers may have to stand out in the dark street and listen.

You will find more entertainment on the main square, **Place du Tertre**. Besides a flock of painters, there are bars, cafés and restaurants aplenty, most offering music. For a truly retro evening, stop at **La Bohème** on the *place* for

Letting time pass in Montmartre.

dinner or drinks. There you can polka and Charleston and cha-cha-cha to the strains of the accordion, and join in loud and joyful French drinking songs.

On the corner of Rue Lepic and Rue Durantin, notice a very quaint house and garden. Dutch painter Vincent Van Gogh lived here in 1887 before moving south. Lepic turns into a lively market street that will carry you down the hill to lower Montmartre.

Red lights: This is **Pigalle** (*Pig Alley* to two generations of American and British soldiers), a gaudy red-light district going as far as Place de Clichy. Beware of the numerous Live Shows along this sexy strip. Though they lure you in with low prices, they hit you up for a stiff drink minimum inside.

The famous **Moulin Rouge** is on Place Blanche. The windmill is neon now and most of the audience arrive by tour bus. Though they still perform a version of French can-can, the girls are wearing feathers these days (mostly on their heads). Champagne obligatory. If you want a more modern scene, go around to

the popular **Le Palace** disco, where disco queen Régine is packing them in once more. The Sunday afternoon Gay Tea Dance here is a Parisian institution. **La Locomotive**, next door to the Moulin Rouge, is Paris's biggest dance venue.

Midway between Montmartre and the Opéra, another bubbly showcase, **Les Folies Bergères**, packs 'em in on the Rue Richer. Some say the long success of the Folies (over 100 years) is due to their peculiar precaution of naming the revues with 13 letter combinations (*Folies je t'aime, Et viva la folie*, etc.). But some credit must go to the gorgeous showgirls, who began undressing as early as 1914, which explains the *Folies* Continental renown.

Boulevard Montmartre is at the heart of the **Grands Boulevards**, traced out by Baron von Haussmann under Napoleon III. The boulevards were designed to open up the city centre and beautify Paris. Most of the buildings along the boulevards date from 1850–70 and create the image of Paris that we still have today. Émile Zola, prolific novelist of

Place du Tertre.

the period, described the immense fortunes that were made on property speculation as Haussmann's plan for the city was implemented.

The **Boulevard des Italiens**, leading up to the Opéra, posed problems. Though level and straight today, it was once a small hill. The hill, wound about with narrow streets and hovels and rife with the odour of the pig market, completely blocked the view of the Opéra. There were few complaints when Haussmann knocked down the slums and levelled the ground, carting the surplus earth away to even out the Champs de Mars.

Lyric visions: The beautiful **Opéra de Paris**, designed by Charles Garnier and completed in 1875, splendidly occupies the central point where the great boulevards converge. This is a favourite quarter for strolling, shopping, or sitting on a café terrace. The opera house is glorious and romantic. Inside, the majestic staircase and rich marble decorations evoke visions of swirling gowns, tuxedos and top hats. On rehearsal days, you can only peep through small portals at the auditorium and stage. But if it's possible, go in to look at the surprising **Marc Chagall Ceiling**. The modern painter's pearly blue image of heaven presents a striking contrast with the gilded luxury of the theatre. At the back, an entrance off Place Charles Garnier leads to the little-known **Musée de l'Opéra**, for lovers of lyric arts. You may be irresistibly drawn to the pavement of the **Café de la Paix**. Known to be the most expensive café in town, it is also admitted to be the most attractive.

Tourists also come to Opéra for the many services offered in the area: the American Express office (banking, tour arrangements and mail); travel, tour and theatre agencies; major banks; duty-free shopping. Two of the largest department stores are nearby on the Boulevard Haussmann, **Galeries Lafayette** and **Printemps**. Both have information booths at ground level.

Boulevard de la Madeleine is a wide fashionable artery leading to the church of the same name. This imposing and squat 19th-century "Greek temple" is an austere note, but a flower market and some high-tone shops dress up the square. One of the most appealing windows is at **Fauchon**. Drool over the displays of delectables from around the world, presented with inimitable French flair. You can take it away in little cartons or enjoy it at the lunch counter. The *truffes au chocolat* are a treat.

If you're still feeling hungry, saunter down the Rue Royale for a gander at **Maxim's** restaurant, the *ne plus ultra* of exclusive (and bulletproof) dining. Maxim's keeps good company in the neighbourhood: Gucci, Dior, Hermès, Courrèges, Laroche, Scherrer, Ungaro, Lapidus and St-Laurent all have boutiques on or around the **Rue St-Honoré** and **Faubourg St-Honoré**.

Back in the centre of town, the visitor can look up the glittering Champs-Élysées, down through the Tuileries to the Louvre, and get a good general feeling for the city's soul. On the left bank, students from the École des Beaux Arts may be wandering out of class, sketchbooks in hand, to head for their favourite café or park.

Left, gypsy musician. Right, window-shopping at Hermès.

L'ÎLE DE FRANCE

You don't have to travel far from Paris for a taste of the amazing diversity which characterises the French landscape. The Île de France region is dotted with castles and monuments, and from Paris a daytripper can choose to visit a glittering palace, stately forest, or quiet garden. Some of these destinations are only a Métro stop away, others are easily accessible by RER or SNCF.

Just outside Paris at the end of Métro line 9, **Sèvres** sits at the bottom of a steep wooded hill. Crossing the bridge to the Seine's left bank, look down at the river escaping the citified *quais* and widening into its natural banks. Porcelaine de Sèvres has been manufactured in this bucolic vale for over 200 years. **Le Musée de la Céramique** is set at the foot of the big sloping park.

The Avenue du Château is the best way to climb the 11 km (7 miles) to the top, where the view from the 17th-century **Terrace de Meudon** is well worth the detour. The **Bois de Meudon**, surrounding the National Observatory, is perfect on a sunny autumn day when the warm golden light dances over the yellow leaves, and the city of Paris glitters in the pale mist like a china toy.

More glitter is in store at **Versailles,** 23 km (14 miles) southwest. RER line C will drop you a short distance from the fabulous **Château de Versailles**.

The palace twinkles on the hilltop as you approach. Louis XIV transformed the simple village and small château into an unequalled display of wealth and privilege. At Versailles, the French court could amuse itself away from the stench and conspiracy of Paris. As a result, it did get rather out of touch: historians debate whether Marie-Antoinette actually said of the starving population during the Revolution, "Let them eat cake," but angry crowds did drag Louis XVI and his wife back to Paris. The château was ransacked, but saved from ruin.

Inside, guides take you through the **King's Apartments**, including his bed-chamber, placed exactly in the centre of the symmetrical palace. The other rooms, including Marie-Antoinette's, are furnished in matchless Louis XIV style. The long **Gallerie des Glaces** is hung with remarkable mirrors facing the French windows which look out over the terrace and the park.

The park was designed by André Le Nôtre, the landscape artist who created the image of the royal garden *à la française*. From the palace steps, you can look down the length of the **Grand Canal** in the form of a fleur-de-lis, which divides the park in two. On each side of the central alley leading to **Apollo's Pool**, the woods are sprinkled with delightful statues, secret groves, goldfish ponds, fountains, flowerbeds and surprises. It is from the bottom of the park, at the far end of the canal, that the beauty of the palace architecture is best appreciated. The building floats on air, buoyed up by the fluffy mass of the trees on either side, capturing the sunlight in its bright windows and gilded ornaments. Don't be fooled by the tricks of

perspective the gardens can play – it's nearly 5 km (3 miles) around the canal! On the northern side of the park, Louis XIV had a smaller residence built where he could escape from the stiff etiquette of the court. The **Grand Trianon** is near the **Petit Trianon** added on by Louis XV, and the **Hameau**, a make-believe village where Marie-Antoinette played milkmaid.

If all this puts you in a mood to pamper yourself, try the tea room at the top of the **Grand Canal**. From the Le Nôtre terrace there is a spectacular view of the Forêt de Saint-Germain. Another royal retreat, **Saint-Germain-en-Laye** is the city's most chic suburb, perched above the Seine since the 12th century.

Impressionist inspiration: To the northwest of here, near the town of Vernon (Autoroute 13 or train from Saint-Lazare), a pink and green country house sits basking in the sunlight and flowers. This is **Giverny**, home of painter Claude Monet until his death in 1926. Visitors are so plentiful on summer afternoons that it is advisable to arrive early in order to enjoy the bright gardens alone. The little pond and Japanese bridge, the wisteria, azalea and water lilies, inspired some of Impressionism's greatest works. New in Giverny is the **Musée Américain** which demonstrates the influence of Monet and French Impressionism on American painting.

Due north, **Saint-Denis Cathedral** is less than 5 km (3 miles) outside Paris. King Dagobert founded an abbey here in 630; the church became first a basilica, then a cathedral. Over the centuries, French kings and queens have been buried in St-Denis. Their tombs are marked with some of the country's finest medieval and Renaissance sculptures. Despite the poor quality of recent renovations, the cathedral represents one of the earliest masterpieces of Gothic architecture.

From the Gare du Nord, you can catch a train farther north to the great forests. In the delightful **Forêt de Chantilly**, the **Château de Chantilly** nestles in a grove. Wild ducks settle in the moat around the blue and white palace. In-

Giverny water lilies.

side, the **Condé Museum**'s collection of Botticelli, Raphael, Giotto and Holbein paintings will amaze you.

On Sunday afternoons from May to September, the waltzing thoroughbreds of the **Musée Vivant de Cheval** in Chantilly offer an impressive display of horsemanship under the magnificent dome of the 18th-century stables. The racecourse here is one of France's most fashionable.

The contingent **Forêt d'Ermononville** boasts an unusual attraction: **La Mer de Sable**, a desert-like area covered in white sand. Big rocks poke out of the curious "Sea of Sand". The amusement park has a Wild West theme.

The largest of the great forests circling Paris is the **Forêt de Compiègne** covering 15,380 hectares (38,000 acres) with oak and beech, ponds and streams, and the hunting trails of kings. The ancient city of **Compiègne** on the banks of the Oise was long a royal residence, as the château testifies. But the Gothic **Hôtel de Ville** steals the spotlight. At the top of its central spire, the oldest bell in France is struck by three figures in pantaloons known as *Picantins.*

Forest excursions: From the centre of the aristocratic little city you can make a number of excursions into the forest. Just outside town, stop at **Les Beaux Monts** for a bird's-eye view of Compiègne and the Oise valley below. From here, a pedestrian circuit has been marked out to guide you through the forest and back in one or two hours.

The **Armistice Wagon** is parked in the clearing where the 1918 and 1940 Armistices were signed between France and Germany. The railway coach is inside a small building which also houses a collection of photos and newspaper records from both world wars. Some of the earlier pictures have to be viewed on stereoscopes. This curious presentation takes nothing away from the photographs, surely among the most eloquent statements on the wars in existence.

The village of **Vieux Moulin** is the perfect place to stop for refreshment after a woodland promenade. Empress Eugénie preferred to relax and go fish-

Picantins in pantaloons at Compiègne.

ing at the nearby **Étangs de Saint-Pierre**. Not far from the *étangs* (ponds) lies the picturebook castle of **Pierrefonds**. It is a strange monument: a medieval castle built in the late 19th century. Architect Viollet-le-Duc undertook the vast restoration for Napoleon III, who used it for hunting and entertaining.

At the fall of the Second Empire, the castle became government property. Empress Eugénie, known as the Countess of Pierrefonds, returned to visit the château in 1912. She stood with other tourists in the emperor's bedroom, where gilded bees and hunting frescoes adorn the walls. She looked again at the spacious reception hall, bold blue and red and satiny gold, and she wept.

The **Château of Vaux-le-Vicomte** was also brutally separated from its owner, but in different circumstances. Nicolas Fouquet was appointed treasurer to Sun King Louis XIV in 1653. He used his privileged position to amass a fortune. A patron of the arts, he supported Molière and Jean de la Fontaine, and organised extravagant parties that were the talk of the town. When he decided to build a country palace, he called on the finest designers: architect Le Vau and landscapist Le Nôtre.

They chose a site 56 km (35 miles) southeast of Paris, near the ancient town of Melun (National Route 4 or 6 or SNCF from Gare de Lyon). The park was Le Nôtre's first major work. The elegant symmetry of the French garden is echoed by the château. The blue water in the pools, the green velvet lawns and the sandy pathways set off the warm stone and slate blue roofs of the château.

When it was completed in 1661 Fouquet organised a grand *fête* to celebrate the king's birthday and inaugurate his exquisite new home. The fountains spewed, musicians played, torchlight sparkled everywhere. A fantastic show including dancing horses (some of them drowned in the moat) was given for the king's enjoyment. But Louis was not amused. He was, on the contrary, outraged at the display of Fouquet's wealth and *panache*. His aide Colbert assured him that the treasurer's

Gone fishing at Étangs de St-Pierre.

fortune had been stolen from the king's own coffers over the years. That same night, as the last of the partygoers stumbled out with the dawn, Fouquet was arrested and imprisoned at Vincennes.

Louis's pride still wasn't satisfied. He ordered Le Vau and Le Nôtre to build another, bigger palace, sparing no expense. They did, and while Fouquet grew old and died in prison, the Sun King and his court shone at Versailles. Visitors can relive the bright moment of the château's history on Saturday nights from May to October in candlelit tours.

Melun sits on the northern edge of the **Forêt de Fontainebleau**, 20,230 hectares (50,000 acres) of oak, beech, birch and pine. There are weird giant rock formations in the forest, complete with local alpinists and climbers who stay in shape by scurrying up them. The station (from Gare de Lyon) is in the suburb of Avon, in the heart of the woods. This is a starting point for cyclists, picnickers, mushroom hunters and bird watchers.

Sounds of satin: The centre of town, is dominated by the rambling **Château de Fontainebleau**. The first royal residence was erected in the 12th century and every subsequent royal inhabitant left his mark on the hunting palace. The most remarkable work was commissioned by François I in the 16th century. In the long, airy gallery and ballroom, you can almost hear the swish of voluminous skirts, the satin dancing slippers, and the music drifting out to mingle with the sounds of the forest.

Perhaps the château bid adieu to regal splendour in 1814, when Napoleon I, who fled here from Paris when his government collapsed, parted company with the Imperial Guards in the aptly named **Cour des Adieux**. Tourists can experience the haughty magnificence of his **Throne Room** (even the kings hadn't thought of installing one at Fontainebleau) and his private apartments. Oddly enough, he chose to live in the same place where Queen Christine of Sweden had had her lover assassinated 200 years earlier. The splendour and magnificence of kings went hand in hand with subterfuge and murder.

Fontainebleau in winter.

A short distance away, **Milly-La-Forêt** is in the valley of the École River. The first thing visitors to the small town notice (by train, get off at Maisse) is the impressive **Market-place**. People have been shopping beneath the massive wooden *halles* since 1479. Now the square is surrounded by high-priced antique shops and property agents, none offering anything as beautiful as the rough-hewn beams of the simple shelter.

Another old tradition in the area is the cultivation of medicinal herbs and flowers. These plants, known as *simples*, were first grown around a 12th-century leprosarium. When it was demolished, only the **Chapelle Saint-Blaise** remained and it still stands today. Poet Jean Cocteau came to decorate the chapel in 1958. His garden flowers grow straight up the walls, around tiny stained-glass windows glowing like lamps in the cool, dim chapel. A frisky yellow cat is poised to leap into the holy water font. Above the altar, Cocteau painted the resurrection of Christ in pure lines and delicate colours. The inscription on the poet's

tomb is also moving in its simplicity: *Je reste avec vous* – "I am still with you".

West of Fontainebleau, in the lovely department of Les Yvelines, **Rambouillet Castle** lends its name to the green forest around it. The castle is the summer home of the president of France, but when he's not in residence visitors can tour the castle and the park. The **Forest** is the region's richest hunting ground, reserved today for the *Chasse à Courre*, running with the hounds.

Rose windows: Another favourite day-trip from Paris is **Chartres**, 97 km (60 miles) southwest of the city, an hour by train from Montparnasse station. The medieval town sits upon a plateau hemmed in by wheatfields, on the banks of the Eure. The first glimpse of the cathedral's lofty spires above the rich plain – exactly as 13th-century pilgrims must have seen them – is unforgettable.

As you enter the cathedral, be sure to take a look at the intricate carvings on the door known as the **Portail Royal**. The 13th-century stained-glass windows represent the world's most remarkable collection of stained glass, measuring a total of 2,499 sq. metres (26,900 sq. ft). The three large **Rose Windows** fill the cathedral with changing patterns of light and colour. Traces of an ancient labyrinth mark the floor. Penitents and pilgrims followed it on their knees to reach the altar. Parts of the crypt below date from the 9th century. If that visit gives you the creeps, climb to the top of the tower, where sunlight and shadows chasing across the fields will lift your spirits.

Chartres is now a protected site, and the old city has been lovingly restored. Besides the beautiful buildings, you will find crafts, shops selling cheeses, cakes and other French delights, and several very good restaurants.

The Eure river banks offer a pleasant promenade after lunch. Behind the **Église Saint-André**, pathways along the river wind all the way to the **Place Saint-Pierre** and the limits of the medieval city, where you can see the old wall that protected the aristocracy of Blois and Champagne for three centuries. If you wish, you can hire an English-speaking guide at the tourist office.

Left, bringing home the bread; and **right**, Cocteau's chapel in Milly-la-Forêt.

EURO DISNEY

Located at Marne-la-Vallée, 32 km (20 miles) east of Paris on a 1,943-hectare (5,000-acre) site one-fifth the size of the city itself, **Euro Disney** is the most popular tourist attraction in France, with nearly twice as many annual visitors as the Eiffel Tower or the Louvre. Although hordes of school buses are the resort's staple diet, many of Euro Disney's attractions stimulate a sophisticated imagination.

France was somewhat of a homecoming for Disney's second non-US venue (the first is in Tokyo), suggest Disney officials, since Walt's family originated in Isigny-sur-Mer, on the Normandy coast (D'Isigny – Disney). Generous financial incentives from the French government might also have influenced the decision.

Disney has enjoyed a love-hate relationship with its hosts since the opening of the park in 1992. President Mitterrand turned down an official invitation to the inauguration, saying it was not his "cup of tea". Publications such as *Nouvel Observateur* and *Libération* tripped over each other in their race to condemn "la folie Disney". Yet 3½ million visitors in the park's first year of operation were French. The park's first language is French, some rides having uniquely French commentaries. Sixty percent of the 12,000 staff are Francophone, although most of them are bilingual French/English.

Whilst the whole site will not be fully developed until 2017, when there will be an MGM studio theme park, new golf course and more hotels, the present resort is impressive enough. Aside from the park itself, there is a complex of American theme bars, shops, and restaurants – known as **Festival Disney** – and six hotels situated just outside the main turnstiles. To the south lies a campsite, whilst to the east stretches the 27-hole golf course, with a putting green the shape of a certain mouse's ears.

On popular days the magic kingdom – on the end of RER line A from Paris –

receives in excess of 40,000 visitors. If you have time and money it is preferable to buy a two-day pass, and spread out your visit. These passes do not have to be used on consecutive days, have no date limit, and offer approximately 20 percent discounts.

What to do: The park can be a daunting place for mild-mannered Europeans, unaccustomed to American-style fun. Decide on your priority attractions, and get to them early, as lines of restless pilgrims form at top rides from 10am onwards. Heading round the park in an anti-clockwise direction avoids the bigger crowds, since the circular Euro Disney train chugs clockwise. Tuesdays and Thursdays are less busy, as is the low season (November to February, not including Christmas and New Year) when prices are reduced.

Here are 150,000 trees, as many as in the whole of Paris; native North American varieties, such as Red Cedar, Honey Locust, and Giant Sequoia, as well as exotic Judas trees, Monkey Puzzle, Cacti and Palms. The park is visited regularly

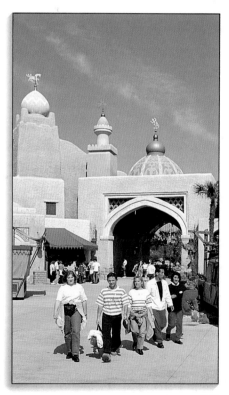

by gardening journalists, there (of course) to undertake serious horticultural studies. The gardens are immaculate, as is the entire complex, with teams of roving cleaners ensuring nothing sullies the Disney brilliance. The code of cleanliness extends to Disney workers, who are not permitted facial hair, earrings, tattoos or short skirts, causing disputes with French trade unions.

Euro Disney theme park is divided into five main areas, or "lands"; a floor plan cloned from the other Disneylands in California, Florida, and Tokyo. Designed by the corporation's "Imagineers", artistic and mechanical wizards who spend their lives thinking up weird and wonderful attractions, this is Disney's most technologically advanced park yet, benefiting from state-of-the-art robotics – Disney's unique "Audio-Animatronics", where life-size, life-like figures speak, sing and dance.

Once through the Victorian turnstiles, already humming along to ubiquitous Disney music, you enter M**ain Street USA**, an evocation of 19th-century small-town America. **City Hall**, on the left, is the central information centre, contact point for lost children and property. Here too is the **Main Street Station**, from where the train circles the park. The station is often crowded, and it is better to board it at one of the other stations on route, such as Frontierland. The bandstand in Main Street square is the best place from which to view the daily parades which traverse the park.

Many of the most popular attractions in the park are found in **Frontierland**, to the left of Main Street, so head here first. **Phantom Manor**, home to some of Disney's most spectacular Audio-Animatronics, provides a high-tech rollicking ride through a haunted house. If the house itself seems vaguely familiar, it may be because it is copied from Hitchcock's *Psycho*. The "dead" tree outside is not actually dead, but specially treated by Disney botanists so that it grows no leaves.

The **Rivers of the Far West**, an artificial lake in the midst of Frontierland, can be enjoyed by Mississippi paddle-

Main Street USA.

158

steamer, keelboat, or Indian canoe. The Indian canoe station, a quiet dead-end, verdant and full of birdsong (taped, but it fools the real birds) is a tranquil contrast to the roller-coaster ride.

From Frontierland, paths lead almost imperceptibly into **Adventureland**. Sparse scrub gives way to lush bamboo and flowers, the twang of Wild-West guitar fading into the beat of African drums. The palms are real, and survive the winter months insulated in foil painted to look like bamboo. Here is another top attraction, the unforgettable **Pirates of the Caribbean** (queues usually move quickly).

Rival to Big Thunder Mountain, the first-ever 360° looping roller-coaster created by Disney, is **Le Temple du Péril**, near **Explorers' Club Restaurant**. Hold onto your stomach as the ore carts plunge through rain forest, and turn upside down above a mock archaeological dig inspired by the *Indiana Jones* saga.

More sedate amusement is found in the **It's a Small World** kingdom, where nationalistic stereotypes are realised in a cheerful puppet kingdom of singing children, first designed by Walt Disney for Pepsi's stand at the 1964 World Fair.

The most popular land for younger children (and thus best visited later in the day, when they have worn themselves out) is **Fantasyland**, containing the centrepiece of the park, Disney's emblem – **Sleeping Beauty's Castle**, or Le Château de la Belle au Bois Dormant. The final stage on the journey around Euro Disney is **Discoveryland**, with its futuristic rides. The top draw here is **Star Tours**, a trip into space with George Lucas's *Star Wars* characters.

The wider resort, Festival Disney and the hotels and camp sites make up a celebration of "Americana" – a direct response to Disney's view of how Europeans view America. **Festival Disney** is the place to get a beer after a long day at the theme park. Open until 2am, the complex boasts flashing neon, country and western music and Cadillacs. The end nearest the lake is more sedate, and more expensive.

A daily parade.

AROUND THE LOIRE

The romantic image of the Loire Valley is quintessentially French; the gentle France of medieval tapestries, the hunt of the Sun King, splendid Renaissance châteaux, Rabelais and gargantuan feasts. What was once a valley of kings has given way to a more bourgeois paradise that can be enjoyed by all, with food and wine of a quality to delight the most discerning traveller.

Between Giens and Angers the Loire Valley is a lush and fertile region, fought over for centuries by a succession of French and foreign protagonists. All along the banks of the mighty river is the architectural evidence; châteaux which range from the gloomy defences of Langeais or Chinon to the exquisite Renaissance detail of Azay-le-Rideau or Chenonceaux, built at a time when pleasure began to predominate over protection. Here too is Chambord, with its spectacular roof once described as "the skyline of Constantinople on a single building," and Villandry with some of the finest formal gardens on France.

Beyond this rich panoply of floodlit battlements and luxurious interiors more rural pleasures await; the gentle landscape of Anjou, the misty woodland of the Sologne, the Orléanais with its half timbered farms and rolling vineyards, the quiet meanderings of the Loire's lesser tributaries; the Indre, Cher, Vienne and Indrois.

The bucolic charms of the region are easily matched by the sophistication of its cities which provide a wealth of magnificent architecture, superb restaurants and elegant shopping. Don't miss the old quarter of Blois, the fine museums of Tours, or the grand parks of Orléans.

But perhaps one of the greatest joys is simply to sit on the river bank and watch the *"avenue qui marche"* flow slowly by on its inexorable journey to the sea.

Preceding pages: formal ornamental gardens at Villandry. **Left,** Chambord, jewel in the night.

ALONG THE LOIRE RIVER

The wealth and beauty amassed over the centuries in the Loire valley is almost beyond belief. This was once the setting for the French court, and courtiers and counts wanted to ensure easy access to the king. But the private domains of the past are now a public showcase of French civilisation. Where all was once designed to exclude the many and please a few, today the visitor is welcomed in parks and palaces.

Set over to the eastern end of the Loire, the little town of **Gien** owes much of its beauty to Anne de Beaujeu, daughter of Louis XI. She was responsible for building the château (now the **International Hunting Museum**), the bridge, the cloisters and church in the late 15th century.

The red and black brick of the château, laid in geometric patterns, is one of the typical styles of the valley. The streets of this bustling little Renaissance town are hung with flags and lined with flowers. *Faiencerie de Gien* (earthenware) is well-known for its bright designs and long history. The riverside factory can be visited only by request (write in advance or telephone 38 67 00 05), but the museum and shop are open daily.

About 23 km (14 miles) downstream from Gien lies the château of **Sully-sur-Loire**. Seemingly afloat along with the ducks and swans around it, the castle has two distinct parts: the early 14th-century fortress and the 17th-century wing added by Sully, finance minister to Henry IV. In the older section, three vast rooms on succeeding floors tell of life in the Middle Ages. Furniture was reduced to large chests which served for storage, seating, even sleeping; dining tables were planks laid over simple trestles; the court slept as many as 12 to a bed. The big drafty rooms were lined with tapestries, which were also used as hanging partitions. The high, keel-shaped timber roof, made of chestnut, is 600 years old. The great tree trunks were soaked and salted, heated and bent,

Below left, Bastille Day parade.

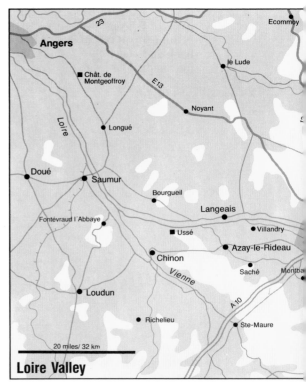

Loire Valley

a process which took 50 years. In the 17th-century wing, the rooms are of more human proportions. The beams are hidden by painted ornamental ceilings and the floors panelled in wood.

Sully-sur-Loire is a rare example of a château with the contrasting architecture of both medieval defensive fortress and Renaissance pleasure palace.

Orléans, where the Loire leaves its northward course to flow southeast, is a modern city whose heart was bombed out during World War II. Its soul, however, lives on in the personage of Joan of Arc; it was here that she successfully resisted the English army before being burnt at the stake. Deprived of its historic buildings, Orléans is now strewn with memorials to her.

Just 18 km (11 miles) outside busy Orléans is the quiet town of **Beaugency**, where an 11th-century bridge provides a view of the river and the town. The tiny streets still have a medieval feel. Market days, with local produce and handicrafts, the smell of roast meats and fresh bread, are particularly atmospheric.

The 15th-century **Château de Dunois** has certainly remained unchanged, except for slight damage incurred during the French Revolution. The museum of traditional regional crafts inside gives an idea of life outside the castle walls. The collection includes nearly 100 *coiffes*, the finely embroidered linen bonnets local women wore religiously until World War II – when they ran out of starch!

The hunting lodge: If going from Beaugency to **Chambord**, plan a route that passes through the **Chambord Forest**. Deer, boar and other wild animals roam the national game reserve freely, and observation towers have been set up for the public. In all, the park covers 5,463 hectares (13,500 acres), surrounded by the longest wall in France.

A few more figures give an idea of the size of François I's "hunting lodge": 65 staircases, 440 rooms, 365 chimneys, 30 years of construction. Other than its size, the most striking feature is the double-spiralled staircase in the centre of the castle, where lords and ladies

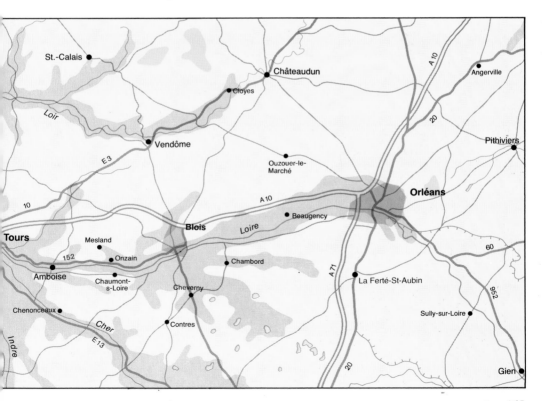

played naughty games of hide-and-seek.

From Chambord to Blois, the traveller can take a delightful route past some less grandiose châteaux, of white tufa stone and slate. At the end of a long alley of stately trees, **Cheverny** rises up gracefully. Though it is still inhabited, visitors can tour the sumptuous 17th- and 18th-century rooms, richly hung with Aubusson and Flemish tapestries. The Viscount and Viscountess Arnaud de Sigalas perpetuate the hunting tradition, and a special *son et lumière* recreates the atmosphere of the royal hunt.

A short distance away is **Fougères**, a charming village off the track of most tourists. The *son et lumière* includes fireworks, fountains and a cast of 60 locals, and well deserves a detour.

To the north, **Blois** was a central stage for courtly intrigue. Louis d'Orléans was assassinated in the château, as were the Guise brothers of the Catholic League. Catherine de Medicis gave up the ghost in the castle after a lifetime of subterfuge and power play. Their stories are told in the spectral *son et lumière*.

In the clear light of day Blois is a gay and sunny place. The château's monumental staircase and its sculpted balconies make a beautiful example of Renaissance design. Though the town itself suffered severely during World War II, the reconstruction was all done in regional style, with slate roofs and brick chimneys. The pedestrian areas near the castle are paved in colourful stone.

The Loire river at nearby **Chaumont** is very wide and the castle's round towers look down upon it from the top of a wooden hill. Catherine de Medicis acquired it in 1560. At the death of her husband Henry II, she forced his mistress, Diane de Poitiers, to leave her palace at Chenonceaux and move here. Visiting the richly furnished rooms, it is hard to relate to Diane's distress.

The lily of the valley: As you cross the River Chaumont, the park and the Loire form a lovely picture. Entering **Onzain**, you are in the **Vallée de la Cisse**, whose winding river flows through pleasant rolling hills, many of which are covered with vineyards for making the local

Deer in the Chambord Forest.

wine, Touraine-Mesland. On the road to **Monteaux**, Owen Watson welcomes visitors to his woodfired pottery shop. The peacocks, and goats roaming freely in the yard will welcome you too.

Downstream, the town of **Amboise** is nestled in around its impressive château. Rich in history, Amboise belonged to the Counts of Anjou and Berry before becoming a part of the French throne in 1434. Charles VIII died here of a concussion he inflicted on himself passing through a low doorway. Visitors take note – and duck!

The murderous Amboise Conspiracy of 1560 was no accident, however, and the cursed château fell from royal favour. Napoleon handed it over to politician Roger Duclos, who demolished two-thirds of it, and World War II damaged a good bit of what was left. Only the facade facing the river reveals the original Renaissance charm. Nonetheless, the château is still famous for its beauty and several unique features: the **Minimes Tower**, with its spiral ramp for mounted horsemen and the **Chapelle**

St-Hubert, where Italian artist Leonardo da Vinci is buried.

The town seems to be a natural extension of the château. The **Rue Nationale** is the colourful main market street, reserved for pedestrians. The essence of a provincial French town is captured in this lively thoroughfare: the sing-song of the merchants, the cafés, the aromas and abundance of fresh produce.

About 500 metres (¼ mile) from the château is **Clos Lucé,** where Leonardo spent the last four years of his life, invited by his patron and admirer, King François I. The house is a museum now, displaying scale models of his precocious inventions, based on the master's drawings. His bedroom and kitchen have been reconstructed and furnished, and a secret tunnel uncovered which linked the house to the château.

Leaving the banks of the Loire, and following the Cher river leads to the **Château de Chenonceaux**. This is perhaps the most elegant of all the Loire valley jewels, renowned for the graceful arches that carry it across the water.

Chenonceaux.

The building rests on pillars planted in the river bed, but might as well be floating on air, light and delicate as it is. The interior is worthy of the architecture.

At night, a *son et lumière* recounts the story of Diane, Henry II's favourite, and his jealous wife, Catherine de Medicis, who could not stand to see so much perfection and not own it.

Recent history touched the château when owner Gaston Menier set up a military hospital in the water gallery during World War I. During World War II, a number of people benefited from the particular situation of Chenonceaux village: the southern exit was in the free zone, while the château entrance was in German occupied territory.

Amboise and Chenonceaux are on the eastern edge of the region called **Touraine**. The city of **Tours** is the centre of this "Garden of France" described by Balzac in *The Lily of the Valley*: "Each step in this land of enchantment allows a fresh discovery of a picture, the frame of which is a river or a tranquil pool in whose watery depths are reflected a château and its turrets, parks and fountains."

As you head towards the centre of Touraine, you'll pass the **Château d'Artigny**, high above the Indre river valley. This place was designed by the famous perfumer François Coty in a pure 18th-century style with spacious lawns and terraces. The château has been converted into a luxury hotel.

Nearby the 10th-century **Château de Montbazon** is mostly in ruins. The eccentric American painter Lillian Whittaker once lived here and fond tales of "La Dame de Montbazon" may still be heard. A small **crêperie** at the foot of the ruins is a nice place to lunch, while sharing the view with a variety of parrots and turtle doves in the aviary.

Tours has a number of interesting monuments (the **Cathedral**, the **Tomb of St-Martin**) and museums at its heart, reached through endless ugly industrial suburbs. Nearly every king, from Saint Louis to François I spent time in the town. The medieval quarter, centred around **Place Plumerau**, is a showcase

Chinon on the Vienne tributary.

of Gothic architecture. One very important event which occurred at Tours was reported in the 6th century by local historian Gregory of Tours. A hundred years earlier, Saint Martin had planted a vineyard around his monastery. One day the dismayed monks discovered that their donkeys had found a way into it and managed to chew off most of the tender young branches. In fact, it must have been heavenly intervention, for the following year's harvest was the best ever. *La taille* (pruning) has been practised as a most important part of viniculture ever since.

The river: Deep in the **Indre valley** lies the river itself, "unravelling like a serpent in a magnificent emerald basin". Honoré de Balzac (1799–1850) loved the valley dearly, for there he passed his most prolific days in the **Château de Saché**. The corpulent author of *La Comédie Humaine* series of 90 novels worked daily from 2am to 5pm when he stayed at Saché.

Inside, devotees will discover a wonderful collection of Balzac memorabilia, including letters and portraits of his lady loves, his manuscripts (which he edited at such length that typesetters refused to work on them more than one hour a day, and that at double pay) and his room, exactly as it was.

The first-floor salon has also retained its character, in part due to the surprising optical illusion of the handpainted wallpaper. The disposition of the furniture and game tables makes it easy to envision the drawing-room intrigues so often described in novels of the period.

Further along the Indre is **Azay-le-Rideau**, a small château of exquisite proportions. The river forms a wide moat around this epitome of Renaissance grace and perfection. The influence of medieval defence architecture is clear, but at Azay all is designed for pleasure. The four turrets are slim and elegant, the crenellations ornamental, and the outlook better for observing clouds reflected in the water than advancing enemies.

The *son et lumière,* every evening from May through September, tells the sorry tale of Philippa Lesbahy, who

Azay-le-Rideau.

dreamed up Azay and supervised its construction. Her husband, who worked in the shadow of the king's treasurer, had trouble keeping the royal account books and his own separate. Scandal broke out among fellow financiers. He fled and Philippa was forced to relinquish her superb home to François I. During the presentation, visitors walk around the park led by torch-bearers dressed in Renaissance costumes.

Touraine's fourth major river is the Cher, and not far from its banks stand **Villandry** and its famous gardens. The three tiers of the garden (the pond, the decorative gardens, the kitchen garden) can be viewed at once from the high terrace of the château. The gardens, planted in low boxwood and yew enclosing flowerbeds, represent the four faces of love on one side, music on the other. The kitchen gardens and herb garden were designed according to documents preserved by medieval monks.

The kitchen garden is like something from *Alice Through the Looking Glass.* Each square describes a different geometric design in contrasting colours that change from year to year in the course of crop rotation. The standard red roses sweetening the air represent the monks tending the vegetable plots.

Sleeping beauties: North of Villandry, on the Loire, the **Château de Langeais** presents a much more severe image. Built as a defensive fortress on the site of a 10th-century stronghold, it has never been altered or added to. The last owner, Jacques Siegfried, oversaw the complete furnishing of the castle in wonderful period pieces before donating it to the French Institute in 1904. Those who are particularly interested in the transition from medieval to Renaissance life will be enraptured by the authentic interiors, the 15th-century Flemish and Aubusson tapestries, the unequalled collection of wooden furniture, lovingly maintained.

Brittany for dowry: In 1491, Charles VIII married Anne de Bretagne in the Langeais castle. Her dowry was the realm of Brittany, which thus became united with France. Her reputation for piety is unsurpassed, and her humility and strength of character shine through the ages in the handsome wedding portrait of the couple as well as in her motto, which she had inscribed on the walls: "If God is with us, who can be against us?"

Cross the Loire and head down the D7, where the many turrets of a tall white castle loom up against the background of the tenebrous forest of Chinon. This is **Ussé**, the castle which inspired Charles Perrault to write *Sleeping Beauty of the Woods.* The furnishings are in poor repair, but children will want to go in to see the wax fairytale figures.

On the other side of the dark forest lies **Chinon** on the River Vienne, in the heart of **Rabelaisie**, the name given this locality in honour of the 16th-century humanist and author, François Rabelais. His satirical works, *Gargantua* and *Pantagruel*, are recommended for those who would like a less stuffy view of the Renaissance. Particularly juicy passages of *Gargantua* describe rather unholy activities at the imaginary Thelème Abbey, where the entrance gate bore the motto: "Do What You Will!"

Villandry.

You can visit his house in nearby **Devinière**. The town of Chinon itself boasts an imposing 10th-century château fort. The English Plantagenet kings spent a lot of time at Chinon, and Charles VII met Joan of Arc here in 1429. There is a **Wine Museum** replete with life-size automatons for kids and wine tasting for adults. Boat trips, carriage rides and steam locomotive excursions are available. These, plus the Vienne river beaches, the *son et lumière*, the medieval market in August make Chinon a fun place to visit.

Now turn back towards the banks of the Loire, passing by **Fontevraud l'Abbaye**. In this restored 12th-century abbey lie the remains of the earliest Plantagenet kings. Four recumbent funeral effigies are the only decoration in the vaulted 90-metre (295-ft) long church. Three of the stone sculptures represent Henry II, his wife Eleanor of Aquitaine and their son Richard the Lionheart. Henry was buried here at his request, though English interests would have preferred that he rested closer to the heart of his kingdom. Eleanor had been the abbess and royal protectoress of Fontevraud. Richard, who succeeded his father to the English throne, also chose to be buried here, next to his beloved parents. The three polychrome sculptures lie side by side. The fourth figure is that of Isabelle of Angoulême, wife of King John Lackland (Richard's brother), and the oldest known wooden monument of this type.

Architecturally, the abbey is celebrated for its large Roman kitchens, with 21 chimneys constructed entirely of stone, though the restoration was completed with some disregard for historical accuracy.

Just across the street in this 12th-century village is a **Regional Museum**, with a very interesting collection of bric-à-brac from past centuries. A visit to the museum is like a trip to someone's attic, though there has been some attempt to organise the objects ranging from neolithic shards to World War II uniforms and including a fine collection of traditional tools used in local trades.

Fontevraud chimneys.

At the crossroads: The route from Fontevraud to **Saumur** (D 947) sums up the Loire valley. Besides the numerous châteaux perched above the majestic river, prehistoric dolmens (stone monuments) and Roman churches and baths testify to a long history of human community in this region at the crossroads of Anjou, Poitou and Touraine.

The caves cut into the high cliffs set back from the river are the result of quarrying to remove tufa, the chalky white stone used to construct most of the Loire valley châteaux. The network of caves created has served to age the fine wines of Saumur, and many of the *grands caves* are open to the public for a tour and a taste. Another use of these cool, dark spaces is the cultivation of mushrooms. The Saumur region is the world's leading mushroom producer; a single cave can produce up to 12 tons in a single day. At Saumur itself, the **Musée du Champignon** offers guided visits of the underground galleries where all the various uses of the caves are demonstrated. Some are dwellings, called *habitations troglodytiques*, and are medieval in origin.

Saumur is also known for its *Cadre Noir* equestrian school and of course its admirable château, housing two museums, **Arts Décoratifs** and the **Musée du Cheval** (Horse Museum).

As you continue on towards Angers, (along route D74), notice the distinguished 18-century **Château de Montgeoffroy** and the long, tree-lined entranceway. This château, resplendent with Louis XIV furnishings, is still inhabited, but open to visitors from May through October.

Angers is the ancient capital of Anjou. The **Château de Foulques** took 100 years to build. The 17 turrets are built in local stone and slate in a striking striped pattern. Formidable from the exterior, the battlements have only a few small openings at the top. From the inside, the view of the grassy moat with its deer and flowers softens the image.

Angers is home to an incomparable tapestry collection. The most famous piece in the collection is the **Apocalypse of St John**, displayed inside the château in a specially constructed building. The world's largest tapestry 107 metres (350 ft) remaining, the Apocalypse was commissioned by the dukes of Anjou in the 14th century. It is an amazing show of complexity, technique and imagination. Each of the 75 panels reveals John, in a small Gothic structure, observing and reacting to his fantastic visions.

On the other side of the river, the **Musée Jean Lurçat** holds that artist's reply to the Apocalypse, *Le Chant du Monde* (Song of the World). Woven at the Aubusson studios from 1957 to 1966, the 10 tapestries are on display in the **Hôpital St-Jean**. This Gothic hospital was built by Henry II Plantagenet in repentance for the death of Thomas à Becket, whose holy head was cut off in Canterbury Cathedral in 1170. Becket is also recalled in the **St-Maurice Cathedral** near the château, in one of a series of 13th-century stained-glass windows in the choir. An audio-visual programme in the cathedral relates the history of Angers, liberally spiced with medieval apocalypse theology.

Left, Saumur leads the world in mushrooms. **Right**, calling the hounds.

POITOU-CHARENTES

Poitou-Charentes is a region where Nature is queen and Tradition her consort. The pace of life is slowed by the weight of centuries, characterised by a strong attachment to the old ways of cultivating, building, distilling and living. One ancient art that is still practised in **Angoulême** is paper-making, for which the city was famous in the 16th and 17th centuries. Today, rag paper is still made in the traditional manner in the towns of Puymoyen and Nersac. This "paper connection" no doubt also explains why a museum here is devoted to the comic strip. The **CNBDI**, or *Centre National de la Bande Dessinée et de l'Image*, was founded in 1982.

A visit to the *ville haute*, or upper city, to see the magnificent 12th-century facade of St-Pierre Cathedral is a must, and from the medieval ramparts there is a splendid view of the Charente valley.

In **Cognac** you can enjoy the famous brandy of the same name. Grapes grown in the region are first turned into wine, then distilled to make Cognac. Curiously, Cognac is never "vintage", that is to say, the year it was made does not figure on the label. The age of a Cognac is determined by a series of highly regulated aging "codes": *Trois Étoiles* from 2½ to four years of age; VSOP (Very Superior Old Pale) from four to 10 years; XO, Napoléon, or Royal if over ten years. Cognac also enters into another speciality of the region, Pineau de Charentes, a fortified wine made by mixing Cognac with grape must. The result is a pleasantly sweet "wine" often served as an apéritif.

A number of private distilleries open their doors to visitors for tours and tasting sessions. One of the most spectacular is the **Château des Valois**, a large part of which was built in the 15th century for Jean de Valois (also called John the Good), but with cellars and a Salle des Casques dating from the 12th and 13th centuries respectively. At the back of the château is the Rue Grande leading toward the centre of the old town and lined with 15th- and 16th-century buildings. Also worth visiting is the **Musée du Cognac**, which not only presents the history of the famous brandy but houses collections of prehistoric, Gallo-Roman, and more recent local artifacts, as well as fine paintings from various periods and countries.

Boats leave regularly in the warm months from Cognac's port to travel down the Charente.

White Isle: The region of **Charente-Maritime** begins where the Gironde river empties into the Atlantic on the Avert Peninsula. The traveller will find the coast more spacious and beautiful moving north towards the **Île d'Oléron**, reached by bridge from Bourcefranc, where gourmets will want to stop and visit the **Oyster Museum** housed in the 17th-century **Citadelle** built by Vauban.

North of Oléron is the **Île de Ré**, accessible by the bridge linking La Pallice Port, just outside La Rochelle, to the Pointe de Sablanceaux. Smaller than Oléron, **Ré La Blanche** is 30 km (18 miles) long and from 100 metres to 5 km (3 miles) wide. The dunes and beaches are made of white sand, giving Ré its surname: White Isle.

At **St-Martin**, remains of Vauban's 17th-century fortifications still surround the town and its 15th-century church. Ré can easily be visited in one day by bicycle, gliding through the vineyards and oyster parks, the cool woods and dunes, on the way to the salt marshes of **Ars-en-Ré**, with its long, sandy beaches, complete with German bunkers.

Back over the bridge is **La Rochelle**, one of France's loveliest ports. The town dates from the 10th century, when it was a fishing village set atop a rocky platform in the middle of the expansive salt marshes. In the following century, a dike was built to dry the land, and now only its name (*roche* – rock) suggests this was once an isolated island.

St-Nicholas Tower and the **Chain Tower** face each other over the 13th-century port where nightly a huge chain was drawn across to keep ships out. The **Lantern Tower** was used as a prison, with graffiti carved there by English soldiers in the 17th and 18th centuries.

Passing through the old gate to the city (Place Barentin), you enter the town centre, now pedestrian only. Many of the houses, with fine vaulted archways, date from the 15th century. On the main square is the high Gothic **Hôtel de Ville**, the town hall and, on Rue Dupaty, the **House of Henry II**, an intricately sculpted Renaissance residence.

Inland and north of La Rochelle is a mysterious region of swamplands and woods. This remarkable national park, **Le Marais Poitevin**, is better known as *La Venise Verte* – Green Venice. Eleventh-century monks took advantage of coastal dyke-building to dig out 1,448 km (900 miles) of waterways, filled from the Sèvre Niortaise river.

At **La Garette** and **Coulon**, local boatmen await tourists with their long forked poles, *pigouilles*. There are 14,974 hectares (37,000 acres) of green silence to discover, under the dome of poplar and oak, on a carpet of water lilies, iris and reeds. The *marais* is used as pasture, and you can see cows gliding by in typical black, flat-bottomed boats.

The regional capital of **Poitiers** is one of the oldest cities in France. It was just north of here that, in 732, Charles Martel stopped the Moorish invasion from Spain, eventually forcing their retreat from France. The architectural richness of Poitiers is rarely equalled elsewhere in France. **Notre-Dame-la-Grande**, with a magnificent, richly sculpted Romanesque facade in the *poitevin* style and 12th-century frescoes decorating the vault of the choir, must be visited but more important still is the church of **St-Hilaire-le-Grand**. The original structure, roofed in wood, was severely damaged by fire in the 12th century. To avoid further fires, the church was rebuilt in stone and columns were constructed to support the weight of new stone vaults. The resulting church with seven naves remains unique in France.

The 11th-century abbey of **St-Savin**, roughly 40 km (25 miles) east of Poitiers on the Gartempe river, has been called "the Sistine chapel of France" and is decorated with the oldest and most beautiful frescoes west of the Alps.

Coming home in *La Venise Verte*.

THE NORTH

History is imprinted in the rock and stained on the grass of northern France. Surrounded by prehistoric menhirs and megaliths, speaking their own ancient language and dressing in traditional clothing at festival time, there's a sense that the people of Brittany are still in touch with their past. Theirs is at times a savage homeland, gripped by Atlantic weather, and with its savagery comes dramatic beauty.

Neighbouring and mellower Normandy is one of France's most fertile areas, its prosperous agriculture producing butter, cheese, cream, meat poultry and fruit, etc. One of these products has become a symbol of France worldwide – the Normandy camembert – but others really have to be sampled on the ground to be properly enjoyed, particularly Normandy cider and Calvados, the brandy distilled from apples.

History has also trampled through Normandy – and comparatively recently. Some 200,000 buildings were destroyed and hundreds of thousands of people killed in the battles of World War II. Along the coast are concrete bunkers and rusting scraps of old tanks. Fortunately the old town centres have been carefully restored.

This corner of France is riddled by rivers: the Seine flows through Rouen on its way from Paris to the sea; the Rance hits the Channel at St Malo, the Epte crosses the rich arable land of the Vexin plateau, and the Orne flows through Caen. Not content to be surrounded by 1,200 km (750 miles) of coastline, Brittany also has its own inland sea in the Gulf of Morbihan, with the largest concentration of seabirds on the Atlantic coast.

But perhaps the most significant of the landmarks of the north is Mont-St-Michel, once in Brittany and now in Normandy, one of Europe's greatest abbeys, perched on an island just offshore. On either side of this lonely abbey are such smart seaside resorts as Deauville, Honfleur and Dinard, where Parisians come for the weekend, seeking peace from the city.

Preceding pages: a farm in Brittany. **Left:** windsurfing in the wild.

NORMANDY AND
LE NORD

How exotic Normandy must seem to a French man or woman from the baked red earth of the southern region of Provence. Here, he or she may find all the strangeness of travelling to a foreign land, but without any of the accompanying complications and difficulties.

In Normandy, the grass is green, the trees large and shady, the half-timbered houses lie by little somnolent rivers. French farmers have been content to go easy on their land. They have left hedges in place, they have not cleaned up every scrap of land that was not high-yield. There are still, for example, ponds with frogs and newts in them.

Walking at dusk beside a perfectly ordinary stream, from a dark clump of trees, comes the pure liquid descant of a nightingale – a bird that has almost disappeared from most European woodlands.

Many sea travellers enter France by the Breton ports of Dinard and St-Malo,

and many by Cherbourg at the tip of the Cotentin Peninsula, or through Caen, capital of Lower Normandy, or through Upper Normandy's Dieppe and Le Havre. But before turning to key destinations in Normandy itself, it is worth mentioning a couple of places which are en route to Normandy from the Channel ports of Calais and Boulogne.

The uneventful gallop from Calais or Boulogne to the Gare du Nord seems to have put some people off getting to know northern France better, so that Picardy, Artois and Flanders – which are anyway rather uninteresting in their landscapes – are more apt to suggest the ordeal of 1914–18 than any associations of pleasant leisure or interesting sightseeing.

Yet no survey of the great religious buildings of France would be complete without a long look at the Cathedral of Notre Dame at **Amiens**, begun in the late 12th century and completed with its soaring spire in the 16th, while, to cater to the needs of the body as well as the spirit, the nearby district of **St-Leu** has a network of interlocking canals designed to bring the

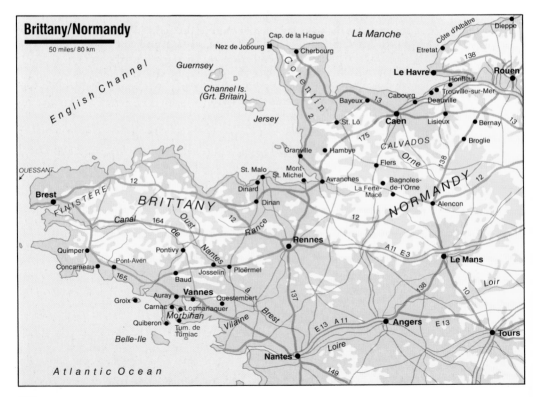

rich produce of that farming region to **Les Hortillonages**, a wide area of market stalls constructed alongside, and in some cases even across, these channels. And when one adds **Lille**, whose art gallery houses so many of the world's most famous paintings, or one remembers **Boulogne** itself, with its medieval *haute ville* rising steeply above the harbour, with huge walls on which one can walk and have a magnificent view – one realises that "**Le Nord**" is much more than an obstacle between the coast and Paris.

Having said that, quality of scenery aside, generalisations about Normandy tend to apply equally well to the relatively small area of Le Nord. In Normandy, there is an overall flavour. The Norman coast, Norman countryside, Norman towns, they all have general characteristics in common, but when one looks at them directly it is only their special quality that one sees.

Caen, for instance, is the powerful, purposive side of Normandy – bustling, businesslike, forever arranging trade fairs and exhibitions, with a lively university and a chamber of commerce that draws attention to itself by flamboyant modern sculpture.

Though there are things in Caen that remind one of the traditional glories of France – a castle, and William the Conqueror's spectacularly beautiful abbey, both in the centre of town – it is primarily a place for doing practical things in. And it is a pleasure to do anything practical in Caen with its excellent bus service and its large and elegant shops set amid pedestrian precincts.

Caen is also a place where one can eat very well and very economically. Those who set a proper value on that nourishing and easily digestible meat – tripe – will naturally want to sample *tripes à la mode de Caen:* down-to-earth Normans are not likely to let a valuable food resource go unappreciated for lack of good preparation. And there is also a variant, *tripes au Calvados*, prepared with a dash of the nectar that the Normans make from their abundant apples.

Bayeux's comic strip: At the opposite extreme is **Bayeux**, set amid the placid

countryside of the northwest, just inland from the Côte de Nacre, and devoted largely to guardianship of the splendours of the past. Of course, the daily worshippers in Bayeux's great cathedral would immediately reject the notion that their religion, rooted in history though it is, belongs to the "past". The **Cathedral** at Bayeux rears up to the sky, austere in outline and extravagantly fanciful in detail, as if every pillar and every stone were leaping passionately towards heaven. This cathedral was for centuries the home of the celebrated **Bayeux Tapestry**, which is both an immortal work of art and an invaluable historical source – you might say, the world's most famous comic strip, setting out in continuous form the story of Duke William's invasion of England in 1066, the defeat and death of the Anglo-Saxon Harold, and the subjugation of England by Normandy. It takes, of course, great pains to tell the story from a Norman point of view.

After 900 years, the tapestry is still extraordinarily vivid and evocative, its two colours hardly at all faded, and its cartoon-like figures arresting and, behind the first impression of comicality, deeply moving. Everyone has seen reproductions of one kind or another, but, even more than most masterpieces, it is worth taking the trouble to go and see the work.

Housed nowadays in a special building, the tapestry has to be approached via a mock-up which prepares the visitor with a photographic preview and also with a sound-track of appropriate noises, culminating in a 14-minute cinema show. Surprisingly, when you get there this seems quite natural, not only because it is done with taste and historical knowledge but because there is an aura of something like show-biz about the tapestry itself, something that can meet this kind of popularisation on its own ground and survive it.

Medieval zoology: Once you get to the tapestry, which is 70 metres (230 ft) long, the best way is to go past it twice; once slowly, taking in the detail, and once at a normal walking pace. Above and below the narrative band are friezes depicting animals – some realistic, some frankly

Left, making Calvados; **right**, the finished product.

mythological, and some on that intermediate ground between the two, a medieval European notion of what animals in tropical countries probably looked like.

When the parleying and mustering and shipfitting and armouring are at last over and battle is joined near Hastings, the figures in the main band become more and more urgent and elongated. They lean forward over their horses' necks, galloping towards the horrible clash with the foe. At the height of the battle, horses somersault and men are replaced by the figures of dead warriors. It is as stark a representation as one would find in some anti-war novel of the 1920s.

The experience certainly sets one thinking about the long, entwining entanglement of France and England. From William in 1066 to the disastrous John in 1204, the dukes of Normandy were also kings of England; after John lost most of Normandy, *Les Îles Normandes,* known nowadays as the Channel Islands, remained with the English Crown of their own free will. The history of this part of Europe has the unity of a patchwork quilt – glaring contrasts that yet somehow form a single entity.

The Calvados region is full of enchanting riverside towns like **Bernay**, **Broglie** and **Hambye** with its ancient abbey. Their older houses, crookedly aligned along narrow streets or the waterside, are half-timbered, and their atmosphere is rural and peaceful. If you strike one of those towns after about nine o'clock at night, don't expect to find anything open. Not even a pub stays awake once people have dispersed for the evening meal.

The cry of seabirds: The coastline of Normandy is as varied and beautiful as everything else about it. Over to the west on the Manche (English Channel) below the Cotentin Peninsula, Normandy has the Breton qualities of wild rockiness, the cry of seabirds and the hurrying of the tide-race.

If Carnac represents the furthest point of Breton religious symbolism on one side, then the furthest point on the other is **Mont-St-Michel**, away to the north and the east, one of the greatest religious buildings in Europe, fit to rank with St

The Bayeux Tapestry.

Peter's in Rome and Chartres and Durham. The first abbey on this site was built after the Archangel Michael appeared to Aubert, Bishop of Avranches. The building that stands now represents some 500 years of work, from the 11th to the 16th centuries, though there are later elements.

Mont-St-Michel is a dangerous place. The abbey stands at the summit of a huge lump of granite, 75 metres (250 ft) above the sea; when the tide is out there are quicksands. And surely this is no accident. This spot was deliberately chosen: dangerous in itself, and constantly in the presence of the most dangerous element of all, the ungovernable ocean. Since the abbey as we know it was begun in the 11th century, it dates from the heyday of Norman power and influence, the noontide of Normandy's importance in the world; and while this knob of rock has been from time immemorial a place of religious meditation and hermitage, as bleak and wild places tend to be, it was these same bold, strenuous Normans who put themselves under the patronage of Saint Michael.

In the traditional Christian view of the universe, the archangels were the highest order of created beings, and Saint Michael had the qualities among archangels that the Normans saw themselves as having: strength, courage, and leadership, the qualities that enabled him to defeat Satan.

Mont-St-Michel makes such a strong impression when seen from a distance, and the heroic cult of the Archangel makes such a strong mental impression when one just sits back and thinks about it, that the main problem for the visitor is to keep hold of these great central threads when he or she actually arrives in the place and is confronted, as usual, with rows of bric-à-brac shops selling rubbish to the tourists, all the detritus of the consumer society at its least dignified.

But one can still hear the Atlantic wind, and look down and see the foam crawling in over the quicksands, the grey dots that are the grazing sheep, and the massive sombre pillars within the great brooding structure of the Hall of the Knights. A noble, inspiring, austere place.

Coastal towns: A few coastal miles to

Mont-St-Michel.

the west and one reaches the two Breton resorts most favoured by holiday-makers, St-Malo and Dinard, which confront each other across the wide estuary of the River Rance.

Granville, the most westerly large coastal town in Normandy, is also almost Breton in its atmosphere. Perhaps its one truly Norman quality is its diversity and practicality, its willingness to have a try at any kind of enterprise. A busy port with docks and warehouses and trucks trundling to and fro, it is also a haunt of the sailing fraternity, who descend on it at weekends throughout the year in their smocks and oilskins and seaboots, with their talk of spinnakers and sternladders, goose-winging and Force Nines.

Granville also is a quiet haven for family holidays, with smooth, golden sands where generations of French children have been happy, and great stretches of butterscotch-coloured rock dotted with shallow pools where the same children can grope for shrimps and crabs.

And on top of all this, Granville is French history, with the old town perched on a great headland staring out at the Channel. The old houses, dominated by the magnificent church of Notre Dame from which one has a total perspective of all the activities of Granville, are solidly made of heavy blocks of stone, ready for any weather the sea may throw at them. They are roofed with dark gray slates, meticulously laid and firmly fixed, exactly like the houses in the corresponding parts of Brittany and Wales.

These slates tell their own story. They are the one form of roofing that will keep out the most torrential and the most driving rain, and when you get to a place where grey slates are common – even if you go there in fine sunny weather and never see rainfall you know that the inhabitants expect rain, a lot of it and often. And when, as in Granville, you see houses with not only the roof but an entire wall slated, the wall that faces the prevailing wind, you know that there are times in the year when the rain comes blasting in horizontally.

Moving north up the Cotentin Peninsula, jutting out into the Channel and

Norman home.

having at its tip the deep-water harbour of **Cherbourg**, one still finds a coast as wild as Brittany's with high cliffs sheltering fine beaches. Those fascinated by ships find themselves at home in Cherbourg, where the busy port has the authentic smell of oil, rotting seaweed and fish-heads, and where a brief stroll down a couple of streets from the waterside will bring you to a beautiful square dominated by the elegant municipal theatre.

Nor is nature far away among these scenes of maritime industry and urban-art. Just to the northwest of the city is the **Cap de la Hague**, a splendid promontory, and a little further south at **Nez de Jobourg**, the cliffs are among the highest in Europe, rearing to an awesome 158 metres (520 ft).

From then on eastward, from the Cotentin Peninsula to bright lights of Deauville and the Côte Fleurie, the cliffs drop down to the low coast and sandy beaches providing the funnel through which the Allied forces poured their men and weapons in 1944.

The **D-Day Beaches**, with their mu-seum and memorials, batteries and bun-kers, still serve as a reminder of the tre-mendous Allied operation of 6 June. The wartime code names remain proudly in place: Utah and Omaha taken by the Americans in the west; Gold, Juno and Sword by the British, Canadians and Poles in the east.

Every part of France suffered terribly from the deep trauma of World War II, but Normandy underwent more physical damage than any other region. To find anything similar one has to go back to the French and Belgian towns that were shelled into rubble in World War I. In 1944, it was the Allied bombardment that did most of the damage – a terrible prospect, but one that the French understood and accepted in the interest of getting back their liberty.

The traveller in Normandy is also for-ever meeting with reminders of the colos-sal effort that went into the rebuilding of towns destroyed in the fighting. Town after town – Caen, Le Havre, Rouen, Avranches, Dunkerque, Boulogne (487 air-raids during the war years) – had to be

Cap de la Hague.

built up from rubble. Where the town was ancient and beautiful, its historic buildings were lovingly recreated stone by stone, in replicas which, now that they have had time to become weathered, have become historic in their own right. There are few real blemishes.

Indeed, the French have never been given the credit that they deserve for this heroic effort. With all the shortages and difficulties of the immediate post-war years, it would have been so easy and so forgivable to put up cheap, shoddy buildings and get on with life. But the French wanted their country back as it had been, and they planned and worked until they had it back.

Essentially Norman: As quick a way as any of indicating the variety that awaits those who wander through Normandy is to take three towns, all within the **Orne** region and a modest distance from each other, so that with a car, or an intelligent use of the train and bus services, they can all be fitted into a single day.

Flers, La Ferté-Macé, and Bagnoles-de-l'Orne are all very different from each other and all offer something essentially French and essentially Norman.

Flers is not a tourist town but a pleasant, bustling, workaday place, very much the centre of a large area of countryside. It has the mandatory château, but does not set out to offer historical romance to the visitor, and its wide, handsome streets are lined with well-stocked shops and good cafés and hotels where the traveller gets value for money without frills.

The huge barn-like parish church, obviously a rebuilt job after the devastation of 1944, dominates a market square that, on the days when the country people bring in their produce, is crammed with stalls and the sort of relaxed, joking, basket-carrying crowd of purchasers that you never seem to see in a supermarket.

The produce stalls in Normandy country towns seem to extend right across the spectrum, from large farms and co-operatives down to smallholders and even families who seem to be selling the small surplus of a cottage garden. Sometimes families actually operate without a stall, simply occupying a few feet of pave-

Countryside commentary on World War II.

BEHIND EVERY MAN

If you *cherchez la femme* in French history, you will come up with a list of influences – for better and for worse. Since the Middle Ages, French women were the ones left behind to keep the home fires burning while their lords went off to the Crusades. Aliénor (Eleanor) d'Aquitaine (1122–1204), who favoured the arts in her enlightened court of Poitiers was one of the first women to mark Gallic history. At first queen of France, she then married the king of England. As her dowry entitled the English crown to a large portion of France, she is considered as partly responsible for the Hundred Years' War. Joan of Arc (1412–31), the Iron Maiden, contributed to ending it before being burned at the stake by the British in the Norman town of Rouen.

Catherine de Medicis (1519–89) was one of the most powerful women in French history. She became queen as the wife of Henry II, but true power came her way after Henry's death in 1559. As regent for her three weak sons, she held ultimate control

over a period of nearly 30 years. Her early love life may have been a source of bitterness to her, however, because Henry was far more interested in his mistress, the lovely Diane de Poitiers. The latter was a prolonged thorn in Catherine's side, because she also became the mistress of Catherine's son King François, inspiring him to engrave on a stained-glass window at Chambord the motto: *Souvent femme varie, bien fol qui s'y fie.* (Women often change, beware he who trusts them.)

Such illustrious names as the Marquise de Monespan (1641–1707) and the Marquise de Maintenon (1635–1719) were the main rays of Louis XIV's Sun Court at Versailles. Their power was derived not only from their looks, but also from their wit. "The four main pastimes of the 17th century were love, gambling, hunting and the official entertainments," declares Nancy Mitford in her biography *The Sun King*. "Love was played like a game, or like a comedy by Marivaux; it had, of course nothing to do with marriage."

Madame de Pompadour (1721–64) remained at Louis XV's side for 20 years. It was the first time that a king chose a woman of the bourgeoisie as his official mistress. As for the unfortunate Marie-Antoinette, she was in fact Austrian. Her famous words "let them eat cake" have long been cited as one of the triggers for the 1789 Revolution and her own demise.

French women have played an important part in intellectual life. Ninon de Lenclos and Madame de Sévigné opened the way for the salons of the 18th century, where writers and philosophers such as Voltaire, Rousseau, Diderot and Chateaubriand entertained all the ladies with clever conversation.

Love has always been a national hobby in France for men and women alike, with the example of the royal courtesans emulated at all levels of the social ladder. The *demimondaines* of the 19th century were kept women by virtue of their looks, and they have been succeeded by the modern-day mistress system, sometimes called *le cinq à sept*, being the time of day between leaving the office and reporting home. Personalities in the public eye continue to have mistresses, and their exposure does them no harm. Indeed, it is said that the system is one of the reasons why the divorce rate has been low in France until recently. ■

Joan of Arc, epitome of a strong French woman.

ment, sitting on cane stools and upturned boxes in front of a few kilos of potatoes.

Flers is, obviously, a historical town because all French towns are that, but it lives in the present and much of its history is of recent date. The Rue de la Banque, at the top of the town's sloping main street, has been renamed the Rue de la IIème Division Britannique, Liberatrice de Flers Les 16 et 17 Aout 1944. That is the kind of history they go in for around here. The charm of Flers for the tourist is precisely that it is so untouristy.

La Ferté-Macé attracts visitors because part of its atmosphere is made up of a kind of "history" that can be tabulated (it has a castle, a modern church with an 11th-century Romanesque tower and a carillon), and there is a *visite commentée* (a guided tour) of the place every Friday afternoon in the season. Perhaps, however, its greatest attraction lies in the unselfconscious way its sloping streets and leaning houses are so obviously home to a community of ordinary country people, getting on with their lives. The trickle of visitors does not disturb the town's daily rhythm. The town has also made its contribution to Norman cuisine with a recipe for tripe (again!) cooked, this time, on skewers.

Part of the magic of La Ferté-Macé comes from its setting amid verdant and peaceful countryside, with small fields and rolling hills. But a few more miles to the south and you strike a town right in the middle of a national park and on the edge of the **Forest of l'Andaine** that even this beautiful setting cannot redeem.

Bagnoles-de-l'Orne owes its existence to the discovery, centuries ago, of thermal springs with curative properties. There is naturally a legend about this (in France, there is a legend about everything), to the effect that Hugues, the Seigneur of Tesse, one day turned loose in the forest a horse of his that had become too old for service. A few days later the same horse turned up again, in rampant form. Hugues mounted and indicated that he wished to be taken to wherever the horse had been and this turned out to be the **Source de Bagnoles**. A few dips therein soon put the veteran Hugues in

The pastoral Pays d'Auge.

magnificent form also, such that he married the Dame de Bonvouloir and begat a numerous second family.

However this may be, the town in its modern form is not devoted to the renewal of fertility but to the treatment of rheumatic disorders, for which purpose it is dominated by huge Institutes and Residences. One has nothing but sympathy for the sufferers from these diseases, who walk slowly along the carefully levelled gravel paths with their aluminum canes. The trouble is that the town itself, like most spas, has set itself to keep up the spirits of the patients and provide amusement for the friends and relatives who accompany them by a determined cheerfulness that extends through every detail of architecture and layout.

A highly engineered lake winds through the centre of town, on which you can hire a pedalo and squeak slowly back and forth. There is a casino, a "Festival of Sir Lancelot du Lac" during the summer, an oval sandy track where children can have rides in carts pulled by tiny Shetland ponies, and long rows of shops selling rubbishy knick-knacks and souvenirs.

Bagnoles-de-l'Orne is worth visiting simply because one's picture of modern Normandy, and modern France, would be incomplete without it. A visitor needs, amid so much beauty and so much historical dignity, the reminder that French bad taste is as lowering to the spirits as the bad taste of any other nation.

But to speak of the variety of Normandy is to remember so many other things, not pre-eminent in any of those three towns; for instance that – hardly less than Brittany, though with a different flavour – it is a place of shrines and auspicious commemorations.

That most lovable and approachable of saints, Saint Thérèse, "the Little Flower", has her personal cult, and the museum that houses her relics is in the little Calvados town of **Lisieux**.

And, at **Rouen** on the River Seine, over towards the eastern boundary of Normandy and upriver from the industrial port of Le Havre, stands the house where Joan of Arc was imprisoned and interrogated. In the **Place du Vieux-Marché**

Norman timbers stuffed with straw.

they have marked the spot on the pavement where she was mercilessly burnt as a witch on 30 May 1431.

If, after contemplating these vestiges of human error, you need to restore your spirits by contemplating the positives of religious faith, the great late-Gothic **Cathedral of Notre Dame** should help you, and so should the **Église St-Maclou**, which contains some of the finest wood carving in France. This medieval church, standing amid streets that match it in age, and the **Grosse Horloge**, arched over an ancient street, emphasise the town's historic dimension. Gustave Flaubert was born here in 1821 and this is where he set his most famous novel, *Madame Bovary*. Rouen is not only the largest city in Normandy physically, but also an important centre for business and industry, as well as France's fourth largest port.

The Seine was also the place where Impressionism was born. Its main instigator, Claude Monet, grew up in Le Havre at the mouth of the river. But it was at the delightful little port of **Honfleur**, the prize of Normandy's holiday coast on the opposite bank, where the artists met and developed their style. Monet spent the last years of his life in a house in the Normandy village of **Giverny**, upstream from Rouen. The house is now a museum, and with its lily-pond garden, it immediately evokes his extraordinary achievement.

Memoirs of the wealthy: But what of the resorts, famous names that occur again and again in the memoirs of the wealthy and powerful of the world?

"Memoirs" is perhaps the operative word. In 1919, German doctors discovered that certain deficiency diseases in children could be alleviated by exposure to sunlight – that the body could, under some circumstances, take in certain vitamins through the skin. Their announcement of this discovery was the shout that started an avalanche. It began the sun-worship that has made holiday resorts out of glaring deserts of the earth and bankrupted the cool and shady places.

Tiny fishing villages in the south of France suddenly began to have visitors not merely in the mild rainy winter but

Horse racing at Deauville.

also in the parching summer. And at the same moment the majestic resorts of the northern coasts, with their miles of smooth sand, their casinos and golf courses and theatre, their row upon row of hotels so magnificent and solid that they seemed built to last forever, began to languish like the equally enormous dinosaurs of old.

They are not dead yet. But to take a holiday at any French resort that faces north is to risk cool weather, even rain. No sun-lover will take that risk.

The battle goes on. **Le Touquet**, set among its lovely pine woods, has an enormous swimming pool. **Cabourg**, favoured by Marcel Proust, has decided to stay fashionable and exclusive, hoping that if you exclude the many you automatically get the discerning few.

Convenient to Paris, **Deauville** still draws TV stars and fashion models to have their photographs taken, and to lure them, the town has constructed a boardwalk a mile long. The élite circle of European polo players that gather yearly keep the anglophile nickname "Doughville" as apt as ever. With its casino, a

theatre, a racecourse, night clubs, and enormous yacht marinas, this resort can hardly be called conquered. And **Trouville**, close by but separated by a small river, offers proximity to all these facilities but a quieter atmosphere.

Of all the traditional northern resorts, perhaps **Dieppe** can be said to have survived best. It deals good-humouredly with a huge volume of English day-trippers and, with its long beach, picturesque 15th-century castle and lively shops and stalls crowding the streets of the old town, has kept its hold on French families too. There is an air of confidence about Dieppe, as if the inhabitants just take it for granted that theirs is a fine town and the rest of the world will always want to come there.

Adding to Dieppe's attractiveness is its proximity to the naive **Pays de Caux** and the **Côte d'Albâtre**. The famed sheer cliffs of **Étretat**, cut with a perfect arch that protrudes into the sea, might well be the best place along the Channel for sighting *les serpents de mer*.

Even if the other northward-facing resorts seem to lack some of Dieppe's confidence, and a faint feeling of whistling to keep up the spirits is perceptible, when the weather is very poor and the holidaymakers indoors, there is definitely a more positive side to the question.

The stampede to the south has taken a lot of pressure off the northern areas of France generally, thereby easing prices and thinning out holiday traffic-jams. France, overall, is a fairly prosperous country, but the northern provinces do not quite share all this prosperity, leaving many Norman country towns with a slightly forgotten air. Hotels are seldom quite full and often keep their prices down to keep business up.

Lovely countryside, then, fine historic towns, breathtakingly beautiful buildings are combined in northern France with relatively empty roads and easy hotel bookings. Add to that Norman food (cream and mushrooms with everything, freshly churned butter, wonderful vegetables to keep you healthy in spite of all the fat and protein) and it becomes a formula hard to resist – especially if, like many modern people, you have never heard a nightingale.

Left, bundled up for winter. **Right**, Monet's *Rouen Cathedral, West Facade, Sunlight*.

BRITTANY

The key to the Breton character is that the people are firstly Atlantic dwellers and secondly Celts. Along with the endurance and patience bred into a people who have had to deal with the most violent of the world's great oceans, they have the rich imagination, the ready recourse to symbol and legend, and the useful ability to lose themselves in dreams that are the mark of the Celt.

Perhaps the best way to introduce oneself to Brittany is to travel, either by road or rail, from Rennes to Vannes. In **Rennes**, though the city is within Brittany and generally regarded as its effective capital, you *feel* you are still in hardworking, realistic, practical Normandy. The town has an immensely important place in French history and, among other things, provided the nation with useful experience in the rebuilding of disaster-stricken cities when the medieval town was almost entirely – a few picturesque streets are still standing – consumed by fire in 1720. It was rebuilt in the severe classical style of the time, elegant but too formal for some tastes and, to speed up the process of getting the citizenry housed, the new buildings were sold off in separate flats, two centuries before this practice became usual.

Today Rennes has two universities, a Citröen car plant and is host to much high-tech industry, notably in electronics and communications. It crackles with energy and sparkles with modernity. In search of Brittany take due note of Rennes – for it, too, is Brittany – and then head southwest to **Vannes**.

At first, you pass through a landscape that, like Normandy, is lush and smiling with plenty. But as mile after mile of westward land slides by, the country becomes rougher and more windblown, the houses lower, the agriculture more basic. Everything combines to remind you that you are penetrating more and more deeply into the westward peninsula of France and that the open Atlantic is around you on three sides.

Vannes is on the coast. Well, almost. It is one of those ports which, partly through silting and partly through the increasing size of ships, has had to put its maritime importance back into history, though you can still sail there in a small boat, with a yacht-basin under the fine old ramparts.

City scenes: Visually, Vannes is delightful. The great ramparts are punctuated by fairytale round towers with tall conical slate hats. Beside the Porte Poterne, there is a *laverie*, a place constructed for the communal washing of clothes, such as one sees in every old French town that has a stream or river, but this one has the most delightful curving and overhanging slate roof.

Inside the walls, in the old town, are the usual half-timbered houses, most of them built by making each floor project a little beyond the one below it (for stability), so that in a narrow street the topmost floors are almost touching. There are also some of those obviously phoney half-timberings – modern constructions across which strips of hardboard have been nailed at random, with no serious attempt to make them look structural. Other buildings

Left, Fest-Noz spinner. Right, Breton produce.

worth looking at are the **Cathedral of St-Pierre** – noble and lofty outside, though rather lowering and forbidding in its interior – and the **Hôtel de Ville**, a striking example of the florid confidence of Western man in the later 19th century, when he assumed that his cultural and material ascendancy would last forever. Beautiful it isn't, but such a bold statement does hold one's attention, and what it must have cost to build is incalculable. In the open space in front of it is a fine swaggering statue of the duc de Richemont, a 15th-century worthy who severely trounced the English and thereby put an end to the Hundred Years' War.

Certainly there is plenty to see in Brittany without leaving the big cities. **Nantes**, although officially no longer a part of Brittany following local government reorganisation in 1972, remains emotionally and economically attached to the old duchy. The city is fascinating in the range of what it contains: a large industrial area centred on the docks and shipyard; a beautiful, austere cathedral whose pale stone, almost luminous in the light from the windows, reminds one of the stone of Canterbury and which does in fact come from the same source; and the wonderful ducal palace, begun by Duke François II and continued by his daughter, the Duchess Anne, who in its chapel married King Louis XII of France, in 1499, thereby uniting France and Brittany. A fascinating woman, physically slight and frail with a limp, but witty, intelligent and well-read, she acted out her important destiny with style.

One cannot, however, stay long in an urban setting if one is to know Brittany for, like Normandy, it is overwhelmingly a rural province. One seems always to be travelling immense distances, chancing across isolated villages that are like places history has passed by. This Breton countryside, wild and lonely, evidently bred a highly differentiated way of life, so that up to the 20th century the Breton costume was very distinctive (elaborate lace headdresses for the women, known as *coiffes*, and for the men black jackets and trousers and wide-brimmed black hats that must have made them look rather like South

Two young Bretonnes in native costumes.

American *gauchos*). These costumes have not entirely disappeared, the people taking to them on ceremonial and festive occasions.

Josselin, in the heart of inland Brittany, is a pleasant place to spend a couple of days. This energetic little town, with its one steep street running down to the river bank, its half-timbering, its bustling Saturday morning street market and friendly, crowded local cafés, really speaks the language of rural Brittany.

The river that runs below the town is the **Oust**, or the **Nantes-Brest Canal**, as it has long been canalised to form part of that important artery. Its rippling waters reflected the dream-like castle of the Rohan family, exactly the kind of castle that a book illustrator would draw to accompany a story of chivalry and enchantment. And across the river, perched on the opposite bank, is the unpretentiously lovely **Chapelle de Ste-Croix**, which speaks of the other side of the Middle Ages – homely, graceful piety.

Cormorants and spoonbills: Josselin, like Vannes, is in Morbihan. The name means "Little Sea" and the **Gulf of Morbihan** is an inlet, effectively a seawater lake, fed by various channels from the Atlantic. It is 20 km (12 miles) wide and from the open sea to the inner shore it reached 15 km (9 miles). It is tidal and dotted with islands, of which the largest are **Arz** and **l'Île des Moines**, each of which supports a few hundred inhabitants, though most of the multitudinous islands are green lumps of solitude amid the advancing and receding waters, and the human beings who frequent the Gulf do so on those movable man-made islands we call boats. They are there in plenty enough, fishing away, and keeping them company is a vast army of seabirds, usually ranging from 60,000 to 100,000 in the Gulf alone, representing the largest concentration of seabirds on the French Atlantic coast. In a number of places (e.g. **Groix, Rohellan, Theriec, Belle-Île, Méaban** and the marsh area of the **Presqu'Île de Rhuys**) there are bird sanctuaries. There, according to the season of the year, you can see oyster-catchers, crested cormorants, Brent geese, hooded mergansers, sand-pipers,

One unlucky ship's coastal graveyard.

plovers, spoonbills, herons and egrets, not to speak of a whole range of gulls.

The connoisseur of coastline can enjoy both wild and stormy, with pounding breakers and rocks hurled far up the beach by the fury of the sea, or alternatively calm, meditative and sheltered. The mouth of the Gulf is guarded by a thin shell of land which makes safe haven for Locmariaquer and Arzon, and further out there is an even thinner finger of shore, running down from Plouharnel to Quiberon, which provides shelter for, among other places, the magical **Carnac**.

Neolithic worship: The very name of Carnac reminds us that the Celtic mind has always been, for want of a better word, "mystical"; the unseen has been as real to the Celt as the seen, the measureless as actual as the measured. This outlook runs seamlessly from Neolithic worship, through the tangled mass of Dark Age legends and myths, to the more ordered but still prodigally rich imaginative landscape of medieval Catholicism.

Carnac is one of the places, perhaps in Brittany *the* place, where one finds this feeling concentrated so strongly that in thousands of years it has not dispersed. The great stone circles and alignments, the raising with frightful labour of those huge everlasting groups of menhirs (single vertical standing stones) and dolmens (hanging stones) by which our ancestors of the Neolithic and Early Bronze Ages marked the places where they enacted their sacred rituals of death and the renewal of life.

Carnac, to employ the sober language of description, consists of three groups of menhirs, variously arranged in patterns of 10 to 13 rows, and also a series of long cairns covering funerary chambers. Time has not left the menhirs entirely intact – it is probable that each row ended in a semi-circle of standing stones which have gone – but still there are nearly 3,000 of them, and the effect is awe-inspiring.

Carnac has, of course, long been carefully investigated and excavated, and many grave goods of fine workmanship have been taken away to museums. (One hopes the people they were intended for can get along all right without them in the **Digging for clams.**

next world). These included beautiful polished axes in greenstone – or, more precisely, jadeite, one of the group of related stones to which the general name "greenstone" is given. Objects made from jadeite have also been found in tombs of the ancient Chinese and of the Indians of North America. In such ways did the religious observances of our remote ancestors girdle the earth and unite all human beings in their most solemn moments.

Fishing on stilts: Back up on the north coast of Brittany, it is a good idea to take a boat trip up the Rance to visit **Dinan**, a beautiful old town some 10 river-miles inland. The voyage begins with an enforced inspection of the hydroelectric dam built in 1966 across the estuary. It is nothing much to look at, but so technologically advanced that it is the only dam in the world that manages to harness both the ebb and flow of the tide.

Once on the river, simpler pleasures take over. The banks are green and wooded, with fine houses to be glimpsed amid wooded estates. The local inhabitants have a quaint method of fishing that involves building small cabins on stilts so as to get right over the tidal flow of the river. On top of these cabins are crossed staves, which, when projected forward, make a square framework for a close-meshed net; this they lower and bring up repeatedly with pulleys. The catch has to be something too small to be fished with a baited hook, but abundant enough to be caught in bulk; something like a whitebait. The stilted huts give the placid northern-European riverside a curious flavour of Borneo, and there is the interest, as one glides by, of whether anything has been caught with all that patient plunging.

Dinan, when it comes in sight, dispels these trivial amusements with something really worth looking at. Rue du Jerzval, rising steeply up the high bluffs that overlook the river, is lined with fine old half-timbered houses, in many of which artist-craftsmen live and work. And from the Jardin Anglais behind the stately **St-Sauveur Church** there is a wonderful view of the river, crossed by a huge viaduct and a reconstructed Gothic bridge.

Casinos and beach huts: As for **St-Malo**

Fishing by pulley on the Rance.

and Dinard, together they form an attractive holiday centre on the Emerald Coast. **Dinard** is modern, with the usual paraphernalia of palm-trees and a casino and beach huts; St-Malo is august, historic, dignified. Perhaps they are both a little too all-or-nothing; St-Malo can be a calmly austere shrine because it can unload its workaday life and its frivolities on to Dinard, and Dinard can have a cheerful spa vulgarity because St-Malo, just over the river, will take care of the refined matters of historicity and beauty.

Being unfair to Dinard will hardly cause its prosperous citizens to lose any sleep. The place has been a successful resort ever since successful resorts came into being. Here, some 80 to 100 years ago, the well-to-do merchants of northern France built their Gothic mansions, with turrets and pillars and buttresses that don't buttress anything, all part of that 19th-century dream of reviving the picturesque side of the Middle Ages, a dream doomed to failure because you can't just skim the picturesqueness off a human society and sell it as if it were cream – it has to rise up naturally from the beliefs and actions and assumptions that underlie it. These amusing monstrosities are probably quite cheerful to live in, with their large pleasant gardens overlooking the sea (Dinard is a conspicuous beneficiary of the Gulf Stream and its climate is very agreeable), but they strike the onlooker as – to use a phrase that George Orwell applied to certain resort hotels in England – "lunatics staring over the asylum wall".

Land's end: Leaving the resorts behind, the coast becomes increasingly wild, rocky and stormy as you move west towards Finistère, the End of the Earth. A good chunk of this weatherbeaten landscape now belongs to the **Parc Régional d'Armorique**, which extends westward from the granitic moorlands of the Mons d'Arrée, along the Crozon Peninsula and across the sea to **Ouessant**. Known to the English as Ushant, this is the most remote of the scores of islands sprinkled around the Breton coast. Of these, 15 are large enough to seduce a permanent population to live on them, and you will not have

Brittany has weird rock formations.

seen Brittany till you have visited at least one of them. Bréhat, on the northern Côte de Granit Rose, and Belle-Île, south of Quiberon, are two of the most accessible and rewarding.

The same can be said for *les enclos paroissiaux*, the parish closes of **northern Finistère**. Begun in the mid-16th-century and completed over the next 150 years, these are grandiose religious ensembles adorned with elaborate granite carvings, their churches, calvaries, ossuaries and triumphal arches absurdly large for the small rural villages that created them. Born of an intense faith spurred by a keen inter-parish rivalry, they now stand in lichen-covered testimony to the fervour and superstition that once gripped the Breton soul. Those at St-Thégonnec, Guimiliau and Lampual-Guimiliau are among the best.

Southern Finistère is known as Cornouaille, so named by the Celts who fled here from Cornwall in the 6th century BC. Here Breton culture remains most evident. In its capital, **Quimper**, you can find specialist shops selling Breton-language books, traditional costume and *keltia musique*, while the old streets around the cathedral have some of the most enjoyable crêperies in the region. A *galette* (buckwheat pancake) and a cup of cider will seem quite appropriate after visiting the city's newly-restored Musée des Beaux Arts, which houses an excellent collection of paintings *sur la thème Bretagne*, including works by Paul Gauguin and the Pont-Aven School.

Pont-Aven lies 34 km (20 miles) east of Quimper, amid a benign countryside of wooded river valleys and secluded coves that reveals the mellow side of Brittany. But before retiring inland, take the short trip out to the *pays* Bigouden to Quimper's southwest. Here the land falls flat to the sea, provoking thoughts of storms, shipwrecks and toiling seaweed gatherers. From the top of the Eckmühl Lighthouse you can survey the Penmarch Peninsula and the immense sweep of the Baie d'Audierne. Such great stretches of coast are virtually as they must have been 2,000 years ago. Even today, a primitive Brittany is not difficult to imagine.

Oyster hunters.

202

Boire sans soif et faire l'amour en tout temps, madame, il n'y a que ça qui nous distingue des autre bêtes. (Drinking without thirst and making love at any time, madame, is all that distinguishes us from other animals.)
— De Beaumarchais, *Le Mariage de Figaro*

Hardly any corner of France lacks vines, but vineyards run riot across the eastern provinces of Champagne, Lorraine, Alsace, Burgundy and the Rhône valley.

Champagne is the most northerly wine producing area of France, and in fact used to be known for its red wines before the delicious fizz came into existence in the 17th century, supposedly discovered by monk Dom Pérignon. Both it and neighbouring Lorraine are celebrated for fine cathedrals, particularly in Reims and Metz.

The very existence of Alsace is a tribute to the ability of human-kind to sort out territorial disputes; over the centuries it has been torn, like a hare between hounds, by the rival powers of France and Germany. Now Alsace lives in peace, doubly endowed by the cultures of both countries, with its capital city of Strasbourg now the seat of the European parliament. Two-thirds of the population in these neat, picture-book villages of Hansel-and-Gretel gingerbread houses speak their own dialect, Elsassdutch, and geraniums burst from every balcony.

Burgundy, at the south of this corridor, is the land of wine, food and dukes which saw itself as the heart of Europe in medieval times. Today's Burgundians believe that paradise begins in the kitchen and ends in the wine cellar, and "better a good meal than fine clothes". And they say they enjoy the TGV (high-speed train) because it allows them to go to Paris and back without missing breakfast or dinner in Burgundy.

Traditional crafts thrive in these regions, but the sophisticated cities of Dijon and the Rhône valley capital, Lyon, support modern industries and cultures. And wherever you go, you can be sure there will always be a sympathetic *cave* open for a little wine tasting around the bend.

Preceding pages: the sign of Hautvilliers Champagne. **Left:** gathering grapes in Hunawihr, Alsace.

CHAMPAGNE

A Frenchman once recounted with a mixture of mirth and dismay his discovery that a bottle of "champanya" sold in Spain bore the caveat "not to be confused with foreign imitations". The name of this French province has become a generic term for sparkling wine, and there is, the French insist, no champagne wine except that which comes from Champagne.

Surrounded by large fields of wheat and sugarbeet whose uniform colours blanket the countryside, **Reims** is the royal road to Champagne. The kings of France were crowned in this city's magnificent cathedral. We tend to think of Gothic as an affair of pointed arches and needle-like spires; here the striking feature is the decoration of coolly imperturbable draped angels, whose reserved smiles contain a whole new aspect of Gothic architecture. For students of art history, the early Gothic **St-Remi Basilica** is to be compared to the classic forms of the cathedral. The **Tau Palace**, with its precious objects and tapestries, was the residence of royalty during their sojourns in Reims. At the **St-Denis Museum** you can almost relive the coronation rites through the paintings that were hung in the streets in honour of the royal arrival.

It would be fun to imagine the damasked and brocaded guests of these festivities with a flute of champagne in hand, bubbles ascending to heaven like the direct link between the king and God. Alas, champagne as we know it didn't come into existence until the 17th century. Its creation is attributed to Dom Pérignon, who allegedly announced its genesis with the words, "Come quickly, I am seeing stars!" Other monks also contributed to the necessary discoveries.

How it's done: The *méthode champenoise* consists of starting and controlling a second fermentation in the spring. Once the wine has been assembled from different vines, a sugary liqueur is added that sets off fermentation in the bottle. Despite thick glass and dense corks wired to the bottles, some 2 to 3 percent regularly explode, proof of this wine's exuberance.

Extending to Vertus, the champagne vineyards are the northernmost in France, making them susceptible to freezing, but also giving the wine its characteristic light acid taste. **Épernay** is the heart of the grape district. Although possessing only one-sixth of the population of Reims, this town produces almost as much champagne. The famed Moët et Chandon establishment gives guided tours of its cellars, and the town's museum includes a historical section on champagne production. Otherwise the town is less interesting, having been greatly rebuilt after World War I. Nearby is **Hautvilliers**, Dom Pérignon's homeland, offering a view of the valley and the rather rare example of an old town transformed both by military destruction and the reconstruction of prosperous wine growers and merchants.

Unlike most other wine regions, in Champagne there are "brand names" that are not designations of varietal or territorial origin, but that of the company assembling and manipulating the wine. These large and famous companies buy

Christian Pol Roger and a double magnum.

the grapes from the growers, and after a first pressing at the harvest site, transfer the incipient wine to their cellars, concentrated in Reims and Epernay.

Great underground galleries and caverns provide the necessary constant cool temperature. Apart from the millions of bottles (and francs!), these cellars are spectacular in themselves. Under Épernay alone they cover some 100 km (60 miles). Each has its fabulous features; Gallo-Roman quarries (Lanson), statues sculpted into the walls (Pommery and Greno), a tour on a small train (Piper-Heidsieck).

The southern part of the province, merging with Burgundy, reaches farther back in history. The museum of **Châtillon-sur-Seine** displays the spectacular Vix collection of bronzes, ceramics and gold jewellery found in a pre-Roman burial site. The town's church has long been of important religious significance. On an exposed plateau, **Langres** is contained in intact Roman ramparts that look out over a valley where modern superhighways follow the line of Roman roads. In the rustic woods around Montier-

en-Der, the timbered and roughcast plaster church of **Lentilles** with its shingled front is one of the best examples of typical Champagne architecture, dating from the 16th century. **Troyes** is a particularly brilliant souvenir of the Renaissance period. The old town has its specific architecture of wood-sided houses whose upper levels jut over the narrow streets. No fewer than nine churches contain marvels of statuary and religious treasures, including the manuscripts saved from the Clairvaux abbey.

In south Champagne west of Chaumont, a 44-metre (145-ft) double-barred Cross of Lorraine in pink granite stands on a hilltop, visible from far across the rolling, chalky plain. It beckons the visitor to the village of **Colombey-les-Deux-Églises**, where Charles de Gualle had his country home and today lies buried in the humble churchyard. The house, a creeper-covered manor, is today a museum full of fascinating de Gaulle memorabilia. Pity about the countless souvenir shops in the village, selling every kind of kitsch to the half-million annual visitors.

Church at Châtillon.

LORRAINE

Hugging the western slopes of the Vosges mountain range in the south, Lorraine extends to the German, Luxembourg and Belgian borders in the north. Long industrialised, towns such as Longwy have become synonymous with the economic difficulties of steel works and coal mines. Nonetheless **Metz**, its regional capital, remains important. In the factory outskirts, trucks laden with beer kegs trundle out of the high brick blocks of breweries. Other industries include printing, and the manufacture of shoes and metal goods.

The Gothic cathedral of the old town is huge. With the largest stained-glass windows in the world, some of them crafted in recent years by Marc Chagall, the 16th-century **Cathedral of St-Étienne** makes a stop in Metz well worthwhile. The 4th-century **Pierre-Aux-Nonnains**, also in Metz, has the distinction of being the oldest church in all of France.

The seat of Nancy: The historic heart of the region is **Nancy**, former seat of the dukes of Lorraine. The hub of this cultural capital is the **Palace Stanislas**, named after Stanislas Lesczcynski, deposed King of Poland, who gratefully accepted the Lorraine duchy from his son-in-law Louis XV in 1735. In extension of the existing city he created a modern rectilinear street plan. The chequered stone esplanade, is enclosed by gilded wrought-iron grillework linking the indispensable trappings of the 18th century, the town hall, the theatre, and the art museum.

In the older town, the renovated houses of the Grande Rue lead to the **Porte de la Craffe**, whose two towers and connecting bastion are impressive reminders of earlier fortifications. Along the way, the **Ducal Palace** is a sober town dwelling. Inside is the **Lorraine Historical Museum**. Next door, the same ticket will let you into the exhibit of pre-industrial traditions. Household objects suggest life in the Lorraine farming towns as can be found in old photos. Housed in a separate museum is the unique **École de Nancy**, the epitome of Art Nouveau or Art 1900, whose flowing lines are applied to a number of buildings in the newer Nancy.

A few miles from the city is **St-Nicolas-de-Port** and its basilica dedicated to the patron saint of Lorraine, who is honoured in a festival every 5 December.

Thousands of crosses: In striking contrast are the memories of World War I. From 1914 to 1918, the Marne valley was part of an immense battlefield straddling the northeast from the Ardennes to Lorraine. The name **Verdun** remains unforgettable. Surprisingly, a good deal of the historic city has survived, including the bishop's palace with a library of manuscripts and miniatures. The main battlefields of Verdun, where 800,000 died in 1916–18, are outside the city to its northeast, on the hills above the River Meuse. A visit today to the giant forts, the grassy remains of trenches, and the towering ossuary of Douaumont, is an immensely moving experience. Today the theme of Franco-German reconciliation dominates. Inside the museum, next to the rooms filled with anguished battle scenes, are happy photos of post-1945 Franco-German exchanges, and nearby lies the plaque

Stained glass in Metz by Marc Chagall.

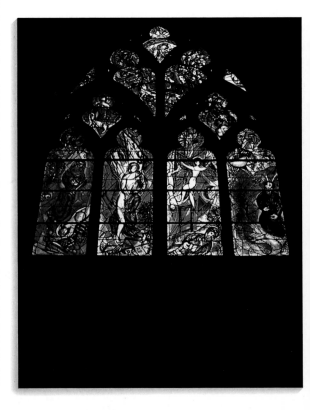

laid in 1987 by Chancellor Kohl and President Mitterrand, pledging their nations to undying friendship.

Arts and crafts: Traditions of art and craft flourish in Lorraine. In **Lunéville** Stanislas created the château and formal gardens that are like a much smaller Versailles. **Baccarat**, from the town of that name, is crystal in all its forms and stages, from workshop to the windows of the modern church. Musicians must not miss **Mirecourt**, where a museum and workshops demonstrate the infinitely delicate art of violin-making. **Domrémy** has the house where Joan of Arc was born, an example of how peasants lived in the 15th century. **Grand** is a Gallo-Roman site, with an amphitheatre and the largest mosaic discovered in France.

The image of **Épinal** is precisely that: images. These illustrations of popular proverbs and homilies were a 19th-century precursor of comics. Printed in thousands, they constituted a virtually infinite rogues' gallery of stereotypes. The local museum specialises in this folk art, from Epinal and abroad. The craft continues, notably at the Pellerin presses where the first images were produced.

A drive towards the **Vosges** is enchanting. From the Lorraine side, the slopes rise quietly in dark green forests. Along the northern and lower range, in the **Lorraine Regional Park** near Sarrebourg, the forest harbours wild boar and roe deer around ponds and reservoirs. The largest, **Étang de Lindre**, is an artificial lake created in the Middle Ages. Ringed with reeds, it is a refuge for water birds, herons, flamingos and storks. From Dieuze local roads form a circuit around the lake, through towns ideal for shoreside walks. **Tarquimpol** is a prime viewpoint.

From Épinal the main highway follows the Moselle river upstream to its source in the high Vosges. **Bussang** and **Gérardmer** are hill resorts famous for fine skiing and hiking trails that lead to innumerable waterfalls. The high passes, known as *ballons*, make your head spin – taking in the panorama that widens from the Alps in the distance to the **Route de Crêtes** that marks the border between Alsace and Lorraine.

View of the Vosges.

ALSACE

With an Alemannic dialect, a Protestant as well as a Catholic tradition, and a distinctly German-style wine, cuisine, folklore and architecture, Alsace demands some explanation.

Originally, Alsace was integrated into the Alemannic kingdom of Charlemagne's succession, and not until 1648 did it become part of France. Meanwhile, its capital Strasbourg retained the right to levy its own taxes and finance a Protestant university. Then, after the French defeat in 1871, Alsace and part of Lorraine were annexed by Bismarck and not returned to France until 1918.

For all these reasons, Alsace had retained its special religious, social and cultural status, including a local dialect that is commonly heard on the city streets.

From June and its internationally renowned classical music festival to the September Musica featuring contemporary compositions, Strasbourg's cultural life never stops. Meanwhile, a European capital of flagpoles, luxury hotels and conference translators dwells in the city's landscaped parks. Indeed, Strasbourg is the seat of the Council of Europe, a 26-member body, and regular host to the European Parliament.

Strasbourg: The city is not actually on the Rhine, but enclosed in a series of basins and canals regulating boat traffic and flood waters. Within the outer rings of modern convention centres and genteel uncramped neighbourhoods is the nutshell of old Strasbourg, a small island formed by the **Ill river**. Numerous bridges cross over the artificial arm of the Ill, channelled in its brick-lined bed. On the facing bank weeping willows droop among a collection of idiosyncratic 19th-century mansions.

From the *quais*, cobbled lanes converge on the **Cathedral**. This, in rosy stone splotched with cream, is like an immense marble cake. When it was finished in the 15th century, the 142-metre (465-ft) steeple was the highest in Europe. This Notre Dame is laden, perhaps even overladen, with decoration, carrying the Gothic idea to its limit. Incessantly modified during its construction, the exterior is layered with lace spires and innumerable statues, as in infinitely reflecting mirrors. Inside, the pulpit and the celebrated Column of Angels are flights of a sculptor's fancy. More recent is the astronomical clock, a multifaced mechanism tracing hourly, daily and yearly celestial movements. When it strikes at 12.30pm, figures of ancient and biblical mythology execute their ordained rounds.

The **Oeuvre Notre Dame** was created in the 1200s to supervise the building of the cathedral, and has been in continuous existence since then. Due to this unprecedented life-span, its museum (Place du Château) has untold treasures. In a Renaissance mansion of lovingly polished wood, the displays range from a very rare series of pre-14th century Jewish epitaphs to a superlative collection of late medieval art, especially paintings of the Lower Rhine school. Most exceptional of all, this museum shows the original master plans for the cathedral. On 6-foot scrolls of parchment the artists drew

Left, gathering the grape. Right, inside the Council of Europe.

and coloured each section of the facades exactly as they were to appear.

The old neighbourhood of the cathedral bustles with the activity of a weekly flea-market. No two buildings on the evocatively named streets (like Old Fishmarket Street) appear to be exactly alike. The typical half-timbered houses seem to have been inflated to giant proportions. Above wide fronts to two or three storeys, the roofs carry up to five gabled windows, one above the other, diminutive in the distance.

Other museums are housed in numerous monuments; the former **Customs House**, bristling with square masonry spikes like chimneys, and the **Grande Boucherie**, or Great Butcher's shop. The **Château des Rohan** boggles the eye with princely chambers of gilt and velvet. Across the river at the Pont du Corbeau, the **Alsatian Museum** is installed in a typical 16th-century Strasbourg dwelling. It displays the distinctive objects of traditional Alsace – square ovens of green tiles, splay-legged chairs with f-holed backs rather like violins, armoires with spiralling columns as thick as small trees.

Congregations and their churches: In keeping with its humanist tradition, Strasbourg is noted for prominent Jewish and Protestant minorities that generate an ecumenical spirit. Protestant congregations are numerous, and their properties likewise, as in the twin churches of **St-Pierre-le-jeune** (one for each confession.) The **St-Thomas Church** and cloister, long a revered Protestant sanctuary, contains the splendid mausoleum of the royal Marshal de Saxe.

Beyond the Place Gutenberg, the waterfront affords a view of firemen placidly fishing from a flat-bottomed skiff behind the station. New buildings with long steep roofs and balconies successfully adapt traditional forms. In the picturesque and traffic-free **Petite France quarter**, a central knot of traditional houses is impecably maintained, with fresh colours and flowers. Along the **Rue des Moulins**, where the river is divided into several channels for the running of mills, buildings have doors at water level. The **Ponts Couverts** are no longer covered bridges, but the

La Petite France quarter of Strasbourg.

square towers of the 14th-century fortifications are still standing. Just upstream is the **Vauban Dam**, designed to block river traffic, and offering a good view of the old city.

Strasbourg has strong connections with two famous Germans, Johannes Gutenberg and Wolfgang von Goethe. It was during his years in the city, 1434–48, that Gutenberg evolved the printing press. Goethe spent a year there as a student in 1770–71. And it was in the pretty village of Sessenheim, to the northeast near the Rhine, that he had his love-affair with a pastor's daughter, Frederike, the inspiration of some of his poems.

Villages and a rose garden: The Alsatian plain between the Rhine and the Vosges is studded with picturesque villages. The noble Rohan family built an extravagant and ostentatious château in **Saverne**, complemented by an immense rose garden. The surrounding countryside north of Strasbourg is a region of ancestral forests and razed castles. **La Petite-Pierre** is the information centre for the **North Vosges Regional Park**, where trails wander

among wildlife preserves. The **Hagenau Forest** shelters hamlets of wooden houses, renowned for colourful festivities, the women coiffed with the giant starched bow of Alsatian folklore. At several points along the border with Germany, it is possible to visit some of the old underground forts of the Maginot Line, built in the 1930s.

The Route du Vin commences with **Molsheim**. In the walled city typically preserved with traditional houses, the **Metzig** is a favourite stop. This museum and wine-tasting cellar is in a beautiful Renaissance building adorned with a double staircase and sculpted balconies.

Obernai is the next stop on the wine road. It is distinguished by a central, covered market-place and an elaborate 16th-century fountain equipped with six buckets. A few miles from the town is the **Montagne Ste-Odile**. From pre-Christian times this spot was both sacred and strategically important, as the 10-km (6-mile) long "pagan wall" attests. This presumably defensive installation continues almost without interruption through the

Sundhouse village festival.

forest, with views towards the remnants of surrounding fortresses. Two chapels remain from the 11th and 12th centuries.

Of all the castles built along the slopes of the Vosges in the Middle Ages, only ruins remain. The European wars following the Reformation, often using the pretext of religious argument to mask simple territorial desires, ran rampage over Alsace. At Nideck and Schirmeck, as at Obernai and Ribeauvillé, desolated towers and fragmented walls stand lost in the forest. At **Haut-Koenigsbourg**, however, the very old ruined castle was completely restored at the beginning of the 20th century by Kaiser Wilhelm II who often stayed there. The vision of red roofs stands out plainly against the mountain foliage. This renovation is more of a reproduction of 15th-century military architecture than a restoration.

Sélestat is one of the old independent cities of Alsace that grouped together as the Decapole to defend the privileges accorded them by the Holy Roman emperor. A traditional market town right in the middle of Alsace, the city has an old medieval section including two city gates. The **Ste-Foy** church is of dusky yellow-pink stone with a slightly bulging central hexagonal tower. In the same stone is the Gothic **St-Georges**. Finally, the city boasts a **Humanist Library** that assembles two scholarly collections of philosophical works.

A shelter for the storks: One of Alsace's most cherished symbols is the stork, who in lore and life nested on chimneys or cartwheels set on a pole for precisely that purpose. By the early 1980s storks were dying out, as few returned from their winter migration to Africa. But now they are again being specially bred in Alsace, in enclosures such as the Stork Reintroduction Centre in the **Kintzheim Château**. This centre is part of the **Volerie des Aigles**, dedicated to the protection of the great and rare birds of prey.

From the narrow plain the Vosges mountains do indeed form a true "blue line", as the saying goes. The foothills are green, the light green of the vineyards shimmering in the sun. The vines touch the walls of **Ribeauvillé**, in the heart of

Stork watching at Mittelbergheim.

the wine-growing region. The town is stretched in a band along the Grand Rue, rising through the busy new town (18th century) to the tower guarding the medieval city. While cars continually climb up the main street, the few side-streets are calm with their shaded, beamed houses. About halfway up, the houses pull back a bit from the street, forming a plaza of several Renaissance stone facades. The curve of an enclosed staircase, a dog's head carved on a beam end, a date set in the lintel over the door, are the details to be admired. At the end of the street an ancient fountain provides a few moments' rest. The perspective continues towards a ruined castle. One of three such châteaux is an hour's walk on the marked path from town. From these high points away from the crowds, there are splendid views both of the valley and the misty peaks above.

In the seemingly endless chain of picturesque towns, **Hunawihr** boasts a stork centre and a fortified church of thick crenellated walls overlooking the valley. The signs indicating **Riquewihr** are intended for hikers, not for drivers. This, a little medieval townlet, is completely enclosed in its protective walls, leaving at least some of the cars outside. The town is a tourist's heaven. Practically every house is a delight of colours, tiles, balconies and flower boxes. Many have cobbled courtyards multiplying the possibilities of little turrets or intricate woodcarvings. Riquewihr's most distinctive trait is its tradition of shop signs of forged iron, old ones as in the **Postal Museum**, and modern ones in the streets. There are also plenty of wine cellars.

Where Schweitzer was born: The town of **Kaysersberg** is one of the most seductive in Alsace. Birthplace of Albert Schweitzer, the old part has the frequent narrow form of the region, enhanced by the **River Weiss**. Near the top of the town, the river traverses a circular plaza united by a fortified bridge and a stone altar, in the shadow of the castle keep perched on the mountain above. The 16th-century houses in narrow alleys are served by numerous Renaissance fountains, although the local wisdom is to prefer wine to water. In addition to the **Schweitzer**

Hot day on the Route du Vin.

House, a small museum is open next door to the Winegrowers' Cellar.

Alsace is synonymous with fruity dry white wine, designated by varietals and not by the land it is grown on. Tiny quantities of red (Tokay) and rosé (Pinot Noir) are produced. Of the seven most common Alsace varietals, the most prestigious are Riesling, Gewürztraminer and Tokay, also called Pinot gris. These wines have a pleasant immediate flavour, but little depth for savouring, as they are generally young. In the informal taverns known as *winstubs* they are always served in attractive glasses with long green stems, and are very popular with fish, seafood and Alsatian specialities such as *choucroute*, *foie gras* and sweet cheese pie. Among the vineyards are orchards of cherries and plums for the famous "white alcohol" fruit brandies.

Second town: Business centre for wine professionals, **Colmar** is the second tourist centre of Alsace. The sculptor Bartholdi, creator of the Statue of Liberty, was born here, and his works are prominent in the town's parks. The old town is a large pedestrian zone of irregularly shaped plazas connected by short streets that detour around historic buildings and churches. The former Dominican monastery contains an impressive manuscript library around a Gothic cloister.

The **Musée Unterlinden**, exceptional overall, is most renowned for the works of the 15th-century artist Martin Schongauer. His masterpiece is the phenomenal Issenheim retable. It consists of a central tableau surrounded by double panels. These panels, painted on both surfaces, have an unearthly glow rendering the saints' tortures and monsters as livid and fantastic as science fiction.

The stroll through Colmar leads to the quarter called **La Petite Venise**, in honour of the little River Lauch and adjacent canal where tanners once cleaned their pelts. Here, as throughout the city, the balconies are lined with flowers, and each half-timbered house has an individualistic touch, a gabled turret or unusual sculptures such as the heads on the **Maison des Têtes**. The **Customs House** is covered in glazed tiles arranged in patterns of green and yellow.

Skyline drive: Leaving Colmar the wine route merges with the **Route de Crêtes**, a skyline drive through the highest and most beautiful part of the Vosges. An Alsace Wine Museum recreating a traditional wine cellar is established in the **Kientzheim Castle**. **Munster** with its celebrated cheese is the appropriate gateway to an itinerary of farm-inns proposing hefty snacks of local cuisine. These little towns have a special homogeneity of high-pitched roofs, red-berried trees and pastoral streams that distinguish them from other regions.

Into the Vosges the valley is quickly left behind; a few fields on the first slopes, and then all is pine and oak forest. From the **Schlucht** and **Hohneck** passes, to the **Ballon d' Alsace**, the mountains are on all sides, the grass of the worn peaks yellowing at the end of summer. Snow and skiing are abundant in winter. From the **Grand Ballon**, the area's highest summit, many hikes are possible. At its foot, **Thann**'s church of rich flamboyant style is comfortably set in the pleasant town. In the former market hall a small museum contains native paintings on wood depicting important events of local memory.

Mulhouse is an industrial city whose past as an independent republic has been erased by war bombings. To make up for this lack, it is a city of museums. The unique **Musée de l'Impressionisme** is devoted to techniques and arts of printed cloth and wall paperings. Another legacy of industrial wealth is the **National Automobile Museum**, a spectacular array of over 500 antique and rare cars. At the fascinating open-air **Eco-Museum**, north of the town, traditional timber-framed houses have been regrouped to form an Alsatian village.

A few miles east among electrical installations on the Rhine is the little-known Romanesque marvel, the eight-sided church of **Ottmarsheim**. South of Mulhouse is a yet-to-be-discovered region, the **Sundgau**, marked by the character of neighbouring Switzerland. In contrast to northern Alsace, the old towns such as **Altkirch** present a muted chiaroscuro palette against the backdrop of the mountainous forests of the Jura.

Typical half-timbered Alsatian home, this one in Itterswiller.

CADET
ROUSSEL

CITOYEN
D'AUXERRE

BURGUNDY

Only minutes from the roar of Paris traffic, the calm, bright Burgundian countryside has come as a welcome shock to more than one visitor travelling south from the French capital. Far north of Dijon, where the powerful dukes of Burgundy (Handsome Philippe or Charles the Bold) controlled an immense kingdom, the Yonne river winds its way to **Sens** through a peaceful valley where ancient glory still clings to the unpretentious Burgundian farmland.

Gothic splendour: Up to 1622 the Archbishop of **Sens** lorded over an area extending all the way to Paris. His palatial lodgings are still an impressive site. They now house a museum devoted to local history with rooms showing a variety of *objets* dating from the Bronze Age to 18th-century artwork.

The **Cathedral-St-Etienne** was the first in France to be built in the Gothic manner. Construction began in the 12th century and work was not completed until 500 years later. In the course of time, this monumental structure was embellished with intricate sculpture, high arches and an impressive series of stained-glass windows. In the adjoining buildings, the church's treasure is remarkable for rare liturgical garments.

Southwest of Sens, the spires adorning the brick and stone château of **St-Fargeau** appear like minarets on the horizon. This is where the *Grande Mademoiselle,* Louis XIV's sister, once lived. Dating from the 15th century, the château was renovated in the mid-17th century by Le Vau, the architect of Versailles.

Many of the rooms have been restored to their original splendour and every summer the grounds are the site of historical re-enactments that trace the history of France from the Hundred Years' War to the liberation of Paris after World War II.

St-Fargeau is situated in an area known as **La Puisaye**. This is rural Burgundy at its best. The hills shimmer in the early afternoon heat and tall trees line the banks of rivers such as the Loing. The area's most famous native daughter is Colette (1873–1953) whose writings remain popular in France today and whose birthplace can be seen in the centre of **St-Sauveur-en-Puisaye**.

Through a network of farm towns, each nonchalantly raising its church steeple, the back roads can, with some determination, be made to lead to **Ratilly**. Here a superbly restored 13th-century château-fort lies hidden in a brambly wood. From the outside it seems like nothing but towers, but just inside the arched entry a cheerful grassy courtyard opens onto a pottery school.

Auxerre, the immemorial capital of northwestern Burgundy, resounds with history, being one of the oldest cities in France. Renaissance houses follow a semi-circular pattern around the **Clock Tower**, which once guarded the 15th-century ramparts. Two churches rival for attention. The **Cathedral-St-Etienne** is recognised by the sharp slope of its asymmetric facade. The medieval sense of Christianity is vivid in this church, from the tympanum's three-

Left, Auxere figurine. Right, bucolic Burgundy countryside.

tiered life of Christ, to the red and blue lives of saints depicted in stained glass. The abbey church dedicated to **St-Germain**, also Gothic, is built on an extraordinary hive of underground chapels. Parts of the church date from the time of Charlemagne and the reddish frescoes go back to AD 850.

From Pontigny to Montréal, the **Serein** (Serene) **river valley** is a quiet haven that merits its name. A major attraction is the small town of **Chablis**, not because it is of any particular architectural interest but because of its world-famous vineyards, stitched like quilts over the hills. Upstream, the little town of **Noyers** has preserved all the charm of its history. The rampart wall is guarded by no fewer than 16 towers circling the arcades of the central square.

Canal country: Beyond the Chablis vineyards is the **Burgundy Canal**. Part of a countrywide network of waterways built for freight transport, the canal is now increasingly used by houseboats, and barges are rented by vacationers looking for a novel way to visit this part of France. Just the width of a single *péniche* (barge), the narrow channel is equipped with locks and wider basins for crossing traffic. Once on a canal, the rest of the world ceases to exist and one can drift down the tranquil waters visiting châteaux from **Tonnerre** to **Bussy-Rabutin**.

Tanlay, passed along the way, is a magnificent sight ensconced as it is in a series of moats, arcades and iron grills. Another château gem, **Ancy-le-Franc**, presents an austerely symmetrical exterior, but the inner courtyard and furnishings are of sumptuous splendour inspired by the Italian Renaissance.

Founded by Saint Bernard, **Fontenay Abbey** is the most complete ensemble remaining in Burgundy of life in a medieval monastery. Solitary and independent at the bottom of a remote valley, all the buildings used when the abbey housed an active community of monks have been preserved. The church and cloister are examples of Cistercian simplicity; intended to be piously modest, without ornamentation of any kind,

Afternoon on the Burgundy Canal.

the bare paving stones and immaculate columns have acquired, in the course of time, a look of grandeur.

Just south of **Fontenay** is the site of a battle decisive in French history and of which it has been rather dramatically stated, "It is here that Gaul died and France was born." **Alise-Ste-Reine** is generally accepted as the site of the battle of Alésia, where the Gauls under Vercingetorix were defeated by Julius Caesar. A monumental statue of Vercingetorix overlooks the Gallo-Roman city where excavations have been under way since 1906. Among the foundations uncovered are those of an early Christian church dedicated to the martyred Reine. Objects from the site are on display at the **Musée Alésia**.

Travelling west, one arrives in **Semur-en-Auxois**, which still retains the flavour of a medieval fortress town, guarded by imposing dungeon towers that overlook the Armançon river. Beyond Semur lies **Époisses**, less well known for its medieval château and Renaissance houses than for its famous cheese. Creamy, pungent and soft, its orange rind is washed with brandy (*marc de Bourgogne*) as it matures in the cellars here. It is the most famous cheese in the region and *must* be tried with a glass of red Burgundy wine.

The Black Mountains: A town of parks and cosy old houses, **Avallon** is the gateway to the **Morvan Region Natural Park**. These first spurs of the **Massif Central** are covered with dense forests, hence the Celtic name *Morvan*, meaning "Black Mountain". Once an inaccessible back-country derided by its richer neighbours, the **Morvan** is now a favoured weekend retreat. Fast streams churning in narrow gorges provide excellent fishing and canoeing. Although not very high above sea level, the landscape gives an impression of mountains, with sheer drops and clefts.

Set on a high hilltop, **Vézelay** offers a splendid view of the surrounding countryside and is in itself one of the most spectacular monuments in all of Burgundy. The majestic **basilica**, reached by walking up the narrow, winding

Interior of the Vézelay Abbey.

streets of the town is remarkable. Founded in the 9th century as an abbey, it was here that Bernard of Clairvaux launched the Second Crusade in 1146. Its long nave is flanked by black and white arches and, faithful to the Romanesque tradition, its entrance is decorated with a superb central tympanum depicting a larger-than-life Christ.

From the **Mont Beuvray**, an ancient wooded plateau, one has a splendid view east over the soft contours of the vineyards toward **Autun**. This town, which celebrated its bi-millennial in 1985, has been an administrative centre ever since Augustus defeated the Gauls. Traces still remain of the Roman roads that led to the town and the quadruple-arched gates of this small provincial city bear witness to its imperial past. The **amphitheatre**, the largest in Roman Gaul, held up to 15,000 spectators. Medieval prosperity left behind the **St-Lazare Cathedral**, whose white sculpted doorway contrasts with the more rustic rock of the church itself. Opposite is the **Musée Rolin**, where it is hard to choose between the seven rooms of Gallo-Roman archaeology and the collections of medieval painting and sculpture. Behind the cathedral the remaining ramparts make a lovely stroll to the ancient Ursulines' keep.

Northeast of **Autun** is the undisputed capital of Burgundy, **Dijon**. This city's many old buildings are in the active city centre, particularly the monumental **Palace of the States of Burgundy**. Arched passageways give access to its spacious courtyards where the light colour of the wide, regular paving stones echoes the pale facades. The **Art Museum**, one of the finest in France, is housed in the oldest part of the palace where French, German and Italian statuary and art dating from the 14th to the 18th century are on display. The **Guard's Hall** contains the museum's most famous tombstones, of three members of the ducal dynasty, sculpted in alabaster and black marble. Also not to be missed is the 14th-century kitchen with its six gargantuan fireplaces an enduring reminder of the splendour of banquets in times past.

Dijon rooftops.

A circular stroll from the palace to the **Square d'Arcy** and back takes in the old quarter with its malls and tiny plazas. **Notre Dame** is a small church full of delightful curiosities, such as the family of figures animated by a clock mechanism. Idiosyncratic old facades line the narrow streets only a few feet from the church walls. Along the pedestrian shopping streets, elegant and antique boutiques have taken up residence with lustrous, low-beamed ceilings and sculptures decorating the upper floors. The **Hôtel Chambellan** is the most striking of a series of Renaissance residences, with its elaborate balconies and staircases hidden away in interior courtyards. Further to the west, **St-Bénigne Cathedral** draws the eye with its tall spire and multicoloured octagonal towers. Coming full circle, the **Palais de Justice** and its neighbourhood are reminiscent of the days when the provincial parliament officiated under the painted and wainscoted ceilings.

Before leaving Dijon, be sure to sample the famous *pain d'épice* (a honey sweetened, anis-flavoured cake/bread) and purchase a jar of the pungent mustard that has been produced here for more than 600 years.

Hills of Gold: What more evocative name than that of the *département* in which all the great vineyards are located, **Côte d'Or**, the "Hills of Gold". Some say the name comes from the gold-coloured leaves that cover the hills in autumn, while others maintain that it is from the great wines or "bottled gold" they produce. No matter, the hills are beautiful and the wines excellent.

The vineyards are quite easy to visit since most of them line the western edge of Highway 74 that runs from Dijon to Chalon-sur-Saône. Here, the names of the towns evoke great vintages: Gevrey Chambertin, Vougeot, Vosne-Romanée, Nuits-St-Georges, Aloxe-Corton, Beaune, Pommard. Continue on further south to visit Meursault, Puligny-Montrachet or Chassagne-Montrachet where the world's best white wines are made. Everywhere one is invited to stop and sample the wine – and invitations

Up to no good.

are hard to refuse when bottles bear of these celebrated names.

Travelling the Wine Route: One of the largest vineyards in Burgundy, the **Clos de Vougeot**, is set back from the road roughly mid-way between Dijon and Beaune. This famous Burgundian vineyard was nurtured by the Cistercians, who greatly contributed to the development of vineyards on lands bequeathed to the order founded by Saint Bernard in **Cîteaux**, to the southeast. The small château of the Clos, built to house wine presses, is also the home of the Chevaliers du Tastevin, a society of connoisseurs whose prizes are coveted.

Directly south of Vougeot is **Beaune** where the jewel-like roof of the **Hôtel-Dieu** made of multicoloured tiles can be seen glimmering in the distance as one approaches. Since the 18th century, Beaune has been the heart of the Burgundian wine trade, and the auction of the *Hospices de Beaune* in the Hôtel-Dieu, a charity hospital historically supported by the wine produced on lands donated by benefactors, is still the high point in the calendar of Burgundian wine lore. Today the building is a museum, and under its splendid multicoloured roof, the long ward contains the original sick beds. The halls off the courtyard house a collection of art work and tapestry crowned by a painting of the *Last Judgment* so detailed it requires a magnifying glass.

Beyond Beaune are the villages that produce the Burgundy whites. These humble stone cottages hardly suggest that here are some of the most sought-after vineyards in the world. It is here the Chardonnay grape is at its best and the names of Meursault and Montrachet are synonymous with excellence.

Approaching **Chalon-sur-Saône**, vineyards are few and far between. Although an industrial centre today, half-timbered houses still crowd around the **Cathedral of St-Vincent** in the old quarter of town. Chalon is also the birthplace of Nicéphore Niepce, the inventor of photography, and has a museum dedicated to him and the history of photography. Chalon also boasts two medieval festivals: *Carnaval*, with an extrava-gant Mardi Gras parade, and the bi-annual *foire des Sauvagines*, an international leather fair (February and June).

Small towns and great churches: Further south in the Saône valley, **Tournus** is the remarkably quiet site of one of the greatest of all the Romanesque churches in Burgundy. **St-Philibert** owes its special beauty to the unretouched surface of its small irregular stones. The exterior, with a square tower and almost no decoration, has a forbidding military appearance. Inside, massive columns of the same yellow stone carry three parallel systems of arches. This austerity is the hallmark of the church, cloister and surrounding monastery buildings dating from the 11th and 12th centuries. Old streets lead down to the river and from the bridge one has a splendid view of the church and its buildings.

Perched on a narrow crest of rock, **Brancion** is a feudal burg delightful to visit. Above the old quarter of the church and marketplace is the crumbling but proud château, one of the few such examples in Burgundy where the dukes' power countered individual fiefdoms.

The Burgundy of the Middle Ages was marked by the great monastic orders whose fervour and ramified organisation revived a spiritual life while profoundly affecting the politics of Christian Europe. The Benedictine rule radiated from **Cluny**, where the abbots were on an equal footing with the Pope until, in the 12th century, the monk Bernard launched a purifying reform, the Cistercian order, named after its headquarters in Cîteaux.

The remains of the Cluny monastery founded in 910 only faintly suggest the secular and spiritual power of this order, whose abbots reigned for life. Five of 15 guard towers remain. The church that was for five centuries the largest of all Christendom was almost entirely destroyed after the French Revolution, leaving a small group of chapels and spires. The cloister, built in the 18th century, was luckier, and the whole immense ensemble can be admired from the central gardens. The town's museum offers an overall view of the rise and fall of Cluny.

Glass pageantry from St-Seine-sur-l'Abbaye.

SANCTUS : EGIDIUS

THE RHÔNE VALLEY

Mâcon marks a transition. Straddling the borderline between Burgundy and the Lyonnais, it is the frontier between northern pointed roofs of slate, and the southern, red, rounded Roman tile. Just outside the city are the vineyards of **Pouilly-Fuissé** vineyards. This white Burgundy wine has a bouquet combining a smoky, dry sensation with a rich taste, making it a much sought-after delicacy.

The rock of **Solutré** rears above the wavy line of hills like a listing ocean liner, giving its name to Solutrean Stone Age civilisations. Prehistoric man used this cliff as a hunting ground, herding deer and wild horses towards the summit and then frightening them into jumping over the edge. The bone yard below extends over 4,000 sq. metres (almost an acre). The panorama, as one walks up the slope, encompasses the black and yellow patchwork of surrounding hills.

Like taciturn troops guarding the vine yards, the **Monts du Beaujolais** are covered with sombre chestnut and pine forests, and there is a local wood industry. But the bell-shaped vines reach high up the slopes, as do the typical farmhouses with living quarters over the cellar.

Technically part of the Burgundy wine region – the nine *crus* have the right to use "Burgundy" on their label – all Beaujolais is actually made from the Gamay grape as distinct from the Pinot Noir of Burgundy. Only Beaujolais Nouveau is produced by accelerated fermentation, and should be drunk within a few months. Normally fermented Beaujolais, produced in 35 villages, is best after two years.

The grapes are harvested in October and the first tastings take place before the end of the month. In **Juliénas** the wine cellar is in a long disused church. At the **Château de Corcelles** the former guard room has been converted into a tasting room. **Belleville** is the commercial centre of an area where the most serious wine-makers work at improving the quality of the traditional Beaujolais. The Beaujolais Nouveau "season" opens with a media bang in mid-November – just a few weeks after the grapes have been harvested. At midnight preceding the date set for the first sale, luxury sports cars and private planes rev their engines for the race to be the first to bring the year's vintage to London, Dublin, or New York.

On the opposite bank of the Saône is a land of solid farm traditions, whose products are the basis of the city-dweller's cuisine. **La Ferme de la Forêt** in **Courtes** is a farm museum, where all activities were concentrated in a single building combining stable, tool shed and dwelling. The chimney topped by a cowl is just one of the signs of the **Bresse** region. The rustic building materials and wood furniture used by generations of the same family are now relics, emblems of a lifestyle that died out in the 1950s.

Bourg-en-Bresse is the capital of a region with a thriving speciality in farm-fatted chickens and capons. At the weekly poultry market thousands of birds, specially prepared in a milk bath after slaughtering, are snapped up by professional buyers. On the outskirts of town the church of **Brou** is a splendid jewel of the Flam-

Left, poet from Pérouges. **Right**, a region of delicacies.

boyant Gothic style. It was commissioned by Archduchess Marguerite of Savoy, as a memorial to her husband, who died in 1504, aged only 24. Inside, the triple-arched rood screen, one of the few left in France, which separates the nave from the choir, is famous for its beautiful stone lattice-work. Seventy-four monks' stalls intricately carved in dark oak line the entry to the choir. Finest of all the splendid marble sculptures are those of the three royal tombs in the choir itself, exquisitely carved with small statuettes and life-size figures of the noble family.

Southwest of Bourg-en-Bresse is the **Dombes**, a marshy plateau with more than 100 lakes, most of them man-made. Large sectors are private hunting grounds, with waterfowl and fish. A system of channels and sluices drains water from one lake to another, for the traditional land use rotating from fish to grain crop.

After the sparse waterscape, **Pérouges** is a return to urban bustle, that of the Middle Ages. The entire town is medieval in character, and thrives on its past. Saved from destruction in the early 20th century, the houses and ramparts have been conscientiously restored and marvellously adapted to modern ideas of space and light. The stone-paved streets encourage a snail's pace ideal for looking into a crooked passageway or window shopping in the boutiques devoted to traditional Bresse crafts, such as blue Meillonas ceramics.

Big city: The high-speed TGV arrives at the central Perrache station, a unique causeway of ramps and escalators leading directly into the city. Central **Lyon**, with the Rhône on one side and the Saône on the other, is compact and ideal for visiting on foot.

The most unusual of Lyon's 24 museums is the **Historical Museum of Fabrics** which covers the development of textile techniques in all ages and from all over the world, and displays some of the rarest and most beautiful materials ever made. The **Museum of Fine Arts** ranks next in importance with a splendid collection of French and European paintings. Lyon was the first town to have a stock exchange and the first place to issue

Below, Brou church. Right, sample ware from Pérouges.

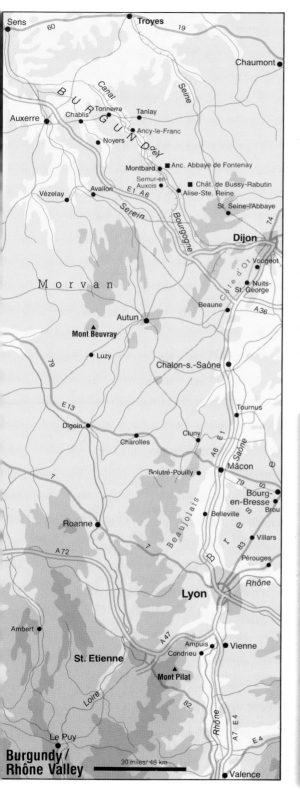

Sens
60
Troyes
19
Chaumont
BURGUNDY
Canal
Seine
Auxerre
Chablis
Tonnerre
Tanlay
Ancy-le-Franc
Noyers
Vézelay
Avallon
Semur-en-Auxois
Montbard
Anc. Abbaye de Fontenay
Alise-Ste. Reine
Chât. de Bussy-Rabutin
E1 A6
Serein
Bourgogne
St. Seine-l'Abbaye
74
Dijon
Vougeot
Côte d'Or
Nuits-St. George
M o r v a n
Beaune
A36
Autun
Mont Beuvray
79
Luzy
Chalon-s.-Saône
E13
Tournus
Digoin
Cluny
E1
Saône
A6
Charolles
7
Solutré-Pouilly
Mâcon
79
Bourg-en-Bresse
Beaujolais
Brou
Belleville
Roanne
Villars
A72
Péronges
Rhône
Lyon
Ambert
A47
Ampuis
Vienne
Condrieu
St. Etienne
Mont Pilat
82
Loire
Rhône
A7 E4
E4
Le Puy
Burgundy /
Rhône Valley
30 miles/ 48 km
Valence

a cheque and the **Printing and Banking Museum** outlines the history of European commerce, as well as having a superb collection of rare books.

The daily rhythm centres on meals, and where food is concerned the Lyonnais do not mess around. The mid-morning *mâchon,* specifically Lyonnais, is no snack, but a meal of *charcuterie*, from sausages and *rosette* salamis to stuffed hocks and hams. Traditional meal times are strictly observed, and after these hours nothing is left in the kitchen. In a city renowned for hearty home cooking, a missed meal is a real loss.

Along the Saône, a tree-lined *quai* extends an unobstructed view over the wide water, with some of its bridges painted red. On the opposite bank lies the city's oldest quarter, **Vieux Lyon**. The restoration of the medieval and Renaissance quarters started some years ago. Typically the Renaissance houses were built round a courtyard, reached from the street through a vaulted passage beneath a house. In each street a few courtyards had another vaulted passage at the back leading

into the next street. These public passages, still in use, are called *traboules*.

A walk offers many discoveries. From the Rue Saint-Jean to the Place du Change, and on to the Place du St-Paul, back down the Rue Juiverie and then the Rue Gadagne, is less than a kilometre altogether. The **Hôtel de Gadagne** is the finest Renaissance mansion in Lyon. It now houses the city's historical museum and a special collection of puppets from all over the world. The **Cathedral of St-Jean** dates from the 11th to the 14th centuries. It contains a remarkable 14th-century astronomical clock, still in working order. At midday, 1, 2 and 3pm bells ring, cocks crow, doors open and puppet figures come out and mime the Annunciation. The building adjoining the cathedral, the former choir school, dates from the same period as the early part of the cathedral.

Above Lyon: The **Fourvière Hill** is reachable on foot by steep *montées,* or by funicular cable cars. It is topped by a rococo **Notre Dame** and a terrace overlooking the city. On the southern slope, the **Museum of Gallo-Roman Civilisation** is a highly original building eminently well-conceived. Built into the hill, from the upper entry a long spiral ramp glides gently down through artifacts such as a chariot wheel, or a smooth bronze Neptune. Windows look out on two Roman theatres, still used for performances.

The other hill rising between the two rivers is **La Croix Rousse,** bastion of the *Canuts,* skilled workers in silk-weaving for generations. From the 15th century to the Industrial Revolution thousands of small workshops painstakingly produced the richly coloured silks. A handful of stubborn craftsmen have maintained the tradition, furnishing the museums and palaces of Europe with the brocades of a bygone era. **La Maison des Canuts** gives demonstrations on different types of looms and patterns. Most spectacular is weaving of Genoa velvet, with 800 *bobines* forming loops cut line by line to give a deep pattern in three-colour relief.

From the **Place Bellevue**, a maze of passages and connecting courtyards winds down to the **Hôtel de Ville**.

The Rhône valley, gateway to Provence, is best seen off the main routes. **Vienne** is full of the echo of its distant glory as a Roman and then episcopal city. Its restored Roman theatre (one of the largest ever built), is used for performances in summer. The **Augustus** and **Livia Temple**, is, with the Maison Carrée at Nîmes, the best example of a Roman temple surviving in France. The **Cathedral of St-Maurice**, built from the 11th to the 16th centuries, has a facade with three portals beautifully carved in the Flamboyant style, still remarkable though its statues were removed during the Wars of Religion. Across the river at **St Romain-en-Gal** a Roman suburb of Vienne has been excavated. Mosaics are shown in a small museum.

From Vienne the **Côtes du Rhône** vineyards stretch south on both sides of the river for 193 km (120 miles) to the **Avignon** region. They produce vast quantities of sound wine, as well as the famous Hermitage and Châteauneuf du Pape. The red Côte Rotie and the white Condrieu, which come from tiny vineyards just south of Vienne, are also first-class.

Left, Lyon is famed for its marionettes. **Right,** serenade in Lyon.

233

234

CENTRAL FRANCE

The region defined as Central France in this book extends from Bordeaux on the west coast, up the Dordogne river into Périgord and thence north-eastwards into Limousin, finally reaching the Auvergne and the Massif Central to the east of Lyon.

This is essentially a pastoral area. The city of Bordeaux, on the Gironde estuary, is both an important port and lies at the centre of a key wine-producing region. At its back, the Dordogne flows gently through some of France's most lovely countryside, which has proved particularly popular with the British holidaymaker. In fact, this has always been a popular place to live; the cave paintings at Lascaux suggest that artistically-gifted hunters were resident here as long as 30,000 years ago. More recent aristocrats have liked it too, and the Dordogne *département* has more châteaux than any other in France.

Périgord is famous for its walnuts, truffles and *foie gras*, the liver paté that results from the controversial force-feeding of geese. Limoges is best known for its porcelain, and the rugged high plateau of the Massif Central produces some of France's finest water from the towns of Vichy and Volvic. Although in the very heart of France, the Auvergne, hoisted high on the Massif plateau as it is, has rarely seized centre stage. This is a land of untouched towns, thermal spas and shepherds, peacefully isolated in their precipitous valleys.

To its west, Central France is well-trodden; to its east it still takes some discovering. The chapters that follow profile both well-known destinations and those that are less familiar but are nevertheless worth seeking out.

Preceding pages: red roofs in the Auvergne town of Le Puy. **Left:** early artwork at Lascaux caves in Périgord.

BORDEAUX

France's sixth largest city and sixth largest port, **Bordeaux** has the appearance of long-standing prosperity. In addition to the wine trade, its merchant marine was active in the slave trade, and later in commerce with French colonies in Africa. Since the 1960s it has also become an industrial centre (aeronautics, etc), thanks partly to the dynamic policies of its Gaullist mayor, Jacques Dulmas.

The urban architecture is cool and spacious, dominated by the regularity of 18th-century construction. The one exception to this pattern is the Romanesque church **Sainte-Croix**, whose elaborately sculpted tympanum is topped by a curiously asymmetric tower added later. Restored and immaculate, Sainte-Croix gives onto a wide cobbled square typical of Bordeaux's modern street lines.

The essence of Bordeaux is to be found along the avenue **Allées de Tourny**. At one end is the **Grand Théâtre**, a purely neoclassical monument of symmetric columns and arches. On the river side opens the gravelled **Esplanade des Quinconces**, the name referring to the arrangement of the trees. In between is the **Maison des Vins**, an indispensable stop for documentation on the different Bordelais vineyards, and in particular those estates open to the public. Just across the street is the well-organised tourism office, which arranges bus tours to a different wine region each afternoon. A foretaste comes without delay in the neighbouring wine stores; the clerks are very knowledgeable about Bordeaux wines. Since medieval times, Bordeaux has exported much of its wine to England, and the rich merchant families still have close British links.

Fittingly, the Bordeaux vineyards begin right on the edge of the city, with **Château Haut-Brion**. Like most of the Bordeaux châteaux, the building in question is not a genuine castle, but rather a stately mansion dating from the 19th-century. The use of the word "château" to designate a wine-producing property is a

Château Margaux welcomes tasters.

Bordelais convention. Also specific to Bordeaux wines is their official classification in multiple categories by *cru* (growth). The original classification of 1855 (amended in 1973) was based on land qualities, price and prestige, and concerned only the Médoc and Sauternes wines. However, although technically a Graves wine, Château Haut-Brion was included – it was too good to be left out.

Graves and Médoc: The name "Graves" refers to the gravelly nature of the soil, producing both red and white wines, sometimes from the same vines. A visit to this region starts with **Labrède**, not a wine-producing château but home of the 18th-century philosopher Montesquieu. The baron's castle, dating from the 15th century, is surrounded by a functioning moat, complete with carp. Not overly large, the interior is partially furnished, and crowned by a vast library.

Unfortunately the famous **Château d'Yquem** is not open to the public, but the nearby **Château Filhot** offers wine tasting and a friendly welcome.

A bit farther is **Roquetaillade**, the best preserved of a series of medieval fortresses built by Pope Clement V. An unusual line of four great towers form the facade, surprisingly austere in the sunny and placid vineyards. Another such fortress, in **Villandraut**, is the backdrop for the Uzestes music festival in late August.

The **Médoc** is the most celebrated of the Bordeaux wine regions, and for many these wines represent the definition and incarnation of the Bordeaux wine that continues to improve over decades. This narrow band of vineyards, stretching northwest from Bordeaux along the coastline of the Gironde estuary, numbers some 180 châteaux. Here, the vines are all grown on slight heights where the soil is more plentiful and less water-logged. At points along the coast are sluice-gates; not to irrigate the land but to drain off excess water, and prevent the tide from moving up the channels. (Tides exist all along the 80-km/50-mile Gironde.)

Most of the Médoc châteaux can be visited, although calling ahead is always recommended. Appointments are necessary for the most famous, such as **Mouton-**

The proprietor of Clos Haut Peyraguey in Sauternes.

Rothschild, with its excessively ornate mansion, and a wine archive where the world's best, rarest and most expensive wines repose for posterity.

The **Château de la Tour de By** (near Lesparre) gives the visitor a particularly warm welcome. After a walk through the vineyards to the lone tower overlooking the estuary, the visit includes a tour of the cellar. "Raising" wine requires many delicate procedures, such as settling the oak casks on chocs and carefully maintaining the same alignment and distribution. These operations are explained in detail by a qualified personnel member, sometimes the wine master himself, who remains available for questions during the sampling. The towns of **Margaux**, **Pauillac**, **St-Estèphe** and **Lesparre** each have wine centres with exhibits and information on their respective wines.

Doves and dunes: If anything can lure a winegrower away from his assembly tanks and glass pipettes, it is the wood pigeon hunting season. The path of these migratory birds is clearly indicated by a sudden array of crude hunters' cabins on stilts,

fabricated out of any spare square of plywood or leftover fence pole available. Some locals recount that it is impossible to get a plumber or carpenter when the wood pigeons come over.

Where the vineyards give out the beach takes over. From the mouth of the estuary along the 207-km (140-mile) coast to **Arcachon**, sandy dunes held down by scrub pine alternate with large inland lakes. While swimming is limited in the high surf, resort towns offer horseback-riding and cycling in the pine forest that is the beginning of the **Landes**. Arcachon and its bay are renowned for oysters and pleasure boating. An immense fine-sand beach is circled by some of Europe's highest dunes. The Landes, sweeping south for 240 km (150 miles), is the largest forest in France and entirely artifical, created out of wasteland in the 19th century. Its timber forms an important part of Bordeaux's export trade.

On the east side of Bordeaux, the small town of **St-Émilion** gives its name to yet another wine district. Honoured by the English as the "King of Wines", the quality has been supervised for eight centuries by an elected council of peers, known as *Jurats*. The deliberations of this brotherhood take place with red-robed ceremony in one of the town's Gothic cloisters. With two monasteries, St-Émilion offers a wealth of religious architecture. The most spectacular is a unique monolithic church. Tunnelled into the steep hillside in the 11th century, the steeple emerges full-blown at street level on the top of the hill. The remains of a cloister mingle with untended greenery.

Not far is the superb Roman villa discovered in **Montcaret** (near Lamothe-Ravel on the road to Bergerac). Extensive foundations of this small community are visible, including ducts for a warm-air heating system, the baths, and above all several complete mosaic floors.

The great novelist François Mauriac (1895–1970) adored his native Bordeaux and the country of the Landes and the Garonne valley. His former country home at Malagar, above the Garonne, is now a museum full of his souvenirs. His masterpiece *Thérèse Desqueyroux* (1927) is set in the brooding Landes forest.

Left, *vendangeur* or grape-picker. **Right**, Bacchus tells all at Mouton-Rothschild.

LIMOUSIN AND PÉRIGORD

Limousin is a centre for the arts of fire – porcelain and enamel; and a land of water – rain and lakes. Still relatively unknown to tourists, the lovely region was off the beaten track until the opening of railways in the late 19th century.

And yet, **Limoges** is a household word for many whose grandmothers treasured this lovely china that graced many a bridal trousseau. Indeed, Limoges has some 30 porcelain workshops of all sizes, many offering guided tours. The **Adrien Dubouché National Museum** has a collection of some 10,000 pieces from all periods. Exhibitions of contemporary Limoges porcelain are held in summer. The exhibition locations vary from year to year.

If china is not your cup of tea, the city abounds in historic sights. Simple and graceful, the eight arches of the 13th-century stone **Pont Saint-Étienne** over the Vienne river marry civil engineering with aesthetic qualities. The **Cathedral of St-Étienne** is a Gothic masterpiece, begun in the 13th century and continued in the Flamboyant style. It was completed in the 19th century. **St-Michel-des-Lions Church**, built from the 14th to 16th centuries, is noted for its stained-glass. The **Musée de l'Évêché**, housed in a former episcopal palace, includes a collection of enamel work. In the summer the city hosts porcelain and enamel expositions.

About 86 km (54 miles) to the east, **Aubusson** is to tapestry what Limoges is to porcelain. The **Centre Culturel Jean Lurçat**, named after the artist who revitalised the art of tapestry-making from the 1930s onward, includes a **Musée de la Tapisserie** which has a permanent exhibition of both contemporary and traditional tapestries.

The **Maison du Vieux Tapissier**, next to the Syndicat d'Initiative, ancestral home of a weaver's family, shows a weaver's workshop as it would have been.

For a change of element, **Lake Vassivière** offers a wide range of outdoor activities. An artificial lake like many others in the region, Vassivière's complex shape provides many quiet inlets for swimming, sailing and canoeing. Horseback-riding is a favourite activity in the region. One of France's many national (as distinct from private) stud-farms is in **Arnac-Pompadour**, whose château evokes the Marquise de Pompadour, mistress of Louis XV. Horse races are held from the beginning of July to the end of September.

One of the region's most spectacular castles is perched above the town of **Coussac-Bonneval**. The exterior is that of a forbidding feudal fortress; one entire wall has no opening whatsoever! Inside the Renaissance courtyard is the reverse, with decoration intended to please, not subdue. And the interior is splendidly furnished.

The **St-Front Cathedral** was originally built in the 12th century but suffered a total reconstruction in the 19th century which completely altered its character. The former building was virtually razed – only the great bell tower was spared. The domed roof (not uncommon in the southwest of France) was rebuilt with five

Left, famous stud farm at Arnac-Pompadour. **Right**, walnut picker.

domes and 17 new towers and turrets. The result has a rather oriental look about it, more like a large mosque than a Christian church.

The surrounding old city, called **Puy-St-Front**, is now a conservation area. The cobbled streets are lined with Renaissance facades, here a doorway topped by a pointed stone arch, there a majestic staircase giving onto a tiny courtyard-foyer. Many buildings have been recently and elegantly restored, housing chic boutiques and architectural firms. Despite these signs of cosy times the modern-day city is not as prosperous as was the Gallo-Roman agglomeration, some say. The **Musée du Périgord** has extensive collections covering all periods.

North of Périgueux on the Dronne river, **Brantôme** has an exceptional charm enhanced by human ingenuity. For pleasure, and the creation of a mill-race, a 16th-century abbot undertook the construction of an elbow-shaped canal that hugs the town in the crook of its arm. The slow green water seems entranced by the long tresses of its own vegetation. The quiet old houses pursue their existence without excessive attention to tourists. On one of the banks is a green park with Renaissance gazebos, formerly the monk's garden. Leading to the **Renaissance Pavilon** and the grounds of the former abbey is a right-angled stone bridge, designed to resist the weight of the water arriving from two directions at once. The abbey buildings include a cave chapel. The bell tower, separate from the church, is a superb 11th-century construction.

Downstream on the Dronne is the superb **Château de Bourdeilles**. In fact, two castles, one feudal, the other Renaissance, the ensemble is bordered by terraces overlooking the cliff edge. The square and crenellated silhouette is dominated by an octagonal keep. The elegance of the 16th-century facades, the regular spacing of the stone-sashed windows, is complemented by lush interior furnishings and tapestries. At the foot of the château is the lord's mill.

The calm verdure along the winding rivers of this part of Périgord give it the

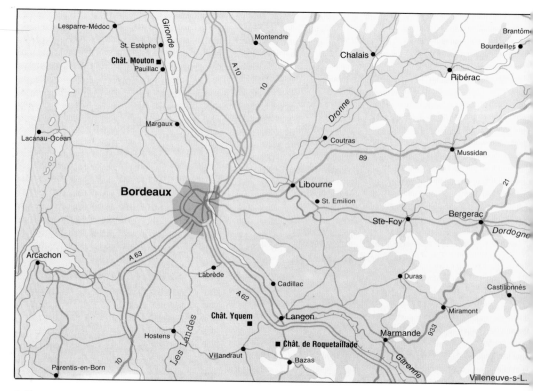

name **Périgord vert**. Walnut trees abound, as do the small water mills originally destined to produce walnut oil. There is also the special type of oak tree under which the elusive truffle is found, with the help of specially trained dogs and pigs. These delicacies, along with the king of provincial specialities, the sumptuous *foie gras,* make Périgord a gastronomic haven. Many fine chefs work in picturesque restaurants such as the Moulin de l'Abbaye in Brantôme.

In a short stretch of the Vézère valley between Montignac and Les Eyzies is the world's most astonishing collection of prehistoric art. The paintings and engravings of the **Lascaux** cave are breathtaking. Between 13,000 and 30,000 years old, perhaps associated with magical rites, the three-colour friezes (black, yellow, red) representing a variety of animals, use a whole range of techniques to obtain perspective, texture and movement.

Unlike other sites, Lascaux has been saved from the irreversible destruction caused by exposure to the air. Closed off in prehistoric times, the cave was not rediscovered until 1940. Due to the preoccupations of the war and ensuing hardships, crowds only started flocking to the site some years later. When an astute official learned in 1963 that a green fungus was growing over the paintings the cave was immediately closed while restoration was still possible. In compensation a partial copy, called **Lascaux 2**, has been created with a great care and skill in the adjacent quarry, and is open to the public. Most of the paintings are reproduced, including a rare human figure visible only with difficulty in the cave itself because it is inside a well. (Tickets for the site must be obtained in advance from the office in Montignac.)

In **Les Eyzies**, where prehistoric skeletons were discovered, a statue of Cro-Magnon man looks out, somewhat bewilderedly, from a ledge over the town's roofs. The **National Prehistory Museum**, presenting archaeological discoveries, is located in a feudal fortress half built into a cliff that shows traces where beams were inserted. The **Tayac Church** with its defensive towers and narrow

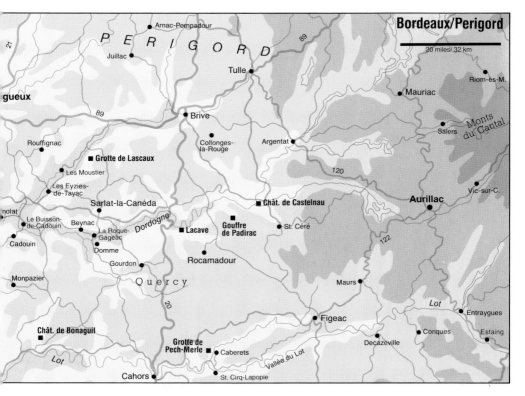

windows is an example of the fortified churches found throughout Périgord.

Literally dozens of important sites are clustered around Les Eyzies. The tourism office organises day-long excursions to many of these sites which avoids long waits in queues, and also rents bicycles. Just down the road is **Font-de-Gaume**, decorated with both paintings and engravings almost as stunning as Lascaux, despite deterioration; the nearby **Combarelles caves** contain engravings. In the same direction, the **Abri du Cap Blanc** is a prehistoric shelter (*abri*) which contains a 13-metre (42-ft) bas relief which includes six horses, a bull, a bison and other animals.

On the other side of Les Eyzies, the town of **Le Moustier** encloses a prehistoric archaeological dig that gave its name to the "mousterian" age. **La Roque-St-Christophe** is a series of cliff dwellings covering a large area that protrudes right over the road on the river bank. Initially inhabited in prehistoric times, the galleries were again reoccupied during the Middle Ages when the resident population feared invasion down below in the valley.

The **Rouffignac caves** are, in fact, the channels of an ancient underground river that dug some 10 km (6 miles) of tunnels. An electric train takes visitors through the dimly lit galleries, the walls dotted with knobs of hard rock that resisted erosion, and furrowed by prehistoric bears' claws. Although the caverns have been known for centuries, the drawings inside were not identified as prehistoric until 1956. Mammoths are the speciality, in a sequence depicting the confrontation of two groups. Sadly, the profusion of drawings on the "great ceiling" must compete with 19th-century graffiti done in candle smoke.

Along the Dordogne: From Sarlat to Bergerac the Dordogne valley combines magnificent views with lovely castles. **Sarlat** is a bustling town that could be the stage for a film set in the Renaissance, the church and episcopal palace creating a breathing space among the interlacing streets that run between the sculpted facades. At **Montfort** begins the almost full-circle bends in the river called *cingles*.

Force-feeding ducks to make their livers swell for *foie gras*.

244

From **Domme** the road plunges down to the river, and across the bridge, a few kilometres west, the village of **La Roque-Gageac** is lodged on the steep slope between the river bank and the cliff edge. A walk through the streets, which alternate between staircase and sidewalk, provides an intimate view of local architecture. At the highest point metal bars jut from the cliff where once a staircase climbed to the plateau above.

At **Beynac-et-Cazenac**, the 13th-century château perched above the town is a vision straight out of a medieval chronicle; the dizzying blank face of the tower keep is softened by the perspective of the surrounding towers and lower buildings, suggesting the multiple functions and activities of a feudal community. While the interior contains a great vaulted hall and frescoes, the view from the towers and terrace is the true spectacle, embracing numerous other castles dotted over the landscape.

Leaving the river for a moment, the **Cadouin Monastery**, on the road from Le Buisson, is an ensemble of sober architecture in an unusual style. The church of yellow stone presents a wide and sternly undecorated facade, the interior a flat transept. The 16th-century cloisters are rich with elaborately sculpted biblical characters. A recently excavated Romanesque chapter hall displays the coffer that contained the relic of the Holy Shroud that was Cadouin's glory – and source of considerable income – until it was proved a fake in 1934.

The Bastides' circuit: Between Limeuil and Trémolat, from the confluent of the Vézère and the Dordogne to the **Cingle de Trémolat**, the Dordogne, placidly immobile in summer, seems to be on all sides at once, the sun penetrating easily to the shallow bed. This picturesque tableau is the setting for comfortable country manor houses; low and large, the red tiled roofs rise to central dovecote tower. Far more than the religious architecture, even more than the military, it is the civil architecture that characterises Périgord.

Of the numerous fortified cities along the **Circuit des Bastides** between the Dordogne and Lot rivers, **Monpazier** is

Troglodyte caves at La-Roque-St-Christophe.

the best preserved. The *bastide* is characterised by a rectilinear street plan around a central square faced by arcades. In Monpazier these arcades are not unified, but vary with each house. Of disparate heights and depths, at the corners the openings for the street are curious lopsided triangles, like a dunce's cap. Monpazier has not only the central *halle* complete with grain measures, but also three of the six original fortified gateways. The church was defaced during the Revolution, the tympanum replaced by an inscription of the official ideology, "The people recognise the existence of the Supreme Being and the immortality of the soul."

Some *bastides* were founded by the English, and some by the French. Monpazier was founded on 7 January 1284, by the English. Both sides sought to win support by granting favours such as the independent, non-feudal status of the *bastides*. These "new towns" of the Middle Ages were often attacked and some changed hands as often as six times during the course of the war. The landscape of Périgord is also characterised by the many fortresses built in the early part of the Hundred Years' War.

The countryside near Cahors is known as the **Quercy noir**, from the dark forests of holm oak which clothe the hills (Latin *quercus* – an oak tree). **Rocamadour** is the area's main attraction; this pilgrims' paradise is an accretion of crypts, chapels and shrines clustered like the cells of a beehive against the cliff. In activity since the body of St Amadour was found uncorrupted in its grave, the ensemble has been considerably changed in modern times, and restored in bad taste. The essential constructions remain, particularly the chapels using the flank of the cliff as a wall. A path of the Stations of the Cross leads up to a château whose terraces overlooking the valley are practically built in thin air.

Fifteen kilometres (9 miles) from Rocamadour, the **Gouffre de Padirac** is an enormous circular chasm or pot-hole, 99 metres (325 ft) across and 103 metres (338 ft) deep. Lifts and staircases take the visitor down to a remarkable system of underground rivers and lakes. The tour takes 1½ hours and covers 2 km (1¼ miles) including 1 km by boat across a spectacular lake. There are more caves at **Lacave** 30 km (18 miles) to the east. A small train and a lift take visitors to the starting point of the tour, which is 2 km (1 mile) through the galleries on foot.

St-Céré is a charming old riverside town which holds an annual classical music festival throughout August. Much of the festival takes place at the château **Castelnau**, 9 km (5 miles) away, near Bretenoux. This château of bright red, rusty rock betraying iron ore is perhaps not as recent as its name "newcastle" suggests, but is remarkably conserved. The long facade dominates the village from steep and unassailable foundations. From the massive wooden portal of the entry to the opposite tower commanding the valley, the evolution of history is visible in the different types of windows, roofs, etc. The interior furnishings are equally splendid.

Continuing north towards Brive and the Limousin, the whimsical **Collonges-la-rouge** is an entire village constructed of red sandstone, making it a most picturesque site favoured by local artisans.

South to Cahors: Originally the "Olt", the **Lot river** received its present name when visiting northerners misunderstood the regional language, *occitan*. From **Cahors** to **Figeac** the Lot valley is relatively wide, producing rich tobacco fields clasped between the sheer white cliffs that lead up to the surrounding plateaux. In the city of Cahors, the river is spanned by the **Pont Valentré**, one of the rare fortified bridges in Europe, counting three defensive towers. Further east, near Cabrerets, the **Pech-Merle caves** combine brilliant rock formations with prehistoric paintings, including enigmatic dots, a negative image of a prehistoric hand outlined in red paint, and a prehistoric footprint. The centre includes a small modern museum and film presentations of the caves. Continuing up the same side of the valley is the best way to see **St-Cirq-Lapopie** from afar. Riding forward like a ship's prow, the church of this small village leads the group of warm ochre-walled houses now occupied by summer trade and crafts.

Château on the Dordogne opposite Beynac.

AUVERGNE AND THE MASSIF CENTRAL

For centuries the **Massif Central** was largely cut off from the rest of France, whose history took place along its perimeter. It was a self-contained, mountainous region of isolated valleys, and its principal common denominator was its remoteness.

But the map shows that numerous rivers, like the fingers of a hand, radiate out from the Massif Central's craggy heights and develop into mighty waterways that snake their way to the Atlantic or the Mediterranean.

The River Lot is one of these. As you travel upstream into the Massif Central, its slow-moving waters are increasingly hemmed in by steeply-rising wooded hills. Just a few kilometres up one of its tributaries, on the legendary pilgrimage route to Santiago de Compostela in Spain, lies the charming village of **Conques**. Its magnificent church, the 11th- and 12th-century **Église Ste-Foy**, and its treasure are one of the marvels of Christian Europe. Little more than a ruin after centuries of neglect, the church was saved in 1837 by the novelist and dramatist Prosper Mérimée, who was also an inspector of historic monuments.

Of Romanesque construction, Ste-Foy's simple barrel-vaulting is given the lofty proportions of a Gothic cathedral. The extraordinary weight of the building has caused the ground beneath it to subside and necessitated sophisticated prosthetic restoration. Unusually, the tympanum radiates an almost irreverent mirth. In the semicircle above the west door, Christ the King presides over the Last Judgment. Of the 117 figures, the grimacing devils and tortured souls are far more amusing than the happy few elected to Paradise. The treasury contains a magnificent, largely 10th-century reliquary of Ste-Foy, a primitive statue covered with successive plaques of gold and decorated with precious stones and intaglios, some of which date from Greek and Roman times.

Cow mountains: Formed by volcanic activity, most recently only 8,000 years ago, the Monts du Cantal – massive, bare hills rather than mountains – seem to bulge skywards as though subjected to huge repressed forces. At their southwest extremity lies the small town of **Aurillac**, whose **Maison des Volcans** is a source of exhaustive information about the area's geological history and its natural park, the **Parc Régional des Volcans**. Extending from Aurillac to Clermont-Ferrand, this vast reserve of volcanic origin is crisscrossed by a network of signposted hiking paths (including one along the Compostela pilgrimage route) that wend their way through forests, grassy meadows dotted with wild flowers, and banks of heather and blueberry. These expanses of unspoilt natural beauty are still used as summer pastures for cows whose milk goes into the making of Cantal cheese and its higher-grade version, Salers. In the old days, a lone cowherd would stay up in the hills for the entire season. The low-slung stone huts called *burons* that dot the slopes would serve as bedroom, dairy and cellar for maturing the 40-kilo

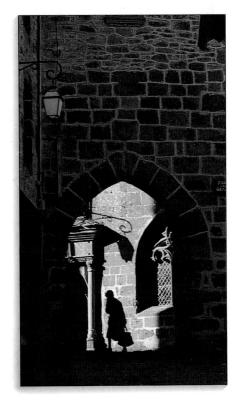

Left, young Auvergnat. Right, shadows and arches in Salers.

(88lb) cheeses. The cowherd's tasks covered every phase of cheese-making, from gathering firewood to boil the water for sterilising the cheesecloths, to filtering the milk and pressing the curd.

Perched above the scenic valley that runs westwards from the Puy Mary, one of the highest Cantal mountains, is the striking little town of **Salers**, which has given its name to a breed of cow, a cheese and an apéritif made from the wild gentian that grows on the surrounding mountains. Significantly, the largely Renaissance town has no château. A long-standing conflict between the townspeople and the local lord culminated in 1666 with a royal order to raze the castle. The lovely houses, notable for their *bartizans* (turrets), spiral staircases and stone window sashes, reflect the prestige the town earned by becoming a bailiwick in the 15th century.

A few kilometres from Salers is the village of Tournemire and its remarkable **Château d'Anjony**. This 15th-century castle overlooks a valley that was once administered by no fewer than four lords, each with his respective castle. It has survived almost intact and been tastefully restored.

The most interesting feature of Anjony are its murals. A miniature chapel tucked into one of the castle's four towers is frescoed from ceiling to floor with a vast anthology of biblical lore in deep reds and sombre blues. In the Salle des Chevaliers the walls tell the tale of the nine knights of legend, the Neuf Preux. The banner identifying King Arthur has been effaced, perhaps indicating disapproval of the English, who ravaged the region during the Hundred Years' War. The ninth knight disappeared when a new window was opened in the wall during the Renaissance.

Lace and spindles: The town of **Le Puy**, in the heart of the Velay region, makes a spectacular sight with its two huge, almost vertical pillars of volcanic rock rising above its roofs. It was an important staging post for pilgrims on their way to Santiago de Compostela. Its steep streets rise to the **Cathedral of Notre Dame**, whose west facade,

Autumn foliage frames Château d'Anjony.

250

reached by a broad flight of steps, is a Romanesque mosaic of yellow, black and reddish stone that seems to float surreally against the sky. The lively geometric patterns of naturally-coloured stone in the outstandingly beautiful, Arabic-inspired cloister make this a less solemn place than might be expected.

Lace-making is a traditional craft in Le Puy, and in many of its lace shops *dentellières* can be seen manipulating dozens of small spindles with incredible speed and dexterity. Work on an intricate tablecloth can take up to a year, so the mind boggles at the number of hours' work that must have gone into of the lace collection in the **Musée Crozatier**.

Perched on top of the largest lava pillar is **Chapelle St-Michel Aiguille** (the name refers to the "needle" of rock), which is reached by a climb of 268 steps. The original sanctuary, the shape of a three-leafed clover, was just large enough for an altar. It was later enlarged by an asymmetrical ambulatory. The intricacy and expressiveness of the tableau of saints sculpted over the doorway contrasts with the touching simplicity of the rough-hewn interior.

Remote and rugged: The road north from Le Puy climbs through uninterrupted colonnades of pine forest to **La Chaise-Dieu**, where even in August a slight drizzle can begin to turn to sleet. This is the remote and rugged site of a grand 11th-century monastery, and the venue of a prestigious classical music festival at the end of August.

In the choir of the abbey-church, the marvellously carved monks' stalls are surmounted by an incomparably rich series of 16th-century tapestries. Contemplating this succession of 11 tableaux, miraculously restored to their original luminous colours, is like walking straight into an illuminated manuscript. Each tapestry, a triptych representing scenes from the Old and New Testaments, is alive with a rich cast of vigorously and naturalistically portrayed characters, from urchins to executioners, who could have come out of a passion play. Another drama is depicted in the Danse Macabre fresco on the

Tuning up in the kitchen.

outer side of one of the stalls, a grim picture in which Death invites a succession of elongated figures, contorted into all the shapes the popular imagination could find, to dance with him.

Ambert was the cradle of the paper industry in Europe. Paper-making techniques, which were thought to have been brought by Crusaders from the Middle East, had spawned some 300 paper mills (*moulins*) in the Ambert region by the 16th century. The surviving **Moulin Richard-de-Bas**, which is included in guided tours of the town, still makes paper the traditional way, sheet by sheet, from a paste of strong cotton fibres. The result, a de luxe article often incorporating fragments of wild flowers, is much sought after by printers of limited editions.

Clermont-Ferrand, the regional capital, originally consisted of two rival towns, Clermont and Montferrand, which merged in the 18th century. There is a startling contrast in Montferrand between the elegant Renaissance architecture of its old quarter and the sprawling Michelin tyre factory. Clermont's **Basilique de Notre-Dame-du-Port** is one of a group of specifically Auvergnat Romanesque churches that are the pride of the Puy-de-Dôme department. Hemmed in on all sides by the houses and narrow streets of the old quarter, the 11th- and 12th-century church takes one by surprise. Steps lead down into a dim nave formed by semicircular arches with fine capitals. Round chapels are arranged like lobes round the apse, and the theme of roundness is repeated in the semicircular tiles of their almost flat roofs.

St-Saturnin is a well-preserved village. Its 12th-century Romanesque church of pale yellow stone bears carved figures of almost casual spontaneity on the outside. The interior is lit from above by pairs of windows whose semicircular arches repeat the pattern of the nave.

On the square in front of St-Saturnin's medieval castle is a remarkable Renaissance fountain, a large sculpted stone basin into which water flows from a central column. The castle itself was restored in the 16th century, when it was

The sleepy village of St-Nectaire.

given a remarkable roof of grey stone tiles (*lauzes*) that protected its main structural elements. But many other features suffered from the gradual encroachment of the town; a jumble of shacks and sheds were built along its moat wall; and its formal gardens were used by farmers. Restoration by volunteers, however, has gradually succeeded in recreating the illustrious past of a castle that was visited by Catherine de Medicis and Marguerite de Valois.

Water worship: The sleepy little town of **St-Nectaire** nestles in a hollow of greenery. It has many typically Auvergnat attributes. Its nutty-flavoured eponymous cheese is renowned all over France. The mineral water from its 40 springs, which inspired the Gauls' water worship, run along conduits deep below the streets. Today, turn-of-the-century hotels cater for families looking for peace and retired people coming to take the waters.

Majestically set on a promontory overlooking the town is **Église de St-Nectaire**, another magnificent example of Romanesque architecture, whose building stone ranges in colour from a deep mossy green to a violet-tinged black. Its nave and choir contain 103 lively capitals, which evoke the miracles worked by St Nectaire.

The partly ruined 13th-century **Château de Murol**, overlooking the village of Murol, near **Lac Chambon**, is an imposing construction. Its thick, copper-coloured walls enclose a complex of cellars, courtyards, staircases, two chapels and living quarters. Only those with a head for heights are advised to visit the rampart walk and watchtower. The castle makes a perfect setting for the historical plays that are performed there in summer.

Not far to the west, on the other side of a high pass that is closed by snow in winter, is the highest point in the Massif Central, the **Puy de Sancy**, on whose slopes the River Dordogne rises. In winter, skiers from the nearby resorts of Le Mont-Dore and La Bourboule have an exhilarating time on the Puy de Sancy, while in summer it is visited for the

Picking
jonquils in
Cantal.

unparalleled view it offers from the summit, encompassing the Monts du Cantal, the Puy de Dôme and, on a very clear day, the Alps. There is a cable car for those who don't want to walk.

A spectacular drive through mountainous terrain leads to **Orcival**, whose 12th-century **Basilique Notre Dame** is another fine and remarkably homogeneous example of Auvergnat Romanesque architecture. Behind the altar there is a striking Black Virgin and Child, a genre of which there are several examples in the Auvergne. Made of wood covered with silver and gold plaques, the sculpture shows the figures in a stiff, front-facing, almost hieratic pose. It is the object of several pilgrimages.

Riom was for centuries Clermont's fierce rival as administrative capital of the region. Its erstwhile importance can be judged from its numerous Renaissance townhouses built of dark volcanic stone. **Sainte-Chapelle**, all that remains of duc de Berry's castle, contains remarkable stained-glass windows. The main attraction of **Église Notre Dame du Marthuret** is its superb 14th-century Gothic statue, *Virgin with Bird*. The **Musée Régional d'Auvergne** has an elegantly presented collection of artifacts dating from pre-industrial rural life. They range from implements used by farmers to traditional furniture such as bench-chests and box-beds.

The little town of **Volvic** is best known for its mineral water, but it also gives its name to a very resistant grey volcanic rock which has been used locally as a building material since the 13th century. The **Maison de la Pierre**, next to the spring, organises guided tours of the lava quarry and a slide-show.

Just to the north of Volvic, the half-ruined **Château de Tournoël** (now being restored) provides a fascinating insight into how people lived in centuries gone by. From the medieval keep to the *châtelaine*'s chambers with their secret entrance, all its elements evoke a precise period and activity. For the modern visitor, the top of the castle affords a breathtaking view; for its medieval occupants it was a vital lookout.

Vichy won a bad name when it was chosen as the seat of the government that collaborated with the Nazi occupation forces. But today it is a pleasant large town that has kept up with the times, unlike some of Auvergne's other spas, whose faded salmon-pink hotels are only a shadow of their former glory. A spacious park planted with rare trees is ideally located next to the River Allier, a salmon-angler's paradise. There are also facilities for water sports, which have attracted a new category of tourist.

The last section of rugged terrain in the Massif Central driving northwards comes with the canyons of the River Sioule. They are succeeded by the rolling country of the Bourbonnais, which in turns flattens into a vast agricultural plain approaching the invisible frontier between northern and southern France.

Abbaye de Noirlac, which is located almost at the geographical centre of France, is that great rarity – a perfectly intact Cistercian abbey. Its 12th-century church, built of light-coloured stone, conveys a powerful simplicity through its total lack of decoration, which the monks regarded as frivolous and distracting. For that reason it is an ideal setting for the summer concerts.

Located in the lordly seclusion of its wooded grounds near St-Amand-Montrond, the splendidly maintained **Château de Meillant** is an example of how successfully the sophisticated Renaissance style could be grafted on to a medieval castle complete with moat. Its courtyard is quintessential Renaissance, with its free-standing chapel, like a miniature cathedral, and its delightfully inventive stairwell towers.

Bourges, an architectural gem, and seat of the duchy of Berry, displays northern artistic influences. Visible for miles around, its flower-girt 13th-century **Cathedral** is indisputably one of the finest Gothic buildings in Europe. Supported by majestic flying buttresses placed at regular intervals, its high, narrow nave is a symphony of vertical lines culminating in superb stained glass. The finest example of the city's Renaissance civil architecture is the 15th-century Gothic house of **Jacques Coeur**, a wealthy merchant and royal treasurer.

The needle-top abbey of St-Michel-d'Aiguille.

SOUTH WEST FRANCE

South West France spans the entire country from the Atlantic coast to the Mediterranean encompassing not just widely differing coastlines, but the wildest reaches of the Pyrenees and the gentlest curve of ancient rivers. It has not just one but three distinct regional identities; the Pays Basques to the west, Catalan Roussillon to the east and between the two, the once independent duchy of Languedoc, which today is witnessing a revival of interest in its ancient origins and the "langue d'Oc" itself.

The Atlantic coast has wonderful long sandy beaches flanked by the huge pine forest of the Landes, and culminating in the fashionable resorts of Biarritz and St-Jean-de-Luz. Beyond, the snow-capped peaks of the Pyrenees stretch all the way to the Mediterranean coast. It is possible to follow the GR10, France's most famous footpath, all the way across, traversing widely varying terrain from high plateau pastures to craggy river valleys, and encompassing a wide variety of activities from skiing to spa visiting, mountain-climbing to caving.

The Roussillon coast offers alternative delights; charming fishing ports like Collioure have attracted artists for over a century, while further along the coast is a string of spanking new resorts distinguished by their golden beaches and modernistic architecture.

Here too is the the superb Romanesque abbey of St-Martin de Canigou and a wealth of smaller churches with fine Romanesque carvings and sculptures.

Inland, Languedoc is Cathar country, its ruined castles and defensive villages marked by years of religous struggle in the Middle Ages. Most distinguished of these is the medieval theme park of Carcassonne, its familiar walls and turrets so controversially restored. Toulouse is the hub, a lively city built of the rosy red brick typical of the region, and combining the pride in the past and innovative plans for the future, typical of this rapidly developing South West corner of France.

Preceding pages: picnic in the Pyrenees. **Left**, surfing at Hossegor.

PAYS-BASQUE PYRÉNÉES

Nearly everyone who heads for the beaches of the Basque coast will drive through **Bayonne**. Some may curse its traffic jams, or the industrial zone, but once on the beaches, most will barely remember having passed the city.

More's the pity. Since it is not located directly on the coast, Bayonne has largely escaped the tourist onslaught, and thus retained a very traditional Basque character. The town is the capital of the Pays Basque, the French part of the Basque country which lies mainly in Spain, home of some 90 percent of Basques. Links across this border are today very close – cultural, social, economic, and alas less desirable. Terrorists of the Spanish Basque militant group ETA have tended to use the French Basque country as a refuge and a base. Spanish Basques are strongly nationalists: but those on the French side, while keen to keep their own culture and traditions, are happy to remain part of France. Many still speak their strange language, all "x"s and "z"s.

Located on the south bank of the River Adour, around the imposing cathedral of **Sainte-Marie**, is old Bayonne. Its narrow streets erupt into wild ecstasy in early August for the city's two-week festival, which includes, of course, bullfights.

For those interested in a more sedate study of ethnographic history, background and traditions of the Basque culture, the **Musée Basque** is located across the **River Nive**. It houses a complete representation of all facets of Basque life and heritage, from sacred art to costumes and furniture to dances and games.

"Discovered" in the mid-19th century by the Empress Eugénie and Napoleon III, who became enchanted with the town, **Biarritz** has long been a charming, luxurious and discreet resort that attracted many famous personalities. And it is still an elegant city of large houses and *salons de thé* (tea rooms).

The beaches of Biarritz extend past the two advances of cliffs, the **Pointe Saint-Martin** and the **Plateau de l'Atalaye**, to the northern beach of **Chambre d'Amour** (love room), famous for its outrageous waves. Hundreds of surfers congregate here, where many of Europe's important surfing competitions take place.

In the heart of Biarritz are the **Promenades**, where steep cliffs fall straight into the ocean. The romantic alleys shaded by tamarisk trees will eventually lead the traveller to the **Rocher de la Vierge** (rock of the Virgin), linked to the mainland by a frail footbridge. The sea rages among the jagged rocks below, but the white Virgin Mary remains unperturbed. The entire Basque coast can be admired from here.

The coastal road winds up and down cliffs before descending into **St-Jean-de-Luz**. Set in the only bay on the coast, St-Jean-de-Luz is a harmonious amalgamation of an accommodating beach resort, a lively Basque town, and an important, and indeed elegant, fishing port.

The heart of St-Jean is extremely Basque in its architecture and spirit. The narrow houses, covered by an over-hanging roof of red tiles, all have the traditional visible beams and cross-beams

Opting for the pool in Biarritz.

painted in brown-red. Halfway down the **Rue Gambetta**, a bustling commercial street, stands the **Church of St-Jean-Baptiste**. It is the largest and the most famous of Basque churches. Externally quite severe with high walls and a massive tower, the splendid interior creates a very striking contrast.

The Rue Gambetta pours onto the **Place Louis XIV**, centre of all nightlife. On the left is the **House of Louis XIV**, where he sojourned in 1660 before marrying Marie-Thérèse, "l'Infante", the daughter of the king of Spain. The **House of the Infante** is a block away, facing the fishing port, which is a beautiful chaos of fishing boats, masts and nets. It is, in fact, the most important tuna port of France.

Aquatic playground: The beaches all around the bay of St-Jean are well-protected from the unpredictable and often raging Atlantic. Three massive jetties at the entrance of the bay break most of the incoming waves.

On the opposite end of the bay lies **Socoa**, a small village with more discreet beaches, behind which looms the **Fort de Socoa**, that once acted as protector of the bay entrance.

The last 10 km (6 miles) of coastal road before reaching Spain are by far the most spectacular. Atop high cliffs, the road ventures precariously near the edge and the view is splendid.

The last French Basque town is **Hendaye**. The gigantic beach, where the tide moves up and down several hundred metres, is virtually unprotected.

Dominating the entire Côte Basque is an enormous symmetrical mountain called **La Rhune**. The road to the base of the mountain is a mere 4 km (6 miles) from St-Jean-de-Luz. One can either begin the climb from **Ascain** or from the pass of **St-Ignace**, 3 km (2 miles) up the road. For the less ambitious there is a cogwheel train leaving from the pass. The view from La Rhune's summit, at 890 metres (2,952 ft) reveals the entire Côte Basque as well as the hills of the backcountry. On a clear day you can also see the endless beaches of the Landes, north of Biarritz, a marvellous mix of white surf and golden sand.

Pelota **is a favourite Basque sport.**

Basque backcountry: Further inland, at the end of a small road, is the adorable Basque village of **Ainhoa**. Its characteristic main street is lined with asymmetrical overhanging roofs, and shutters and beams painted with Basque inscriptions.

Deep in the heart of the Basque country, **St-Jean-Pied-de-Port** once was the capital of the province Basse-Navarre. Rich with a heritage dating back to the Middle Ages, St-Jean was a traditional stop on the pilgrimage route to Santiago de Compostela. The *haute ville,* on the right bank of the Nive, is where the pilgrims paraded into the town that always received them with joy. All the houses along that street are built with the unique red sandstone of Basse-Navarre.

In order to leave the gift shops and crowds behind, take a scenic road leading westward to **St-Étienne-de-Baigorry**, 11 km (7 miles) away. A perfectly charming little village encased in the surrounding, deep green mountains, St-Étienne exemplifies the calm and romantic atmosphere of Basque backcountry. A Roman arched foot-bridge straddles a torrent that separates the town into two distinct quarters, once vicious rivals.

Pau, situated above the valley of the Gave, provides the best perspective on the central section of the Pyrenees. On an elevation, slightly away from the mountains, Pau's **Boulevard des Pyrénées** offers the most panoramic view of the entire chain. On the balustrade along the edge of the boulevard are little notches, which, if aligned with the lighting rod of the tram factory below, will enable the mountain buff to pick out each peak, and learn its name and elevation.

Historically, Pau is the birthplace of Henry IV, venerated king of France who during his reign (1589–1610) managed to put an end to the horribly bloody Wars of Religion. The castle located at the end of the Boulevard des Pyrénées is a charming Renaissance palace, rare for the region, inside which hang close to 100 Flanders and Gobelins tapestries.

The Pyrenees: Extending from the Atlantic Ocean to the Mediterranean Sea, the **Pyrenees** form a massive and continuous chain along the Spanish border,

Basque shepherd.

with an extraordinarily varied physiognomy. Due to the deep and forbidding transversal valleys that slice through the range, several distinct cultures and ways of life dwell in its various provinces.

Its ski resorts and year-round spas, along with the endless mountain trails throughout the range, bring visitors of all kinds to the Pyrenees. Though the relatively warm climate tends to shorten the ski season, it also provides less adverse weather conditions.

The Pyrenees are also renowned for the numerous spas which are scattered throughout the range, where one can bathe in various types of spring water that will cure a multitude of ailments.

There are three basic routes into the chain. The traditional and most rewarding method is by foot. One principal trail, **GR 10**, links the Atlantic Ocean to the Mediterranean. To hike the entire trail could take two months, but GR 10 does offer several shorter ideal trips into the highest mountains.

Another popular way to discover the Pyrenees is by bicycle. The entire chain can be traversed in a gruelling week and a unique experience.

The landscape is no less spectacular by car. **La Route des Pyrénées**, D918/D618, begins on the Atlantic coast in St-Jean-de-Luz and winds through the magnificent mountains to the Mediterranean.

The ascent: Leaving St-Jean-de-Luz, the route soon leaves behind the bustling crowds of the coast. The Atlantic Pyrenees are characterised by dense, green forests and gently terrain. Soon, however, the road enters the Basque province of **Soule**, where it will become slightly steeper. At the wide pass of **Osquich**, the Basques catch hundreds of ringdoves by stretching large nets between trees.

The road then descends into the valley of the **Aspe**, crosses it and climbs again into the thick forest of **Bois du Bager**.

It is not until the road re-emerges from the forest in the midst of high mountains, that you are hit by the beauty. If coming from Pau, the surprise is replaced with anticipation, since the road plunges straight into the mountains.

The magnificent valley of the **Ossau**

river begins in **Izeste**. The landscape becomes more and more splendid with each mile as the peaks of the high Pyrenees appear one by one. One can choose to continue along this road (D943) in the direction of the Spanish border. The road climbs steadily nearer to the **Pic du Midi d'Ossau**, an isolated peak which plunges spectacularly into its surrounding lakes. In **Gabas**, one can take the 15-km (9-mile) footpath, or the cog train, up to the lake of **Artouste**, a lovely mountain lake above tree level, at an elevation of 1,989 metres (6,524 ft). From the lake, the Pic du Midi can be admired.

If one sticks to D 918, the journey is no less rewarding. The road climbs eastward, passing **Eaux-Bonnes**, a popular spa, and **Gourette**, an important ski resort at 1,400 metres (4,600 ft). Above Gourette the road opens onto fields where herds of sheep graze in the summertime. Finally at the top of the pass, the **Col d'Aubisque**, one is surrounded by rocky peaks and grassy slopes.

After the pass, the road continues precariously suspended on a cliffside until it reaches another pass (**Soulor**). It then winds slowly down towards **Argelès-Gazost**, deep in the valley. South of Argelès is the big thermal resort of **Cauterets**, whose springs since Roman times have been thought to benefit sterile women. Aptly, it has also been fertile in literary romance. Victor Hugo womanised there; Georges Sand discovered the thrills of adultery; Chateaubriand, in a visit in 1829 to soothe his rheumatism, met the elusive young Occitan girl who was to haunt his life.

The shrine: Thirteen km (8 miles) north of Argelès is the most important Catholic shrine in the kingdom of the Vatican, **Lourdes**. Nestled in a valley at the foot of the highest Pyrenees, Lourdes is unique. On the one hand, the magnificent surroundings and picturesque old town contribute to the climate of unrelenting hope and spiritual devotion. On the other hand, the thousands who crowd the streets of Lourdes each year in search of miracles and healings, physical or emotional, create a grim atmosphere of despair.

The origins of Lourdes as a shrine date

Bird hunters.

back to 1858, when the 14-year-old Bernadette Soubirons first saw the apparition of the "beautiful lady" in the cave of **Massabielle**, on her way to catechism. That year, the Virgin Mary was to appear before Bernadette 18 times. The miracle drew crowds at once, and in 1864 a sanctuary, along with a statue of Notre Dame de Lourdes, was built at the entrance of the cave. In 1871, a splendid neo-Gothic basilica was built above it.

Today some 6 million annual visitors come to Lourdes, including thousands of disabled and ailing faithful. Many are pushed up to pray by the shrine in wheelchairs. Some even arrive on wheeled stretcher beds, so desperate is their situation. Needless to say, this is not a town filled with laughter and nightlife. It is nonetheless fascinating for the casual visitor who will probably never experience anything else like it.

At **Luz-St-Sauveur**, leave the D918 on your left and plunge into the deep, harsh **Gorges of St-Sauveur**: they will lead you straight to the world-famous natural wonder of the **Cirque de Gavarnie**. A mysteriously unreal "monument", Gavarnie has awed countless writers and painters.

From the town of **Gavarnie** one can reach the cirque either by horse or by foot in one hour. From the **Hôtel du Cirque**, 5 km (3 miles) up the trail, one is already blessed with a dazzling view of the mountain. The cirque is actually made up of three semicircular superimposed shelves, the top shelf being a succession of peaks, all above 3,000 metres (10,000 ft). Waterfalls tumble from shelf to shelf. It is possible to walk to the bottom of the largest, the **Grande Cascade**.

The pass of **Tourmalet**, at 2,114 metres (6,934 ft) is the highest of the French Pyrenees. The jagged terrain is very unique, and above the pass, the **Pic du Midi de Bigorre**, (accessible by car) at 2,865 metres (9,397 ft), dominates the entire mountain chain.

The route then continues down and up over two splendid passes (Aspin and Peyresourde), before winding down to Luchon. Tired hikers and bikers will be especially rewarded by what's in store.

The faithful at Lourdes.

Bagnères (meaning baths) **de Luchon** is the spa par excellence, by far the most important spa of the Pyrenees. The Romans already exploited the springs of Luchon in the 2nd to 4th centuries AD. Excavations have led to the discovery of three large swimming pools with marble floors. The 80-odd springs that feed Luchon yield a water particularly appropriate for the treatment of respiratory ailments. Hence Luchon has drawn its celebrities from actors, singers and politicians. The ski resort of **Superbagnères**, above the valley of the Lys, will give you a magnificent view.

The road travels north of Luchon, then east again towards St-Girons. There one meets the River Salat, a stream favoured by kayakers. The road winds through the gorges of Ribanto and then climbs towards the Col de Port. From the pass, or better yet from the **Pic d'Estibat** (1,663 metres or 5,455 ft) a couple of miles away, the division of Central to Eastern Pyrenees is evident. To the west extend the high, majestic peaks that surround Luchon, smooth and even. To the east begins the rocky and rugged terrain of the Eastern Pyrenees.

Pure rocks: On the easy descent towards **Foix**, the landscape changes significantly. Rich, tall trees become scarce, giving space to the short, bristly bushes that grow in between the rocks. The valleys are obstructed by rocky stumps. In Foix, the three towers of the medieval castle dominate the city from atop a rocky peak.

The region around Foix was a stronghold of Catharism, until the faith's complete extinction in the mid-13th century. Cathars, whose name derives from the Greek word "pure", were reformists of the increasingly corrupt and decadent medieval Catholicism. They became persecuted in the 13th century throughout the Eastern Pyrenees and Languedoc. Early in the 13th century, well aware of their precarious position vis-à-vis the rest of Catholic France and the Vatican, the Cathars began to build their chapel fortresses atop the high *rocs* that are so prevalent in the mountains to the east of Foix. Hence, the **Pays de Foix** is sprinkled with the ruins located atop unreachable heights.

The area where the most spectacular and renowned Cathar castles still stand is along the road between Foix and **Quillan**. Beyond the **Pain de Sucre** (sugar loaf), the ruins of **Roquefixade** can soon be discerned atop a natural wall of rocks. Ahead looms the silhouette of the **Roc of Montségur**, symbol of the holocaust of the Cathars.

Built in 1204, Montségur was a haven for a community of the purest members of the Cathar faith. It soon became a prestigious site of pilgrimage and thereby a challenge and potential danger to the Catholic church and French crown. In July 1243, the *roc* was besieged. By the spring of the following year, the fortress, weakened by repeated attacks and lack of food, decided to surrender after obtaining the promise that the inhabitants of Montségur would remain unharmed. However, the Cathars of the village refused to take part in the negotiations or to deny their faith. They opted for martyrdom; on 16 March 1244, 207 Cathars descended from Montségur onto the gigantic burning stake of the **Prats des Cramats** (field of the cremated), in *occitan* language. This was a fearful blow to Catharism.

Yet in some upland villages the heresy lingered on into the 14th century – as related by social historian Emmanuel Le Roy Ladurie in his best-selling book *Montailloux* (1978), the vivid account of medieval life in one such village, on a plateau southeast of Foix. The village still has the crumbling ruins of its feudal château.

The road from Foix into the high peaks of the Eastern Pyrenees follows the course of the **River Ariège**. First it crosses **Tarascon-sur-Ariège**, supposed site of the hidden grail of the Cathars. Next is **Ax-les-Thermes**, a serious spa dating back to the Romans.

The road after Ax-les-Thermes follows the Ariège, now a torrent, until the valley widens above the tree line. Cattle graze on the barren slopes, and often wander onto the road in search of grass. Here, finally, is the pass of **Puymorens** (1,915 metres or 6,281 ft), gateway to Roussillon and last major obstacle before the Mediterranean.

Typical Pyrenean clifftop monastery, St-Martin-de-Canigou.

ROUSSILLON AND LANGUEDOC

Although half of the Languedoc-Roussillon administrative French region, **Roussillon** is most distinguished by its Catalonian identity. Local architecture, landscapes and lifestyles all have a largely Spanish flavour, and the language of Catalan is widely spoken here. Indeed, some of Roussillon's older inhabitants still stubbornly refer to the city of Barcelona as their capital.

Coming from the Pyrenees, the road winds down steeply, passing the ski resort of **Font-Romeu**, into a very wide valley that separates France and Spain, and gives the impression of being already near sealevel. Yet at the fortified town of **Mont-Louis**, the road suddenly plunges into the steep and narrow gorge of the **Caranca**, and does not level off until it reaches the town of Prades.

Prades and its surrounding villages are built at the foot of the **Pic du Canigou** and provide some of the best scenic and cultural treats of all the region. The favoured town of the cellist Pablo Casals, who died in 1973 aged 97, Prades holds a commemorative music festival from late July to early August in the magnificent surrounding of the 11th-century abbey of St-Michel-de-Cuxa.

Up the road, at the foot of the Pic's wooded heights, the spa **Vernet-les-Bains** is cooled by a vociferous mountain torrent. From the nearby village of **Casteil** is the steep ascent (on foot only) to the spectacularly sited monastery of **St-Martin de Canigou**, superbly restored and one of the finest examples of Romanesque architecture in the region.

The forbidding road to the Pic du Canigou leaves from the pass of **Millières**. It is 16 km (10 miles) to the **Chalet-Hotel des Cortalets** where one must leave the car for the two-hour walk to the top of the Pic. The panorama at the top more than justifies the effort. At 2,784 metres (9,132 ft), the Canigou looks out over the Pyrenees and towards the Mediterranean, sometimes as far as Montpellier.

A French Catalonia: Anyone falling from the sky and landing in the middle of Perpignan's **Place Arago**, paved with marble, lined with palm trees, and straddling the flowered canal, would be sure that he had dropped in on Spain. **Perpignan**, long time the second city of Catalonia, has fully kept its Spanish flavour. A city of moderate size (pop. 120,000) and only moderate touristic appeal, its streets are lively.

The best way to reach the heart of the city is through the **Castillet**, along the canal. This medieval gate sided by two massive brick towers is the emblem of Perpignan, and opens onto its oldest streets. Straight ahead, the **Loge de Mer**, **Hôtel de Ville** (city hall) and the **Palace of Deputation** are three adjacent 15th-century facades of extraordinary beauty, whose inner courtyards have the delicacy and ornate splendour of Spanish palaces. The **Place de la Loge**, paved with pink marble, is reserved for pedestrians and captures the festive nightlife.

The gem of the Catalonian coast, the chosen paradise of kings past, the inspiration of great 20th-century painters like Matisse, Braque and Picasso, is **Collioure**, the goddess of Roussillon.

Encased in a small, rocky bay, the Albères mountains practically pushing the town into the sea, Collioure has managed to escape any of the development that has devoured the coast of Roussillon down to **Argelès-sur-Mer**, 10 km (6 miles) away. The horseshoe-shaped bay is separated in two halves by the 13th-century **Royal Castle** of the king of Mallorca. On the sea side of the castle is the bustling old town, full of cafés, shops and art galleries. At the extremity of the horseshoe, caught between the bay and sea, stands the church, adjacent to the ancient lighthouse that now serves as a bell tower. The rose dome atop the tower is the trademark of romantic Collioure.

Having endured 17 different dominations and sieges over the ages, the population has acquired an independent, although hospitable, character that seems almost oblivious to the tourist onslaught of July and August. The divine month of September brings a much slower pace.

The rocky coast south of Collioure is particularly scenic and refreshing, but beware of July and August traffic jams.

Perpignan has kept its Spanish flavour.

The narrow road winds up and down across Port-Vendres and Banyuls, all the way to charming **Cerbère**, the last port before Spain.

Land of Oc: Although it no longer has definite boundaries, the ancient region of **Languedoc** extends basically from the Rhône valley to the Garonne at Toulouse.

The area benefited considerably from the Roman occupation of the 1st to 4th centuries. Its early cultural and intellectual development, led by cities like Toulouse and Montpellier in the Middle-Ages, gave Languedoc a sense of pride and independence from the French crown.

The apogee came in the 13th century when Catharism, the movement aimed at Christian reform, gained popularity and power throughout Languedoc. The king of France joined forces with the Vatican to crush the heretics, which, in turn, weakened and destroyed much of the region, ensuring its permanent attachment to the kingdom of France.

Today the landscape of Languedoc offers much variety, from wide river valleys and rugged gorges to the popular resorts on the coast. Its cities are regenerating themselves as centres of artistic activity and architectural innovation.

Big city: "Pink city at dawn, red in the raw sun, mauve at dusk." This popular phrase is amazingly close to the truth. The only material yielded by the plain of the Garonne, the red brick, has given **Toulouse** its special trademark. From the 9th to 13th centuries, Toulouse enjoyed complete autonomy, and the Toulousians lived a life of prosperity and leisure.

Today Toulouse is the fastest developing city in France, boasting an extremely advanced technological and intellectual community. Concorde, for example, was created here, and the university established in 1229 is the second largest in France. Yet, despite its remarkable industrial development and enormous university, Toulouse has also managed to retain the fun-loving atmosphere prevalent throughout the Midi.

Entering Toulouse from the south, stop a quarter of the way across the modern bridge **St-Michel** to admire the perspective of old Toulouse. The churches are

Toulouse's red brick is its special trademark.

easily recognisable, and at sunset reflect a deep red or mauve.

The centre of Toulouse is at the **Place du Capitole**. The Capitole, Toulouse's city hall, also houses the theatre and opera house. Its facade, 130 metres (425 ft) long and ornate with pink marble columns, dates from the mid-18th century while the inner courtyard is Renaissance.

Nearby is the Rue du Taur, which leads to both the 11th-century Roman basilica **St-Sernin**, with its magnificent bell tower, and **Notre Dame de Taur**. Taur is the Latin word for bull and Notre Dame de Taur was erected in the spot where martyr Saint Sernin (of the Basilica) was buried after being dragged about Toulouse by one of those brutal beasts.

Two blocks from the Capitole towards the river stands **Les Jacobins**, a complex of church, convent and cloister. Restored in the 1970s, the imposing brick walls remind one of a fortress, but the interior displays the Flamboyant Gothic style, celebrated for its palm-tree vaulting.

Off to the right of the Capitole is the pedestrian street of **Rue St-Rome**. Along with the noisier **Rue d'Alsace-Lorraine** running parallel, these streets have the liveliest shopping. Beyond the Place Esquiro 1 which connects the two streets, begins the hushed medieval quarter.

Nightlife centres about **Place du President Wilson** and the **Allée Roosevelt** that emanates from it. Parisian-style cafés line the pavements while outdoor musicians provide entertainment.

Toulouse-Lautrec's home town: Albi la Rouge is situated on the banks of the River Tarn, which meanders through the region to which it gives its name. Albi, the birthplace of Henri de Toulouse-Lautrec, is a city with an extremely rich historical and artistic heritage.

Because in the 12th and 13th centuries Albi was a haven for the Cathars, religious heretics are often referred to as *Albigeois*. It was not, therefore, until 1282, after most Cathars had been massacred, that the Catholic bishop of Castanet initiated the construction of the **Cathedral of Albi**. As a show of force to any who might aspire to heresy, it was conceived externally as a fortress, a style that was to

The medieval city of Carcassonne.

characterise many Gothic cathedrals in Languedoc. Its giant, barren walls of bright red brick dwarf the old town.

But while the exterior is as plain and austere as a cathedral could be, the decoration of the interior is exquisite. The walls are all painted with religious scenes or intricate patterns. A wall of arches, in Flamboyant Gothic style, encloses the choir in the middle of the nave.

Adjacent to the cathedral is the old episcopal palace that now houses the **Museum Toulouse-Lautrec** which contains Toulouse-Lautrec's early work. It also owns some of the more famous portraits, and works illustrating his life in Paris. A stroll outside the building will take you around the dungeon, down into the flower gardens below, and a magnificent view over the Tarn.

The old town surrounding the cathedral is a labyrinth of small streets lined with red brick houses and an interesting mix of antique shops, used clothing, children's books and old records stores, art galleries and exotic restaurants.

While the Tarn at Albi is wide and majestic as it meanders westward, 100 km (60 miles) to the east the magnificent Gorges of the Tarn begin, the river carving extraordinary canyons through steep limestone cliffs. Les Detroits (the straits) the most impressive section of the Gorges, start from the town of Le Rozier. Here the river is but a few metres wide with the cliffs towering more than 300 metres (1,000 ft) above.

Just a few kilometres upstream of the town of **Les Vignes**, where the river widens, is the **Point Sublime**. Slightly on an elevation and at the corner of a bend, this point offers the most breathtaking perspective on the Gorges of the Tarn.

Victory with a pig: Halfway between Toulouse and the Mediterranean Sea, along what was once the Spanish border, **Carcassonne** is without question the only medieval monument of its kind in Europe. Built on a hill of 50 metres (160 ft), the fortified town dominates the plain.

Legend has it that after Charlemagne had besieged the city for five years, one Dame Carcas gathered all the last bits of grain remaining in the starved-out city,

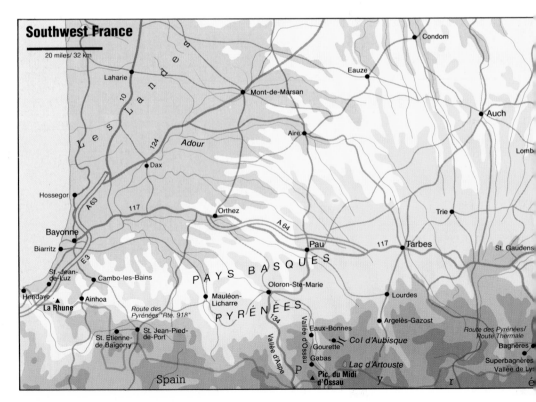

fed them to a stray pig, and ordered the animal to be thrown over the ramparts. On landing, the stuffed beast burst, scattering grain at the feet of Charlemagne's army. Amazed at the apparent abundance of food, Charlemagne called for negotiations, and Dame Carcas answered with victorious trumpet blasts: whence the name "*Carcas sonne!*" (Carcas rings).

Aside from its romance, the uniqueness of Carcassonne lies in its two sets of intact fortifications, which surround a tiny town of 350 inhabitants overlooking the modern city. The first ramparts were built by the Romans in the 3rd and 4th centuries AD. They were later improved upon in the 13th century under St Louis, for fear of a Spanish invasion.

During the Middle Ages, the town housed 4,000 inhabitants, and in periods of siege, up to 10,000 would take refuge inside the fortifications. The two sets of walls rendered the city absolutely impregnable; if a group of enemy soldiers managed to climb over the first set, they would only find themselves trapped in between the two ramparts.

Early detection of Carcassonne's beauty in the 19th century by the author Prosper Merimée led to its restoration by the controversial 19th century architect Viollet-le-Duc, who rebuilt it in what he considered to be medieval style, complete with dubious pepperpot towers.

After crossing the drawbridge, or **Porte Narbonnaise**, and passing a few tourist shops, you reach the heart of the bustling little town, filled with cafés and restaurants, bakeries and antique shops. A nocturnal visit to the medieval **Château Comtal** is particularly impressive, and during June and July a cultural festival is held here, using its fabulous outdoor amphitheatre for a stage. Walking between the ramparts, one can follow the entire perimeter of Carcassonne and admire the combination of Roman and medieval construction methods.

The plains: The journey between Carcassonne and Montpellier is a pleasant one, through endless fields of grapevines, along the banks of slow rivers and roads lined with plane trees. This is the growing region for the abundant Corbières and

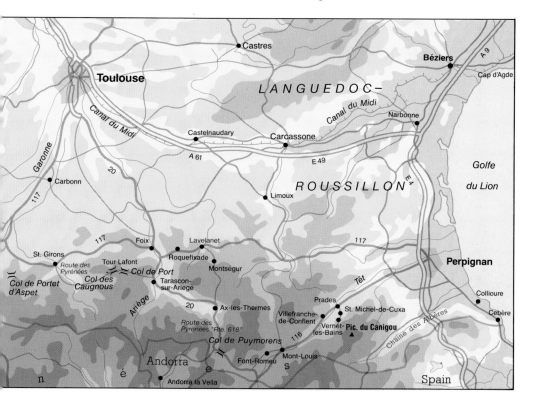

Minervois wines, robust reds that are becoming increasingly popular.

The roads are often accompanied by the friendly **Canal du Midi**, which links the Mediterranean with the Atlantic via the Garonne river, and is a favourite playground for vacationers on rented houseboats. **Narbonne**, once the capital of the Roman region of *Narbonensis Prima*, is today a shadow of its former self. It is worth visiting for its well restored medieval quarter, the excellent archaeological collection housed in the Archbishop's Palace, and next to it, the remarkable **Cathedral of St-Just**, with its beautiful stained glass and tapestries and 14th-century cloisters. Note that despite its vast size, the cathedral today is only the choir of the gigantic structure originally planned.

The city of **Béziers**, 80 km (50 miles) from Montpellier, prospered under the Roman occupation. However, the crusade against the Cathars in 1209 reduced the city to ruins. Since the 19th century, thanks to the growing wine market, Béziers has regained its vitality, and is today a quiet city typical of the Midi. Life is taken at an unhurried pace along the plane-tree shaded esplanades where the *Biterrois* (inhabitants of Béziers) play *pétanque*, or sip pastis over a lively conversation about rugby.

The Coast: During the 1960s the Languedoc-Roussillon coast began a major development programme which has resulted in a string of new and highly popular resorts, some, like Cap d'Agde and La Grand-Motte, complete with dramatic (if controversial) modern architecture – but all, fortunately, still interspersed with miles of windswept, sandy beaches.

Sète stands out as the most authentic town along this coast, its bridges and canals reminiscent of Venice, and its seafood restaurants unsurpassed anywhere, particularly popular with the fishermen who still frequent the port.

Set a few kilometres inland from the Mediterranean, **Montpellier** is the capital of the Languedoc-Roussillon region and one of the liveliest and youngest cities in the Midi. It has been revitalised by a dynamic mayor and a programme of

Playing boules.

274

avant-garde, public architectural developments, such as the Antigone project.

Montpellier vaunts one of the France's largest universities. Most important is its medical school, which is both the oldest in France, dating back to the early 13th century, and reputedly one of the best.

The old town of Montpellier is confined to the very centre of the city, which embraces all of the active student and social life. The best starting point into this section is the **Place de la Comédie**, a large oval, often known as l'Oeuf, in front of the Theatre Opera house.

From here, the **Rue de la Loge** leads to the **Place Jean Jaurès**, perhaps the liveliest square of the city. During the day, a market of fresh fruit and meat, clothes and jewellery bustles until early afternoon. Once cleared, the square is filled with tables and chairs from the surrounding cafés. In the evening, it is a popular meeting place for students and the well-heeled of Montpellier.

Rue de la Loge soon meets up with the **Rue Foch** that, in turn, climbs to the **Promenade du Peyrou** at the top of the hill. The Promenade consists of wide alleys lined by tall trees and flowerbeds, with an imposing statue of Louis XIV at its centre. From here, the sunset over the Cévennes mountains is splendid.

The late 17th-century style of this garden is well out of character with the rest of old Montpellier, whose architecture dates from the 14th and 15th centuries. Though the facades along the side streets around Rue de la Loge are quite austere, the curious visitor who pushes open some of the heavy doors will step into magnificently elaborate courtyards.

The 14th-century **Cathedral of St-Pierre** is the only church in Montpellier to have survived the Wars of Religion. Attached to it is the **Faculté de Médecine**, with its **Musée de l'Anatomie** not recommended for those with weak stomachs. Across the boulevard lies the **Jardin des Plantes** (botanical garden). It is a peaceful retreat and the oldest garden in France, founded in 1593 by Henry IV.

Secretive mountains: The distant mountains of **Cévennes** offer some breathtakingly spectacular natural formations,

Château-le-Champ in the Cévennes.

along with the solitary peace of mountain trails. Amongst the large *massifs* are several *causses*, which are the elevated, extremely dry plateaux, divided by very deep gorges, through which flow some of the major rivers of Languedoc.

The Cévennes rise abruptly about 60 km (36 miles) north of the Mediterranean. Considering the proximity to the sea, the climate is drastically cool, with temperatures of 18–21°C (65–70°F) in the summer, and chilly winds constantly blowing over the more elevated points. The winters can be harsh, with freezing winds and regular snowfalls. Now protected as a national park, the Cévennes provide an ideal break, in the summer, from the torrid heat of lower Languedoc. They could still be classified as virtually undiscovered by European vacationers.

En route from Montpellier is the once remote Romanesque abbey of **St-Guilhem-le-Désert**, tucked into the head of a ravine overlooking the gorge of the Hérault river. Close by the caverns of the Grotte des Clamouses can be explored. At the foot of the Cévennes the **Grotte des Demoiselles** are reputedly the most spectacular caves in the region. The central chamber of the cave, dubbed the cathedral, is 120 by 80 by 50 metres (395 ft long, 262 ft wide and 164 ft high).

Following the flow of the **River Hérault** northward will lead to the looming **Cirque de Navacelles**, an immense natural amphitheatre created by the **River Vis**, 300 metres (1,000 ft) deep and 1.6 km (1 mile) in diameter.

Continuing along the course of the Hérault, the pretty road ultimately leads to the highest peak of the Cévennes, the **Mont Aigoual** (1,567 metres or 5,140 ft). From here the view is magnificent. On a clear day one can see the Alps to the east, the Mediterranean to the south, and the Pyrenees to the southwest.

The entire region surrounding the Mont Aigoual is full of foot trails, marked by the code GR, followed by a number. These trails are well-travelled in the summer and have mountain lodges along the way. Still further north, however, in the area known as **Lozère**, one can easily lose oneself on deserted paths.

Adjacent to the Cévennes on the eastern side, 100 km (60 miles) northeast of Montpellier, lies the region known as the **Ardèche**. Situated on high plateaux that resemble the *causses*, and are given to abrupt descents, this area marks the eastern edge of Languedoc. The Ardèche river, which gives its name to the region, follows a particularly picturesque course towards the Rhône.

While canoeing and kayaking are prevalent throughout all of Languedoc, the Ardèche is most ideal. The section beyond the village of **Vallon Pont d'Arc** is especially scenic and challenging. The river has dug incredibly deep and large gorges that are equally spectacular when viewed from the river or from the road 400 metres (1,300 ft) above. At **Pont d'Arc** the river has pierced a passage through the rock, which has now grown into a beautifully symmetrical arch.

For the canoeist-kayaker, the river runs at a reasonable speed with challenging rapids. It is best to descend prior to mid-July, as the water level becomes too low thereafter. Around Vallon Pont d'Arc are numerous locations for canoe rental.

Left, important discussion at the local café. Right, paddler at the Pont d'Arc.

INTO THE ALPS

In contrast to the neighbouring countries of Switzerland and Italy, the French Alps have never been particularly thickly populated: there was always enough room elsewhere in the country not to force farmers up into the back-breaking and barely cultivable terrain dominated by Mont Blanc, the highest peak in Europe.

In days gone by the alpine passes became impossible in winter, and travellers had to avoid the mountains altogether, with the result that the higher valleys were almost deserted when the weather closed in. The skiing industry has changed all that, and the more remote and high the valley, the more likely it is to ring with shrieks of delight and despair; if skiing has done one thing, it has certainly brought blasphemers closer to heaven.

Summer in the Alps presents rather a different picture, with some of the purpose-built ski resorts looking less than elegant without their winter shroud of snow. But the range of summer activities they offer, from paragliding to absailing down mountain rivers, is remarkable.

A little lower down there are landmarks aplenty. Briançon is the highest town in Europe at 1,320 metres (4,334 ft). And then there's the monastery at Chartreuse, where the monks still distil the well-known liqueur of the same name. In fact, Savoie, the region which incorporates most of the French Alps, is particularly known for its gastronomical specialities.

And then there's Geneva, itself just over the border into Switzerland, but filled with Frenchmen commuting in daily and surrounded by hills and spas that are on the French side of the border, on the shores of the elegant lake.

Preceding pages: Alpine bar with a glacier view at Chamonix. **Left:** a TGV penetrating into the mountains.

THE FRENCH ALPS

When the great and thoroughly humane English poet Shelley wrote the famous lines "Mont Blanc yet gleams on high," the Alps already represented Europe's earthly paradise, a kind of new Arcadia in the centre of an already congested, socially unequal and, to the eyes of the Romantic poets, industrially polluted Europe. Jean-Jacques Rousseau was born within view of the French Alps in the city of Geneva, which has always been a French town though now officially part of the Swiss Confederation. Rousseau's idea of "the noble savage" is still very influential in Western society and, at least indirectly, draws millions of visitors to the Alps every year: to attempt to recover a possibly lost innocence – or just to breathe clean air.

Europe's highest mountain: Any account of the French Alps should start with **Mont Blanc**, the highest mountain in Europe at 4,800 metres (15,780 ft), which rises above the border town of **Chamonix**. Regarded from any viewpoint, with its famous broad shoulders, the mountain is deservedly famous.

At the top, the great chains of the Alps, stretching from Italy to Austria, seem like tiny mountain ridges far below. In the spring accomplished climbers and guides, with a bit of luck, climb the mountain during two days on their skis and spend their final night some two hours from the summit. Then they go to sleep just as new snow begins to fall. The next morning they climb to the summit of the mountain in the very early hours, and then spend the entire day skiing all the way back down to Chamonix in fresh deep powder snow. That night in the Chamonix bars they will laugh and cry about one of the greatest days in their lives.

Mont Blanc comes down upon Chamonix in the form of the **Bossons Glacier** (7 km/4 miles), which may be seen quite closely at the entrance to the **Mont Blanc Tunnel**. With its length of 11.5 km (7 miles), it was the longest road tunnel in the world until 1978, and at its highest point, the tunnel's roof reaches nearly 2,470 metres (8,100 ft) in altitude. The tunnel links Chamonix to the Italian resort of **Courmayeur**, now less than 20 km (12 miles) away.

The tourist can take the same trip to Italy and return via the spectacular cable-car network which goes up from Chamonix to the **Aiguille de Midi** (3,800 km/ 12,500 ft), traverses the top of the famous **Vallée Blanche** spring ski run and the **Géant Glacier** to the **Pointe Helbronner** where hundreds of year-round skiers may be found, and then descends to the village of **Entreves**, near Courmayeur. The trip is one of the most spectacular, if somewhat harrowing, voyages of its kind in the world. For those who prefer something with their feet on the ground, a train goes up from Chamonix to **Montenvers** with a view onto the end of the **Vallée Blanche** and the **Mer de Glace** (Sea of Ice).

Truthfully, cowbells are heard no more in the Chamonix region. The town has become a full-fledged tourist resort year round, and the pastures and herds of cattle have been replaced by hotels, swimming pools and restaurants. In its centre, how- **Alpine splendour.**

ever, like most Alpine resorts, it remains an old-fashioned mountain town, with a sophisticated international clientele.

St-Tropez of the Alps: Not far from Chamonix (35 km/22 miles) is **Megève**, the "St-Tropez of the Alps". Like Gstaad in Switzerland, Megève is frequented by the rich and famous. It is also a summer resort set in pine forests, with foothills and mountain streams, that has retained its alpine charm. Megève is the home of Émile Allais, who developed the modern "French Method" of ski technique. This old village with turreted houses has a very famous ski school.

The hometown of famed French skier Jean-Claude Killy, **Val-d'Isère** constitutes for many the finest ski area in all of Europe, together with the more recently developed **Tignes**. The trails go up to 3,750 metres (12,300 ft) and, as in Chamonix, skiing continues all year long. From both Megève and Val-d'Isère are splendid views of the French and Italian faces of Mont Blanc. It is said that in Val-d'Isère-Tignes you can ski for a week without taking the same lift twice.

In the summer, Val-d'Isère is a tourist centre very near the French national **Parc de la Vanoise**, one of the more important reserves of Alpine flora and fauna, well worth the visit by cablecar up to **Mont Bochor** (2,070 metres/6,650 ft). Footpaths for properly equipped hikers lead through wild and spectacular domains.

Further to the south is **Briançon**, a military town and home of the *Chasseur Alpin,* the French army's mountain brigade. At 1,320 metres (4,334 ft) it is the highest town in Europe. Another ancient Alpine place, with narrow streets and wooden balconies, it is the gateway to the valley of **La Vallouise** and the **Parc National des Écrins**, the largest of the six French national parks (91,800 hectares/226,850 acres). Dominated by its fortress, the old part of town remains much as it was in the time of Louis XIV. Narrow streets make automobile traffic virtually (blessedly!) impassable.

The big city of the French Alps is **Grenoble**, birthplace of Stendhal, famous author of *The Red and the Black*. It is a true city, with chemical, computer and

Below left, between runs at Val de Thorens; right, Megève.

microchip industries, and all the noise and rush of modern traffic. It is also an old and respected university town, though the university complex has been moved out to the suburbs. The Winter Olympic Games of 1968 gave Grenoble a boost into the modern age that has marked it forever. A superb view may be had from the **Fort of the Bastille**, easily reached in five minutes from the centre of the town. The **Beaux Arts**, **Dauphinois** and **Stendhal museums** all testify to a rich cultural heritage, as do the library and the modern sculptures that have been erected in the huge patio of the Hôtel de Ville.

The monks' liqueur: 35 km (22 miles) from Grenoble is the famous **Monastery of La Grande Chartreuse**, where to this day the monks distill a rather well-known liqueur. In 1084 the bishop of Grenoble dreamed of seven stars announcing the arrival of seven travellers, led by Saint Bruno, who had decided to live in complete isolation from the vexatious world. The good bishop then led them to the mountain chain of La Chartreuse, which gave its name to the Carthusian Order of monks. They built their famous monastery there, well-removed from all other human habitation.

The Carthusians live essentially in solitude and engage in religious devotion, study and manual labour. They meet only three times each day in the chapel. They eat together only once a week, on Sunday in the refectory. The monastery was destroyed by an avalanche in 1132 and has been nearly destroyed by fire on eight different occasions. The present buildings date from 1688.

Needless to say, the monastery is closed to visitors. But the monks have built a Carthusian museum depicting the history of the Order and their daily life. Of particular interest are the representations of the monastery itself and of the monks passing their solitary lives in prayer.

Nearby **Chambéry** brings the visitor back down to earth. The town became the capital city of the dukes of Savoy in 1232. To this day it remains a largish town, defended by its fortress. Its best-known monument is the **Fontaine des Éléphants**, built in 1838 as a memorial to one of the town's benefactors, the Count de Boigne, and his rollicking adventures in colonial India. The château was erected as the home of the first of the rulers of Chambery and then of the dukes of Savoy. From the **Place du Château** there is a fine view of the old centre of town.

Chambéry's was the scene of numerous famous marriages, including those of French King Louis XI and Charlotte of Savoy. One of the more famous French Gothic churches, building work was started in 1408. Chambéry also offers the **Savoy Museum** and the 13th-century **Cathedral of St-François de Sales**.

Chambéry is associated with perhaps the most famous French romantic, the creator of the revolutionary social contract, Jean-Jacques Rousseau. In 1728, at the age of 16, Rousseau, then an apprentice engraver who had been badly treated by his employer, ran away from his Calvinist home in Geneva. Two km (1 mile) from Chambéry is **Les Charmettes**, the cottage, completely restored as it was in his day, which he shared for six years with Madame de Warens. She had been converted back to Catholicism from Cal-

Reaching the heights.

vinism and was working to reconvert others. As indicated in his *Confessions*, Rousseau was at least converted to Madame Warens, if nothing else.

Resort spas and Roman baths: The neighbouring spa of **Aix-les-Bains** is known as a centre for the treatment of rheumatism, and the remains of Roman baths testify to past fame and elegance, as does its name, derived from *aquae Gratianae* (Baths of Emperor Gratian). After the fall of the Roman Empire, the baths fell into disuse, but were rebuilt between 1779 and 1783.

Today's resort has as its centre the **National Thermal Baths**, the **Municipal Park**, the **Palace of Savoy** and the more recent **casino**. During the summer season particularly, there is much activity around the two ports and the beach on **Lake Bourget**. The hot baths are open all year long, with sulfuric waters and two hot pools for the cure of rheumatism.

The lake and small city of **Annecy** are both associated with Jean-Jacques Rousseau. It was here soon after his flight from Geneva that he first met Madame de Warens. Like most cities around **Lake Geneva** on both the French and Swiss sides, Annecy was a lake-dweller town in prehistoric times, and derives its name from an ancient Roman estate, the *Villa Aniciaca*. Annecy proper developed in the 12th century, when its fortress was constructed. Its most famous citizen, aside from Rousseau, was St François de Sales, who became a priest in 1593, at age 26, and entered into the raging wars of Reformation with the Calvinists.

Today Annecy is a small industrial city involved in the manufacturing of points for ballpoint pens, razor blades and fashionable jewellery. The main street, the **Rue Ste-Claire**, is lined with ancient arcaded buildings intersected by canals. Cars are forbidden in parts. The **Saint-François church**, built in the 17th century, and the **Palace de l'Isle** (12th century), which should be visited together with the 16th-century **château** and the **Cathedral of Saint-François de Sales**, constitute the major landmarks.

Geneva, the frontier town: Nearby **Geneva** is no longer a part of France – strictly speaking. Nonetheless, the world-

Annecy's old prison.

famous international city is the main aircraft entry point to the French Alps and figures prominently in the history and activities of the area. People who live in Geneva tend to ski and go for excursions in France, and the offices of the busy city are filled with *frontaliers,* French citizens who cross the borders daily.

The two famous French spas on the shores of Lake Geneva (*Lac Léman,* between France and Switzerland; depth 1,015 ft/310 metres; area 143,325 acres/ 58,000 hectares; the largest entirely inland body of water in Europe), are **Thonon-les-Bains** and **Évian-les-Bains**. The road along the lake from Geneva passes by the picturesque French village of **Yvoire**, which juts out into the lake and is justly famous for its restaurants and its narrow gabled streets. Part of the 14th-century ramparts still stand, and numerous medieval houses bedecked with flowers. Here visitors must park their cars at the gates of the fortress wall and make their way down to the port on foot.

Thonon-les-Bains specialises in waters with a high mineral content and the cure of intestinal disorders. On the **Place du Château** stood a fortress of the dukes of Savoy (from whom, of course, the entire area takes its historical name) which was destroyed by the French in 1589. The **Chablais Museum** is devoted to the folklore of the region. At the **Church of Saint Hippolyte** (12th to 17th centuries), Saint François de Sales also preached the return to Catholicism to the wavering believers in the area.

Évian-les-Bains, with its casino, is internationally famous. Much of the construction along the lakeside dates from 1865, when the city fathers decided to develop "Évian Water" and turn the small fortified city into a spa. The baths are open all year round and Évian produces 40 million bottles per month on average. The **Jardin Anglais** (English garden) fronts the lake near the port, where the Lake Geneva paddle-wheel steamers carry tourists to the famous towns all around the lake and make repeated journeys from Évian to **Lausanne** (on the Swiss side) to provide transport for French people working daily in Switzerland.

The summer green of Les-Praz-de-Chamonix.

From June to September it is possible to make a complete tour of Lake Geneva from Évian. The steamers of the *Compagnie Générale de Navigation* link up a total of 42 ports on both French and Swiss sides of the lake. In season there is a night crossing from Évian to Lausanne with an orchestra for dancing.

Resorts: The Lake Geneva area of the French Alps is called **Le Chablais**. The Swiss border, at **St-Gingolph**, is the gateway to the resort area known today as **Les Portes du Soleil**, or the Gateway to the Sun, a complex involving eight French and six Italian resorts, most notably Morzine and Avoriaz, and several other more recently developed ski towns on both French and Swiss (Champery, Les Crozet) sides of the Alps.

Developed over the past 20 years, Les Portes du Soleil is now a vast series of sun and snow bowls where the downhill skier may hiss from one lovely ski area to another, the cross-country skier may trek to his heart's content, staying the night in different towns, and the mountain climber and hiker consider himself in a true outdoorsman's paradise. **Morzine** is in a particularly well-placed situation where six beautifully wooded valleys come together. **Avoriaz** is an example of a completely modern French town constructed purely for tourism – winter and summer. Its architecture of high-rise wood does not please everybody, but the skier on holiday in Avoriaz can put his skis on in front of his apartment building, ski away, and return right to the doorstep. The nightclubs, *dancings* and restaurants are linked by indoor passages, and baggage transport is by horse-drawn sleigh.

From the hundreds of look-out points in the Portes du Soleil area, the tourist will have still another glimpse at one of Europe's most lovely mountains. And as the poet Shelley found, an image of the spiritual power of nature on the human imagination, in the flow of the River Arve down from the Alps through Chamonix, to Lake Geneva, into the Rhône and on to the Mediterranean, so the Alps themselves still serve as a source of spiritual and physical refreshment. Mont Blanc is still there. And it is unforgettable.

Hardy Savoyard.

THE SOUTH OF FRANCE

The South of France has been a glamorous holiday destination, both winter and summer, for more than a century and its enduring popularity accounts for millions of visitors every year. Along the South East coast of the Mediterranean the star-studded names of the Côte d'Azur are strung like a glittering necklace; Cannes, Nice, Monte-Carlo, Antibes and St-Tropez.

Their plentiful pleasures include not only sun and sea but magnificent modern art museums and medieval architecture, glorious perfumes and exotic flower gardens, world class yachts, casinos, and film and jazz festivals. It is a region best appreciated through the eyes of the many artists inspired by its luminous light and dazzling colours; Picasso's nymphs and sea urchins, Matisse's balcony views of Nice, Dufy's triangles of white sails on a blue sea.

Today Provence has acquired almost as mythic a status as the coast, and during the summer months it can seem almost as popular; vast crowds flock to the theatre festival in Avignon, the bullfight *feria* in Nîmes and the gypsy pilgrimage to Saintes Maries-de-la-Mer. But there is more – some of France's finest Roman remains are here, including the amphitheatre in Arles, the theatre in Orange and the extraordinary Pont du Gard.

Always in the background are the windswept mountain plateaus, river gorges and lavender terraces of Provence and Jean de Florette country. The region is famous for its *villages perchés*, hamlets that cling to inaccessible mountain crags like an organic part of the landscape, the terraces of tiny stone houses offering the visitor a glimpse of medieval life. And Provence provides wonderful walking country whether you choose to clamber over the dry maquis and sunbleached rocks of the Luberon, or explore verdant river gorges of tumbling streams and rushing waterfalls.

An unfailing treat is market day in any small town in Provence; the air a rich melange of peaches, figs and miniature *fraises des bois* (wild strawberries), earthy mushrooms, pungent blue cheeses, honey-scented Cavaillon melons and bunches of dried herbs. Best of all perhaps, once the shopping is done, is to sit peacefully over big cups of *café crème* in a quiet village square, limeflowers dropping gently on to the table.

Preceding pages: lake at Canyon du Verdon in Haute Provence. **Left**, sitting pretty in St-Tropez.

PROVENCE

The breeze is deliciously sweet, the sun is already warming the earth, and yet the air remains sharp and dry, like the taste of wine. Everywhere are the fragrances of honey, thyme, lavender, all the herbs of the nearby hills.

– Cézanne

Drive down from the north and you gradually enter into that magical, light-infused world of the Mediterranean, where the rolling hills are terraced with vines and olive trees. Under a sky as blue as that of Greece, black cypress trees bend in the gentle breeze, and everywhere is the scent of lavender and pine.

This is Provence, sensuous land of honey-gold, hazy-amber, pine-green and chalky-white: a feast for the five senses. Stretching from the marshy Camargue, with its famous wild horses and birds, to the Alpine foothills where fields of flowers are grown for France's perfume industry, most of Provence is a dry but fertile land whose austere pine forests are in constant danger of sweeping fires.

Provence is a place where the myth of the French people comes alive, the French as open-air and relaxed and full of *joie de vivre*. There is plenty of laughter here, good wine, late hours and warm smiles. The passionate Provençal people have witnessed civilisation succeed civilisation over thousands of years and, although independent in character, have learned the advantage of accepting the influence of Italy, Spain and the Arab world. Vestiges of this turbulent past are scattered across the region.

Bullfights and Romans: The 2,000-year-old Roman amphitheatres at **Arles**, **Nîmes** and **Orange** still echo with thundering hooves and desperate cries, when summer bullfights draw enormous crowds to these former gladiatorial arenas. Nîmes is home to France's top bullfighting school and each May hosts the **Feria de Pentecôte** series of bullfights, the best attended festival in Europe. In Arles the noble bull is not killed. Instead 10 white-suited matadors attempt to snatch a red ribbon from its tossing horns; a far more skilful and exciting contest.

In addition to the bulls, the arena at Nîmes is summer venue for rock concerts and sporting events. Nearby, the ancient temple of the **Maison Carrée** is a fine example of Roman architectural flair with its delicate Ionic columns. Next door the avant-garde **Centre d'Art Contemporain** is a far less elegant memorial to latter-day taste.

Nîmes is also the spiritual home of blue jeans. Blue durable cloth was imported from Egypt by Nîmois tailors as early as the 17th century. In 1848 Levi-Strauss, a Californian, discovered the cloth in America, and used it to make work clothes for farmers . The cloth he ordered had the mark "de Nîmes", and "Denim" was born.

Twenty kilometres (12 miles) northeast of Nîmes is the spectacular **Pont du Gard**, one of the finest remaining Roman aqueducts in the world. Spanning half a mile over the river Gardon, its massive stones have stood intact for

over 2,000 years. Provençal legend tells that the devil built the aqueduct in return for the soul of the first traveller across it. A rabbit bounded over and the devil, unimpressed with his catch, threw himself into the river 45 metres (150 ft) below. The view from the top tier of arches is breathtaking.

Orange, at the northern tip of Provence, was also a thriving Roman settlement and boasts a majestic amphitheatre complete with 3-metre (10-ft) high statue of Emperor Augustus and the original **Arc de Triomphe**, built in 26 AD. Surrounding Orange, the area of the **Vaucluse** is richly fertile. In May the sweet melons of **Cavaillon** are carried up to Paris for the French president's delectation. In early summer wild morel mushrooms, sweet tomatoes and peppers colour the fields. In October the grape and olive harvests begin. This is also home to the Provençal truffle: furtive figures roam the hills in early spring seeking its priceless flesh. The dark, earthy vegetable has a strong smell attractive to pigs. The rich earth also nourishes some of France's most famous vineyards, in particular those at **Châteauneuf-du-Pape** which are famous for their strong red and flavourful white wines.

Northern Provence: This is a beautiful land of hills and woods much of which has national park status. Nature rules this barren countryside – the violent Mistral wind roars down the Rhône bending street-lights and tearing the ears off unsuspecting donkeys. **Vaison-la-Romaine** suffered a tragic flood in 1992 in which 30 people drowned. The area is recovering and proceeds from tourists visiting the Roman ruins are helping to restore the village. **Fontaine-de-Vaucluse**, where poet Petrarch spent 16 years composing ballads for Laura, is Europe's largest natural spring with a 400-metre (1,300-ft) deep pool. Jacques Cousteau almost drowned here and nobody has yet plunged to the bottom of the spring's secret.

Capital of this region, **Avignon** is a walled city of history, refinement and culture. The Popes moved here from

Toro, toro à **la Nîmes**.

Rome in 1309 at the behest of King Philippe the Handsome. For 70 years Avignon was the centre of European religion, art and prostitution. The clerics and brothels are long gone, but the palace remains the most breathtaking sight in Provence. The **Palace of the Popes** is superb inside and out with its silent cloisters, cavernous halls and imposing ramparts. Leading from the palace, **Place de l'Horloge** is the place to sip a *pastis* and wonder why the Popes ever left. The famous "Pont d'Avignon", **Pont St Bénézet**, on which the nursery rhyme dances, is a disappointing four-arch ruin tumbling into the Rhône.

To the east of Avignon lies the **Lubéron National Park**, made famous by Peter Mayle's international bestseller *A Year in Provence*. Relatively untarnished, despite the roaring trade in genuine *Year in Provence* T-shirts, the Lubéron retains a mystic attraction. Mayle lives in **Ménerbes**, but the small villages of **Oppède-le-vieux** and **Gordes** have far more charm. Here too is the moon-scape of **Roussillon** and its incredible rock formations of red ochre. Today the Lubéron is one of the most fashionable places to live in France: Brigitte Bardot and Sean Connery have houses here, along with the *crème* of Parisian society.

For fewer crowds and more countryside, head north to the sleepy vine-fringed villages of the **Haut-Var** with their legends of flying donkeys and fire-breathing dragons. The **Abbaye du Thoronet** is a beautiful 12th-century monastery hidden in the hills on the way to the **Gorges du Verdon**, France's Grand Canyon. The Verdon cuts through limestone cliffs which plunge to the torrent 600 metres (2,000 ft) below. From here stretch the **Alpes de Haute Provence**, a wild, barren landscape leading up into the French Alps.

South of Avignon the land flattens, punctuated only by the rock outcrop of **Les Baux de Provence**. This medieval citadel inspired Dante's view of hell in *Inferno*. Today the wind tears at the twisted rock from which bauxite was first mined in 1822. Its desolate summit

Avignon's Palais des Papes.

provides an unforgettable panorama over the **Crau Plain** to the flower-clad slopes of **Les Alpilles**. If you can afford it, seek shelter from the wind and the tourists at Jean-André Charial's restaurant, **L'Oustau de Baumanière**, well worth its two Michelin stars.

Soul cities: The soul of Provence lies in **Arles**. In among the pretty nests of red roofs and soft stone the splendid **St-Trophime Cathedral** chimes out its relaxed charm each hour, while the statue of Frédéric Mistral, poet of Provence, and the man responsible for reviving the Provençal language and traditions at the turn of the century, gazes down benignly. Above all, this is a place to wander and sit, following in the footsteps of Van Gogh who lost his sanity in the sun-dappled cafés and neighbouring heat-swirled fields. The Saturday market, when gypsies gather from surrounding villages with their guitars, is eternally lively.

Arles is the gateway to **La Camargue**, a wild place of lagoons, rice fields and cowboys. The *gardians* ride white horses and tend to the herds of black bulls that roam the marshes. In summer, thousands of flamingos congregate on the lagoons, turning the water pink. Today the best way to experience the Camargue is still on horseback (organised excursions). **Les Saintes-Maries-de-la-Mer** is the gypsy capital of the world. In late May thousands of travellers flock to the village for the festival of the black Madonna, when a statue of the Virgin is carried into the sea surrounded by white horses. The statue is kept in the crypt of the village church, along with a terrifying effigy of a woman whose stare follows you around. The beach here is one of the longest in Provence: kilometres of white sand and shallow water. To the east, the salt works at **Salins-de-Provence** turn sea into mountains of salt.

Handsome, aristocratic **Aix-en-Provence**, city of fountains and tree-lined avenues, is the intellectual heart of Provence. Between 1487 and the Revolution the Supreme Court of France sat here, and today Aix still boasts one of

Picking tomatoes.

296

Europe's most prestigious universities. Its ancient streets, 17th-century residences and numerous squares are reminiscent of Paris, and like the capital, Aix adores its "beautiful people". A Sunday afternoon in a café on the **Cours Mirabeau** is a lesson in crafted chic. Adjust your sunglasses, pout, and watch the world and his poodle go by.

Aix derives its name from the Latin for water, *aquae*. Water is everywhere and fountains trickle in every corner. The **Fontaine des Quatre Dauphins** is one of the most beautiful in a small square of 17th-century hotels. During the 19th century, novelist Émile Zola's father was the engineer responsible for building aqueducts to improve Aix's water circulation. Zola grew up in the city along with his friend, painter Paul Cézanne. One of the best ways to see Aix is by taking the **Cézanne Trail**, following a free leaflet from the tourist office. Bronze plaques mark sites from the painter's life. North of the cathedral on Avenue Paul Cézanne, **L'Atelier Paul Cézanne** preserves the artist's studio and house – his cape and beret hang where he left them. Modern art is found at the **Fondation Vasarely**.

Aix is the place for markets, and on Saturdays the **Place de l'Hôtel de Ville** and **Place des Prêcheurs** are filled with stalls of garlic, tomatoes, beans, olive oil, spicy sausage and riotous flowers.

Dominating Aix, the **Montagne Ste Victoire** was painted by Cézanne in over 60 of his paintings. Strikingly triangular when viewed from the picturesque hamlet of **Le Tholonet**, the mountain is a naked contortion of white rock. Cézanne collapsed on one of the paths leading to the mountain, and died in Aix in 1906. The magical light of Ste Victoire attracted numerous other artists – Picasso himself is buried under the shadow of the rock, at his former chateau in **Vauvenargues**.

Gateway to the Mediterranean: South of Aix, **Marseille** is France's oldest and second biggest city. Founded by Greek traders in 600 BC, the gateway to the Mediterranean, the Orient and beyond has been a bustling port for centuries.

Market at Aix-en-Provence.

Marseille's reputation as the "Chicago of France" was built on tales of Mafia, financial corruption and drugs. In the 1960s and '70s this was the infamous "French Connection" providing drugs for the United States. More recently Marseille has done much to clean up its image. The Mafia has moved down the coast and today the city is a vibrant, spicy concoction, worthy of its most famous dish, the *bouillabaisse*. According to legend this thick fish stew was invented by Aphrodite that she might put her husband Hephaestus to sleep in order to sneak out with her lover, Ares. Today the **Vieux Port** has a colourful fishmarket and many seafood restaurants. (Beware! Most of the seafood has been cargoed down from Scandinavia, and unfrozen that morning.)

Running from the port is **La Canebière**, or "Can o'beer" as it was to British sailors of the last century. Marseille's most famous street, the boulevard is a human tide of different nationalities by day and an empty wasteland at night. The streets around the

Canebière are lively, with the **Opera House** a focal point for music-lovers and prostitutes. On nights when the American navy is in town this area becomes a farcical stage as fur-wrapped opera buffs weave their way daintily through crowds of drunken, singing, whoring sailors.

Whilst commonsense is required in the city at night, Marseille's nightlife is surprisingly quiet. The Good and the Bad head to the nightclubs in Aix, whilst the rest of them are in bed by 10 o'clock. When the local football team, Olympique de Marseille (owner: Bernard Tapie), are playing at home the city is a ghost town until the final whistle of the match when, if the team has won, the streets erupt into a noisy party.

Marseille is still a great port, and as such has welcomed immigrants from all round the Mediterranean basin. Tales of racism are not without foundation, but Marseille deals successfully with its urban tensions. North Marseille is a concrete land of megalithic apartment blocks hastily constructed in the 1960s to house immigrants after the Algerian War. To the south are elegant 17th-century townhouses. Climb to **Notre-Dame-de-la-Garde**, the white church which is spiritual home of the city. A golden Virgin looks seaward, and at sunset time stops and Marseille appears the most beautiful place on Earth.

To the east is **Aubagne** whose rough white rock hills were home to Marcel Pagnol and his stories of Provençal lust and revenge: *Jean de Florette* prayed in vain for water in the parched fields, and *Manon des Sources* stalked the herb-scented ravines. Accessible only on foot or by boat, **Les Calanques** comprise a stretch of France's most beautiful coastline. In their midst is **Cassis**, a picture-postcard fishing village, famous for its golden beach and fragrant white wine which tantalises the palate with savours of rosemary, gorse and myrtle – the herbs which cover these hills. Just to the east, the 350-metre (1,000-ft) sea cliff of **Cap Canaille** is the highest in Europe and offers an unforgettable view over Cassis, the Calanques and the Mediterranean.

Left, Paul Fouque, famed crèchemaker. Right, Marseille port bustles with life.

CÔTE D'AZUR

Despite its popularity the Côte d'Azur has succeeded in maintaining its allure and remains for many the classic image of a summer holiday; glorious blue sea, almost guaranteed sunshine, waving palm trees and serious suntans. Debate as to the precise definition of the Côte d'Azur continues to rage, especially among property developers anxious to claim some of the magic. This chapter follows the coast, and samples the secrets of the interior from Marseille to the Italian border.

Between Marseille and Toulon is the least developed part of this much abused coastline. Here the shore is distinguished by the Calanques, steep-sided fjords carved out of the limestone cliffs, best appreciated by boat from Cassis.

Cassis is a charming small port, today a chic resort of fully restored village houses with a popular beach. It is a perfect place to sample *bouillabaisse*, the famous fish stew of the Mediterranean, accompanied by Cassis white wine, one of the best and lightest white wines in the region. A little further down the coast is Bandol, home to another of the finest wines in Provence.

To the north the view only improves. The high ridge of **Le Gros-Cerveau** (the Big Brain) overlooks vineyards, orchards and fields of flowers – and, on clear days, the distant harbour of Toulon. By the D11, around Gros Cerveau, one proceeds fairly quickly into wilder country, through the **Gorge d'Ollioules**, a hill-village with ruinous basalt houses holding fast to the side of a long-extinct French volcano. Down the road, is the lofty **Mont Caume** whose panorama extends from the shipyards of La Cietat on the west to Cap Benat, a *presqu'île* (peninsula) on the coast of the Massif des Maures.

A royal harbour: The prefecture of the *département* of the Var, **Toulon** has been France's most important naval base since the royal navy was established. An amphitheatre of limestone hills, covered with pine, screens its deep natural harbour, one of the Mediterranean's most attractive. The surrounding hills are crowned by the star-shaped forts built by Vauban, Louis XIV's great military architect and engineer. Toulon was severely damaged during World War II and much of the post-war building is ugly, especially along Quai Stalingrad, where boats depart for tours of the harbour and nearby islands. Toulon is famous for the work of 17th-century sculptor Pierre Puget, who began his career carving ships' figureheads, and two of his best works, the *Atlantes*, can be seen on the *quai*. Works by his followers can be seen in the **Musée Naval**, along with models of the many ships once made in Toulon.

Quai Stalingrad separates the port from the old town of Toulon which is at least as louche and authentic as Marseille, with streets like Place Puget and Rue d'Alger abounding in sleazy bars and cheap hotels. The best time to visit is during morning market hours, especially the famous fish market on Place de la Poissonnerie.

The islands of gold: Today **Hyères**, northeast of Toulon along the coast, is made up of a *vieille ville* and a newer area with modern villas and boulevards lined with

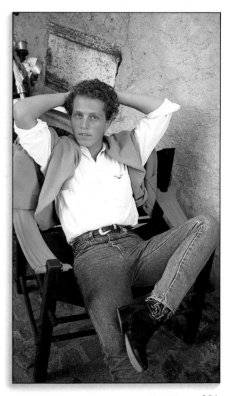

Left, the yachts of Monaco. **Right**, cool in Cannes.

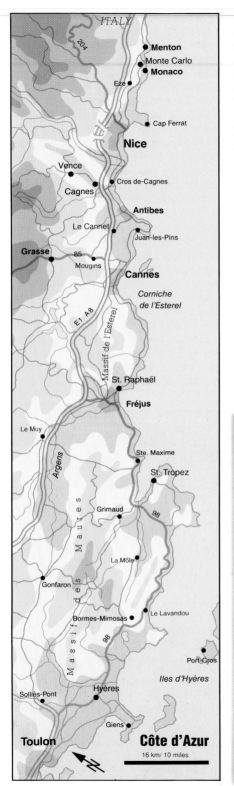

Côte d'Azur

16 km/ 10 miles

date palms. This was an ancient and medieval port, but it is now 4 km (2 miles) from the sea. Hyères was the first "climatic" resort on the Côte d'Azur. Indeed, from the 18th century until 1939 a British colony flourished here, visited by Queen Victoria herself. It was described by American novelist Edith Wharton, who had a villa in the old town as, "the warm peaceful temperate heaven of the Greeks".

Hyères has long been a centre for seriously *sportif* French as well, its subtropical climate providing the ideal opportunity for sailing, scuba-diving, windsurfing and water-skiing. The busy atmosphere of a modern town combines charmingly with its backdrop of faded *belle époque* grandeur. The 14th-century château is built on the Casteou hill, above the twisting medieval streets of the old town. Nearby is the 13th-century **Church of St-Louis**, a marriage of Italian Romanesque and Provençal Gothic. Within the old town, entered via its 13th-century gate, is the Place Massillon, where there is a food market every day, especially good for Arab and Provençal delicacies.

No tan lines here.

Presqu'Île de Giens, once one of the Iles d'Hyères, is connected to the mainland by sand bars. The **Salins des Pesquiers** is the only salt marsh still worked on the Côte.

Most of the forest on **Porquerolles**, the largest of the three islands, and **Port-Cros** next to it burned in the 1890s so that they now resemble rugged hilltops lushly planted with semitropical vegetation – which is, in fact, what they are; part of the very old mountain system to which the Maures and Esterel massifs belong. The Îles d'Hyères and Massif des Maures are schistous rock, while the colourful Massif de l'Esterel is famous for its blood-red porphyry. Sunlight reflected by mica in the rock is the origin of the name bestowed long ago, *Îles d'Or* or golden islands.

It takes a morning or afternoon to walk from the north coast of Porquerolles, with its sandy beaches, surviving pines, heather, and myrtle to the *phare* (lighthouse) on its rugged south coast. Or make one of the half-day or all-day walks on Port-Cros, the highest, hilliest and, because of its springs, greenest island. All

of Port-Cros, including its seabed, is a nature preserve.

The navy bought **Île du Levant**, the easternmost island, in 1892 for a firing range. Comparatively barren, it is now an aircraft engine testing centre. Sharing Île du Levant is the well-known nudist colony, **Héliopolis**. Today, when facilities for nudists are all over France and topless sunbathing has become normal on the Riviera, Héliopolis is less sensational than when it was founded in 1931.

Sun-worship between the wars manifested itself in the nudist camp movement, the decorative arts (the sun motifs of Art Deco), and the increasing popularity of summer resorts on the Côte d'Azur. Non-nudists are welcome at Héliopolis, as long as they uphold the tradition of respecting everyone's privacy.

Massif des Maures: In the Middle Ages these islands and their tiny islets belonged to monks who were constantly at risk from pirate raids and until the 18th century the shore opposite, the wild, wooded, hilly region called the **Massif des Maures**, was almost deserted for fear

The plunging coastline of the Massif des Maures.

of pirates. Only the well-fortified fishing and hill-villages like St-Tropez and its upland neighbours were inhabited.

The demand for sea-and-sunbathing accommodation transformed the Maures coast into a lively strip of resorts – some, so far, less spoiled than others – and traditional local industries like bottle-cork and briar pipe manufacturing took second place to tourism.

The Maures's uncrowded inland roads pass through charming villages, ravines with waterfalls, and forests of carefully cultivated cork-oak and chestnut. Visitors are rewarded with glimpses of the sea; an abandoned 18th-century monastery, **Chartreuse de la Verne**; a medieval town, **La Garde-Freinet**, built around ruins of a Saracen castle with gardens designed by André Le Nôtre, who worked for Louis XIV at Versailles; and a market town, **Draguignan**, formerly the prefecture and now the centre of commercial wine production in the Maures (reds and rosé).

The damage from forest fires, a serious problem here, is very noticeable from the **Corniche des Maures**, the spectacular coastal road from **Le Lavandou** (a pleasant fishing village protected by Cap Bénat – although, like the others, overdeveloped – whose name evokes its fields of lavender) to **La Croix-Valmer**, a resort that grows one of the better Côte-de-Provence wines.

St-Tropez: At the eastern end of the Maures, **St-Tropez** looks north across the Golfe de St-Tropez. Thus the quayside cafés receive the famous golden evening light and the bay's stunning sunsets. Today this once tiny fishing village receives up to 10,000 visitors in the summer, becoming a sort of Mediterranean extension of the Left Bank of Paris, with all that this implies in terms of parking and expense.

The writer Colette and other Parisians complained as early as the 1920s that "S'trop" was too crowded. Today even the yachts number in the thousands. French painters and writers had discovered it by the end of the 19th century and kindly recorded their findings. Paintings by these artists, some showing the pretty

Setting sail in St-Tropez.

village in its unspoiled state, have been collected in the **Musée de l'Annonciade**, a converted 16th-century chapel.

The port was blown up in 1944, but the lovely pink and ochre houses have been reconstructed. Bikinis, an American import refined by the French, struck the beaches at the end of the war. In 1957, the director Roger Vadim filmed his then unknown wife, Brigitte Bardot, wearing even less, on one of the beaches at St-Tropez, starting the national craze for her and the beaches.

Fortunately it is still possible to head for the hills to get away from holidaymakers who assemble every summer to watch celebrities and each other. Several villages in the Maures have their own elaborate way of preparing *marrons glacés,* the delicious sugary chestnut that comes foil-wrapped. A tour could be built around them. Or since this is the place for it – squeeze into discos and onto the beaches (**Tahiti** and **Pampelonne** are still the best-known). Shop in designer boutiques, admire the eclectic Hôtel Byblos, try to get a table somewhere and order a white Cassis, the best Côte white wine, or one of M. Ricard's anisettes, and watch the mob. There are motorboat tours of the port and of Port-Grimaud.

Port-Grimaud is a recent resort built in the style of a Provençal village, except that each house has its own waterfront and boat mooring. Built by architect François Spoerry in 1966, this Provençal Venice has its detractors, but has nevertheless proved popular, contributing to the purported future of the Var as the "Florida of Europe".

Peaches and forest fires: Fréjus and **St-Raphaël**, grown together, divide the Massif des Maures from the Massif de l'Esterel. Fashionable St-Raphaël with its casino and **Museum of Underwater Archaeology** is another reminder that Monte-Carlo is up ahead. The plateau of Fréjus, like Hyères, used to lie on the sea. Its name derives from *Forum Julius;* it was founded by Julius Caesar as one of the important trading centres of Transalpine Gaul. At Fréjus, Augustus built the galleys that won the Battle of Actium. Here there are important Roman ruins,

In the evening sun at St-Tropez.

including the 10,000-seat arena where Picasso liked to watch bullfights. Hour-long tours are available of the Roman city and the episcopal city with its outstanding 5th-century baptistry, cloisters dating to the 12th century, and cathedral with parts as early as the 10th century.

Fréjus is famous for peaches. But the hills nearby also contain moving reminders of the last days of French colonialism: a mosque built between 1914 and 1918 by Sudanese soldiers and a cemetery with Buddhist shrine where 5,000 Annamite (Vietnamese) soldiers who fought in World War I are buried.

The Romans built with porphyry taken from the Massif de l'Esterel that lies between the Golfe de Fréjus and Golfe de Napoule, where strata of yellow, green, blue and purple run together with the red for which it is famous. Ragged red cliffs, occasional red beaches, lichen-covered rocks and islets contrast with the intense blue of sea and sky. The **Corniche de l'Esterel** follows the promontories and long, deep indentations of the coast, linking beach resorts and isolated panoramic view point. The **pic du Cap Roux**, a 452-metre (1,483-ft) peak visible 48 km (30 miles) out to sea, and **pic de l'Ours** inland provide highly-rated views.

The Aurelian Way (*Via Aurelia*) that connected Gaul to Rome, one of the triumphs of civil engineering in which southern France abounds, passed through the Esterel. Early on, escapees from galleys and other criminals hid in its gorges and dense forest. Smaller in area than the Massif des Maures, the Esterel is even wilder and more rugged. Highwaymen and a weird, unwelcoming landscape discouraged visitors until the 19th century, when Charles Lenthéric, an engineer, wrote: "To the geologist and the botanist it is a most remarkable upheaval of eruptive rocks, whose mineral wealth and remarkable flora call for minutest investigation. To the traveller and the artist it is a piece of nature's most wonderful scene painting." Forest fires, once set deliberately in battle, continue to destroy the Esterel's oak and pine, laying bare the immense chunk of igneous rock.

Cannes: Lord Brougham discovered

Forest fires plague the Massif d'Esterel.

Cannes at the eastern end of the Esterel in 1834 when it was among the least important fishing villages on the coast; in his wake arrived wintering British and Russian royals and aristocrats and a few rich Americans, attracted by the constant climate and lovely setting.

Competition for the *palme d'or* at the international film festival, begun in the late 1940s to rival the competition held in Venice, consolidated its reputation for sophistication and glamour. One of the most fashion-conscious seaside promenades in the world, palm-lined **Boulevard de la Croisette**, divides a long row of luxury hotels, galleries, boutiques and other expensive speciality shops from the sweep of beach. Nowadays people come to Cannes just to see who else is there.

Cannes and its setting should be viewed from the **Pointe de la Croisette** at the eastern end of the promenade (where the original "Palm-Beach" is located) and from the *vieille ville,* known as **Le Suquet,** just west of it. One of the most spectacular views is that from the **Observatoire de Super-Cannes**, north of the point.

The Îles des Lérins off Cannes are called **St-Honorat** and **Ste-Marguerite** after the 4th-century monk who founded an important monastery on one and for his sister who established a nunnery on the other. The monastery declined due to pirate depredations and by the 18th century had become a "monks' galley" for disgraced priests.

Richelieu built a fort on Ste-Marguerite, which was improved by Vauban. It is a melancholy place where Dumas's "Man in the Iron Mask" was imprisoned.

Picasso country: Two of the 20th century's most important artists spent their last years above Cannes: Pierre Bonnard (1867–1947), at **Le Cannet** and Pablo Picasso (1881–1973) at **Mougins**. From Mougins, in 1937, Picasso first visited nearby **Vallauris**. Returning in 1947, he combined his gifts for painting and sculpture in fashioning thousands of ceramics at the Madoura Pottery, where copies are still sold.

Ancient Gaul had sent ceramics to Rome, and the potters of Vallauris had long practiced their craft. Picasso revital-

The Carlton's strip in Cannes.

ised the village industry, living there until the mid-1950s. He gave one of three bronze castings of his *Man with a Sheep* to Vallauris on the condition that it be placed in the square, where it is today.

In the barrel-vaulted, deconsecrated 12th-century chapel where the ceramicists gave Picasso a 70th birthday banquet, he painted the *War and Peace* with War on one wall and Peace opposite, a controversial work conceived during the war in Korea. In order to complete it, Picasso isolated himself in his studio on **Rue de Fournas** in Vallauris, formerly a perfumery, for two months.

The artists who painted on the Côte d'Azur during the past century have responded strongly to the earlier art of southern France – from naive *sandos* and ex-votos reminiscent of Mexico to the remains of the Romans and Greeks, and much earlier primitive art. Thus Picasso's suggestion, not acted on, that his chapel be visited by torchlight like the paleolithic cave paintings at Lascaux.

Just outside the little walled village of Biot to the north, also famous for its glassworks, is the **Fernand Léger Museum**, with its gigantic ceramic panels and mosaics exhibited on the exterior walls of the building, a spectacularly colourful sight burnished by the strong sun of the Midi. Beyond is the plain of Valbonne, the vast **Sophia-Antiopolis** technology park, and above it, the delightful town of **Grasse**, a sheltered retreat of pink villas and palm trees.

Grasse was the home of another important artist, Jean-Honoré Fragonard. Here he lived in the 17th-century country house that is today the **Fragonard Villa-Museum**. In the museum, one of several interesting ones in Grasse, are copies of his masterpiece – the *Progress of Love* panels painted for Mme Du Barry. Notice the cascades of flowers.

Grasse has had perfume distilleries since the 16th century. Two of them, Fragonard and Melinard, give tours that explain the difference between *enfleurage,* extraction and distillation, methods of obtaining the essences that are sent to Paris. There is also a new **Musée International de la Parfumerie**, housed in an

Sculpture garden in St-Paul-de-Vence.

elegant 18th-century mansion, where you can observe the entire history of perfume manufacture, see a remarkable collection of perfume bottles and best of all, smell the perfumed plants themselves in a rooftop greenhouse.

"Au fond," Picasso said about one of his neighbours on the Côte d'Azur, *"il n'y a que Matisse"* ("After all is said and done, there is only Matisse.") Matisse (1869–1954) may have been the greatest 20th-century artist and he considered his **Chapelle du Rosaire**, (Chapel of the Rosary) painted for the Dominican nuns at **Vence**, northeast of Grasse by D2210, his masterpiece. Indeed, he gave to it much of his time between 1948 and 1951.

Matisse's chapel (av. Henri-Matisse) is a finely tuned synthesis of architectural elements, the most important being stained glass and the white walls on which their coloured light falls. In his villa not far away, the bedridden artist was in the habit of making large wall drawings with a thick, longhandled brush and india ink. These became the chapel's mural-sized black line drawings on white tile.

In another mode, the invalid at Villa La Rêve had also begun to make gouache-painted *papiers découpés* (paper cut-outs). He called this "drawing in colour" with his scissors, and it is the method he used to design the windows and vestments. Picasso so admired the chasubles, designed at Nice where Matisse had worked intermittently since 1916, he was inspired to attempt a bullfighter's cape. Green, red, violet, rose, black and white chasubles were worn by the priest according to the liturgical calendar. The nuns' habits were black and white. It is only during Mass, therefore, that the success of Matisse's scheme can be correctly judged. His designs are in a gallery next to the chapel.

St-Paul-de-Vence to Antibes: It has often been pointed out that the modern artists who worked along the Mediterranean, from Claude Monet to those of the present, were attracted by the quality of the light. This will vary from one fishing or hill-village to the next. It has, by all accounts, always been especially fine at **St-Paul-de-Vence** directly south of Vence. A walled town with 16th-century ramparts

Antibes boasts the Picasso museum.

almost intact, St-Paul was discovered by artists (among them, Paul Signac and Bonnard) in the 1920s. **La Colombe d'Or** at the entrance to the village, an exclusive hotel and restaurant patronised by famous entertainers, has developed from the café where painters met more than half a century ago to enjoy each others' company, the view of the Mediterranean or the Alps over terraced hillsides, the healing warmth and fresh air.

Today the Colombe d'Or has a priceless art collection of works originally donated by visiting artists; in the garden are Léger mosaics, a Calder mobile and an exquisite Braque dove (best seen by visiting the restaurant, an expensive but memorable experience).

St-Paul itself is a perfectly formed hill village complete with walls ideal for strolling round and admiring the vista of swimming pools, villas and cypresses as far as the eye can see. It is however extremely popular and its narrow winding main street becomes jammed with visitors. Just outside the village **The Fondation Maeght** occupies a white concrete and rose brick structure designed by Spanish architect J.L. Sert. In addition to the 20th-century paintings and space for temporary exhibitions in the building itself, there are several outdoor sculpture areas among the pines with works by Alberto Giacometti and others. Of the outstanding collections of contemporary art east of Toulon, the Fondation is probably the best known.

Antibes and **Cap d'Antibes** face Nice and St-Jean-Cap-Ferrat across the Baie des Anges (Bay of Angels). Here sandy French beach turns into Italian shingle. The "Antiopolis" of the Greeks, Antibes was a Roman arsenal and, until 1860, the first French port west of the Var. Today **Port-Vauban** is the centre of Mediterranean yachting, sheltering some of the world's most expensive yachts. Remains of the Vauban-built ramparts now constitute the seawall and the imposing Fort Carré can still be seen to the north. On a terrace overlooking the sea is the Grimaldi château, originally a 12th-century building, reconstructed in the 16th-century and now home to the magnificent Picasso

Nice flower market.

310

Museum. It contains a remarkably unified collection of more than 50 works Picasso painted here in 1946 when he was offered the keys to the château to use as a studio. The light and intense colour of the south and the antiquity of the Mediterranean inspired many of his major works like *La Joie de Vivre*, *Night Fishing at Antibes* and the *Antipolis Suite*.

Juan-les-Pins, south of Antibes, has an active nightlife: many clubs close with the Riviera casinos at 4am. The very expensive villas and hotels are hidden by high walls and vegetation; but take D2559 around Cap d'Antibes for the coastal views, the sailor's offerings at the **Sanctuaire de la Garoupe**, and the **Thuret Garden**, named after the horticulturist who acclimatised a number of the tropical plants that give the Côte what the French call its "African" appearance. At the southern tip, visit the bar or swim in the pool at the glamorous **Hôtel du Cap Eden Roc** ("Hôtel des Etrangers" in *Tender is the Night*).

Nice, the prefecture of the Alpes-Maritimes, is France's fifth largest city.

Writer Graham Greene, who lived in Antibes, famously criticised the corruption of Nice in *J'Accuse: The Dark Side of Nice* in 1982, anticipating the scandal surrounding the downfall of Nice's flamboyant right-wing mayor, Jacques Médecin in 1990. It has its sunny side, too, but the ideal time to hunt for it may not be during the summer explosion.

Nice was a resort by the mid-18th century. The style of its architecture, from medieval to early 20th-century, is Genoese but it was the British who created the **Promenade des Anglais**. Today the promenade is like a 3-km outdoor café leading to the **Quai des États-Unis**.

Nice is divided by what remains of the Paillon river, now a mere trickle and covered over with promenades and hanging gardens, dominated by the new **Acropolis** convention centre and the **Musée d'Art Moderne et Contemporain** with its collection of modern works, especially the Nice school of Yves Klein, Martial Raysse, Caesar and Arman. To the east is the **old town** of Nice, a charming, bustling maze of winding streets and

Running the Promenade des Anglais, Nice.

pastel houses. The Cours Saleya is the promenade between the old city and the sea, famous for flea and flower markets.

Cimiez to the north has recently excavated Roman ruins, including baths and an amphitheatre often used for festivals. There is also the newly renovated **Matisse Museum**, which contains many of his drawings, all his bronzes, and was specially designed to house his masterpiece, *Messages Bibliques*, and has the biggest single collection of his work.

The Riviera Corniches: Until 1860, when France annexed Nice, the Var river was the French border. The **Var Corniche** (Avenue Auguste-Renoir from Cagnes) follows the west bank of the river, tamed since the 19th century. A once controversial motorway (the A8), completed in 1980, runs along the opposite bank a few miles north from Nice before turning east to tunnel through several mountains.

The Alpes-Maritimes between Nice and Menton, on the Italian border, plummet to the sea, producing some of the most spectacular scenery along the coast. For the adventurous prepared to explore beyond the coast a whole new world awaits in the hinterland of the Alpes-Maritimes; high mountain peaks, plunging gorges, clear sparkling rivers and crowning the most inaccessible craggy peaks, the famous *villages perchés* (perched villages). Some, like **Ste-Agnès**, **Gorbio**, **Peille** and **Peillon**, are only a few miles inland, and yet provide an immediate and welcome contrast to the urbanised coast. Peillon in particular, though barely out of the Nice surburbs, rises to dizzy heights amongst pines and olive groves, and provides extraordinary views from its steep, twisty little streets.

Three *corniches,* one above the other, traverse the 30 km (20 miles) from Nice to Italy. The *grande corniche,* highest and most breathtaking, follows the military road built by Napoleon in 1806. After Nice the coastline changes dramatically, wide bays giving way to towering craggy cliffs. Here, **Villefranche** is a surprisingly unspoilt little town, built round its harbour, one of the deepest in the world, and until recently home

Painting perfumed soaps in Èze.

to the American 6th fleet. It is well restored with a huge 16th-century citadel, and lovely pastel-painted Italianate houses along the seafront. Here there are lots of lively bars, and on the Quai Courbet is the 14th century Chapelle St-Pierre with a candy-coloured facade and an interior decorated by Jean Cocteau who spent his childhood in Villefranche.

Beyond is the luxurious enclave of **Cap Ferrat**, though the 10-km (6-mile) drive around the perimeter offers only glimpses of celebrity villas and glorious gardens secreted behind serious security systems. The **Musée Ephrussi de Rothschild** gives a hint of the lifestyle, with 7 hectares (17 acres) of whimsical garden spread right along the crest of the Cap with views on all sides. The pink and white *belle époque* villa was built to house the personal art collection of the Baroness Ephrussi de Rothschild and includes a magnificent variety of 18th-century furniture, porcelain, carpets, and paintings, with ceilings specifically designed to accommodate her Tiepolo paintings.

Just the other side of the Cap is **Beaulieu-sur-Mer**, which lays claim to the best climate on the coast, protected from the north wind by a great rock face. It is thus a popular retirement town, with many elegant rest homes and genteel hotels, surrounded by softly waving palm trees. It also boasts some of the best hotels on the Riviera, and was where the British and Russian gentry used to spend their winters. Worth a visit is the **Villa Kerylos**, a complete reconstruction of a Greek villa with marble columns and cool courtyards open to the sea and sky, and housing a large collection of mosaics, frescoes and furniture.

The tiny village of **Èze**, perched high above the sea, is today restored to the last stone; a bijou museum of medieval detail, with charming features to be seen at every turn; medieval chimneys, Romanesque windows and tiny rooftop gardens. But its current prosperity belies its troubled past. For most of its history Èze has been nothing but a charred ruin, razed successively over several centuries, enslaved by Saracens,

The Jardin Exotique in Èze.

its citizens regularly tortured and burned. Even in the 1920s the village was almost completely depopulated, described thus by Sir Frederick Treves in *The Riviera of the Corniche Road*: "It is a silent town and desolate. On the occasion of a certain visit the only occupant I came upon was a half-demented beggar who gibbered in an unknown tongue." Today what little remains of the château is surrounded by the **Jardin Exotique**, a fine collection of cacti and succulents. On the Place du Planet look out for the 14th-century White Penitents' **chapel** with a 13th-century Catalan crucifix with a smiling Christ.

High up on the *grande corniche* beyond Èze there is a dramatic view of Monaco from the Roman monument at **La Turbie**. The name La Turbie comes from the Latin, *tropaea*, meaning trophy, and the village is named after the vast monument which was erected to commemorate the conquest of the 45 Alpine tribes who had been attacking Romanised Gaul. It was built between 13 and 5 BC probably using the en-slaved tribes as labour. The names of the tribes are inscribed on the monument, the longest intact Roman inscription to have survived. The structure was once 50 metres (165 ft) tall and visible for miles, and even now at 35 metres (115 ft) is still spectacular. Only one other similar trophy is known, in Rumania.

High rollers: Between the 1870s and 1930s, changing laws and fashions made **Monte-Carlo** the roulette capital of Europe, and the wintering place of the very rich and of mothers with eligible daughters. Prince Rainier III has diversified his economic base by turning the tiny country into the Miami of the Mediterranean. Nonetheless some pleasure-seekers still hesitate before entering this strange principality (that some accuse of being filled with thieves). Passports are not required except in the casinos and *le parking* is in another country.

Sea, skyscrapers and mountains form concentric circles around the tiny headland that is **Monaco**. Like many Americans in 1956, Mrs Kelly is said to have believed her daughter was engaged to the Prince of Morocco. Tourism in Monaco doubled within a few years of Grace Kelly's televised wedding in **St Nicholas' Cathedral** on Le Rocher, alongside the **Oceanographic Museum** and the **Palais des Princes**, Rainier's official residence. From the Palace, where a daily changing of the guard is still performed, a stroll through the old quarter leads to the cathedral and exotic gardens, and a labyrinth of covered passages, tiny squares and tinkling fountains. The Rock is flanked by two harbours, the artificial Port de Fontvieille and the original Port de Monaco. From here to Monte-Carlo, on its skyscraper studded hill, *belle époque* villas are giving way to more high-rise sprawl, and the epithet and the appearance of Hong Kong on the Med.

A little further along the coast, **Menton**, pretty and well-protected, was the home of a large British colony until 1914 and remains more reserved than its Côte neighbours. Its famous lemon trees flower and bear fruit almost continuously. There is *fête du citron* (lemon festival) on Shrove Tuesday (early February) with floats and a parade of prize lemons.

Left, the high-rolling Monte-Carlo casino. **Right**, Menton's lemon festival on Shrove Tuesday.

CORSICA

Reachable by air or car ferry from France, the French island of **La Corse**, pointed north toward the Genoan Riviera across the Ligurian Sea, is one of the Mediterranean islands that look like a mountain thrust from the water. First called "Corsica" by the Romans whose settlements are being excavated at the modern resort of **Aléria**, at **Mutola** near **Calvi**, and at **Mariana** near **Bastia**, it is southern Europe's most mountainous and least densely populated large island.

Since the early 1960s, the island has been visited increasingly by tourists – despite the bombs that have been planted by the FLNC (Front Libéral National Corse) or other small separatist organisations. Fortunately, such activity is now more a recent memory than a reality.

Corsica is unique in having belonged to France since the end of the 18th century without to this day becoming quite French. Every year the beauty of the island, the sun, and this quality of being and not being French attract a million Frenchmen. Among the tourists are Corsicans or their descendants who work in France, frequently in government service jobs (15 percent of French policemen are Corsican), but who intend to return to the economically undeveloped island to draw their pensions.

Like a rollercoaster: Corsica is one of those surprising small geographic entities possessing a variety of landscapes through which one passes as if on an amusement park ride: high mountains; the desert of **Les Agriates** lakes, dammed fairly recently for agriculture and power generation; chestnut groves on the **Massif de Castagniccia**; the laricio pines used by the Romans for masts; vineyards on the southeastern plain often tended by *les pieds-noirs* (repatriated French Algerians) and North Africans; the brilliant bay at **Porto** encircled by red granite cliffs and guarded by one of the 70 medieval Genoese watch towers on the 1,000-km (620-mile) coast. Nowhere are the beaches – some of the best in Europe –

Preceding pages: typical Corsican interior. Below left, the rocky coast of Bonifacio.

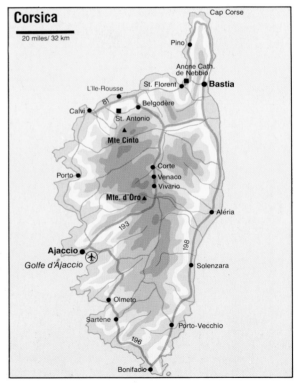

Corsica

20 miles/ 32 km

Cap Corse
Pino
Anone Cath. de Nebbio
L'Ile-Rousse
St. Florent
Bastia
Calvi
Belgodère
St. Antonio
Mte Cinto
Porto
Corte
Venaco
Vivario
Mte. d'Oro
Aléria
Ajaccio
Golfe d'Ajaccio
Solenzara
Olmeto
Sartène
Porto-Vecchio
Bonifacio

found to be as urbanised and unattractive as many along the Côte d'Azur.

Visitors to the island can watch or take an active part in almost any mountain or sea sport. Winter skiing has begun at **Haut-Asco** below the 754-metre (2,475-ft) **Monte Cinto,** the highest peak, while during the summer all the ports are crowded with pleasure boats. Crystal clear water off the beaches encourages underwater swimming. And, even between the French official holiday dates of 14 July and the end of August, it is possible to make lonely forest walks and fish undisturbed in clear mountain streams.

Ajaccio and Bastia: The 8,721-sq. km (3,367-sq. mile) island, in area about a third the size of the Italian island of Sardinia 14 km (9 miles) south, consists of two French *départements*: **Corse-de-Sud** with its prefecture at **Ajaccio** (Ah-YAH-Cho) on the west coast, and **Haute-Corse** with its prefecture at Bastia on the east. If mountainous **Cap Corse** above Bastia is the finger pointing accusingly toward the oppressive Genoans who ruled Corsica for 484 years, Haute-Corse makes a fist and Corse-du-Sud makes the wrist.

Like Menton on the Côte d'Azur, Ajaccio, birthplace of Napoleon, celebrates the Bonapartes. The birthday of "the little corporal," who had to learn French when he went off to military school on the mainland – the Corsican dialect is a variant of Italian – is celebrated with fireworks and parades on 15 August. Visit his birthplace, the baptismal font, the **Salon Napoléonien** in the Hôtel de Ville by the wonderful markets, and perhaps most interesting, the **Palais Fesch** built by his uncle. Here are remnants of one of the great 19th-century art collections and a Bonaparte crypt.

Take the incredible narrow-gauge railway to Bastia or hire a driver to negotiate the mountains. The **Musée Ethnographique Corse** in the *bastia* (citadel) for which the city was named guides one through centuries of oppression from prehistory to Hitler, explains Corsican "vendettas", the local heroes Paoli and Pezzo, and the process by which the *maquis* (the typical fragrant undergrowth) gave its name to the French Resistance.

Below, goat-milking in Venaco. **Overpage:** moving sculpture in Paris.

TRAVEL TIPS

GETTING THERE

BY AIR

Air France is the main agent for all flights to France from America and other European countries; as well as its own services it also handles bookings for smaller operators such as Air Littoral, Air Vendée and Brit Air. These smaller operators offer direct flights from British cities to various provincial airports in France. For those travelling via the UK, British Airways has frequent flights to France from London and several regional airports.

Travellers from America and other countries can get direct flights to Paris and other major destinations, such as Nice and Lyon via Air France and most national airlines, although for long-haul passengers a charter flight to London, then onward from there may work out cheaper.

Nouvelles Frontières offer some of the most competitive fares on both scheduled and charter flights to Paris and London from the US and Canada. Availability of charter flights is variable; details from their offices at:
London: 11 Blenheim Street, London W1. Tel: 071-629 7772.
New York: 12 East 33rd Street, New York NY. Tel: 212-779 0600.
Montreal: 800 Boulevard de Maisonneuve Est., Montreal, Quebec H2L 4M7. Tel: 514-288 4800.

Other low-price charter flights can be obtained through discounters, although France is not as well served by these as other European destinations.

Students and young people can normally obtain discounted charter fares through specialist travel agencies in their own countries. In the UK try Campus Travel, tel: 071-730 3402 for your nearest branch. Campus is part of the international group USIT, whose main US address is the New York Student Centre, William Sloane House YMCA, 356 West 34th Street, New York, NY 1000l. Tel: 239-4247 6955024.

Paris is served by two airports: Roissy–Charles de Gaulle, 23 km (15 miles) outside the city via the A1 or RN2, tel: (1) 48.62.12.12; and Orly, 14 km (9 miles) from the centre via the A6 or RN7, tel: (1) 49.75.52.52. An automatic train, Orlyval, runs between the two airports roughly every 5 minutes from 5.50am to 11.48pm.

Air France operates a rail package with flights available from 16 airports around the UK and Ireland (not Heathrow) to Paris, then onward by train to one of 3,000 stations around the country. These inclusive tickets can also be combined with a 15-day France Vacances rail pass (*see also By Train*).

BY SEA

There are several ferry services operating from the UK, the Republic of Ireland and the Channel Islands to the northern ports of France. All of them carry cars as well as foot passengers. Hovercraft crossings are fast, but more dependent on good weather than the ferries. The new Seacat catamaran service offers the quickest crossing but, like the hovercraft, can only carry a limited number of cars. The ports of Boulogne, Calais and Le Havre offer direct access by motorway to Paris; there is almost direct motorway access also via Dunkerque and Caen.

Brittany Ferries sails from Portsmouth to Saint-Malo and Caen, Cork (Eire) and Plymouth to Roscoff, and a cheaper Les Routiers service from Poole to Cherbourg (summer only). Details from Wharf Road, Portsmouth PO2 8RU, tel: 0705-82770l; or from Millbay Docks, Plymouth PL1 3EW. Tel: 0752-221321.

Hoverspeed operates hovercraft from Dover to Calais and Boulogne (crossing time approx. 30 minutes). The Seacat catamaran runs between Boulogne and Folkestone. Details of all services from Hoverspeed Ltd, Marine Parade, Dover CT17 9TG, tel: 0304-240101; central reservations: Maybrook House Queens Gardens, Dover CT12 9UQ. Tel: 0304-240241.

North Sea Ferries connect travellers from the north of England and Scotland to France, via their Hull-Zeebrugge route. Situated 56 km (35 miles) from the French border, Zeebrugge gives good motorway access to Paris region. The overnight services offer entertainment and a five-course dinner and breakfast are included in the fare. Contact the company at King George Dock, Hedon Road, Hull HU9 5QA. Tel: 0482-795141.

P & O European Ferries operate the short sea routes from Dover to Calais and Boulogne, as well as Portsmouth to Le Havre and Cherbourg. Fares and schedules from P & O, Channel House, Channel View Road, Dover CT16 3BR. Tel: 0304-203388.

Sally Line ferries use the smaller ports of Ramsgate and Dunkerque. Details from 81 Piccadilly, London W1V 9HF, tel: 071-409 2240; for reservations: Argyle Centre, York Street, Ramsgate, Kent CT11 9DS. Tel: 0843-595522.

Sealink Stena Line ferries operate from Dover to Calais (the fastest shipping route at 90 minutes), Southampton to Cherbourg, and Newhaven to Dieppe. Details and reservations for all services are available from Charter House, Park Street, Ashford, Kent TN24 8EX, tel: 0233-647047. Personal bookings can be made at Sealink Stena Line Travel Centre, Victoria Station, London SW1.

Irish Ferries offer a service from Rosslare to Le

Havre and Cherbourg, with ferries leaving daily from 1 April to mid-September to one of the two ports. It currently runs a service once weekly from Cork to Le Havre and Cherbourg from June–August. Contact them at 2-4 Merrion Row, Dublin 2. Tel: 610-511.

Emeraude Lines runs a ferry from Jersey in the Channel Islands to St-Malo, also from Guernsey in summer. Information from Gare Maritime, BP16, 35041 St-Malo Cedex. Tel: 99.40.48.40.

SNCM (Société Nationale Maritime Corse Méditerranée) operates car ferries from Marseille, Nice and Toulon to the Corsican ports of Bastia, Calvi, Ile Rousse, Ajaccio, Propriano and Porto-Vecchio. Information from them at Division Passages, 61 Boulevard des Dames, 13002 Marseille, tel: 91.56.62.05, fax: 91.56.36.66; or 179 Piccadilly, London W1V 9DB. Tel: 071-491 4968.

CMN (Compagnie Méridionale de Navigation) also operates the sea route between Marseille and Ajaccio in Corsica. Their headquarters are at 9 boulevard Sampiéro, 20000 Ajaccio, tel: 95.21.20.34, fax: 95.20.99.40; or telephone Marseille 91.90.01.37, fax: 91.56.24.48.

BY RAIL

France has a fast efficient rail network operated by the SNCF (Société Nationale des Chemins de Fer de France). Their much praised TGV programme is developing all the time, offering comfortable express services from Paris to Lyon and the southeast and to Le Mans, Rennes and Bordeaux in the west and southwest.

For visitors travelling from Paris, the train is a comfortable way to reach any major destination in France with most express services offering refreshments (and even play areas for young children). There are five stations serving the provinces from Paris, so check which one you need before setting off. Getting across country by rail is less easy. Car and bicycle hire is available at most main stations – as a package with your rail ticket if you prefer (details from French Railways).

Tickets may be booked for through journeys from the UK, including ferry travel, from any British Rail station; BR travel centres can supply details of continental services, or contact British Rail International Enquiries, Victoria Station, London SW1. Tel: 071-834 2345.

Some passengers can obtain discounted fares, e.g. young people under 26 can buy a return ticket to Paris for as little as £40. Holders of a senior citizen's rail pass can pay an extra £7.50 for a Rail Europe card which then entitles them to a 50 percent reduction on fares; a Family Rail Europe card is also available for family groups of a minimum of three and maximum of eight people, which can be used to purchase cheaper tickets. Details of these deals can be obtained from the International Rail Centre at Victoria (as BR address *see above*). Eurotrain, tel:

071-730 3402 also offers 30 percent of standard two-month return tickets for those under 26.

Any rail ticket bought in France must be validated by using the orange automatic date-stamping machine at the entrance to the platform. Failure to do so incurs a surcharge.

RAIL PASSES

There are several rail-only and rail combination passes available to foreign visitors. These must always be bought before departing for France. In the UK a France Vacances Pass offers unlimited rail travel on any four days within 15 days or any 9 days within a month. This can also be purchased in conjunction with an Air France-Rail ticket.

Visitors from North America have a wider choice of passes, apart from the basic Railpass (Vacances Pass). For example, a France Rail 'n' Drive pass offers a flexible rail and car rental package, while the Euraildrive Pass offers a similar deal throughout 17 European countries. The Fly Rail and Drive Pass combines internal flights on Air Inter with train travel and car hire within a 15-day period. A Eurailpass for first-class travel is available for various periods from three to 15 months; while a Eurail Youthpass offers one or two months' travel for visitors under 26.

Similar passes are available to travellers from other countries, although the names of the tickets and conditions may vary slightly.

MOTORAIL

Motorail takes the strain out of driving long distances to your holiday destination while allowing you the freedom of your own car once you arrive. Some services operate during the summer only from the channel ports e.g. Boulogne to Biarritz, Brive, Bordeaux, Toulouse, Narbonne; Calais to Nice; Dieppe to Avignon and Fréjus. Also useful for ferry users are the routes from Lille to Avignon, Brive and Narbonne. There are over 30 motorail routes out of Paris, some of which depart daily all year round. Tickets can be booked to include cross-channel ferries with Sealink Stena, P & O or Hoverspeed.

CHANNEL TUNNEL

The much delayed Channel Tunnel will offer fast, frequent rail services between London and Paris (expected journey time is three hours), and other cities. It is expected to be in use by the beginning of 1994, but won't be fully operational until the fourth quarter of 1994.

USEFUL ADDRESSES

Information and reservations for all the above services are available in the **UK** from French Railways Ltd, French Railways House, 179 Piccadilly, London W1V 0BA. Tel: 071-499 2153.

In the **US** from Raileurope Inc: 226-230, Westchester Avenue, White Plains, NY 10604; 360 Post Street, San Francisco, CA 94102, tel: 415-982 1993; 100 Wilshire Boulevard, Santa Monica, CA 90401, tel: 213-451 5150; II E. Adams Street, Chicago, IL 60603, tel: 312-427 8691; 800 Corporate Drive, Suite 108, Fort Lauderdale, FL33334, tel: 305: 776 2729; 6060 N. Central Expressway, Suite 220, Dallas, TX 75206, tel: 214-691 5573.

In **Canada** from Raileurope Inc: 2087 Dundas East, Suite 204, Mississauga, ONT L4X IM2, tel: 416-602 4195; 643 Notre Dame Ouest, Suite 200, Montréal, QUE H3C 1HB, tel: 514-392 1311; 409 Granville Street, Suite 452, Vancouver, BC V6C IT2.

In **Australia** and **New Zealand** details are available from Thomas Cook Travel offices.

SNCF has a central reservation office in Paris, tel: (1) 45.65.60.60 and a telephone information service in English on (1) 45.82.08.41; in French (1) 45.82.50.50. The SNCF office in Paris is at 10 place de Budapest, 75436 Paris Cedex 09. Tel: (1) 42.85.60.00, fax: (1) 42.85.63.78.

Most French railway stations accept payment by Visa and Amex.

BY COACH

Eurolines is a consortium of almost 30 coach companies, operating in France and throughout Europe. They operate services from London (Victoria) to many major French destinations. Some (e.g. Paris) are daily, others are seasonal. One of the cheapest ways of reaching France, discounts are available for young people and senior citizens. The ticket includes the ferry crossing (via Dover) and National Express coaches have connections with the London departures from most major towns in the UK.

For details contact Eurolines UK, 52 Grosvenor Gardens, Victoria, London SW1W 0AU, tel: 071-730 0202; or in France at the Gare Routière Internationale, 3-5 Avenue de la Porte-de-la-Villette, 75019 Paris, tel: (1) 40.38.93.93, fax (1) 40.35.01.31.

BY CAR

Almost all the motorways in France are privately owned and subject to tolls (credit cards are usually acceptable). The trip from the northern ports to the south of France costs almost £40 (US$60) in tolls one-way. The benefits of paying for the use of the motorway can be seen in the high standards of maintenance of the roads and the frequent rest areas, picnic sites and catering facilities.

Free motorway maps are often available at motorway service stations/cafeterias and are useful as they mark the position and facilities of all the rest areas on the route.

If speed is not of the essence and you intend to make the drive part of your holiday, follow the green holiday route signs to your distination – these form part of a national network of *bison futé* routes to avoid traffic congestion at peak periods. You will discover parts of France you never knew existed and are more likely to arrive relaxed. The first and last (*rentrée*) weekend in August and the public holiday on 15 August are usually the worst times to travel, so avoid them if you can. (For further details about driving in France, *see Getting Around*.)

TRAVEL ESSENTIALS

VISAS & PASSPORTS

All visitors to France need a valid passport. No visa is currently required by visitors from any EC country or from the US, Canada or Japan. Nationals of other countries do require a visa. If in any doubt check with the French consulate in your country, as the situation may change from time to time. If you intend to stay in France for more than 90 days at any one time, then a *carte de séjour* must be obtained (again from the French consulate) – this also applies to EC members until restrictions are relaxed.

MONEY MATTERS

The Franc is divided into 100 centimes. A 5-centime piece is the smallest coin and the F500 note the highest denomination bill.

Banks displaying the *Change* sign will change foreign currency and in general, at the best rates (you will need to produce your passport in any transaction). If possible avoid hotel or other independent bureaux which may charge a high commission. Credit cards are widely accepted, but Visa is by far the most common and can now be used in hypermarkets and many supermarkets. Access (Mastercard/Eurocard) and American Express are also accepted in many establishments.

Eurocheques, used in conjunction with a cheque card, drawn directly on your own bank account, can be used just like a cheque in the UK and are commonly accepted. Apply for these, or if you prefer, travellers' cheques, from your own bank, allowing a couple of weeks before your departure.

For the fastest weekend refunds anywhere in the world.

Ensure your holiday is worry free even if your travellers cheques are lost or stolen by buying American Express Travellers Cheques from;

Lloyds Bank	Leeds Permanent Building Society[*]
Royal Bank of Scotland	Woolwich Building Society[*]
Abbey National[*]	National & Provincial Building Society
Bank of Ireland	Britannia Building Society[*]
Halifax Building Society[*]	American Express Travel Offices.

As well as many regional building societies and travel agents.

[*]Investors only.

Not all travellers cheques are the same.

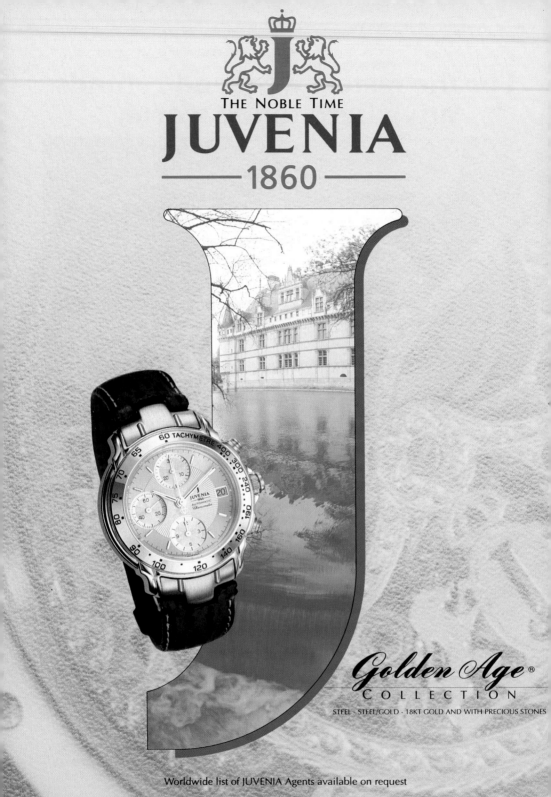

THE NOBLE TIME

JUVENIA
1860

Golden Age ®
COLLECTION

STEEL - STEEL/GOLD - 18KT GOLD AND WITH PRECIOUS STONES

Worldwide list of JUVENIA Agents available on request

JUVENIA MONTRES SA - 2304 LA CHAUX-DE-FONDS - SWITZERLAND
Tel. 41/39 26 04 65 Fax 41/39 26 68 00

If you enter France directly from another European Community country, you need make no declaration to Customs for goods brought in for personal use. However, try bringing in enormous amounts of cigarettes or alcohol and you may be asked to prove that they're not for resale (e.g. you're a hopeless addict or there's a family wedding coming up).

All personal effects may be imported into France without formality (including bicycles and sports equipment). It is forbidden to bring into the country any narcotics, pirated books, weapons and alcoholic liquors which do not conform to French legislation.

GETTING ACQUAINTED

GOVERNMENT & ECONOMY

France has roughly the same population as Britain (around 56 million), but has more than twice the land area to accommodate them (551,500 sq. km/ 212,96 sq. miles). The capital, Paris, is the country's largest city (pop. 8.7 million), followed by Lyon (1.2 million) and Marseille (1.1 million).

France is made up of 22 regions, including Corsica (covered fully in *Insight Guide: Corsica*) and overseas territories such as Guadaloupe, Martinique and New Caledonia. Each region comprises several *départements* or counties. French *départements* are identified by an individual number which is used as a handy reference for administrative purposes, for example it forms the first two digits of the postcode in any address and the last two figures on vehicle licence plates. The *département* numbers follow a simple alphabetical order, i.e. Ain is 01, Aisne is 02 and so on.

Each *département* is divided into a number of disparately-sized communes whose district councils control a town, village or group of villages under the direction of the local mayor. Communes are responsible for most local planning and environmental matters. Decisions relating to tourism and culture are mostly dealt with at regional level, while the state controls education, the health service and security.

France first became a republic in 1792 after the abolition of the monarchy. Constitutional change resulted in the establishment of the Second, Third, Fourth and the current Fifth Republic, which was instituted when General de Gaulle became Prime Minister in 1958. The President, who holds a powerful office, is elected for a term of seven years. He (so far it has always been a man), appoints the Prime Minister as head of government. Parliament is made up of two houses, the National Assembly and the Senate.

In recent history France has been ruled by a very centralised form of government, but under the socialists (1981–86) the Paris-appointed *préfets* lost much of their power as the individual *départements* gained their own directly elected assemblies for the first time, giving them far more financial and administrative autonomy. Each *département* still has a *préfet*, but the role is now much more advisory. The *préfecture* is based in the county town of each *département*.

France is an important industrial nation in terms of EC and world markets, with over 30 percent of the working population employed in industry: primarily in car production, steel, textile and aircraft industries. Its stake in the area of information technology is also growing. Agriculture is still extremely important, although now only around 6 percent of the country's workforce is involved in farming; many farms are still very small-scale affairs, with dairy produce, wine and wheat being the main exports. Another continuing growth area of the economy is tourism and indeed, many areas of the country rely heavily on this trade as a major source of income.

GEOGRAPHY & CLIMATE

That tourism is a major economic force in France is hardly surprising given the delightful diversity of landscape the country enjoys. With its natural boundaries being formed by seas and oceans, mountains and rivers, and each region in turn offering its own particular geographical features of forests, farmland or windswept moors it certainly does not lack in variety.

The highest mountains are to be found in the east; the Alps' highest peak is Mont Blanc at 4,807 metres (15,770 ft); the longest river is the Loire at 1,005 km (625 miles). Bounded on the north and west by the English Channel and the Atlantic and in the southeast by the Mediterranean, France boasts 3,000 km (1,860 miles) of coastline.

The French climate is varied and seasonal. In the north it is similar to that of southern England, while in the south summer temperatures can frequently rise to over 30°C (86°F). Springtime is often suggested as the best time to see the capital, and indeed the temperature then is ideal for sightseeing, but be prepared for showers. In the autumn, mornings can be quite sharp, but by midday the skies are usually clear and bright.

Many areas of France have quite distinct micro-climates and the weather can change rapidly. Beware in the south of very heavy thunderstorms and hailstorms which can cause damage not only to crops, but also to personal property. The Midi has its own particular *bête noire*, the fierce wind known as the Mistral which mostly appears in winter and spring, but which may blow up at other times, and is known to have a very depressing effect on the local population.

TIME ZONE

For most of the year, France is one hour ahead of Greenwich Mean Time, so if it is noon in Paris, it is 11am in London, and 6am in Washington DC.

CULTURE & CUSTOMS

Each region enjoys its own culture and customs, which have grown up and survived over a long history. France does not have a "national dress" as such but traditional costumes are often worn during local pageants and festivals.

Some of the best examples can be seen in Brittany, during the regular *pardons*, when the women can be seen in their finest lace. *Pardons* are religious festivals, but many of the local events in France are a celebration of local produce, and take place at the appropriate season – such as wine festivals and apple fairs in the autumn; flower festivals in the spring and summer. Local tourist offices give information about these, as well as municipal museums (too numerous to list in this guide) which often give a fascinating insight into the history of the culture and customs of an area.

WEIGHTS & MEASURES

The metric system is used in France for all weights and measures, although you may encounter old-fashioned terms such as *livre* (roughly one pound weight – 500 grams) still used by small shopkeepers.

For quick and easy conversion remember that 1 inch is roughly 2.5 cm, 1 metre roughly equivalent to a yard, 4 oz is just over 100 g and a kilo is just over 2 lbs. As a kilometre is five-eighths of a mile, a handy reckoning whilst travelling is to remember that 80 km = 50 miles, thus 40 km = 25 miles. Accurate conversions are given below:

Weight
3.5 oz = 100 grammes (g)
1.1 lb = 500 grammes
2.2 lb = 1 kilo (kg)
Length
0.39 in = 1 centimetre (cm)
1.094 yard = 1 metre (m)
0.62 mile = 1 kilometre (km)
Liquid
2.113 pints = 1 litre (l)
0.22 Imp gallon; 0.26 US gallon = 1 litre
2.2 Imp gallons; 2.6 US gallons = 10 litres

TEMPERATURES

Temperatures are always given in celsius (centigrade). For conversion to fahrenheit, see below:

0° C	=	32° F
10° C	=	50° F
15° C	=	59° F
20° C	=	68° F
25° C	=	77° F
30° C	=	86° F

ELECTRICITY

Electric current is generally 220/230 volts, but still 110 in a few areas. Current alternates at 50 cycles, not 60 as in the US, so take a transformer for shavers, travel irons, hairdryers etc. This also takes care of the fact that outlet prongs are different.

BUSINESS HOURS & PUBLIC HOLIDAYS

Office workers normally start early – 8.30am is not uncommon – but often stay at their desks until 6pm or later. This is partly to make up for the long lunch hours (from noon or 12.30pm for two hours) which are still traditional in banks, shops and other public offices. Many companies are beginning to change to shorter lunchbreaks as employees appreciate the advantages of getting home earlier to families in the evening.

A list of major public holidays is given below. It is common practice, if a public holiday falls on a Thursday or Tuesday for French business to *faire le pont* (literally bridge the gap) and have the Friday or Monday as a holiday too. Details of closures should be posted outside banks etc. a few days before the event but it is easy to be caught out, especially on Assumption day in August, which is not a holiday in the UK.

New Year's Day (1 January); Easter Monday (but not Good Friday); Labour Day (Monday closest to 1 May); Ascension Day; 8 May to commemorate the end of World War I; Whit Monday (Pentecost); Bastille Day (14 July); Assumption Day (15 August); All Saints Day – Toussaint (1 November); Armistice Day (11 November); Christmas Day (25 December), but not Boxing Day (26 December).

Banks are normally open Monday–Friday 8.30am–noon and 1.30–5pm but these hours may vary slightly.

THE WORLD IS FLAT

Its configuration may not be to Columbus' liking but to every other traveller the MCI Card is an easier, more convenient, more cost-efficient route to circle the globe.

The MCI Card offers two international services—MCI World Reach and MCI CALL USA—which let you call from country-to-country as well as back to the States, all via an English-speaking operator.

There are no delays. No hassles with foreign languages and foreign currencies. No foreign exchange rates to figure out. And no outrageous hotel surcharges.

If you don't possess the MCI Card, please call the access number of the country you're in and ask for customer service.

The MCI Card. It makes a world of difference.

With MCI CALL USA and MCI WORLD REACH services, reaching around the world has never been easier.

To reach around the world, use your MCI Card or call collect.° Just select the number next to the country you're calling from. An English-speaking operator will put your call through to anywhere in the 50 States as well as a growing list of participating World Reach countries#

Austria	022-903-012	Germany††	0130-0012	Peru‡	001-190
Belgium	078-11-00-12	Greece	00-800-1211	Poland	0*01-04-800-222
Bolivia	0-800-2222	Hungary	00*-800-01411	Portugal	05-017-1234
Brazil	000-8012	India**	000-127	Saudi Arabia	1-800-11
Chile	00*-0316	Ireland	1-800-551-001	Slovak Rep	00-42-000112
Colombia	980-16-0001	Israel	177-150-2727	Spain#	900-99-0014
Cyprus	080-90000	Italy	172-1022	Sweden	020-795-922
Czech Rep	00-42-000112	Kenya**	080011	Switzerland	155-0222
Denmark	8001-0022	Kuwait	800-MCI (800-624)	Turkey	99-8001-1177
Dominican Republic	1-800-751-6624	Lebanon	425-036	UAE	800-111
Ecuador	170	Mexico%	95-800-674-7000	United Kingdom	0800-89-0222
Egypt†	355-5770	Netherlands	06*-022-91-22	Uruguay	000-412
Finland	9800-102-80	Norway	050-12912	Venezuela+	800-1114-0
France	19*-00-19				

#Country-to-country calling may not be available to & from all MCI CALL USA locations. Certain restrictions apply. *Wait for second dial tone. **Available from most major cities. †When dialing outside of Cairo, dial 02 first. ‡When dialing outside of Lima, the access number is 190. +Limited availability. °Collect calls to U.S. only. In some countries, public phones may require deposit of coin or phone card for dial tone. %Service from public telephones may be limited. Rate depends on call origin in Mexico. ††Service available on a limited basis in eastern Germany © MCI International, Inc., 1993. MCI, its logo, and all other MCI products and services mentioned herein, are proprietary marks of MCI Communications Corporation.

COMMUNICATIONS

POSTAL SERVICES

Provincial post offices – Postes or PTTs (pronounced *pay-tay-tay*) are generally open Monday–Friday 9am–noon and 2–5pm, Saturday 9am–noon (opening hours are posted outside); in Paris and other large cities they are generally open continuously from 8am–7pm. Exceptionally, the main post office in Paris is open 24 hours every day, at 52 Rue du Louvre, 75001 Paris.

Inside major post offices, individual counters are marked for different requirements – if you just need **stamps**, go to the window marked *Timbres*. If you need to send an urgent letter overseas, ask for it to be sent *par exprès*, or through the Chronopost system which is faster, but very expensive.

Stamps are often available at tobacconists (*tabacs*) and other shops selling postcards and greetings cards. Letters within France and most of the EC go for FF2.50 for up to 20g; FF3.70 for airmail to Ireland, the US and Canada; and FF4.10 for Australia.

Telegrams (cables) can be sent during post office hours or by telephone (24-hours); to send a telegram in English dial 16-1 42.33.21.11. Expect to pay around FF75 for a minimum of 15 words to the US, Canada or the UK.

For a small fee, you can arrange for mail to be kept *poste restante* at any post office, addressed to **Poste Restante**, Poste Centrale (for main post office), then the town's post code and name, e.g. 16000 Angoulême. A passport is required as proof of identity when collecting mail.

Many post offices have coin-in-slot **photocopying** machines.

Telex, Minitel information service (useful for directory enquiries) and **fax** facilities are available in the main post office in most major towns.

TELEPHONES

The French telephone system, once quirky, is now one of the most efficient in the world. That is not to say that you can be guaranteed to find telephone boxes (*cabines publiques*) that are always operational, but most are. Telephone numbers have been rationalised to eight figures, given in sets of two, e.g. 99.44.63.21., the only codes necessary are for dialling into or out of Paris or overseas. To dial Paris from the provinces, dial 16.1, then the subscriber's number; to dial out of Paris, just dial 16 then the number.

International calls can be made from most public booths, but it is often easier to use a booth in a post office – ask at the counter to use the phone, then go back to settle the bill – but you have no record of the cost of the call until the end.

Coin-operated phones take most coins and card phones are now very common and simple to use. It is worth purchasing a phone card (*une télécarte* – currently F50 or F120) if you are likely to need to use a public call box, as many are being converted to take cards and in some towns are far more numerous now than coin-operated ones. Cards are available from post offices, stationers, railway stations, some cafés and tobacconists. Several main post offices now also have telephones that can be used with credit cards.

If you use a phone (not a public call box) in a café, shop or restaurant you are likely to be surcharged. Some hotels and cafés now have computerised public telephones whereby the caller receives a printed statement of the details of his call on payment of the bill at the bar – a useful asset for business travellers.

To make an international call, lift the receiver, insert the money (if necessary), dial 19, wait for the tone to change, then dial the country code (*see below*), followed by the area code (omitting any initial 0) and the number.

International dialling codes: Australia 61; Canada 1; Ireland 353; UK 44; US 1.

Useful numbers: operator services 13; directory enquiries 12.

Note that numbers will be given in pairs of figures, unless you ask for them to be given *chiffre par chiffre* (singly).

Some main post offices in France have now replaced their traditional telephone directories with the computerised **Minitel** system. Members of the public can use this free of charge to look up any number in the country. The instructions (in French) are fairly simple to understand, and you simply tap in the name of the town, *département* and person (or company) whose number you seek for it to be displayed on the small screen, connected to the telephone. It can also be used in the same way as yellow pages to find, for example, all the dry cleaners listed in a particular town.

If you need to make a phone call in rural areas, or small villages with no public phone, look out for the blue plaque saying *téléphone publique* on private houses. This means the owner is officially required to allow you to use the phone and charge the normal amount for the call.

You cannot reverse charges (call collect) within France but you can to countries which will accept such calls. Go through the operator and ask to make a PCV (pronounced *pay-say-vay*) call. Telephone calls can only be received at call boxes displaying the blue bell sign.

To take advantage of cheap rates, use the telephone weekdays between 10.30pm and 8am and at weekends after 2pm on Saturday when you will have 50 percent more time for your money.

MEDIA

Newspapers: Regional newspapers, as in the US, contain national and international as well as local news, and are often read in preference to the national press. The main national dailies are *Le Monde* (good for a liberal overview of political and economic news), the more conservative *Le Figaro* and the communist papers, *Libération* and *L'Humanité*. *Le Point* and *L'Express* are the major weekly news publications. British and American dailies, notably *The Times*, *The European* and the *International Herald Tribune* are widely available in major towns and cities.

Television: Viewers can receive the two main national channels: TF1 (commercial) and Antenne 2 (state-owned but largely financed by advertising); as well as FR3 which offers regional programmes. French houses are beginning to be defaced by satellite dishes. Cable TV provides access to Britain's BBC channels.

Radio: France Inter is the main national radio station (l892m long wave), it broadcasts English-language news twice a day in summer (generally 9am and 4pm). During the peak holiday period, other local stations sometimes put out English bulletins. On the Mediterranean, Riviera Radio (106.3 and 106.5 kHZ) broadcasts 24 hours a day in English. The BBC's Radio 4 can be received on longwave (198 kHZ).

EMERGENCIES

SECURITY & CRIME

Sensible precautions regarding personal possessions is all that should really be necessary when visiting France. Theft and other crime exists here as elsewhere but it is not a serious problem as far as tourists are concerned.

Drivers should follow the rules of the road and always drive sensibly. Heavy on-the-spot fines are given for traffic offences, such as speeding, and drivers can be stopped and breathalysed during spot checks. The minimum fine for speeding is FF1,300 and immediate fines of up to FF30,000 can be levied for drink-driving offences (if you do not have enough cash, you will be required to pay a deposit). Police are fairly visible on the main roads of France during the summer months.

LOST PROPERTY

If you lose something on a bus or the métro, first try the terminus to see if it has been handed in. In Paris, after 48 hours, you can go to the Bureau des Objets Trouvés, 36 Rue des Morillons, 75015 Paris, tel: 48.28.32.36. You will have to pay 4 percent of the value of any item reclaimed through this office.

To report a crime or loss of belongings, visit the local gendarmerie or *commisariat de police*. Telephone numbers are given at the front of local directories, or in an emergency, dial 17. If you lose a passport, report first to the police, then to the nearest consulate (*see Useful Addresses*). If you have the misfortune to be detained by the police for any reason, ask to telephone the nearest consulate for a member of the staff to come to your assistance.

HEALTH CARE

The International Association for Medical Assistance to Travelers (IAMAT) is a non-profit-making organisation which anyone can join, free of charge (although a donation is welcome). Benefits include a membership card, entitling the bearer to services at fixed IAMAT rates by participating physicians, and a Traveller Clinical Record, a passport-sized record completed by the member's own doctor prior to travel. A directory of English-speaking doctors, belonging to IAMAT, and on call 24 hours a day, is published for members' use.

IAMAT offices:
US: 736 Center Street, Lewiston NY 14092. Tel: 716-754 4883.
Canada: 1287 St Claire Ave W.,Toronto M6E 1B9. Tel: 416-652 0137; 40 Regal Road, Guelph. Ontario N1K 1B5, Tel: 519-836 0102.
New Zealand: PO Box 5049, Christchurch 5.
Switzerland: 57 Voirets, 1212 Grand-Lancy, Geneva.

For minor ailments it may be worth consulting a pharmacy (recognisable by its green cross sign), which have wider "prescribing" powers than chemists in the UK or US. They are also helpful in cases of snake or insect bites and identifying fungi.

If you need to see a doctor, expect to pay around FF100 for a simple consultation, plus a pharmacist's fee for whatever prescription is issued. The doctor will provide a *feuille des soins* which you need to keep to claim back the majority of the cost (around 75 percent) under the EC agreement. You have to attach to the *feuille* the little sticker (*vignette*) from any medicine prescribed to enable you to claim for that too. Refunds have to be obtained from the local *Caisse Primaire* (ask the doctor or pharmacist for the address).

BREAK THE LANGUAGE BARRIER!

If you travel internationally, for business or pleasure - or if you are learning a foreign language - TI's electronic language -products can make communication a lot easier.

The **PS-5800** is a versatile 3-language dictionary with 30,000 entry words in each language. Available in English/German/French or English/Italian/French, it includes, travel sentences, business words, memory space to build and store your own vocabulary, currency and metric conversions, and more.

The **PS-5400** is a powerful 5-language translator fea-

turing up to 5,000 words and 1,000 structured sentences in English, German, French, Italian, and Spanish. Travel-related sentences, conveniently grouped by category, facilitate conversation in the language of your choice. To keep you on time and on top, there's also world time, alarm reminders, calculator, and metric conversions.

The **PS-5800** and **PS-5400**. Two pocket-sized ways to break the language barrier!

For more information, fax your request to:
Texas Instruments France, (33) 39 22 21 01

INSIGHT GUIDES

COLORSET NUMBERS

▶ *What is the
significance
of the number
that appears
in a triangle
on the spine
of each
Insight Guide?
Each number,
in fact, is a
color code
identifying the
background
color of the
spine. Line up
all titles from
No. 100 to
300 for a
full set of
Insight Guides
and your
book-shelves
will radiate a
dazzling
rainbow of
world travel.*

In cases of medical emergency, either dial 15 for an ambulance or call the Service d'Aide Médicale d'Urgence (SAMU) which exists in most large towns and cities – numbers are given at the front of telephone directories.

The standard of treatment in French hospitals is generally high, and you should be able to find someone who speaks English to help you. You may prefer to try to get to either the American Hospital at 63 Boulevard Victor-Hugo, 92292 Neuilly, tel: (1) 47.47.53.00; or the British Hospital Hortford, 3 Rue Barbes, 92300 Levallois, tel: (1) 47.58.13.12, both just outside Paris. Show the hospital doctor or authorities your E111 and you will be billed (once you are back home usually), for approximately 25 percent of the cost of treatment.

GETTING AROUND

MAPS

A first essential in touring any part of France is a good map. The Institute Géographique National is the French equivalent of the British Ordnance Survey and their maps are excellent. For route planning, IGN 901 is ideal at a scale of 1:1000,000 or 1" = 16 miles (1 cm:1 km); the Michelin M911 at the same scale shows just motorways and main roads which is a good clear presentation if you do not plan to go off the beaten track.

For more detailed maps, the IGN Red Series (1:250,000, 1 cm:2.5 km) covers the country on 16 sheets at a good scale for touring. Michelin also produce regional maps at a similar scale (1:200,000, or 1" = 3 miles approx.). These sheets are also available bound as a Motoring Atlas including route planning maps, Paris area map and several town plans. Collins also produce a good atlas based on the IGN's regional maps.

Another particularly good series for touring are the Telegraph (Recta Foldex) maps which cover France on four maps: northwest, northeast, southwest and southeast.

IGN's Green Series (1:100,000, 1" = 4 miles or 1 cm: 1km) are more detailed, local maps which cover the whole of France on 74 sheets. These are useful for travellers with a single main destination, and also quite good for walking. Serious walkers though will need IGN's highly detailed 1:50,000 and 1:25,000 scales (Blue Series). Other specialist maps for walkers and climbers are produced by Didier

Richard (Alpine maps), while the IGN produces detailed maps of the Pyrenees and the national parks of France.

Michelin publish town plans, as do Blay, but local tourist offices often give away their own town plans free of charge.

In France, most good bookshops should have a range of maps, but they can often be bought more cheaply in hypermarkets or service stations. Motorway maps can often be picked up free of charge at rest areas.

PUBLIC TRANSPORT

BY BUS

Details of routes and timetables are generally available free of charge either from bus stations (*gare routière*) which are often situated close to rail stations, or from tourist offices. They will also give details of coach tours and sightseeing excursions which are widely available.

BY TRAIN

Information on services is available from stations (Gare SNCF). If you intend to travel extensively by train it may be worth obtaining a rail pass before leaving home (*see Getting There*). These tickets can be used on any journey, otherwise individual tickets need to be purchased, but check on any discounts available, e.g. the Carte Couple for married couples travelling together on off-peak services. Children under 4 travel free, from 4 to 12 for half-fare. People travelling in groups of 6 or more can also obtain discounts (20–40 percent depending on numbers).

All tickets purchased at French stations have to be put through the orange machines at the stations to validate them before boarding the train. These are marked *compostez votre billet*.

PARIS METRO & RER

The Paris métro is one of the world's oldest subway systems and some of its stations are almost historic monuments. Despite that, it is quick and efficient. The métro operates 5.30am–12.30am; its comprehensive map and signalling make it virtually impossible to get lost; the lines are identified by number and the names of their terminals. It operates in conjunction with the RER, suburban regional express trains, which operate on four lines, identified as A–D.

Flat fare tickets are valid for both the subway and the bus, and cost around FF5.50 for a single fare, but a book (*carnet*) of 10 gives a considerable saving at around FF34.50. Buy them at bus or métro stations and some tobacconists.

Another option is the Paris-visite card which is valid for three or five consecutive days on the métro, bus and railway in the Paris/Ile de France region.

It also gives discounted entry to various tourist sites; available from main métro and SNCF stations and the airports. For shorter stays, buy the Formule 1 card, which allows an unlimited number of trips in any one day on the métro, bus and suburban trains and the night buses (it extends as far as Euro Disney). Buy it from métro offices or the Central Tourist Office in the Champs Elysées.

PRIVATE TRANSPORT

Car hire is expensive if rentals are organised locally (*see Car Hire*), but bikes (*vélos*) are fairly readily available, often from cycle shops. Local tourist offices keep information on hire facilities. French Railways have them for hire at around 200 of their stations; they do not necessarily have to be returned to the same station. Bikes can be carried free of charge on buses and some trains (Autotrains), on other, faster services you will have to pay.

Travelling by a combination of bike and bus or train can be an excellent way of touring, and relieves you of some of the legwork. For further information *see Cycling* in the *Sports* section of this guide.

DRIVING

British, US, Canadian and Australian licences are all valid in France and you should always carry your vehicle's registration document and valid insurance (third party is the absolute minimum, but full cover is strongly recommended).

Additional insurance cover, which can include a get-you-home service, is offered by a number of organisations including the British and American Automobile Associations and Europ-Assistance, 252 High Street, Croydon CR0 1NF, tel: 081-680 1234; in the US: Europ Assistance Worldwide Services Inc, 1133 15th Street, Suite 400, Washington DC 20005, tel: 202 347 7113.

The Automobile Club National is the umbrella organisation of France's 40-odd motoring clubs. It will assist any motorist whose own club has an agreement with it. Contact them at 9 Rue Anatole-de-la-Forge, 75017 Paris. Tel: (1) 42.27.82.00, fax: (1) 40.53.90.52.

RULES OF THE ROAD

The minimum age for driving is 18; foreigners are not permitted to drive on a provisional licence.

Full or dipped headlights must be used in poor visibility and at night; sidelights are not sufficient unless the car is stationary. Beams must be adjusted for right-hand drive vehicles, but yellow tints are not compulsory.

The use of seat belts (front, and rear if fitted) and crash helmets for motorcyclists is compulsory. Children under 10 are not permitted to ride in the front seat unless fitted with a rear-facing safety seat, or if the car has no rear seat.

PRIORITE A LA DROITE

An important rule to remember is that priority on French roads is always given to vehicles approaching from the right, except where otherwise indicated. In practice, on main roads the major road will normally have priority, with traffic being halted on minor approach roads with one of the following signs:
STOP
Cédez le passage – give way
Vous n'avez pas la priorité – you do not have right of way
Passage protégé – no right of way

Particular care should be taken in towns, where you may wrongly assume you are on the major road, and in rural areas where there may not be any road markings (watch out for farm vehicles).

Note that if a driver flashes the headlights it is to indicate that he has priority, **not** the other way round. Priority is always given to emergency services and also public utility vehicles e.g. gas, electricity and water companies.

The French recently changed the rules concerning roundabouts. In theory, drivers already on the roundabout now have priority over those entering it – but beware, some drivers still insist that priority belongs to the drivers entering a roundabout.

SPEED LIMITS

Speed limits are as follows, unless otherwise indicated: 130 kph (80 mph) on toll motorways; 110 kph (68 mph) on other motorways and dual carriageways; 90 kph (56 mph) on other roads except in towns where the limit is 50 kph (30 mph). There is also a minimum speed limit of 80 kph (50 mph) on the outside lane of motorways during daylight with good visibility and on level ground. Speed limits are reduced in wet weather: toll motorways 110 kph; dual carriageways 100 kph; 80 kph on other roads.

On-the-spot fines can be levied for speeding; on toll roads, the time is printed on the ticket you take at your entry point and can thus be checked and a fine imposed on exit. Nearly all motorways (*autoroutes*) are toll roads.

Note that stringent parking regulations are in force in Paris, making it an offence to park in many streets in the city centre.

Autoroutes are designated **A** roads and national highways **N** roads. **D** roads are usually well maintained, while **C** (local roads) may not always be so.

You must carry a red warning triangle to place 50 metres (165 ft) behind the car in case of a breakdown or accident. In an accident or emergency, call the police (dial 17) or use the free emergency telephones (every 2 km/1 mile) on motorways. If another driver is involved, lock your car and go together to call the police. It is useful to carry an European Accident Statement Form (obtainable from your insurance company) which will simplify matters in the case of an accident.

Unleaded petrol (*essence sans plomb*) is now widely available in France. If in doubt, a map showing the location of filling stations is available from main tourist offices.

For information about current road conditions, contact the Inter Service Route line tel: (1) 48.94.33.33 (this is a recorded announcement in French and not always terribly clear).

MOTORCYCLES & MOPEDS

Rules of the road are largely the same as for car drivers. The minimum age for driving machines over 80cc is 18. Crash helmets are compulsory. Dipped headlights must be used at all times. Children under 14 years are not permitted to be carried as passengers.

CAR HIRE

Hiring a car is expensive, partly because of the high sales tax (TVA) – 33 percent on luxury items. Some fly/drive deals work out reasonably well if you're only going for a short visit. French Railways offer a good deal on their combined train/car rental bookings. Weekly rates often work out better than a daily hire and it can be cheaper to arrange hire in the UK or US before leaving for France. The minimum age to hire a car is 23, or 21 if paying by credit card and the hirer must have held a full licence for at least a year.

The central reservation offices of the major car hire companies are listed below. Car hire anywhere in France can be arranged through them or via their agencies abroad. To hire a car locally, check in telephone directories or ask at tourist offices.

Autorent: 98 Rue de la Convention, 75015 Paris. Tel: (1) 45.54.22.45, fax: (1) 45.54.39.69.

Avis: Tour Franklin, 92042 Paris-La-Défense Cedex 11. Tel: (1) 49.06.68.68, fax: (1) 47.78.98.98.

Budget/Milleville: 1 Rue des Hauts-Flouviers, 94517 Thiais. Tel: (1) 46.86.65.65, fax: 46.86.14.13.

Citer: 125bis Rue de Vaugirard, 75015 Paris. Tel: (1) 44.38.60.00, fax: (1) 40.56.08.08.

Eurodollar/Mattei: Place des Reflets, Z.I. Parc Nord II, 165 Avenue du Bois-de-la-Pie, B.P. 40002, 95911 Roissy-Charles-de-Gaulle Cedex. Tel: (1) 49.38.77.00, fax (1) 49.38.77.02.

Europcar/National/InterRent: 65 Rue Edouard-Vaillant, 92100 Boulogne. Tel: (1) 49.10.55.55, fax: (1) 46.20.47.81.

Eurorent: 42 Avenue de Saxe, 75007 Paris. Tel: (1) 45.67.82.17, fax: (1) 40.65.91.94.

Hertz: 4 Avenue du Vieil-Etang, 78180 Montigny-le-Bretonneux. Tel: (1) 30.45.65.65, fax: (1) 30.58.46.21.

ROUTES

Following a tourist circuit, or route is a sure way of getting to see the major sites of a region. Tourist offices will help with suggestions, but the Caisse Nationale des Monuments Historiques et des Sites have published a very useful leaflet showing some 64 historic routes throughout France. For a copy of the leaflet, write to them at 62 Rue Sainte-Antoine, 75004 Paris. Tel: (1) 42.74.22.22.

Some of the routes are quite long, such as the one which takes in the greatest cathedrals in France (Chartres, Strasbourg, Rouen, etc.) and one covering the parks and gardens of the Beauce, Berry and Loire Valley; but it also suggests many shorter circuits which are quite manageable in a day or two, such as the route des Ducs de Normandie or the Quercy Marches road.

You can travel southeast from Paris all the way as far as Lyon, following the route Historique Buissonière, taking in such sites as Auxerre, Paray-le-Monial, Vézelay and Château-Chinon among others on the way. Another suggestion is following the William the Conqueror trail, mostly around Normandy, which can be picked up at either the port of Caen or Le Havre.

For further information about historic routes and monuments contact: Demeure Historique, 57 Quai de la Tournelle, 75005 Paris. Tel: (1) 43.29.02.86.

TAXIS

Taxis are most readily available at airports and railway stations. In Paris there are almost 500 taxi ranks, but be careful in the capital to hail only a genuine taxi (with a light on the roof); other operators may charge exorbitant fares. Taxi drivers in Paris operate on three tariffs:

Tariff A 7am–7pm
Tariff B 7pm–7am
Tariff C at night in the suburbs and during the day in the outlying districts of Hauts-de-Seine, Seine Saint-Denis and Val-de-Marne, when the taxi has no client for the return journey.

A 10 percent tip is usual. Any complaints about Paris taxis should be addressed to Suivis taxis, Préfecture de Police, 36 Rue des Morillons, 75015 Paris. Tel: 45.31.14.80.

INLAND WATERWAYS

One of the most pleasant ways of exploring a small corner of France is on board a narrowboat or one of the other craft that can be hired on many of the country's navigable canals and rivers.

Holidays on inland waterways have become extremely popular in recent years and choices range from a simple day or half-day cruise, to piloting your own hired boat, or enjoying the luxury of the so-called hotel barges, where you just sit back and relax while the navigation and catering is all taken care of for you. Burgundy is particularly favoured by internal waterways, the Canal de Bourgogne is the longest, connecting the river Yonne in the north to the Saône in the south.

Devotees of canal architecture will wish to incorporate into their trip the aqueduct at Briare. This masterpiece of engineering, whose foundations were laid by the engineer Eiffel's company, was built in 1896 to connect the Briare and the Loire lateral canals, to enable freight to be carried all the way from the Channel to the Mediterranean. The Briare canal itself was built by Sully in the early 17th century and served as a prototype for all France's later canal-building.

Other popular options for boating holidays are the canal du Midi, the Nantes-Brest canal in the southwest and the little Rhône-Sète canal which finishes on the Mediterranean coast. The mysterious green waterways of the Marais Poitevin, in the area known as "Green Venice" just inland from La Rochelle, have their own particular charm and are ideal for day trips.

Even if you have never navigated before, you will feel confident after a minimum of instruction (foreigners require no permit or licence). Several companies offer "package" holidays afloat including travel arrangements. A selection is given below:

Abercrombie and Kent, Sloane Square House, Holbein Place, London SW1W 8NS. Tel: 071-730 9600. Canal and river barges in Alsace, Burgundy and the Rhône; hotel barges in Burgundy and the Loire.

Blakes Holidays, Wroxham, Norwich NR12 8DH. Tel: 0603-784131, fax: 0603-782871. Offer the widest choice of boats, operating in all areas.

Crown Blue Line, 8 Ber Street, Norwich, Norfolk NR1 3EJ. Tel: 0603-630513, fax: 0603-664298. Wide range of cruisers on all main waterways.

Eurocamp, Edmundson House, Tatton Street, Knutsford WA16 6BG. Tel: 0565-633844. One of the leaders in the packaged camping holiday field, now operating canal holidays in most areas.

Hoseasons Holidays Abroad, Sunway House, Lowestoft NR32 3LT. Tel: 0502-500555, fax: 0502-500532. Operates on the canals in Burgundy, Brittany, Alsace and the Mediterranean.

World Wine Tours, 69-71 Banbury Road, Oxford OX2 6PE. Tel: 0865-310344. Luxury holiday barges operating in Alsace, Burgundy and the Canal du Midi.

Agencies in the US include:

Abercrombie and Kent, 1420 Kinsington Road, Oak Brook, Illinois 60521-2106. Tel: 1-800-323 7308.

French Country Waterways, PO Box 2195, Duxbury, Massachusetts 02331. Tel: 1-800-222 1236.

If you prefer to book direct in France, try the Service Loisirs Accueil in the individual *départements* (*see Useful Addresses*) or contact one of the following companies (this is just a selection of the many operators):

Bateaux de Bourgogne, SRLA Yonne, 3-4 Quai de la République, 89000 Auxerre. Tel: 86.52.18.99.

Bateaux Parisiens, 1 Port de la Bourdonnais, 75007 Paris. Tel: (1) 47.05.50.00, fax: 45.56.07.88
Blue Line Bourgogne, La Gare d'Eau, Saint-Usage, 21170 Saint-Jean-Losne. Tel: 80.29.12.86.
Crown Cruisers, Port de la Jonction, 58300 Decize. Tel: 86.25.46.64.
Locaboat Plaisance, Quai du Port-au-Bois, 89300 Joigny. Tel: 86.91.72.72.
Maine Anjou Rivières, Le Moulin Chenillé Changé, 49220 Le Lion d'Angers. Tel: 41.95.10.83, fax: 41.95.10.52.
River Palace, BP 249, 44008 Nantes Cedex 01. Tel: 40.20.24.50.

The following French operators offer holidays on luxury hotel barges:
Aquarelle, Port de plaisance, Quai Saint-Martin, 89000 Auxerre. Tel: 86.46.96.77.
La Belle Aventure, 89000 Auxerre. Tel: 86.81.44.77.
Navigation et Technique, Port du Canal, 21370 Plombières-lès-Dijon. Tel: 80.45.44.60.
Péniches-Hôtels de France, 21140 Villeneuve-sous-Charigny. Tel: 80.97.21.27.

If you are navigating for yourself, a map or guide to the waterway is essential. These are often provided as part of a package deal, otherwise you will need to take your own. Crown Blue Line produce large format map-guides for their own clients, which are now available to the general public; ECM map-guides are well-produced strip maps with all navigation aids, boating serives and tourist information. Vagnon map-guides are also very good, with some colour photography.

RAMBLERS

There are countless opportunities for exploring France by foot; given the time you could cross the whole of France north-south or west-east by following footpaths. All the main footpaths in France form part of the national network of long-distance footpaths (Sentiers de Grandes Randonnées or GR). The routes are numbered for easy identification, e.g. the GR.1 takes you around Paris and the Ile de France, covering a distance of 395 miles (630 km).

The French Ramblers' Association, Fédération Française de la Randonnée Pédestre (FFRP) based at 8 Avenue Marceau, 75008 Paris, tel: (1) 47.23.62.32, fax: (1) 47.20.00.74., publishes Topoguides (guide books incorporating IGN 1:50,000 scale maps) to all France's footpaths but they are available only in French. These guides are available in good bookshops in France, or in the UK try Stanfords of Covent Garden. The IGN Blue series maps at a scale of 1:25,000, are ideal for walkers.

A good basic guide book for serious walkers is Rob Hunter's book *Walking in France*, while *Classic Walks in France* by Hunter and Wickers, suggests 20 great tours in the most beautiful areas of the country. Both are published by Oxford University

Press. Robertson McCarta are gradually compiling a comprehensive series of regional walking guides to France based on the French Topoguides mentioned above; titles include *Walks in Dordogne*, *Coastal Walks in Normandy and Brittany* and *Walks in Corsica*.

Each *département* has its own ramblers' organisation (operating under the FFRP umbrella) which arranges a variety of activities throughout the year: guided walks taking a day, a weekend or more, as well as walks with a particular theme, flora, or wildlife, for example. For more information, contact the Centre d'Information Sentiers et Randonnée, 64 Rue Gergovie, 75014 Paris. Tel: (1) 45.45.31.02. Tourist offices will also give information about local clubs and events.

Various walking holidays with accommodation either in hotels or under canvas are available. Some are organised through package tour operators in the UK, others are bookable through the French tourist offices and other local organisations. The Service Loisirs Accueil in several *départements* (*see Useful Addresses*) offer walking holidays, and a selection of other operators is given below:

FRANCE

Clés de France, 13 Rue Saint-Louis, 78100 Saint-Germain-en-Laye. Tel: (1) 30.61.23.23. The national organisation for holidays in France's regional parks. **Les Quatre Chemins**, 25 Rue aux Raz, 71400 Autun. Tel: 85.52.07.91. Walking and other activity holidays in the Morvan.

BRITAIN

Headwater Holidays, 146 London Road, Northwich CW9 5HH. Tel: 0606-48699. Holidays in the Loire Valley, Auvergne and other popular areas.
Ramblers Holidays, Box 43, Welwyn Garden City, Herts AL8 6PQ. Tel: 0707-331133. Wide range of tours, including the Cévennes, Alps, Pyrénées and Corsica.
Sherpa Expeditions, 131a Heston Road, Hounslow TW5 0RD. Tel: 081-577 2717. Independent guided walks in many areas for a fortnight or just a weekend.
Waymark Holidays, 44 Windsor Road, Slough SL1 2EJ. Tel: 0735-516477. Touring or centre-based holidays in the Auvergne, Provence, Alps and Pyrénées.

Independent travellers can take advantage of low-priced accommodation offered in *gîtes d'étapes*, hostels offering basic facilities which are to be found on many of the GR routes and in mountain regions. For more information contact the Gîtes de France organisation (*see Where to Stay*). If you prefer a little more comfort, there is a group of hotels in the Massif Central which have signed a charter guaranteeing a good welcome to hikers. Information from Rand'Hotel, Chamina, BP 21, 8 Rue de Verdun, 15130 Arpajon-sur-Cère. Tel: 71.64.54.23, fax: 71.63.53.58.

HITCHHIKING

With sensible precautions, hitchhiking can be an interesting and inexpensive way to get around France. Would-be hitchhikers may be discouraged by the difficulty of getting a lift out of the channel ports, so it may be worth taking a bus or train for the first leg of your journey. Hitching is forbidden on motorways, but you can wait on slip roads or at toll booths. Allostop is a nationwide organisation which aims to connect hikers with drivers (you pay a registration fee and a contribution towards the petrol). Tel: (1) 42.46.00.66.

WHERE TO STAY

HOTELS

Hotels are plentiful in the main towns of France and along the main highways, but those in the smaller country villages can be the best. All hotels in France conform to national standards and carry ☆-ratings, set down by the Ministry of Tourism, according to their degree of comfort and amenities. Prices (which are charged per room, rather than per person) range from as little as FF90 for a double room in an unclassified hotel (i.e. its standards are not sufficient to warrant a single star, but is likely to be clean, cheap and cheerful), to FF550 for the cheapest double room in a ☆☆☆☆ luxury hotel.

Hotels are required to show their menus outside the hotel and details of room prices should be visible either outside or in reception, as well as on the back of bedroom doors. It is possible for a hotel to have a one-☆ rating, with a ☆☆ restaurant. This is ideal if you are on a budget and more interested in food than fading wallpaper or eccentric plumbing.

When booking a room, you should normally be shown it before agreeing to take it; if it doesn't suit you, ask to be shown another (this may sound odd advice, but rooms can vary enormously within the same building). Prices are charged per room; supplements may be charged for an additional bed or a cot (*lit bébé*). You may be asked when booking if you wish to dine, particularly if the hotel is busy – preference should not, but may in fact be given to hungry customers as there is not a lot of profit in letting rooms alone. Also the simple request, "*On peut dîner ici ce soir?*" will confirm that the hotel's restaurant is open (many are closed out of season on Sunday or Monday evenings).

Lists of hotels can be obtained from the French Government Tourist office in your country or from regional or local tourist offices in France. It is also worth buying from your local French Tourist Office the *Logis et Auberges de France* guide. This is an invaluable guide to a very good and reasonably priced network of family-run hotels who aim to offer a friendly welcome and good local cuisine. The guide can be bought in bookshops in France but it is more expensive. It can be used to book hotels before travelling (for the central reservation office in Paris, tel: (1) 45.84.83.84). Some tourist offices will make hotel bookings for you, for a small fee (usually around FF15).

Several other hotel chains and associations offer central booking facilities. These range from the very cheap and simple groups such as the Balladins chain, which has almost 100 very modern ☆ hotels, to the Concorde group of 28 ☆☆☆☆ and de-luxe hotels. A list of central booking offices is given below, with UK and US booking offices mentioned where available.

Altéa/Mercure, 7 Allée du Brévent, 91021 Evry Cedex Résinter. Tel: (1) 60.77.27.27, fax: (1) 60.77.21.08. 160 ☆☆☆ hotels.
UK office, tel: 081-741 4655, fax: 081-748 3542.
Balladins, 20 Rue du Pont-des-Halles, 94656 Rungis Cedex. Tel: (1) 49.78.24.61, fax: (1) 46.86.41.44. 91. ☆ budget-priced hotels.
Campanile, 31 Avenue Jean-Moulin, 77200 Torcy. Tel: (1) 64.62.46.46, fax: (1) 64.62.46.61. 225 ☆☆ to ☆☆☆☆ hotels.
UK office, tel: 081-569 6969, fax: 081-569 4888.
Climat de France, 5 Avenue du Cap-Horn, ZAC de Courtaboeuf, BP 93, 91943 Les Ulis. Tel: (1) 64.46.01.23 or 05.11.22.11 (toll-free in France), fax: (1) 69.28.24.02. 150 ☆☆ hotels.
UK office, tel: 071-287 3181.
Concorde Hotels, 35-37 Grosvenor Gardens, London SW1W 0BS. Tel: 0800-181591, fax: 071-630 0391.
Formule 1, Immeuble le Descartes, 29 Promenade Michel-Simon, 93163 Noisy-le-Grand. Tel: (1) 43.04.01.00, fax: (1) 43.05.31.51. 178 ☆ budget-priced hotels, offering a booking service from one hotel to another in the chain.
Ibis/Urbis, 6-8 Rue du Bois-Briard, 91021 Evry Cedex. Tel: (1) 60.77.27.27, fax: (1) 60.77.22.83. 170 ☆☆ hotels.
UK office, tel: 071-724 1000, fax: 081-748 9116.
Minotels France Accueil, 85 Rue du Dessous-des-Berges, 75013 Paris. Tel: (1) 45.83.04.22, fax: (1) 45.86.49.82. 150 ☆☆ and ☆☆☆ hotels.
UK office: France Accueil, 10 Salisbury Hollow, Edington, Westbury, Wilts BA13 4PF. Tel: 0380-830125; or Minotels Great Britain, 5 Kings Road, Cleveleys, Lancs FY5 1BY. Tel: 0253-66266, fax: 0253-866251.
US office: Minotels Europe, 683 South Collier Boulevard, Marco Island, Florida 33037. Tel: 813-394 3384 (toll free: 1-800-336 4668), fax: 813-394 3384.

In Canada: Tours Chanteclerc, 65 Rue de Brésoles, Montréal, Québec H2Y 1V7. Tel: 514-845 1236, fax: 514-845 5794.

The following are hotel groups which do not have central booking facilities. Most of these groups offer something other than the average hotel. Each group produces its own brochure or list of hotels, available from the addresses below, but bookings have to be made with the individual establisments.

Châteaux-Demeures de Tradition et Grandes Etapes de Vignobles, BP 40, 13360 Roquevaire. Tel: 42.04.41.97, fax: 42.72.83.81. 112 elegant ☆☆☆ hotels, particularly in wine-growing regions.
Moulin Etape, Moulin de Chameron, 18210 Bannegon. Tel: 48.61.83.80, fax: 48.61.84.92. 49 former mills offering ☆ to ☆☆☆☆ accommodation.
Les Nids de France, 15 Rue Verdun, 78800 Houilles. Tel: (1) 39.68.95.41. 42 ☆☆ family hotels.
Rand'Hotel, Chamina, BP 21, 8 Rue de Verdun, 15130 Arpajon-sur-Cère. Tel: 71.64.54.23, fax: 71.63.53.58. 42 ☆ to ☆☆☆ hotels in the Massif Central, catering particularly for hikers.
Relais et Châteaux, 9 Avenue Marceau, 75116 Paris. Tel: 47.23.41.42, fax: (1) 47.23.38.99. 146 independently-owned hotels and restaurants in former castles and other historic buildings (guide available from French Government Tourist Offices abroad). UK information office: 28 Basil Street, London SW3 1AT.
Les Relais du Silence, 2 Passage Duguesclin, 75015 Paris. Tel: (1) 45.66.77.77, fax: (1) 40.65.90.09. 145 ☆☆ to ☆☆☆☆ hotels in particularly tranquil settings.

It is not possible here to offer a very comprehensive list of hotels for the whole of France, for which we recommend the *Michelin Red Guide*. The following is just a small selection of hotels in each region of France to suit all budgets. Star ratings are given thus ☆☆; CC: means credit cards. Prices are given for double room (not per person), these should be taken as a rough guide only.

PARIS

The Paris Tourist Office has several Welcome Bureaux which will book your first night's accommodation if you apply in person, they are situated at the following places:
Central office, 127 Champs Elysées, 75008. Tel: (1) 47.23.61.72. Open: daily 9am–8pm except Christmas Day and 1 January.
Gare du Nord, 18 Rue de Dunkerque, 75010. Tel: (1) 45.26.94.82. Open: daily 8am–9pm, Sunday 1–9pm. Closes 8pm out of season, and all day Sunday.
Gare de l'Est, Hall d'Arrivée, 75010. Tel: (1) 46.07.17.73. Open: Monday–Saturday 8am–9pm (8pm out of season).

Gare de Lyon, at Sortie Grandes lignes, 75012. Tel: (1) 43.43.33.24. Open: Monday–Saturday 8am–9pm (8pm out of season).
Eiffel Tower, Champ de Mars, 75007. Tel: (1) 45.51.22.15. Open: May–September daily 11am–6pm.
Gare d'Austerlitz, at Arrivée Grandes Lignes, 75013. Tel: (1) 45.84.91.70. Open: Monday–Saturday 8am–3pm.
Gare Montparnasse, 15 Boulevard de Vaugirard, Arrivée Grandes Lignes, 75015. Tel: (1) 43.22.19.19. Open: Monday–Saturday 8am–9pm (8pm out of season).

LUXURY

Hôtel de Crillon ☆☆☆☆, 10 Place de la Concorde. 75008. Tel: (1) 44.71.15.00, fax: (1) 44.71.15.02. Centrally situated near the Arc de Triomphe. CC: Amex, Diners, Visa. Rooms: FF3,300–3,800.
George-V ☆☆☆☆, 31 Avenue George V, 75008. Tel: (1) 47.23.54.00, fax: (1) 47.20.40.00. Famed for its stylish elegance. CC: Amex, Diners, Visa. Rooms: FF2,850–3,850.
Hilton International ☆☆☆☆, 18 Avenue de Suffren 75015. Tel: (1) 42.73.93.00, fax: (1) 47.83.62.66. Offers a great view of the Eiffel Tower. CC: Amex, Diners, Visa. Rooms: FF1,650–2,300.
Plaza-Athénée ☆☆☆☆, 25 Avenue Montaigne, 75008. Tel: (1) 47.23.78.33, fax: (1) 47.20.20.70. Convenient for the Champs Elysées. CC: Diners, Visa. Rooms: FF2,780–2,890.
Ritz ☆☆☆☆, 15 Place Vendôme, 75001. Tel: (1) 42.60.38.30, fax: (1) 42.60.23.71. Unashamed luxury on one of the most famous squares in the capital. CC: Amex, Diners, Visa. Rooms: FF2,900–3,900.
Royal Monceau ☆☆☆☆, 37 Avenue Hoche, 75008. Tel: (1) 45.61.98.00, fax: (1) 42.56.90.03. Very central. CC: Amex, Diners, Visa. Rooms: FF2,250–2,650.

MODERATE

Alexandre Montparnasse ☆☆, 71 Boulevard de Vaugirard, 75015. Tel: (1) 43.20.89.12, fax: (1) 43.22.77.71. Handy for the antique shops of the Village Suisse and the Beaugrenelle quarter. CC: Amex, Visa. Rooms: FF420–500.
Ducs de Bourgogne ☆☆, 19 Rue du Pont-Neuf, 75001. Tel: (1) 42.33.95.64, fax: (1) 40.39.01.25. By the Pont Neuf, the oldest bridge in Paris. CC: Amex, Diners, Visa. Rooms: FF520–620.
Saint-Germain ☆☆, 50 Rue du Four, 75006. Tel: (1) 45.48.91.64, fax: (1) 45.48.46.22. On the left bank, near the Luxembourg Gardens. CC: Amex, Diners, Visa. Rooms: FF400–690.
Saint-Louis ☆☆, 75 Rue Saint-Louis-en-Ile, 75004. Tel: (1) 46.34.04.80, fax: (1) 46.34.02.13. Set on the "island" of Saint-Louis. Rooms: FF620–720.

Saint-Thomas-d'Aquin ☆☆, 3 Rue Pré-aux-Clercs, 75007. Tel: (1) 42.61.01.22, fax: (1) 42.61.41.43. Handy for the Eiffel Tower and the relatively new Musée d'Orsay. CC: Amex, Diners, Visa. Rooms: FF410–480.
Urbis Sacré Coeur ☆☆, 100 Boulevard Rochechouart, 75018. Tel: (1) 46.06.99.17, fax: (1) 42.55.42.26. Ideal for Montmatre and the Moulin Rouge. CC: Amex, Visa. Rooms: FF360–400.

BUDGET

Grand Hôtel l'Evêque ☆, 29 Rue Cler, 75007. Tel: (1) 47.05.49.15, fax: (1) 45.50.49.36. Limited facilities, but inexpensive. Rooms: FF185–380.
Marignan ☆, 13 Rue du Sommerard, 75005. Tel: (1) 43.25.31.03. In the Latin Quarter. Rooms FF180.
Mont Blanc ☆, 11 Rue Victor, 75015. Tel: (1) 48.28.16.79. CC: Visa. Rooms: FF175–320.
Rouen ☆, 42 Rue Croix-des-Petits-Champs, 75001. Tel: (1) 42.61.38.21. Small hotel, convenient for the Forum des Halles. CC: Visa. Rooms: FF180–290.
Titania ☆, 70 bis, Boulevard Ornano, 75018. Tel: (1) 46.06.43.22. Handy for Montmartre and the Moulin Rouge. Rooms: FF130–250.
Wilson ☆, 10 Rue de Stockholm, 75008. Tel: (1) 45.22.10.85. Cheap, but close to the posher quarters. Rooms: FF210.

ILE DE FRANCE

The Euro Disney resort has its own hotels – see *Things to Do* section for information.
Adagio Paris Sèvres ☆☆☆, 11-13 Grande Rue, 92310 Sèvres. Tel: (1) 46.23.20.00, fax: (1) 46.23.02.32. Convenient for the National Museum of Ceramics. CC: Amex, Diners, Visa. Rooms: F795.
Angleterre ☆☆, 2bis Rue de Fontenay, 78000 Versailles. Tel: (1) 39.51.43.50, fax: (1) 39.51.45.63. Moderately priced accommodation near the Château de Versailles. CC: Amex, Visa. Rooms: FF320–350.
Aux Tilleuls, 2 Route de Champagne, 77810 Thomery. Tel: (1) 60.70.06.62. Family-run hotel, not far from Fontainebleau. CC: Mastercard, Visa. Rooms: FF70–220.
Campanile St Denis Basilique, 14 Rue Jean Jaurès, 93200. Tel: (1) 48.20.74.31, fax: (1) 48.20.74.26. Not too far from central Paris, near Saint-Denis cathedral. CC: Amex, Visa. Rooms: FF330.
La Chasse ☆☆, 2-4 Rue de la Chancellerie, 78000 Versailles. Tel: (1) 39.50.00.92, fax: (1) 39.51.77.27. Family-run Logis; menus start at FF100. CC: Amex, Diners, Mastercard, Visa. Rooms: F230–290.
Climat de France ☆☆, 32 Avenue de la Victoire, 77100 Meaux. Tel: (1) 64.33.15.46, fax: (1) 60.23.11.64. One of the Climat group of hotels. CC: Amex, Visa. Rooms: FF260–285.
Napoléon ☆☆☆, 9 Rue Grande, 77300 Fontainebleau. Tel: (1) 64.22.32.65, fax: (1) 64.22.20.87. Convenient for the Fontainebleau

Palace and Barbizon. CC: Amex, Diners, Visa. Rooms: FF650–990.

Pavillon Henri IV ✩✩✩✩, 21 Rue Thiers, 78100 Saint-Germain-en-Laye. Tel: (1) 34.51.62.62, fax: (1) 39.73.93.73. Unashamed luxury; convenient for the Château de Saint-Germain-En-Laye. CC: Amex, Diners, Visa. Rooms: FF1,000–1,900.

Pullman Versailles ✩✩✩✩, 2 bis Avenue de Paris, 78000 Versailles. Tel: (1) 39.53.30.31, fax: (1) 39.53.87.20. Perfect for visitors to the Versailles Palace and its environs. CC: Amex, Diners, Visa. Rooms: FF690.

LOIRE VALLEY & WESTERN LOIRE

ANGERS: MAINE-ET-LOIRE

Anjou, 1 Boulevard Mar. Foch, 49100. Tel: 41.88.24.82. Large rooms in a recently modernised old hotel. CC: Amex, Diners, Mastercard, Visa. Rooms: FF270–450.

de France, 8 Place Gare, 49100. Tel: 41.88.49.42. Comfortable hotel, convenient for the major sights. CC: Amex, Diners, Mastercard, Visa. Rooms: FF280–400.

AMBOISE: INDRE-ET-LOIRE

Le Choiseul, 36 Quai Charles Guinot, 37400. Tel: 47.30.45.45. Beautifully refurbished 18th-century mansion; garden and swimming-pool. Recommended restaurant. CC: Mastercard, Visa. Rooms: FF380–680.

AZAY-LE-RIDEAU: INDRE-ET-LOIRE

Le Grand Monarque, 3 Place de la République, 37190. Tel: 47.45.40.08. Nice rooms overlooking garden. CC: Amex, Diners, Mastercard, Visa. Rooms: FF180–450.

BLOIS: LOIR-ET-CHER

Le Relais Bleu du Château, 22 Rue Porte Côte, 41000. Tel: 54.78.20.24. Restored, set below the château; inexpensive restaurant in pretty interior courtyard. Rooms: FF250.

Savoie, 6 Rue Ducoux, 41000. Tel: 54.74.01.17. CC: Amex, Mastercard, Visa. Rooms: FF140–260.

CHATEAUBRIANT: LOIRE ATLANTIQUE

La Ferrière, Route de Nantes, 44110. Tel: 40.28.00.28. Rooms: FF190–220.

CHÂTEAU DU LOIR: SARTHE

La Gare, 170 Avenue Jean-Jaurès, 72500. Tel: 43.40.00.14. CC: Mastercard, Visa. Rooms: FF100–220.

CHENONCEAUX: INDRE-ET-LOIRE

Le Bon Laboureur et Château, 6 Rue du Dr. Bretonneau, 37150. Tel: 47.23.90.02. Very popular, fills quickly. CC: Amex, Diners, Mastercard, Visa. Rooms: FF280–400.

CHINON: INDRE-ET-LOIRE

La Boule D'Or, 66 Quai Jeanne d'Arc, 37500. Tel: 47.93.03.13. Family-run Logis on the quayside. Rooms: FF240

CHOLET: MAINE-ET-LOIRE

Le Belvédère, Lac de Ribou, 49300. Tel: 41.62.14.02. Just outside town; original menu. Closed: 23 July–

22 August. CC: Amex, Diners, Mastercard, Visa. Rooms: FF270–320.

DESCARTES: INDRE-ET-LOIRE

Le Moderne, 15 Rue Descartes, 37160. Tel: 47.59.72.11. Small hotel, well restored. CC: Diners, Mastercard, Amex. Rooms: FF180–250.

LA FLÈCHE: SARTHE

Le Relais Cicero, 18 Boulevard Alger, 72200. Tel: 43.94.14.14. Quiet 17th-century house set in a private garden. CC: Mastercard, Visa. Rooms: FF270–450.

FONTEVRAUD-L'ABBAYE: MAINE-ET-LOIRE

La Croix Blanche ✩✩, Place des Plantaganêts, 49590. Tel: 41.51.71.11. Delightful hotel overlooking the abbey; good food. CC: Mastercard, Visa. Rooms: FF162–412.

Le Domaine de Mestré, Mestré, 49590. Tel: 41.51.75.87. The abbey's farmhouse. Rooms: FF250.

MONTREUIL-BELLAY: MAINE-ET-LOIRE

Splendid and Relais de Bellay (annexe), 139 Rue du Docteur Gaudrez, 49260. Tel: 41.53.10.00. Comfortable rooms and good food. Swimming-pool at the annexe. CC: Visa. Rooms: FF180–350

NANTES: LOIRE-ATLANTIQUE

Astoria, 11 Rue de Richebourg, 44000. Tel: 40.74.39.90. Near the station, but fairly quiet. CC: Visa. Rooms: FF280–350.

ORLÉANS: LOIRET

Jackhotel, 18 Rue Cloître Saint-Aignan, 45000. Tel: 38.54.48.48. Small and central with a garden. Rooms: FF220–300.

Les Cècres, 17 Rue Mar. Foch, 45000. Tel: 38.62.22.92. CC: Amex, Diners, Mastercard, Visa. Rooms: FF180–370.

SANCERRE: CHER

Panoramic, Rempart des Augustins, 18300. Tel: 48.54.22.44. Modern hotel, with beautiful views. CC: Amex, Mastercard, Visa. Rooms: FF200–270.

SAUMUR: MAINE-ET-LOIRE

Anne d'Anjou, 32 Quai Mayaud, 49400. Tel: 41.67.30.30. One of the region's best hotels; pretty rooms. CC: Amex, Diners, Mastercard, Visa. Rooms: FF230–360.

Le Clos des Bénédictins, Saint-Hilaire-Saint-Florent, Saumur. Tel: 41.67.28.48. New hotel in peaceful setting, 3 km from the town. CC: Visa. Rooms: FF200–340.

TOURS: INDRE-ET-LOIRE

Bordeaux, 3 Place Maréchal Leclerc, 37100. Tel: 47.05.40.32. CC: Amex, Diners, Mastercard, Visa. Rooms: FF270–420.

Jean Bardet, 57 Rue Groison, 37100. Tel: 47.41.41.11. Elegant villa in a tranquil park; outstanding restaurant. CC: Amex, Diners, Mastercard, Visa. Rooms: FF420–900.

VENDÔME: LOIR-ET-CHER

Le Vendôme, 15 Faubourg Chartrain, 41100. Tel: 54.77.02.88. CC: Mastercard, Visa. Rooms: FF200–350.

ABBEVILLE: SOMME

De France ☆☆, 19 Place du Pilori, 80100. Tel: 22.24.26.42. At the centre of town. CC: Amex, Diners, Visa. Rooms: FF200–280.

ALENÇON: ORNE

Du Grand Cerf ☆☆☆, 21 Rue St-Blaise, 61003. Tel: 33.26.00.51.

AMIENS: SOMME

Le Postillon ☆☆☆, 19 Place au Feurre, 8000. Tel: 22.91.46.17. Near the cathedral. CC: Amex, Visa. Rooms: FF460–600.

BAYEUX: CALVADOS

Grand Hôtel du Luxembourg, 25 Rue des Bouchers, 14403. Tel: 31.92.00.04. It is quite grand. Rooms: FF320–520.

BOULOGNE-SUR-MER: PAS-DE-CALAIS

Métropole ☆☆, 51 Rue Thiers, 62200. Tel: 21.31.54.30. Nice hotel with a garden. CC: Amex, Visa. Rooms: FF175–300.

CAEN: CALVADOS

Le Relais des Gourmets ☆☆☆☆, 15 Rue de Geôle, 14300. Tel: 31.86.06.01. In a central location, with traditional restaurant. Rooms: FF240–430.

CALAIS: PAS-DE-CALAIS

Meurice ☆☆☆, 5 Rue E.-Roche, 62100. Tel: 21.96.92.89. Good service and restaurant. CC: Amex, Diners, Visa. Rooms: FF270–360.

CHERBOURG: MANCHE

Le Louvre ☆☆, 2 Rue H. Dunant, 50100. Tel: 33.53.02.28. No restaurant. CC: Visa. Rooms: FF160–220.

CHÂTEAU THIÉRRY: AISNE

De la Girafe ☆, Place Aristide Briand, 02400. Tel: 23.83.02.06.

COMPIÈGNE: OISE

De Flandre ☆☆, 16 Quai de la République, 60200. Tel: 44.83.24.40. Simple but good. CC: Diners, Visa. Rooms: FF150–270.

DEAUVILLE: CALVADOS

Le Royal ☆☆☆☆, Boulevard Cornuché, 14800. Tel: 31.98.66.34. Majestic hotel; some rooms have good sea views. Rooms: FF900–1,600.

DIEPPE: SEINE-MARITIME

La Présidence ☆☆☆, Boulevard de Verdun, BP 32, 76204. Tel: 35.84.31.31. Spacious and central. Rooms: FF340–530.

DINAN: CÔTES-D'ARMOR

Avaugour ☆☆☆, 1 Place du Champ, 22100. Tel: 96.39.07.49. Has a garden and excellent restaurant. CC: Amex, Diners, Visa. Rooms: FF330–440.

DINARD: ILLE-ET-VILAINE

Reine Hortense, 19 Rue de la Malouine, 35800. Tel: 99.46.54.31. Elegant old hotel. Closed: mid-November to Easter. CC: Amex, Diners, Visa. Rooms: FF770–1,200.

GRANVILLE: MANCHE

Marmotte ☆, 57 Avenue des Matignons, 50400. Tel: 33.50.05.05. Moderately priced with rooms from around FF100.

LE HAVRE: SEINE-MARITIME

Foch ☆☆, 4 Rue de Caligny, 76600. Tel: 35.42.50.69. Quiet surroundings near the marina. CC: Amex, Diners, Visa. Rooms: FF175–280.

HONFLEUR: CALVADOS

Le Cheval Blanc ☆☆☆, 2 Quai des Passagers, 14602. Tel: 31.89.13.49. Near the harbour; good restaurant. Rooms: FF320–620.

MONT-ST-MICHEL: MANCHE

Les Terrasses Poulard ☆☆☆, Intra Muros, 50116. Tel: 33.60.14.09. Modern and offering all the comforts. CC: Amex, Diners, Visa. Rooms: FF320–770.

LAON: AISNE

Angleterre ☆☆☆, 10 Boulevard de Lyon, 02000. Tel: 23.23.04.62. In the lower town. CC: Amex, Diners, Visa. Rooms: FF170–350.

LILLE: NORD

Carlton, 3 Rue de Paris, 59000. Tel: 20.55.24.11. Central, modernised hotel, one of the best in town. CC: Amex, Diners, Visa. Rooms: FF450–740.

LE MANS: SARTHE

La Closerie, Route de Laval, 72000. Tel: 43.28.69.92. One of the Best Western chain, has a garden and good restaurant. CC: most. Rooms: FF340–450.

QUIMPER: FINISTÈRE

Le Griffon ☆☆☆, 131 Route de Bénodet, 29000. Tel: 98.90.33.33. Modern hotel just south of the town, with own swimming-pool. CC: Amex, Diners, Visa. Rooms: FF380–440.

RENNES: ILLE-ET-VILAINE

Du Guesclin, 5 Place de la Gare, 35000. Tel: 99.31.47.47. At the town centre. CC: Amex, Diners, Visa. Rooms: FF300–340.

ROUEN: SEINE-MARITIME

De Dieppe ☆☆☆, Place Bernard-Tissot, 76000. Tel: 35.71.96.00. Convenient for the station, but quiet rooms. CC: Amex, Diners, Visa. Rooms: FF350–520.

du Gros Horloge ☆☆, 91 Rue du Gros Horloge. Tel: 35.70.41.41. Near the famous clock in the old part of town. Rooms: from FF150.

ST-BRIEUC: CÔTES-D'ARMOR

Ker Izel, 20 Rue du Gouët, 22000. Tel: 96.33.46.29. Centrally located. CC: Visa. Rooms: FF220–280.

ST-MALO: ILLE-ET-VILAINE

Elisabeth, 2 Rue des Cordiers, 35400. Tel: 99.56.24.98. One of the Châteaux-hôtels chain in the Ville Close. CC: Amex, Diners, Visa. Rooms: FF300–500.

ST-OMER: PAS-DE-CALAIS

Le Bretagne ☆☆, 2 Place du Vainquai, 62500. Tel: 21.38.25.78. Quiet and comfortable. CC: Amex, Visa. Rooms: FF220–420.

LE TOUQUET: PAS-DE-CALAIS

Manoir ☆☆☆, Avenue du Golf, 62520. Tel: 21.05.20.22. Popular with golfers. CC: Amex, Visa. Rooms: FF570–1,100.

VANNES: MORBIHAN

Manche-Océan ☆☆☆, 31 Rue du Lt. Col.-Maury, 56000. Tel: 97.47.26.46. One of the Inter-Hôtel chain. CC: Amex, Diners, Visa. Rooms: FF190–270.

EASTERN FRANCE & BURGUNDY

AUTUN: SAÔNE-ET-LOIRE

Hôtel Saint-Louis, 6 Rue de l'Arbalète, 71400. Tel: 85.52.21.03. Attractive old coaching inn. CC: Amex, Diners, Visa, Mastercard. Rooms: FF100–320.

AUXERRE: YONNE

Hôtel Normandie ☆☆, Boulevard Vauban, 89000. Tel: 86.52.57.80. Attractive hotel with small garden, near the centre. CC: Amex, Diners, Visa, Mastercard. Rooms: FF240–280.

BEAUNE: CÔTE-D'OR

Hôtel Central ☆☆☆, 2 Rue Victor Millot, 21200. Tel: 80.24.77.24. Central, comfortable and a good restaurant. CC: Visa, Mastercard. Rooms: FF400–450. Closed: January.

BESANÇON: DOUBS

Altea ☆☆☆, 3 Avenue E. Droz, 25000. Tel: 81.80.14.44. Modern chain hotel on the river. CC: Amex, Diners, Visa. Rooms: FF340–540.

BOURBONNE-LES-BAINS: HAUTE-MARNE

Les Lauriers Rose ☆☆, Place des Bains, 52400. Tel: 25.90.00.97. Closed: November–April. Rooms: FF115–320.

BOURG-EN-BRESSE: AIN

Hôtel Terminus ☆☆☆, 19 Rue A. Baudin, 01000. Tel: 74.21.01.21. Comfortable hotel, a completely renovated Napoléon III building, in lovely grounds. CC: Amex, Diners, Visa, Mastercard. Rooms: FF245–330.

CHABLIS: YONNE

Hostellerie des Clos ☆☆, 18 Rue Jules Rathier, 89800. Tel: 86.42.10.63. Pleasant rooms overlooking a garden. CC: Visa, Mastercard. Rooms: FF230–520.

CHALONS-SUR MARNE: MARNE

D'Angleterre ☆☆☆, 19 Place Mgr Tissier, 51000. Tel: 26.68.21.51. Small, elegant hotel. Rooms: FF380–600.

CHARLEVILLE-MÉZIÈRES: ARDENNES

Le Cleves ☆☆☆, 43 Rue de l'Arguebuse, 08000. Tel: 24.33.10.75. Centrally situated. CC: Amex, Diners, Visa. Rooms: FF225–370.

COLMAR: HAUT-RHIN

Terminus Bristol ☆☆☆, 7 Place de la Gare, 68000. Tel: 89.41.10.10. Central hotel with good restaurant, specialities fish and game. CC: Amex, Diners, Visa. Rooms: FF320–520.

COLOMBEY-LES-DEUX EGLISES: HAUTE-MARNE

Motel Les Dhuits ☆☆☆, on the RN 19, 52330. For pilgrims to de Gaulle's burial place. Rooms: FF220–380.

DIJON: CÔTE-D'OR

Urbis Central ☆☆, 3 Place Grangier, 21000. Tel: 80.30.44.00. Modernised rooms in old house; central with a good restaurant. CC: Amex, Diners, Visa, Mastercard. Rooms: F290–310.

Le Jacquemart ☆☆, 32 Rue Verrerie, 21000. Tel: 80.73.39.74. Friendly, inviting hotel in the old quarter. CC: Visa, Mastercard. Rooms: FF248–285.

EPERNAY: MARNE

St-Pierre, 1 Rue Jeanne-d'Arc, 51202. Tel: 26.54.40.80. Small, moderately-priced hotel, but good. Rooms: FF70–140.

GÉRARDMER: VOSGES

Bas-Rupts ☆☆☆, outside town on the D486, 88400. Tel: 29.63.09.25. In a peaceful mountain site, a hotel of the Relais du Silence chain. CC: Amex, Diners, Visa. Rooms: FF300–600.

LANGRES: HAUTE-MARNE

de l'Europe ☆☆, 23-25 Rue Diderot, 52200. Tel: 25.87.10.88. Fine old hotel with good traditional restaurant. CC: Amex, Diners, Visa. Rooms: FF125–310.

LUXEUIL-LES-BAINS: HAUTE-SAÔNE

Hôtel Beau Site ☆☆☆, 18 Rue Georges-Moulinard, 70302. Tel: 84.40.14.67. Spa hotel.

LYON: RHÔNE

Carlton, 4 Rue Jussieu, 69000. Tel: 78.42.56.51. A good central base. CC: Amex, Diners, Visa. Rooms: FF330–600.

Grand Hôtel des Beaux Arts, 73 Rue du Président-Herriot, 69000. Tel: 78.38.09.50. Set right between the Rhône and the Saône. CC: Amex, Diners. Rooms: FF330–560.

MÂCON: SAÔNE-ET-LOIRE

Terminus ☆☆, 91 Rue Victor-Hugo, 71000. Tel: 85.39.17.11. Boasts a swimming-pool and garden. CC: Amex, Diners, Visa, Mastercard. Rooms: FF252–270.

METZ: MOSELLE

Royal Concorde ☆☆☆, 23 Avenue Foch, 57000. Tel: 87.66.81.11. Old hotel with modern facilities. CC: Amex, Diners, Visa. Rooms: FF450–530.

MULHOUSE: HAUT-RHIN

Wir ☆☆, 1 Porte de Bâle, 68100. Tel: 89.56.13.22. Moderately priced rooms and a recommended restaurant. CC: Amex, Diners, Visa. Rooms: FF160–300.

NANCY: MEURTHE-ET-MOSELLE

Grand Hôtel de la Reine ☆☆☆☆, 2 Place Stanislas, 54000. Tel: 83.35.03.01. If you can't afford to stay here, just go to admire this listed building. CC: Amex, Diners, Visa. Rooms: FF500–1,000.

NEVERS: NIÈVRE

Château de la Rocherie ☆☆, on the RN7, 58000. Tel: 86.38.07.21. Small château in quiet setting; good food. CC: Amex, Diners, Visa, Mastercard. Rooms: FF160–300.

NOGENT-SUR-SEINE: AUBE

Beau-Rivage, 20 Rue Villers aux Choux, 10400. Tel: 25.39.84.22. Small hotel and restaurant. Rooms: FF95–180.

NUITS-SAINT-GEORGES: CÔTE-D'OR

Hostellerie la Gentilhommière ☆☆☆, Vallée de la Serrée, 21700. Tel: 80.61.12.06. Modern comfort with separate restaurant in a former hunting lodge. CC: Amex, Diners, Visa, Mastercard. Rooms: FF300.

ORNANS: DOUBS

De France ✩✩✩, 51-53 Rue P. Venier, 25290. The other side of the river from Impressionist Courbet's birthplace. Tel: 81.39.04.09.

REIMS: MARNE

Le Boyer Les Crayères ✩✩✩✩, 64 Boulevard Henri Vasnier, 51100. Tel: 26.82.80.80. Ultimate luxury in this Relais et Châteaux hotel and superb restaurant. CC: Amex, Diners, Visa. Rooms: FF990–1,790.

De la Paix, 9 Rue Buirette, 51100. Tel: 26.40.04.08. Less pricey, highly recommended and centrally situated. CC: Amex, Diners, Visa. Rooms: FF370–510.

ST-MÉNÉHOULD: MARNE

Le Cheval Rouge ✩✩, 1 Rue Chanzy, 51800. Tel: 26.60.81.04. Small hotel with own restaurant. Rooms: FF200–350.

SEDAN: ARDENNES

De l'Europe ✩✩, 5 Place de la Gare, 08200. Tel: 24.27.18.71. By the station. Rooms: FF170–230.

SENS: SENS

Hôtel de Paris et de la Poste ✩✩✩, 97 Rue de la République, 89100. Tel: 86.65.17.43, fax: 86.64.48.45; S8910PARI. Has a charming restaurant; or meals on the terrace. CC: Amex, Diners, Visa, Mastercard. Rooms: FF350–520.

STRASBOURG: BAS-RHIN

Hannong ✩✩✩, 15 Rue du 22-novembre, 67000. Tel: 88.32.16.22. Elegant old hotel, convenient for the old town, plus a good wine bar. CC: Amex, Diners, Visa. Rooms: FF330–480.

Monopole-Métropole ✩✩✩, 16 Rue Kuhn, 67000. Tel: 88.32.11.94. Handy for Petite France. CC: Amex, Diners, Visa. Rooms: FF350–550.

TROYES: AUBE

De la Poste ✩✩✩✩, 35 Rue Emile Zola, 10000. Tel: 25.73.05.05. Excellent accommodation. CC: Amex, Visa. Rooms: FF340–900.

VERDUN: MEUSE

Le Coq Hardi ✩✩✩, 8 Avenue de la Victoire, 55100. Tel: 29.86.36.36. The restaurant is recommended, but quite pricey. CC: Amex, Diners, Visa. Rooms: FF180–420.

HEART OF FRANCE

ANGOULÊME: CHARENTE

De Bordeaux, 236 Route de Bordeaux, 16000. Tel: 45.91.60.66. Pleasant hotel and restaurant. CC: Amex, Diners, Visa. Rooms: FF300–360.

ARCACHON: GIRONDE

Le Nautic ✩✩, 20 Boulevard de la Plage, 33120. Tel: 56.83.01.48. By the beach with panoramic views. Rooms: FF180–395.

AUBUSSON: CREUSE

de France ✩✩, 6 Rue des Déportés, 23200. Tel: 55.66.10.22. A family-run Logis de France. CC: most. Rooms: FF160–350.

AURILLAC: CANTAL

Grand Hôtel St-Pierre, Promenade du Gravier, 15000. Tel: 71.48.00.24. Good central hotel and pleasant restaurant. CC: Amex, Diners, Visa. Rooms: FF220–370.

BORDEAUX: GIRONDE

Le Bayonne ✩✩✩, 15 Cours de l'Intendance, 33000. Tel: 56.48.00.88. Situated in one of the most interesting quarters of the city. Rooms: FF330–370.

Grand Hotel Français, 12 Rue du Temple, 33000. Tel:56.48.10.35. Charming 18th-century mansion offering modern facilities and comfort. CC: Amex, Diners, Visa. Rooms: FF330–370.

BRIVE: CORRÈZE

La Truffe Noire ✩✩✩, 22 Boulevard Anatole-France, 19100. Tel: 55.92.45.00. Has a garden; restaurant specialises in local dishes. CC: most. Rooms: FF380–660.

Le Montauban ✩✩, 6 Avenue Edouard-Herriot, 19200. Tel: 55.24.00.38. A Logis de France hotel. CC: most. Rooms: FF140–220.

CAHORS: LOT

Le Terminus ✩✩✩, 5 Avenue Ch.-de-Freycinet, 46000. Tel: 65.35.24.50. Near the station with a good restaurant. CC: Amex, Visa. Rooms: FF185–300.

LA CELLE-DUNOISE: CREUSE

Hostllerie Pascaud ✩✩, 23800. Tel: 55.89.10.66. Central with lovely river views. CC: most. Rooms: FF120–170.

CLERMONT-FERRAND: PUY-DE-DÔME

Altea, 82 Boulevard Gergovia, 63000. Tel: 73.93.05.75. An attractive example of a chain hotel; mountain views. CC: Amex, Diners, Visa. Rooms: FF320–570.

COULON

Le Central ✩, 4 Rue d'Autremont, 79510 Coulon. Tel: 49.35.90.20. Charming little hotel at the heart of the Marais Poitevin. CC: Mastercard, Visa. Rooms: FF180.

LES EYZIES: DORDOGNE

Le Centenaire, Le Rocher de la Penne, 24620. Tel: 53.06.97.18. Well situated for sightseeing and with good facilities. Closed: November–31 March. CC: Visa. Rooms: FF370–520.

GOURDON: LOT

Le Bissonier ✩✩✩, 46300. Tel: 65.41.02.48. Logis de France in this attractive market town.

LIMOGES: HAUTE-VIENNE

De La Paix, 25 Place Jourdan, 87000. Tel: 55.34.36.00. The hotel is also a phonograph museum, with a good selection on view in the restaurant. CC: most. Rooms: FF180–300.

MARGAUX: GIRONDE

Relais de Margaux ✩✩✩✩, Chemin de l'Ile Vincent, 33460. Tel: 56.88.38.30. A luxury hotel in a lovely park right by the Château Margaux vineyard. Rooms: FF975–1,250.

MONT-DORÉ: PUY-DE-DÔME

Le Puy-Ferrand ✩✩, Pied du Sancy, 63240. Tel: 73.65.18.99. At the foot of the Puy Sancy, peaceful hotel with good amenities and own grounds. CC: Amex, Diners, Visa. Rooms: FF220–360.

MONTLUÇON: ALLIER
Grand Hôtel du Lion d'Or, 19 Rue Barathon, 03100. Tel: 70.05.00.62. Own restaurant.

MOULINS: ALLIER
de Paris, 21 Rue de Paris, 03000. Tel: 70.44.00.58. Attractive hotel and a good restaurant. CC: Amex, Diners, Visa. Rooms: FF300–720.

NIEUL: HAUTE-VIENNE
La Chapelle St-Martin, 87510. Tel: 55.75.80.17. A Relais et Châteaux hotel just outside Limoges, swimming-pool. CC: most. Rooms: FF620–1,350.

NOTH: CREUSE
Château de la Cazine ✩✩✩, La Souterraine, 23300. Tel: 55.89.61.11. Lovely pink brick hotel near Guéret; own grounds and swimming-pool. CC: most. Rooms: FF360–1,020.

PEYRAT-LE-CHÂTEAU: HAUTE-VIENNE
Auberge du Bois de l'Etang ✩, 38 Avenue de la Tour, 887470. Tel: 55.69.40.19. An attractive, moderately-priced Logis de France. CC: most. Rooms: FF125–250.

POMPADOUR: CORRÈZE
Auberge de la Marquise ✩✩, Avenue des Ecuyers, 19320. Tel: 55.73.33.98. Logis de France with own garden. CC: most. Rooms: FF230–275.

ROCAMADOUR: LOT
Ste-Marie ✩✩, Place des Shenais, 46500. Tel: 65.33.63.07. Closed: November–March. CC: Visa.

LA ROCHELLE: CHARENTE-MARITIME
Le Champlain ✩✩✩, 20 Rue Rambaud, 17000. Tel: 46.41.23.99. Lovely old hotel with garden. CC: Amex, Diners, Visa. Rooms: FF300–450.

ROYAN: CHARENTE-MARITIME
Grand Hôtel ✩✩✩, 195 Avenue de Pontaillac, 17200. Tel: 46.39.00.44. Practically on the beach, with its own garden. CC: Visa. Rooms: FF300–420.

ST-CIRQ-LAPOPIE: LOT
Auberge du Sombral ✩✩, 46330. Tel: 65.31.26.08. Country inn. CC: Visa. Rooms: FF200–320.

ST-EMILION: GIRONDE
Auberge de la Commanderie ✩✩, Rue des Cordeliers, 33330. Tel: 57.24.70.19. Family atmosphere and good food at the heart of the medieval town. Rooms: FF180–320.

SAINTES: CHARENTE-MARITIME
Le Bois St-Georges ✩✩✩, Rue de Royan-Cours Genêt, 17100. Tel: 46.93.50.99. A Relais et Silence hotel in a charming setting. CC: Visa. Rooms: FF300–920.

TULLE: CORRÈZE
Le Limouzi ✩✩✩, 16 Quai de la République, 19000. Tel: 55.26.42.00. Centrally situated with attractive restaurant. CC: most. Rooms: FF190–210.

UZERCHE: CORRÈZE
Hôtel Teyssier ✩✩, Pont Turgot, 19140. Tel: 55.73.10.05. Attractive old hotel near the centre. CC: most. Rooms: FF145–290.

VICHY: ALLIER
Regina ✩✩✩, 4 Avenue Thermale, 03200. Tel: 70.97.53.77. Well-sited old hotel with own garden. CC: Amex, Visa. Rooms: FF250–520.

AIRE-SUR-L'ADOUR: LANDES
Chez l'Ahumat, 2 Rue des Ecoles, 40800. Tel: 58.71.82.61. Simple hotel with good value restaurant. CC: Visa. Rooms: FF90–145.

ALBI: TARN
Chiffre ✩✩✩, 50 Rue Séré-de-Rivières, 81000. Tel: 63.54.04.60. Good, central hotel. CC: Amex, Diners, Visa. Rooms: FF270–430.

AMÉLIE-LES-BAINS: PYRÉNÉES-ORIENTALES
Le Roussillon ✩✩, Avenue Beausoleil, 66110. Tel: 68.39.34.39. Has its own garden and swimming-pool. Rooms: FF220–240.

ARGELÈS-GAZOST: HAUTES-PYRÉNÉES
Le Reais ✩✩, 25 Rue du Maréchal-Foch, 65400. Tel: 62.97.01.27. Good mountain views and enticing restaurant. CC: Visa. Rooms: FF150–250.

AUCH: GERS
de France ✩✩✩✩, Place de la Libération, 32000. Tel: 62.05.00.44. A Relais et Châteaux establishment on the main square, run by the county's most notable chef, André Daguin. CC: Amex, Diners, Visa. Rooms: FF300–1,150.

AX-LES-THERMES: ARIÈGE
Des Pyrénées, 09110. Tel: 61.64.21.01. A family-run Logis de France hotel.

BAGNÈRES-DE-BIGORRE: HAUTES-PYRÉNÉES
Le Florida ✩✩, 65200. Tel: 62.95.03.84. A convenient base for sight-seeing; sports facilities include tennis, swimming and golf.

BAGNÈRES-DE-LUCHON: HAUTE-GARONNE
Bellevue, 31110. Tel: 61.79.01.65. A Logis de France, closed: November and December.

BAYONNE: PYRÉNÉES-ATLANTIQUES
Aux Deux Rivières, 21 Rue Thiers, 64100. Tel: 59.59.14.61. Central hotel. CC: Amex, Diners, Visa. Rooms: FF350–550.

BIARRITZ: PYRÉNÉES-ATLANTIQUES
Régina et Golf ✩✩✩, 52 Avenue de l'Impératrice, 64200. Tel: 59.41.33.00. Fine hotel with sea views and excellent facilities. CC: Amex, Diners, Visa. Rooms: FF530–1,300.

BISCAROSSE PLAGE: LANDES
Océan Hôtel ✩✩, 99 Avenue des Iris, 40600. Tel: 58.78.27.27. Has a tennis court. Rooms: FF280–350.

CAPBRETON: LANDES
Aquitaine ✩✩, 66 Avenue de Lattre de Tassigny, 40130. Tel: 58.72.38.11. Has a swimming-pool. Rooms: FF170–270.

CANET-EN-ROUSSILLON; PYRÉNÉES-ORIENTALES
St-Georges ✩✩, 45 Promenade Côte Vermeille, 66140. Tel: 68.80.33.77. Resort hotel with own swimming-pool. Rooms: FF160–300.

CARCASSONNE: AUDE
Montmorency ✩✩, 2 Rue Camille St-Saëns, 11000. Tel; 68.25.19.92. A good base for exploring the old Cité; has a garden and swimming-pool. CC: Amex, Diners, Visa. Rooms: FF220–320.

CASTRES: TARN

L'Occitan ☆☆☆, 81100. Tel: 63.35.34.20. A Logis de France hotel with swimming-pool, tennis and golf.

CONDOM: GERS

des Trois Lys ☆☆☆, 32100. Tel: 62.28.33.33. Renovated hotel just down the road from the cathedral, with swimming-pool and tennis court.

CONQUES: AVEYRON

Sainte-Foy ☆☆☆, Rue Principale, 12320. Tel: 65.69.84.03. Stands in its own garden near the abbey. CC: Amex, Visa. Rooms: FF300–350.

CORDES: TARN

Du Vieux Cordes ☆☆☆, 81170. Tel: 63.56.00.12. A well-equipped Logis in a charming old building, plus a good restaurant. CC: Amex, Diners, Visa. Rooms: FF270–420.

DAX: LANDES

Du Parc ☆☆☆, Place Thiers, BP 76, 40100. Tel: 58.56.79.79. By the river; popular with curistes. CC: Amex, Diners, Visa. Rooms: FF280–430.

EUGÉNIE-LES-BAINS: LANDES

Les Prés d'Eugénie ☆☆☆☆, 40320. Tel: 58.05.06.07. The famous establishment of master chef, Michel Guérard. CC: Amex, Diners, Visa. Rooms: FF1,000–1,4000.

FOIX: ARIÈGE

Pyrène ☆☆☆, on the RN 20, south of town, 09000. Tel: 61.65.48.66. Boasts a swimming-pool and tennis court. CC: Visa. Rooms: FF240–330.

GAVARNIE: HAUTES-PYRÉNÉES

des Voyageurs ☆, 65120. Tel: 62.92.48.01. Stands in its own grounds with swimming-pool and tennis court.

LOURDES: HAUTES-PYRÉNÉES

Galilée-Windsor ☆☆☆, 10 Avenue Peyramale, 65100. Tel: 62.94.21.55. Good sporting facilities in this large hotel next to the holy grotto. CC: Amex, Visa. Rooms: FF420.

MIMIZAN: LANDES

Au Bon Coin ☆☆☆, 34 Avenue du Lac, 40200. Tel: 58.09.40.84. By the lake, away from the bustle of the beach. CC: Amex, Visa. Rooms: FF480–560.

MONTAUBAN: TARN-ET-GARONNE

Mapotel Ingres ☆☆☆, 10 Avenue de Mayenne, 82000. Tel: 63.63.36.01. A Best Western hotel, well situated. CC: Amex, Diners, Visa. Rooms: FF280–420.

NARBONNE: AUDE

Du Languédoc ☆☆☆, 22 Boulevard Gambetta, 11100. Tel: 68.65.14.74. A good hotel of the Mapotel chain. CC: Amex, Diners, Visa. Rooms: FF190–400.

PAU: PYRÉNÉES-ATLANTIQUES

Continental ☆☆☆, 2 Rue du Maréchal-Foch, 64000. Tel: 59.27.69.31. Smart hotel near the centre. CC: Amex, Diners, Visa. Rooms: FF300–500.

PERPIGNAN: PYRÉNÉES-ORIENTALES

Climat de France ☆☆, 170 Guynemer, R.P. Kennedy, 66000. Tel: 68.66.00.00. Large, comfortable, good value chain hotel. Rooms: FF290.

ST-JEAN-DE-LUZ: PYRÉNÉES-ATLANTIQUES

Chantaco ☆☆☆☆, Golf de Chantaco, 64500. Tel: 59.26.14.76. Luxurious amenities in a beautiful Spanish-style building. Good restaurant. CC: Amex, Diners, Visa. Rooms: FF750–2,000.

ST-JEAN-PIED-DE-PORT: PYRÉNÉES-ATLANTIQUES

Les Pyrénées ☆☆, 19 Place Charles-de-Gaulle, 64220. Tel: 59.37.01.01. Mountain views, fine restaurant, garden, swimming-pool – what more could you ask? CC: Amex. Rooms: FF500–770.

ST-LARY-SOULAIN: HAUTES-PYRÉNÉES

Altea Christal Parc ☆☆☆, 65170. Tel: 62.99.50.00. Well-equipped chain hotel in this popular skiing resort.

TOULOUSE: HAUTE-GARONNE

Grand Hôtel de l'Opéra ☆☆☆☆, Place du Capitole, 31000. Tel: 61.21.82.66. Elegant hotel with a fine restaurant at the heart of the old city. CC: Amex, Diners, Visa. Rooms: FF450–1,200.

du Clocher de Rodez ☆☆, 14 Place Jeanne-d'Arc, 31000. Tel: 61.62.42.92. Old established hotel and restaurant. CC: Amex, Diners, Visa. Rooms: FF200–330.

ALPS

ALLEVARD: ISÈRE

Les Pervenches ☆☆, Route de Grenoble, 38580. Tel: 76.97.50.73. A hotel of the Relais de Silence chain, so peaceful. CC: most. Rooms: FF250–320.

ALBERTVILLE: SAVOIE

Le Roma, on the RN 90, 73200. Tel: 79.37.15.56. Modern and efficient. CC: Amex, Diners, Visa. Rooms: FF280–420.

AIX-LES-BAINS: SAVOIE

Le Manoir ☆☆☆, 37 Rue George 1er, 73100. Tel: 79.61.44.00. A comfortable hotel and restaurant in the Relais du Silence group. CC: Diners, Visa. Rooms: FF300–500.

L'ALPE-D'HUEZ: ISÈRE

La Christina ☆☆☆, Rue Maurice Pajon, 38750. Tel: 76.80.33.32. Good views and a tennis court. CC: most. Rooms: FF512–678.

ANNECY: HAUTE-SAVOIE

Le Belvédère ☆☆ Chemin du Belvédère, 74000. Tel: 50.45.04.90. Offers wonderful views of the lake and superb restaurant. CC: Visa. Rooms: FF150–350.

BRIANÇON: HAUTES-ALPES

Le Mont-Porel ☆☆, 5 Rue R.-Froger, 05100. Tel: 92.20.22.88. Small hotel, convenient for the ski lift. CC: Amex, Diners, Visa. Rooms: FF250–320.

CHAMBÉRY: SAVOIE

Prince Eugène de Savoie, Esplanade Curial, 73000. Tel: 79.85.06.07. Stylish hotel, set in its own garden. CC: Amex, Diners, Visa. Rooms: FF280–510.

CHAMONIX: HAUTE-SAVOIE

Auberge du Bois Prin ☆☆☆☆, 69 Chemin de l'Hermine, Les Moussoux, 74400. Tel: 50.53.33.51. High class by friendly hotel with good restaurant. CC: Amex, Diners, Visa. Rooms: FF630–1,200.

DIVONNE-LES-BAINS: AIN
Château de Divonne ☆☆☆☆, 01220. Tel: 50.20.00.32. Delightful mansion, convenient for Divonne and Geneva; good mountain views. Rooms: FF450–1,100.

GAP: HAUTES-ALPES
Clos ☆☆, 20ter, Avenue Cdt-Dumont, 05000. Tll: 92.51.37.04. In a quiet spot with good views and a garden. CC: Visa. Rooms: from around FF250.

GRENOBLE: ISÈRE
D'Angleterre ☆☆☆, 5 Place Victor-Hugo, 38000. Tel: 76.87.37.21. CC: Amex, Diners, Visa. Rooms: FF460–540.

MÉGÈVE: HAUTE-SAVOIE
Au-Vieux Moulin ☆☆☆, Rue Ambroise-Martine, 74120. Tel: 50.21.22.29. Traditional Alpine hotel and restaurant with a swimming-pool. Rooms: FF350–670.

MONTÉLIMAR: DRÔME
Relais de l'Empereur ☆☆☆, 1 Place Max Dormoy, 26200. Tel: 75.01.29.00. Centrally situated hotel and restaurant. CC: Amex, Diners, Visa. Rooms: FF330–470.

NANTUA: AIN
De l'Embarcadère, Avenue du Lac. 01130. Tel: 74.75.22.88. Modern hotel and restaurant right by the lake. Rooms: FF250.

TIGNES: SAVOIE
Le Ski d'Or, Val Claret, 73320. Tel: 79.06.51.60. A member of the Relais and Châteaux group, with a good restaurant. CC: Visa. Rooms: FF720–920.

VAL-D'ISÈRE
Christiana ☆☆☆☆, 73150. Tel: 79.06.08.25. Luxurious hotel with great views. CC: Visa. Rooms: FF1,000–1,400.

VALENCE: DRÔME
du Grand St-Jacques, 9 Faubourg St-Jacques, 26000. Tel: 75.42.44.60. Rooms from around FF200.

VILLARD-DE-LANS: ISÈRE
Le Pré-Fleuri ☆☆, Avenue Albert Pietri, 38250. Tel: 79.95.10.96. Quiet hotel set in a garden. CC: most. Rooms: FF330–340.

PROVENCE & COTE D'AZUR

AIGUÈS-MORTES: GARD
St-Louis ☆☆☆, 10 Rue Amiral Courbet, 30220. Tel: 66.53.72.68. Closed: January to mid-March. Rooms: FF375–395.

ALÈS: GARD
Orly ☆☆, 10 Rue d'Avejan, 30100. Tel: 66.52.43.27. Moderately priced accommodation. CC: Amex, Diners, Visa. Rooms FF200.

ANTIBES: ALPES-MARITIMES
Mas de la Pagane, 15 Avenue du Mas-Ensoleillé, 06600. Tel: 93.33.33.78. Attractive old farmhouse in central position. CC: Visa. Rooms: FF250–450.

ARLES: BOUCHES-DU-RHÔNE
D'Arlatan ☆☆☆☆, 26 Rue du Sauvage, 13200. Tel: 90.93.56.66. An extremely old house, the former mansion of the Counts of Arlatan de Beaumont. CC: Amex, Diners, Visa. Rooms: FF420–630.

AVIGNON: VAUCLUSE
Cité des Papes ☆☆☆, 1 Rue J.-Villar, 84000. Tel: 90.86.22.45. Well sited near the former Papal Palace. CC: Amex, Diners, Visa. Rooms: FF280–460.

BEAULIEU-SUR-MER: ALPES-MARITIMES
La Réserve de Beaulieu, 5 Boulevard Leclerc, 06310. Tel: 93.01.00.01. Luxurious villa on the coast with private beach and swimming-pool. CC: Amex, Diners, Visa. Rooms: FF700–2,400.

BÉZIERS: HÉRAULT
Splendid ☆☆, 24 Avenue du 22-aout, 34500. Tel: 67.28.23.82. No restaurant. Rooms: FF250.

CAGNES-SUR-MER: ALPES-MARITIMES
Le Cagnard, Rue du Pontis-Long, 06800. Tel: 93.20.73.21. Charming hotel near Grimaldi castle, a member of the Relais and Châteaux group. CC: Amex, Diners, Visa. Rooms: FF320–1,300.

CANNES: ALPES-MARITIMES
Carlton Intercontinental, 58 Boulevard Croisette, 06322. Tel: 93.68.91.68. Famous waterfront luxury hotel. CC: Amex, Diners, Mastercard, Visa. Rooms: FF2,000–3,500.

EZE: ALPES-MARITIMES
Château Eza, 06360. Tel: 93.41.12.24. Accessible only on foot (baggage transported by donkey), this wonderful old castle has superb views and antique furnishings. CC: Amex, Diners, Visa. Rooms: FF1,000–3,500.

CAP D'AGDE: HÉRAULT
St-Clair ☆☆☆, Place St-Clair, 34300. Tel: 67.26.36.44. Hotel/restaurant with good amenities, including swimming-pool and tennis. CC: Visa. Rooms: FF390–550.

FRÉJUS: VAR
Résidence du Colombier ☆☆☆, Route de Bagnols, 83600. Tel: 94.51.45.92. More like a motel with rooms in bungalows. CC: Amex, Diners, Visa. Rooms: FF340–500.

GRIMAUD: VAR
La Boulangerie, Route de Collobrières, 83310. Tel: 94.43.23.16. Simple comfort in the Maures hills with a swimming-pool. CC: Visa. Rooms: FF250–300.

JUAN-LES-PINS: ALPES-MARITIMES
Belles Rives, Boulevard Baudoin, Juan-les-Pins, 06160. Tel: 93.61.02.79. Former home of Scott and Zelda Fitzgerald on the edge of the town. CC: Amex, Diners, Mastercard, Visa. Rooms: FF800–2,500.

MARSEILLE: BOUCHES-DU-RHÔNE
Novotel Pharo, 36 Boulevard Ch.-Livon, 13000. Tel: 91.59.22.22. Modern, comfortable hotel, convenient for sightseeing around the old port district. CC: Amex, Diners, Visa. Rooms: FF480–550.

MENDE: LOZÈRE
Urbain V ☆☆, 9 Boulevard Théophile-Roussel, 48000. Tel: 66.49.14.49. Good-sized hotel with a restaurant. CC: Amex, Visa. Rooms: FF310.

MENTON: ALPES-MARITIMES

Chambord ☆☆☆, 6 Avenue Boyer, 06500. Tel: 93.35.94.19. Well situated, just off the Promeande de Soleil. CC: Amex, Diners, Visa. Rooms: FF350–470.

MONACO

Hermitage, Square Beaumarchais. Monaco. Tel: 93.50.67.31. Beautiful Edwardian architecture offering comfortable rooms. CC: Amex, Diners, Mastercard, Visa. Rooms: FF1,000–2,800.

Paris, Place du Casino, Monaco. Tel: 93.50.80.90. Monaco's most famous luxury hotel. CC: ???most. Rooms: FF1,400–2,800.

MONTPELLIER: HÉRAULT

Demeure des Brousses ☆☆☆, Route de Vaugières, 34000. Tel: 67.65.77.66. Has a swimming-pool and good food in an old farmhouse restaurant. CC: Amex, Diners. Rooms: FF390–610.

NICE: ALPES-MARITIMES

Négresco, 37 Promedande des Anglais, 06000. Tel: 93.88.39.51. Furnished with antiques and dominating the Baie des Anges. CC: Amex, Diners, Mastercard, Visa. Rooms: FF1,200–2,200.

Windsor, 11 Rue Dalpozzo, 06000. Tel: 93.88.59.35. Moderately priced, but central. CC: Amex, Diners, Mastercard, Visa. Rooms: FF375–600.

NÎMES: GARD

Les Tuileries ☆☆☆, 22 Rue Roussy, 30000. Tel: 66.21.31.15. Small hotel without a restaurant. Rooms: FF370.

ST-JEAN-CAP-FERRAT: ALPES-MARITIMES

Brise Marine, 58 Avenue Jean Mermoz, 06230. Tel: 93.76.04.36. Small hotel with some rooms overlooking the sea; attractive terraced garden. CC: Visa. Rooms: FF250–600.

ST-TROPEZ: VAR

Le Yaca, 1 Boulevard d'Aumale, 83990. Tel: 94.97.11.79. A lovely old Provençal residence in the town with a swimming-pool and garden. CC: Amex, Diners, Visa. Rooms: FF850–1,1650.

STE-ENIMIE: LOZÈRE

Du Commerce ☆☆, 48210. Tel: 66.48.50.01. Situated right on the River Tarn, with a private beach. CC: Amex, Visa.

SÈTE: HÉRAULT

Impérial ☆☆☆, Place E. Herriot, La Corniche, 34200. Tel: 67.53.28.32. A Mapotel by the sea. Rooms: FF385–450.

VENCE: ALPES-MARITIMES

La Roseraie, Avenue Henri-Giraud, 06140. Tel: 93.58.02.20. Small friendly hotel in a 1930s villa with a pretty garden and swimming-pool. CC: Amex, Visa. Rooms: FF250–400.

BED & BREAKFAST

Bed and breakfast accommodation is available in much of France (mostly in rural areas) in private houses, often on working farms, whose owners are members of the Fédération Nationale des Gîtes Ruraux de France.

This means that the accommodation is inspected by a local representative of the Fédération to ensure that standards are maintained in accordance with its "☆" rating (which in fact is shown by ears of corn on a scale of one to four). They can be booked for an overnight stop or a longer stay. Breakfast is included in the price (from around FF120 for one person, FF180 for a couple) and evening meals – usually made with local produce and extremely good value – are often available.

Staying with a family in this way provides an ideal opportunity really to get to know the local area and its people. A brochure of all recognised Gîtes-Chambres d'hôtes is available from regional tourist offices and some are bookable through the Gîtes de France office in London (*see Self-Catering*).

B&B Abroad, offer a straightforward bed and breakfast service which can include ferry bookings if desired. They will book accommodation at your chosen destination and overnight stops en route. Contact: 5 Worlds End Lane, Green St Green, Orpington, Kent BR6 6AA. Tel: (0689) 855538.

Café-Couette is a Paris-based organisation offering B&B, or as they call it, *Hébergement chez l'habitant*. Contact them at 8 Rue de l'Isly, 75008 Paris. Tel: (1) 42.94.92.00, fax: (1) 42.94.93.12.

Bed and Breakfast 1 is a similar operation run by two young Parisians, offering accommodation in more than 300 homes in the capital. They operate from 7 Rue Campagne Première, 75014 Paris. Tel: (1) 43.35.11.26, fax: (1) 40.47.69.20.

For B&B on a slightly grander scale, try **Château Accueil**. This is a group of owners of some 70 private châteaux who offer luxury accommodation and usually evening meals in their own homes. Information from Marquis de Chénerilles, Président, Château de Gerfaut, 37190 Azay-le-Rideau. Tel: 47.45.40.16, fax: 47.45.20.15. Reservations are made through Concept Service, 6 Rue du Général-Leclerc, 93310 Saint-Ouen-L'Aumone. Tel: (1) 34.64.51.30, fax: (1) 34.64.63.32.

They can also be booked in the UK through **Château Welcome**, PO Box 66, 94 Bell Street, Henley on Thames RG9 1XS, tel: 0491-578803; or in Canada through Tours Chanteclerc, 65 Rue de Brésoles, Montréal, Québec H2Y 1V7, tel: 514-845 1236; and at 100 Adelaide Street West, Toronto, Ontario M11 1S3. Tel: 416-867 1595.

Châteaux en Vacances offer a similar service, but guests have to stay for at least two days and booking and payment must be made in advance. For further details contact FIPE/Châteaux en Vacances, BP4, 78220 Viroflay. Tel: (1) 30.24.18.16, fax: (1) 42.65.14.42.

Also operating just in the Loire Valley and western France is **La Vie de Château**, a group of 140 private owners of châteaux and manor houses who welcome paying guests. Information from La Vie de Château, 9 Rue Henri-Pape, 75013 Paris. Tel: (1) 45.80.01.01, fax: (1) 45.65.94.14. Book through B & D de Vogue Tours SARL at the same address, tel:

(1) 05.00.51.47 (toll-free in France), fax: (1) 45.61.94.14.

If you do not wish to book anything in advance, just look out for signs along the road (usually in the country) offering *chambres-d'hôtes*. You will be taking pot luck, but you may be delighted by the simple farm food and accommodation on offer.

SELF CATERING

France has what is probably Europe's best network of self-catering holiday cottages. The **Fédération des Gîtes Ruraux de France** was set up around 40 years ago with the aim of restoring rural properties (by means of offering grants to owners) on the condition that these properties would then be let as cheap holiday homes for the less well-heeled town and city dwellers. These *gîtes* (literally: a place to lay one's head) have now become extremely popular with the British in particular, as an inexpensive way of enjoying a rural holiday in France. The properties range from very simple farm cottages to grand manor houses and even the odd château.

The properties are all inspected by the Relais Départemental des Gîtes Ruraux de France (the county office of the national federation) and given an *épi* (ear of corn) classification. The *gîtes* are completely self-catering (in many cases expect to supply your own bedlinen), but most have owners living nearby who will tell you where to buy local produce (and if on a farm, often provide it). One salutary note: many of these cottages are on farms, and as such, are surrounded by wildlife so if you are squeamish about the odd mouse in the kitchen, stay in a hotel. But the properties should be, and generally are, kept clean and in good order.

Many *gîtes* are rather off the beaten track and a car, or at least a bicycle is usually essential. Bicycles can often be hired locally or sometimes from *gîte* owners. Car hire is expensive, but some fly/drive packages still make this a relatively inexpensive way to visit the region, as gîtes can cost as little as FF1,000 a week for the whole house.

Gîtes can get heavily booked in high season, so start the process in the New Year. If you wish to deal directly with France, contact the Maison des Gîtes de France, 35 Rue Godot-de-Mauroy, 75009 Paris. Tel: (1) 47.42.20.20, fax: (1) 47.42.73.11. They will provide addresses of the individual Relais Départementaux who each produce a list of all the *gîtes* in their *département*. Alternatively, you can book through the London booking office: Gîtes de France, 178 Piccadilly, W1V 9DB. Tel: 071-493 3480. For a £3 membership you have the choice of hundreds of *gîtes* all over France.

The main ferry companies also offer *gîte* holidays in association with the Gîtes de France office in London – apply to the ferry companies for their brochures (*see Getting There* for addresses). Many other tour operators and private individuals also offer self-catering accommodation, ranging from a simple farm cottage to an apartment in a luxurious château. Sometimes these properties are official *gîtes* and so have to conform to the Féderation's standards, but others are not subject to any form of inspection at all.

CAMPING

There is a good choice of campsites in France, many of them situated near lakes or rivers. The Regional tourist offices (*see Useful Addresses*) each produce their own lists of all recognised sites, with details of ☆-rating and facilities.

As with other types of holiday accommodation, the sites can get booked up in high season, so do consider advance booking. Members of the Camping Club or Camping and Caravanning Club of Great Britain may make use of their booking services. The Michelin Camping/Caravanning Guide lists sites which accept (or insist on) pre-booking.

The Camping Service at 69 Westbourne Grove, London W2 4UJ, tel: 071-792 1944, can book sites either from their own brochure of ☆☆☆ and ☆☆☆☆ sites or certain others and will also book ferries. A camping *carnet* is useful (some sites will not accept a booking without one).

Campsites, like hotels have official classifications from ☆ (minimal comfort, water points, showers and sinks) to ☆☆☆☆ luxury sites with more space to each pitch, and offer above-average facilities, often including a restaurant or takeway food, games areas and swimming-pools. The majority of sites nationwide are ☆☆. Average prices are around FF12 per person per night at a ☆ site, to around FF22 at a ☆☆☆☆ site.

If you really like to get back to nature, and are unimpressed by the modern trappings of hot water and electric power, look out for camp-sites designated "Aire naturelle de camping" where facilities will be absolutely minimal and prices to match. These have a maximum of 25 pitches so offer the opportunity to stay away from some of the more commercial sites (which can be huge).

The FFCC Guide (*see Useful Publications & Addresses*) lists over 2,000 such sites nationwide.

Some farms offer "official" sites too under the auspices of the Fédération Nationale des Gîtes Ruraux (*see Self-Catering*) – these are designated *Camping à la ferme*, again facilities are usually limited but farmers are only allowed to have six pitches and if you are lucky you will get to know and enjoy the farm life and some of its produce.

Another option, currently becoming popular on some sites, are wooden huts which are rather more attractive than caravans, but offer the same sort of facilities. For details of sites and rentals contact Huttes de France, tel: 73.34.18.48.

Packaged camping holidays are now very popular with British holidaymakers and ideal for other overseas visitors too, as all the camping paraphernalia is provided on the site – you only have to take

K P M

KÖNIGLICHE
PORZELLAN
MANUFAKTUR
Berlin

BERLIN MASTERPIECES

ROCAILLE,
Breslauer Stadtschloß
The unusual reliefs and
opulent embellishments
of this rococo design
places extremely high
demands on the artistic
abilities of the craftsmen.

SCHINKEL Basket
Design: app. 1820
by Karl Friedrich Schinkel.

KURLAND, *pattern 73*
The first classicistic service
made by KPM was created
around 1790 by order of
the Duke of Kurland.

KPM BERLIN · Wegelystraße 1 · Kurfürstendamm 26a · Postal address: Postfach 12 21 07, D-10591 Berlin · Phone
(030) 390 09 - 226 · Fax (030) 390 09 - 279 · U. K. AGENCY · Exclusif Presentations, Ltd. · 20 Vancouver Road
Edgware, Middx. HA8 5DA · Phone (081) 952 46 79 · Fax (081) 951 09 39 · JAPAN AGENCY · Hayashitok Co., Ltd.
Nakano-Cho. Ogawa. Marutamachi · Nakagyo-Ku. Kyoto 604 · Phone (075) 222 02 31 / 231 22 22 · Fax (075) 256 45 54

Our history could fill this book, but we prefer to fill glasses.

When you make a great beer, you don't have to make a great fuss.

your personal luggage. Many companies now offer this type of holiday, mostly with ferry travel included in the all-in price. Like other package tours, the companies have couriers on the sites to help with any problems.

It is interesting to note that where such companies have taken over sections of existing sites, that facilities have improved to meet the demands of their customers and so benefit all campers. Many companies offer good opportunities for sports and leisure, such as wind-surfing or surfing; often the equipment, and sometimes instruction too is covered by the cost of the package. Be warned, though, that some of the sites are very large, so might not suit those who wish to get away from it all.

CAMPING VAN HIRE

Motorhomes or camper vans can be hired and picked up in France at many locations. Contact the Caravan and Camping Service, 69 Westbourne Grove, London W2 4UJ. Tel: 071-792 1944. Some Hertz hire offices also have them available. Also try in France:
Bourgogne Evasion, Garage Moderne SA, 156 Avenue de la République, BP 30, 71210 Montchanin. Tel: 85.78.52.11.
Bidaut Caravanes, Route de Dijon, 39100 Sampans. Tel: 84.82.09.50, fax: 84.82.60.32.

USEFUL PUBLICATIONS & ADDRESSES

The French Federation of Camping and Caravanning Guide (FFCC), lists 11,300 sites nationwide, and also shows which have facilities for disabled campers. Available from Springdene, Shepherd's Way, Fairlight, E. Sussex TN35 4BB. Price £7.95.
Michelin Green Guide – Camping/Caravanning France. Very informative and also lists sites with facilities for the disabled. Published annually in March, £5.95.
Camping and Caravanning Club, 11 Lower Grosvenor Place, London SW1.
Caravan Club, East Grinstead House, East Grinstead, Sussex RH19 1UA.

YOUTH HOSTELS

Holders of accredited Youth Hostel Association cards may stay in any French hostels which are in fact run by two separate organisations; Fédération Unie des Auberges de Jeunesse (FUAJ), 27 Rue Pajol, 75018 Paris, tel: (1) 46.07.00.01, fax: (1) 46.07.93.10 which is affiliated to the International Youth Hostel Federation; and the Ligue Française pour les Auberges de Jeunesse (LFAJ), 38 Boulevard Raspail, 75007 Paris, tel: (1) 45.48.69.84. Expect to pay around FF60 per night.

The British **YHA** publishes the *International Youth Hostel Handbook, Vol. I* (revised each March), which includes all the hostels in the region, price £5.99 by post from Youth Hostel Association, 14 Southampton Street, London WC2E 7H7. Tel: 071-836 8541. They also handle membership queries. Tel: 071-836 1036.

In the US apply to the **American Youth Hostels Inc**, PO Box 37613, Dept USA, Washington DC 20013/7613. Tel: 202-783 6161.

Gîtes d'Etapes offer hostel accommodation and are popular with ramblers, climbers and horse riders (some offer stabling). All official *Gîtes d'Étapes* come under the auspices of the Relais Départementaux des Gîtes Ruraux. These are a popular form of cheap accommodation particularly in the national parks. Prices are similar to youth hostels – around FF50 per night for basic accommodation, but up to FF110 or more in the more luxurious establishments which may be on farms offering riding facilities and/or stabling. You do not have to be a member of any organisation to use them.

FOOD DIGEST

France enjoys a reputation throughout the world for its fine cuisine and good wine. Indeed, the French pay very serious attention to their food and it is only recently that fast foods have started to creep into French supermarkets, and on to the high streets. It may be argued, however, that the French have always enjoyed convenience foods provided by their splendid *traiteurs* and *charcutiers*. Visit a delicatessen (*charcuterie*) and pick a selection of their prepared dishes for a delicious picnic.

Each region of France has its own specialities: the creamy sauces of Normandy, the traditional confits of duck and goose in the southwest, choucroute in the east, coq au vin in Burgundy and wonderful seafood all around the coast. In Paris, you will find restaurants serving dishes from all over the country, as well as ethnic food, particularly from North Africa and Indo-China.

Some of the most famous and popular restaurants in Paris are listed below, as well as some more homely, moderately priced establishments that offer good traditional cuisine, without the frills.

TOP-CLASS RESTAURANTS

Expect to pay around FF500 per head à la carte. **La Coupole**, 102 Boulevard du Montparnasse, 75014. Tel: (1) 43.20.14.20. Ever-popular cavernous hall in art deco style. Serves good *choucroute*, *steak au poivre* and huge platters of seafood.

La Closerie des Lilas, 171 Boulevard Montparnasse, 75006. Tel: (1) 43.26.70.50. Once the haunt of Joyce and Hemingway and still popular with artists and intellectuals.

Drouant, Place Gaillon, 75002. Tel: (1) 42.65.15.16. Art deco style meeting place of the Paris literary set.

Le Fouquet's, 99 Avenue des Champs-Elysées, 75008. Tel: (1) 47.23.70.60. Very trendy; mingle with the "in" crowd of Paris.

Le Grand Vefour, 17 Rue du Beaujolais, 75001. Tel: (1) 42.96.56.27. Admire the magnificent ceiling and the view of the Palais-Royal gardens.

Maxim's, 3 Rue Royale, 75008. Tel: (1) 42.65.27.94. One of France's most famous restaurants which aims to recreate the atmosphere of the *belle époque.*

Le Procope, 13 Rue de l'Ancienne Comédie, 75006. Tel: (1) 43.26.99.20. Has been opening its doors to the "glitterati" of Paris (including Voltaire and Balzac) since 1686.

TRADITIONAL RESTAURANTS

Here you can try menus from different regions of France.

L'Ambassade d'Auvergne, 22 Rue du Grenier Saint-Lazare, 75003. Tel: (1) 42.72.31.22. Auvergnat specialities, including *choux farci* (stuffed cabbage).

Le Dôme, 108 Boulevard du Montparnasse, 75014. Tel: (1) 43.35.25.81. Just along the road from the other famous café, La Coupole, this is the most popular seafood restaurant in Paris – try the *bouillabaisse* (fish stew).

L'Escargot Montorgueil, 38 Rue Montorgueil, 75001. Tel: (1) 42.36.83.51. Specialises in snails prepared in many different ways.

La Fermette Marbeuf, 5 Rue Marbeuf, 75008. Tel: (1) 47.20.63.53. Traditional cuisine served in a wonderful *fin-de-siècle* setting.

Au Trou Gascon, 40 Rue Taine, 75012. Tel: (1) 43.44.34.26. Specialities from the southwest, including *foie gras* and *cassoulet* (pork and bean stew).

BUDGET RESTAURANTS

Good value local eating houses offering simple fare, often for as little as FF70 a head.

Batifol, 15 Place de la République, 75003. Tel: (1) 42.77.86.88.

A La Cloche des Halles, 28 Rue Coquillière, 75001. Tel: (1) 42.36.93.89.

La Crémaillère, 15 Place du Tertre, 75018. Tel: (1) 46.06.58.59. Mingle with the artists and tourists at the heart of Montmartre.

L'Hippopotamus, Place de la Bastille, 75004. Tel: (1) 42.72.98.37. Try the char-grilled meat dishes.

Le Petit Gavroche, 15 Rue Sainte-Croix de la Bretonnerie, 75004. Tel: (1) 48.87.74.26.

Restaurant des Beaux-Arts, 11 Rue Bonaparte, 75006. Tel: (1) 43.26.92.64.

ETHNIC RESTAURANTS

Charly de Bab-el-Oued, 95 Boulevard Gouvion Saint-Cyr, 75017. Tel: (1) 45.74.34.62. North African cuisine.

Chez Vang, 10 Rue de la Grande Truanderie, 75001. Tel: (1) 40.26.09.36. Indo-chinese specialities.

Dominique, 19 Rue Bréa, 75006. Tel: 43.27.08.08. Home cooking for the Russian émigrés of Paris.

Le Grand Chinois, 6 Avenue de New York, 75016. Tel: (1) 47.23.98.21. Chinese.

Institut de Monde Arabe, 1 Rue des Fossés Saint-Bernard, 75005. Tel: (1) 46.33.47.70. North African restaurant offering a splendid view of the Seine and Notre Dame.

WINE

Vines have been cultivated in France since the ancient Romans first planted them. To exclude wine from the dinner table is almost like forgetting the salt and pepper. It is not regarded as a luxury; everyday wine (*vin de table*) is produced for everyday consumption. On the other hand France produces some of the finest vintages in the world, and the pomp, ceremony and snobbery that accompany their production show just how important it is to the culture and economy of France.

Encyclopaedias have been written about French wine and it is not the intention here to give detailed information about all the vineyards of France. The main regions of wine production are Bordeaux (clarets and sweet sauternes), Burgundy – which some say produces the finest wines in the world, Champagne (only wine from here produced by the *Méthode Champenoise* can truly call itself champagne), the Loire valley where we find Muscadet and other dry white wines, and Alsace which produces white wine of a similar style to its German neighbours. A lot of red wine now is also produced in Languedoc and Provence, but these have not yet acquired the cachet of the great wines of Burgundy and Bordeaux.

Reading the label: Wines are graded according to their quality and this must be shown on the label. The grades are as follows:

Vin de Table, usually inexpensive everyday table wine. Quality can be variable.

Vin de Pays, local wine.

VDQS (*Vin délimité de qualité supérieure*). Wine from a specific area, and of higher quality than a *vin de table.*

AOC (*Appellation d'origine contrôlée*). Good quality wine from a specific area or château where strict controls are imposed on the amount of wine produced each year.

If the label bears the words "*mis en bouteille au château*" it has been bottled at the vineyard. This is also indicated by the words, *récoltant* or *producteur* around the cap; the term *négociant* means that it has been bought by a dealer and usually bottled away from the estate. However, this is not necessarily to the detriment of the wine; there are many excellent *négociants* in business today.

The French are fiercely proud of their wines and keen to educate visitors about their production. In all the regions of wine production you will find roadside signs offering visits to cellars open to the public for tours, tastings and sale of wine. The following organisations disseminate information about wines and viticulture, organise courses and produce lists of cellars open to the public:

Centre de Documentation et de Dégustation du Vin, 45 Rue de Liancourt, 75014 Paris. Tel: (1) 43.27.67.21.

Fédération Interprofessionelle des Vins de Bourgogne, 12 Boulevard Bretonnière, 21200 Beaune. Tel: 80.22.21.35. Also at 389 Avenue de Lattre de Tassigny, 71000 Mâcon. Tel: 85.38.20.15.

Comité Interprofessionel du Vin de Champagne, 5 Rue Henry-Martin, 51200 Epernay. Tel: 26.54.47.20.

The Professional Trade Council for Bordeaux Wines (CIVB), 1 Cours du 30 Juillet, 33000 Bordeaux. Tel: 56.00.22.66.

Some tourist organisations in France offer wine tours and holiday courses, mostly lasting a weekend. For more information, contact the professional bodies or the Loisirs Accueil services in the *départements* (*see Useful Addresses*).

THINGS TO DO

There is an old saying "*Paris – ce n'est pas la France.*" These days one might modify it to "*Euro Disney – ce n'est pas la France*". There has been so much hype about this new resort that it is important to remind ourselves that just as Paris, important as it is, cannot represent the true diversity of what France has to offer, Euro Disney is just a small dot on the map.

WALT'S WORLD

The £2.2 billion **Euro Disney Resort** opened to much fanfare, and some disparagement from a few quarters, in 1992. It offers 29 major attractions set in five themed "lands", plus a golf course, hotels and campsite, and is the reason for many families venturing near Paris in the first place.

Euro Disney is 32 km (20 miles) east of Paris, in the suburb of **Marne-la-Vallée**. To get there by car, you need to leave Paris by the A4, but you can avoid the hassle of getting out of Paris by taking the RER train (Line A), from Auber, Châtelet or Etoile; trains run right into the Euro Disney complex.

Completion of the final stages of Euro Disney's development is not scheduled until 2017, when the theme park will cover an area one-fifth the size of Paris itself. In the meantime, you can expect to find all the usual Disney attractions of the five key theme kingdoms – Fantasyland, Discoveryland, Main Street USA, Frontierland and Adventureland – grouped around Sleeping Beauty's Castle, known here as Le Château de la Belle au Bois Dormant. State-of-the-art special effects of rides such as Phantom Manor (Frontierland), the ultimate ghostly encounter, Pirates of the Caribbean (Adventure Land) and Star Tours (Discoveryland), a trip into the World of Star Wars, are impressive.

But there are also more traditional, roller-coaster thrills to be had on Big Thunder Mountain Railroad, where a seemingly runaway mine train scares eager children witless (be warned: this is the most popular attraction; during busy periods, people have to queue for more than two hours). More sedate favourites such as Peter Pan's Flight, Voyages of Pinnochio and It's a Small World (all in Fantasyland) appeal to younger children.

In order to get the most out of the entrance price be sure to allow a full day (9am–midnight), although a 2-day Disney "Passport" is good value. Entrance includes unlimited use of all rides. Where costs tend to mount up is on souvenirs and food – there is a shop and theme restaurant/café on every corner – and Disney has also recently dropped its no-alcohol policy to improve revenue. If one of your aims is to return to childhood for the day, then part of that experience has to be not to count the cost.

Euro Disney's address is BP 105, 77777 Marne-la-Vallée Cedex 4. Tel: (1) 64.74.30.00; for reservations in English tel: (1) 49.41.49.10.

PLACES OF INTEREST

The listing below covers a variety of different activities: technical visits, parks and gardens, miniature railways and so forth. Some of the suggested venues are quite particular to each individual region and are well worth seeking out.

All the places listed are open daily, morning and afternoon (not including public holidays) except where otherwise specified. Most close for a long lunch break – noon or 12.30 until 2 or 2.30pm, although many of the major sites stay open throughout the day at high season. Opening times are subject to change, so if making a special journey it is wise to check. Expect to pay an entrance fee at most venues. A list of museums and art galleries, arranged section by section, is given under the heading of *Culture Plus*.

Most major towns offer guided tours – enquire at the Office de Tourisme or Syndicat d'Initiative, just the main sights are listed here.

PARIS & THE ILE DE FRANCE

The oldest part of Paris, founded by the Romans and called Lutetia, is the **Ile de la Cité**, now the site of the **Notre Dame cathedral** and the **Palais de Justice**. It has now expanded out to cover 20 *arrondissements* (districts), but it is still small enough to cover on foot, and this is one of the best ways to discover the capital. Paris of course is always changing, but the turn of the century will see enormous new developments: The area known as the Marais is becoming a fashionable district, inhabited by business people and politicians; La Villette has seeen much hi-tech development with its new **City of Science and Industry**; the Bastille's new opera house has regenerated the 11th and 12th *arrondissements*; the district of La Défense is set to become the biggest business centre in Europe; while there are plans to make Bercy in the east the first international centre for the food and wine industry.

Bois de Boulogne, vast wooded park which has always been a favourite with Parisians with its seven lakes, a children's amusement park and farm, plus the Parc de Bagatelle flower garden.

Bois de Vincennes, floral gardens, children's amusements, boating lakes and a zoo. Tel: (1) 43.43.84.95 (zoo only).

Catacombes, Service des Visites, 1 Place Denfert-Rochereau, 75014 Paris. Tel: (1) 43.22.47.63. Unusual collection of bones from the old cemeteries of Paris. Closed: Monday.

Centre International de l'Automobile, 25 Rue d'Estienne-d'Orves, 93500 Pantin. Tel: (1) 48.43.79.14. Car exhibitions of vehicles owned by private individuals and car manufacturers.

Centre de la Mer et des Eaux, 195 Rue Saint-Jacques, 75005 Paris. Tel: (1) 46.33.08.61. Aquarium and oceanography centre. Closed: Monday.

Cimetière du Père-Lachaise, Boulevard de Ménilmontant, 75020 Paris. This famous old cemetery attracts many tourists who wish to visit the graves of its famous "residents" such as Chopin, Proust and Oscar Wilde. Other notable burial places are at Montparnasse and Montmartre.

Cité des Sciences et de l'Industrie, 30 Avenue Corentin Cariou, 75019 Paris. Tel: (1) 40.05.80.00. Discover the universe at this exciting new centre which includes a planetarium and an Inventorium (demonstrations workshops suitable for 3 to 9 year olds). Closed: Monday.

Egouts de Paris, Place de la Résistance, 75007 Paris. Tel: (1) 47.05.10.29. Visit Paris underground by way of the sewers, 11am–4pm except Thursday and Friday.

France Miniature, 25 Route du Mesnil, 78990 Elancourt. Tel: (1) 30.51.51.51. Well presented models of 150 historic monuments, villages and other scenes. Open: April–October.

Jardin des Enfants des Halles, Forum des Halles, 105 Rue Rambuteau, 75001 Paris. Six worlds of adventure for children ages 7–11 to discover.

Jardin Fleuriste, 3 Avenue de la Porte d'Auteuil, 75016 Paris. The city's greenhouses – open to the public 10am–5pm.

Jardin du Luxembourg, created by Marie de Médicis on the Left Bank. Games areas and puppet shows for children.

Jardin des Plantes, 57 Rue Cuvier, 75005 Paris. Tel: (1) 40.79.30.00. Medicinal herbs and plants are grown here.

Mirapolis, BP 8568, 95808 Cergy-Pontoise Cedex. Tel: (1) 34.43.20.00. France's first theme park exploring the history and legends of France.

Montmartre: climb up to this delightful district, or take the funicular railway, and explore its little winding streets and watch the painters at work in the Place du Tertre. Usually full of tourists.

Palais de la Découverte, Avenue Franklin D. Roosevelt, 75008 Paris. Tel: (1) 40.74.80.00. Planetarium. Closed: Monday.

Parc Océanique Cousteau, Forum des Halles (level 3), 75001 Paris. Tel: (1) 40.26.13.78. Representations of the famous marine explorer's undersea world, all shown without a drop of water. Closed: Monday.

Parc de Saint-Vrain, 91770 Saint-Vrain (off Autoroute du Sud). Tel: (1) 64.56.10.80. African game reserve featuring wild animals in a prehistoric setting; safaris by boat or car. Open: April–October.

Rock 'n' Roll Hall of Fame. Tel: (1) 40.28.08.13. Waxworks gallery featuring all the heroes of the contemporary music business in the Forum des Halles.

Thoiry Wildlife Park and Zoo, on the RN11, 78770 Thoiry-en-Yvelines. Tel: (1) 34.87.40.67. The largest African game park in Europe, 45 km (28 miles) from Paris.

LOIRE VALLEY TO THE ATLANTIC COAST

ANGERS: MAINE-ET-LOIRE

Arboretum Gaston Allard, Rue Château Allard. Tel: 41.48.57.01. Attractive park, open all year. The leisure park on Maine lake has sports facilities for all ages. Open: all year.

APREMONT: CHER

Attractive medieval village; visit the floral park in the grounds of the château. Open: Easter to mid-September, not Tuesday.

ARTENAY: LOIRET

Le Moulin de Pierre d'Artenay, on the RN20. Built in 1848, this is one of the many windmills in the area which has been restored and is now open to the public. Open: April–October.

BOUIN: VENDÉE

Ostréiculture. Tel: 51.49.85.66. Guided visit to an oyster farm, plus tastings. By appointment only, April–September.

BRION: MAINE-ET-LOIRE

Omlande, Le Bois Thomas. Tel: 41.57.43.19. Animal and amusement park with a miniature train. Open: Easter–September.

CHÂTELAIS: MAINE-ET-LOIRE

Domaine de la Petite Couère. Tel: 41.92.22.51. Reconstructed village square with old shops, exhibitions and collection of vintage vehicles. Also an animal park with a tourist train. Opened in 1990.

CHÂTEAUNEUF-SUR-CHER: CHER

Animal park in the grounds of the château featuring exotic species. Closed: November–April, except Sunday afternoons. Tel: 48.60.64.21.

CHAVANNES: MAINE-ET-LOIRE

La Magnanerie Silk Farm, Chavannes, 49200 Le Puy Notre Dame. Tel: 41.52.29.16. Silk farm in a former troglodyte dwelling. Open: June–October Saturday and Sunday afternoons, (plus Tuesday–Sunday afternoons June and July).

CHEMILLÉ: MAINE-ET-LOIRE

Jardin des Plantes Médicinales, l'Albarel. Tel: 41.30.35.17. Garden of medicinal plants, best seen mid-May to mid-October, but open all year.

CHINON: INDRE-ET-LOIRE

Centrale Nucléaire de Chinon, on D7 45 km (25 miles) west of Tours. The first nuclear power station in France; it was decommissioned in 1973 and is now open the public. Information from CPN de Chinon, Services Relations Publiques, BP 80, 37420 Avoine. Tel: 47.98.97.07.

A narrow-gauge **steam train** operates from Chinon for a round trip to Richelieu and back (120 minutes) on Saturday and Sunday afternoons from mid-May to mid-September, plus Tuesday and Wednesday mornings in June and July. Tel: 47.58.36.29.

CHOLET: MAINE-ET-LOIRE

Parc de Loisirs de Ribout. Tel: 41.62.12.77. Pony rides, and sports facilities. Open: all year.

LE CROISIC: LOIRE-ATLANTIQUE

Ocearium, Avenue St Goustan. Tel: 40.23.02.44. Good aquarium devoted entirely to Atlantic sea creatures; unusual tunnel aquarium 11 metres (36 ft) long.

DÉNÉZÉ-SOUS-DOUÉ: MAINE-ET-LOIRE

Caverne Sculpté, cave showing hundreds of carved figures dating back to the 16th century in a remarkable underground site. Open: afternoons Easter to mid-November (all day July and August; weekends out of season). Information from DAP, 49700 Dénézé-sous-Doué. Tel: 41.59.15.40.

DOUÉ-LA-FONTAINE: MAINE-ET-LOIRE

Parc des Ecuries Foulon, former park of the ruined château, now a magnificent rose garden.
Parc Zoologique des Minières. Tel: 41.59.18.58. Specialising in exotic domestic animals.
Le Moulin Cartier, the last windmill built in Anjou. Open to the public; also wine tasting available. Information from Percher Frères, Viticulteurs, 49700 Les Verchers-sur-Layon. Tel: 41.59.11.56.

LA FAUTE-SUR-MER: VENDÉE

Zoo Parc de Californie. Tel: 51.27.10.48. Open: Easter–1 November.

GENNES: MAINE-ET-LOIRE

The many megalithic monuments (dolmen and menhirs), together with an amphitheatre constitute an open-air museum. Winter opening is restricted to Saturday afternoon and Sunday.

LA FLÈCHE: SARTHE

The **Military School** (Prytanée) is of interest, particularly for its 17th-century chapel.
Zoological Park, at Tertre Rouge, just outside the town.

LE MANS: SARTHE

The old part of town, especially Rue de la Reine Bérangère, is worth a visit for its medieval houses. See too the Cathédrale Saint-Julien.

MAULEVRIER: MAINE-ET-LOIRE

Parc Oriental, Japanese-style park with pagoda and 200 species of trees; place of pilgrimage for Buddhists. Open: afternoons, plus Tuesday–Friday morning in summer.

NANTES: LOIRE-ATLANTIQUE

Nantes has several pleasant gardens, including the Jardin des Plantes with a collection of over 400 camelias (opposite the station), the park of Le Grand Blottereau around an 18th-century château and the Ile de Versailles, on the banks of the Erdre.

NOYANT-LA-GRAVOYÈRE: MAINE-ET-LOIRE

La Mine Bleue. Tel: 41.61.55.60. Former slate mine, reopened as a tourist site. Wearing hard hats, visitors are taken around by means of a miner's train. Also at the site is the Saint-Blaise leisure park. Open: June–October (closed: Tuesday).

OBTERRE: INDRE

Haute-Touche safari park, Route d'Azay, Obterre, 36290 Mézières-en-Brenne. Tel: 54.39.20.82. Open: April–November.

ORLÉANS-LA-SOURCE: LOIRET

Floral park with roaming wildlife where a tourist train runs in summer (except Friday). Closed: mornings mid-November to 1 April. Tel: 38.63.33.17.

LA POISSONNIÈRE: MAINE-ET-LOIRE

L'Arche. Tel: 41.72.21.09. Amusement park with mini-golf, miniature train, etc. Open: 1 April–1 November.

PONCÉ-SUR-LOIR: SARTHE

Arts and Crafts Centre, Paillard Mill. Watch the various artists at work: pottery, glass-blowing, woodwork etc. Closed: Sunday.

ST-MALO-DE-GUERSAC: LOIRE-ATLANTIQUE

The **Rozé animal park** is concerned with the wildlife on the marshlands. Open: April–October. Tel: 40.91.17.80. See too the **Maison d'Eclusier** (lock-keeper's house). Open: 1 June–30 September. Tel: 40.88.42.72.

SAUMUR: MAINE-ET-LOIRE

Ecole Nationale d'Equitation, St-Hilaire-St-Florent. This famous riding school is open to the public and the Cadre Noir cavalry puts on regular displays in the summer. Information from the tourist office or the school, BP 207, 49400 Saumur. Tel: 41.50.21.35.

SAVONNIÈRES: INDRE-ET-LOIRE

Petrifying caves (*grottes pétrifiantes*), 14 km (8 miles) west of Tours, where objects have literally been "turned to stone". See to the Gallo-Roman cemetery and displays of prehistoric fauna and fossil collection.

TURQUANT: MAINE-ET-LOIRE

Moulin de la Herpinière, restored windmill. Closed: Monday and January. Tel: 41.51.75.22.

LE VAL-HULIN: MAINE-ET-LOIRE

Troglo Tap, Le Val Hulin, 49730 Turquant. Tel: 41.51.48.30. A cave in the cliffs, renowned in the last century for producing *pommes tapées,* an apple delicacy popular with the British navy. Visits and tastings: weekends April–October (daily June–September).

VILLANDRY: INDRE-ET-LOIRE

Do not miss the formal Renaissance gardens of the château on the D7, 17 km (10 miles) west of Tours. Supplementary entrance fee for the castle. Open: mid-March to mid-November.

NORMANDY, BRITTANY & THE NORTH

AMIENS: SOMME

Hortillonages, Boulevard de Beauville. The hortillonages are fascinating market gardens established on a network of tributaries of the Somme and Avre. They can be visited by flat-bottomed boat (departures from 54 Boulevard de Beauville). For information, tel: 22.92.12.18.

Parc Zoologique de la Hotoie, 139 Rue du Faubourg de Hem. Tel: 22.43.06.95. One of the major zoos in France with animals kept in pleasant natural settings. Open: 1 April–31 October, closed: Monday.

AMFREVILLE-SUR-ITON: EURE

La Mare Hermier, visit a producer of foie gras; tasting possible and sale of produce.

ANEVILLE-SUR-SCIE: SEINE-MARITIME

Visit the apple orchards of the Duchy de Longueville and see the cider makers at work. Tel: 35.83.32.76. Open: Monday–Friday morning.

ARGOULES: SOMME

Les Jardins de Valloires. Tel: 22.23.53.55. Botanical gardens, specialising in roses and rare shrubs; also has thematic gardens. Sale of rare plants. Closed: February.

AUVERS: MANCHE

Cidrerie Héroult Filts. Tel: 33.42.04.24. Farm producing cider, pear perry and calvados. Open to the public: Monday–Friday, plus Saturday morning May–September.

AUZOUVILLE-SUR-SAÂNE: SEINE-MARITIME

Le Gloopi. Tel: 35.83.23.47. Leisure park with 70 amusements. Open: 1 April–30 October.

BAIE DE SOMME: SOMME

Well preserved natural environment and bird reserve which can be explored by means of a little tourist train (trips 1–3 hours depending on place of departure). Trains leave from Crotoy, St-Valéry-sur-Somme, Noyelles, and Cayeux-sur-Mer. Information from Chemin de Fer de la Baie de Somme, Gare, 80230 St-Valéry-sur-Somme. Tel: 22.26.96.96.

BELLEAU: AISNE

Cimetière Americain du Bois de Belleau, World War I cemetery in a beautiful wooded setting,

dedicated to the Americans that fell. Some 2,350 servicemen are buried here. Guided visits possible.

BELLEFONTAINE: MANCHE

Le Village Enchanté. Tel: 35.59.01.93. The Enchanted Village, a fairytale land with various attractions. Open: Easter–30 September.

BLAINVILLE-SUR-MER: MANCHE

Coopérative d'Aqua-Culture. Tel: 33.47.13.47. An oyster farm, also producing mussels and other shellfish. Open: daily except weekend.

BREST: FINISTÈRE

Conservatoire Botanique, 52 Allée du Bot. Tel: 98.02.63.14. Houses a collection of threatened species from all over the world.

Océanopolis, Rue de Kerbriant, Port de Plaisance du Moulin Blanc. Sealife centre.

CAMEMBERT: ORNE

La Maison du Camembert. Tel: 33.39.43.35. Discover how the famous local cheese is made; sale of produce. Open: Easter–November.

CAP SIZUN-GOULIEN: FINISTÈRE

Bird reserve. Tel: 98.70.13.53. Mostly nesting and migratory colonies. Open: mid-March to August; close up tours available Monday and Thursday mornings in July and August.

CHAMOUILLE: AISNE

Parc de l'Ailette, leisure park with bathing and pedalo boats, a sandy beach and 18-hole golf course. Tel: 23.24.79.02; 23.24.83.99 for the golf course.

CHAMPREPUS: MANCHE

Modern zoo where the comfort and environment of the animals is paramount. Ninety species of animals and birds. Open: 15 march–11 September. Tel: 33.61.30.74.

CHAVIGNON: AISNE

Ateliers de l'Abeille, on the RN 2 between Soissons and Laon. Tel: 23.21.61.62. This is the biggest producer of honey in Picardy. Living museum and tastings possible. Closed: Tuesday.

CHEMIN DES DAMES: AISNE

In the southern Aisne valley some 200 underground quarries served as shelters for soldiers during World War I. They were cut out of stone almost 2,000 years ago and have been decorated by the soldiers that sheltered there. Guided tours possible (enquire at Laon tourist office, tel: 23.20.45.54).

CLERÈS: SEINE-MARITIME

Parc du Bocasse. Tel: 35.33.22.25. Leisure park with many attractions including pedalo, an enchanted river, etc. Open: 1 March–31 October.

COMBRIT: FINISTÈRE

Parc Botanique de Cornouaille. Tel: 98.56.64.93. One of the best in France, with over 3,500 species.

COMPIÈGNE: OISE

Visit a replica of the railway wagon where the ceasefire was signed at the end of World War I in a clearing of the Compiègne forest. Closed: Tuesday between Easter and Whitsun.

COUTANCES: MANCHE

Parc l'Evêque, unusual medieval park, founded in the 11th century, recently restored; home to much wildlife. Open: weekends only 15 May–1 November (daily July–August).

CRÉCY-EN-PONTHIEU: SOMME

The Crécy forest offers many leisure oppportunities; by car you can follow the trail of the Vieux Chênes (Ancient Oaks), and of course there are many marked footpaths.

CREUSE: SOMME

La Ferme d'Antan. Tel: 22.38.98.58. Visit this farm which has been organised as it would have been at the turn of the century; old tools and methods can be observed.

DINARD-SAINT-BRIAC: ILLE-ET-VILAINE

Barrage de la Rance, world's first tidal power factory offers visits in English.

ECOUCHÉ: ORNE

La Marionnetterie, Le Moulin. Tel: 33.35.17.97. Puppetmakers open to the public, with possible the largest permanent exhibition of puppets in Europe. Phone for an appointment. Open: all year.

ENGLANCOURT: AISNE

Atelier Artisanal de Vannerie, 21 Rue du Bicentenaire, 02120 Chigny. Tel: 23.63.38.16. Basket-weaving workshop open to the public who can take a hand in making the products.

EPRETOT: SEINE-MARITIME

Le Canyon, 76430 St-Romain-de-Colbosc. Tel: 35.20.42.69. Leisure park with 50 different amusements, including carousels. Open: daily June–August; Wednesday and weekends March–May and September to mid-November.

ERMENONVILLE: OISE

Parc Jean-Jacques Rousseau, Rue René de Girardin. Tel: 44.54.01.58. Part of the former vast estates of the Marquis de Girardin, this well preserved garden is a testament to the art of gardening in the 18th century. Open: every afternoon June–30 September; Wednesday and weekends only October–November; Sundays only 15 January–31 May. Closed: mid-December to mid-January.

ESSIGNY-LE-GRAND

Le Mémorial. Tel: 23.63.38.16. Reconstructed scenes from World War I, plus documents and other material. Closed: August.

FLAMANVILLE: MANCHE

Centrale Nucléaire de Flamanville. Tel: 33.08.95.95. ext: 4100. Guided tour and exhibition at the nuclear station. Take some form of identity with you. Open: daily (afternoons only Sunday and school holidays).

FORT MAHON: SOMME

Aquaclub Côte Picardie, Promenade du Marquenterre. Tel: 22.23.33.29. Exciting waterpark with many facilities including wave pools and giant toboggans. Open: Easter–September.

GIVERNY: EURE

The house and gardens (easily recognisable from his famous paintings) of Claude Monet. Tel: 32.51.28.21. Visit too the Museum of American Impressionists. Tel: 32.51.94.65. Both open: April–31 October, closed: Monday.

GOLFE DU MORBIHAN: MORBIHAN

Inland sea with more than 365 tiny islands, a handful of which are inhabited. Of particular interest are the Ile de Groix, for its mineral deposits, the exhibition at Fort d'Hedic on Hoedic and the Ile d'Houat for its cliffs and dunes.

IFFENDIC, ILLE-ET-VILAINE

Base de Loisirs de Trémelin. Tel: 99.09.70.40. Leisure and animal park.

ILE DE BATZ: FINISTÈRE

Jardin Colonial. Tel: 98.61.76.76. Garden of exotic plants.

ILE DE TATIHOU: MANCHE

A natural environment of sandy moors and dunes, with an observatory for bird-watching, plus a scientific cultural centre and maritime museum. Tel: 33.23.19.92.

ISNEAUVILLE: SEINE-MARITIME

Le Jardin de Papillons. Tel: 35.61.31.22. Huge tropical glasshouse where butterflies from Asia, Africa and the Americas can be observed flying free. Open: May–October.

LAMBALLE: CÔTES D'ARMOR

Haras (national stud), one of the largest in France, breeding farm horses as well as thoroughbreds. Tel: 96.31.00.40. Open: mid-July to mid-February.

LAZ: FINISTÈRE

Parc de Loisirs de Laz. Tel: 98.26.82.47. Leisure park with mini-golf, a 550-metre luge run and other amusements.

MENEZ MEUR-HANVEC: FINISTÈRE

Parc d'Armorique near Daoulas. Tel: 98.21.90.69. Animal park. Open: daily June–September, otherwise Wednesday and Sunday only.

MERLIEUX ET FOUQUEROLLES

A natural wooded site, ideal for walking, it includes aquariums (tel: 23.80.18.33), an educational farm (bookings necessary 1 month ahead, tel: 23.20.45.54) and an information centre (the Maison de l'Aisne, tel: 23.80.13.26).

MUZILLAC: MORBIHAN

Parc Zoologique du Château de Branféré, le Guerno. Tel: 97.42.94.66. Some animals roam free. Open: Easter–November.

PLAILLY: OISE

Parc Astérix, near the A1 (exit at Survilliers or Plailly). Tel: 44.62.34.34. Meet all your favourite characters from the famous Astérix books at this theme park; see too the dolphin lake.

PLEMEUR-BODOU: CÔTES D'ARMOR

Planetarium; also the **radôme des télécommunications** (radar station) are open to the public April–October. Nearby the **Centre Ornithologique de l'Ile Grande** has a permanent exhibition. Tel: 96.91.91.40.

PLEUGUENEC, ILLE-ET-VILAINE

Parc et Château de la Bourbonsais. Tel: 99.60.40.07. Animal park and gardens; also château open to the public every afternoon.

Etang au Duc, bird reserve.

PLOUGUERNEAU: FINISTÈRE
Phare Ile Vierge, lighthouse. With 392 steps to climb, it is the highest in Europe. It is one of several open to the public around the coast. Enquire at local tourist offices for information.

LE POMMIER: MANCHE
Chèvrerie de la Huberdière, Le Pommier, 50790 Liesville-sur-Douve. Tel: 33.71.01.60. Cheesemaker, offering visits and tastings.

PONT SCORFF: MORBIHAN
Kerruisseau. Tel: 97.32.60.86. Zoo and exhibition of local fauna. Open: daily Easter–October, otherwise Saturday–Tuesday only.

RENNES: ILLE-ET-VILAINE
Jardins du Thabor, 10 hectares (25 acres) of gardens in the town centre.

ST-GOAZEC: FINISTÈRE
Parc de Trévarez. Tel: 98.26.82.79. Floral gardens. Open: afternoons April–September, weekends October–March.

ST-MARTIN-DE-LANDELLE: MANCHE
Ange Michel leisure park. Tel: 33.49.04.74. Has amusements for adults and children as well as a craft and agricultural museum. Open: weekends Easter–September (daily, except Monday, 20 June to mid-September).

ST-QUENTIN-EN-TOURMONT: SOMME
Parc Ornithologique de Domaine du Marquenterre, vast bird sanctuary which can be visited by the tourist train departing from the neighbouring Baie de Somme (*see listing*). Together, these two reserves provide 2,300 hectares (5,685 acres) of protected environment for wildlife. See too the **Maison de l'Oiseau** and the **Valloires gardens**. Open: 1 April–11 November. Tel: 22.25.03.06.

SENE: MORBIHAN
Réserve Naturelle de Falguérec, bird reserve. Closed: Monday in July and August.

TREGOMEUR: CÔTES D'ARMOR
Parc Zoologique de Moulin de Richard. Tel: 96.79.01.07. 10 hectares (25 acres) of woods where animals roam freely.

VANNES: MORBIHAN
Parc du Golfe, equatorial park principally for the breeding of tropical butterflies (over 500 species).

VARENGEVILLE-SUR-MER: SEINE-MARITIME
Moutiers floral park. Tel: 35.85.10.02. Botanical gardens which have won international acclaim. Open: Easter–November.

EASTERN FRANCE & BURGUNDY

ARCY-SUR-CURE: YONNE
Les Grottes. Tel: 86.40.90.63. A network of vast caves with remarkable limestone concretions which can be explored by following a 900-metre (2,950-ft) underground walk (easily accessible to the elderly or disabled). Open: mid-March to mid-November.

ARLAY: JURA
Jurafaune, wildlife park, set around the ruins of a medieval fortress, specialising in birds of prey. Birds in flight 4–5pm. Open: daily 15 June–15 September, Wednesday and weekends from Easter to 1 November.

ARNAY-SOUS-VITTEAUX: CÔTE-D-OR
Zoo de l'Auxois. Tel: 80.49.64.01. 3,000 animals, plus adults' and children's amusements, a restaurant and lakeside picnic spot.

AZE: SAÔNE-ET-LOIRE
Les Grottes. Tel: 85.33.32.23. Two caves open to the public – one is prehistoric and a very rare example of its type, the other boasts an underground river. Accessible to all (no stairs). Also an archaeological museum. Open: Easter–September, Sunday only in October.

BAIRON: ARDENNES
The **Lac du Bairon** has been organised partly for sports and leisure use, and partly as a nature reserve.

BAUMES-LES-MESSIEURS: JURA
Grottes et Cascades, in a remarkable site in the Jura plateau, you can explore the waterfalls and underground caves which are illuminated with special lighting effects. Open: mid-March to mid-October.

BELVAL: ARDENNES
Le Parc de Vision, vast park of woods and footpaths with observation towers; it has animals roaming half wild, including bison, board moose and deer.

BÈZE: CÔTE-D'OR
Visit the caves and take a boat ride along the underground river. Superb illuminations. Open: daily May–September, weekends only in April. Tel: 80.75.31.33.

BLANZY: SAÔNE-ET-LOIRE
The machines and galleries of the old mine have been rebuilt and opened to the public with an exhibition, *Mine and Men*, telling the story of the life and work of miners since the industry began. Open: Saturday and Sunday afternoons May–September (every afternoon July–August). Information from Mme Lotte, 20 Rue Paul Valéry, 71450 Blanzy. Tel: 85.58.40.02.

BOURBONNE-LES-BAINS: HAUTE-MARNE
La Bannie wildlife park.

BUFFON: CÔTE-D'OR
Buffon Forges. Tel: 80.89.40.30. An 18th-century "model factory", with most of its buildings still intact; audiovisual exhibition of the traditional iron and steel work of northern Burgundy. Open: every afternoon June–September, plus Wednesday–Friday mornings in July and August.

CHAMOUX: YONNE
Cardo-Land is a most unusual site; in a wooded park, 7 km (4 miles) from Vézelay. Tel: 86.33.28.33. The sculptor Cardo has created an imaginary prehistoric world of life-size creatures from the sea and land; plus a museum of prehistory and paleontology and the decorated cave. Open: daily June–August; September–October and April–May open at weekends, public and school holidays.

CHARBONNIÈRES-LES-SAPINS: DOUBS

Dino-Zoo, 16 Rue du Château. Tel: 81.59.22.57. A prehistoric animal park with model dinosaurs in a natural environment. Open: 1 March–30 November.

CHARLEVILLE-MÉZIÈRES: ARDENNES

St-Laurent wildlife park is just outside the town. Tel: 24.57.39.84.

CHATILLON-SUR-MARNE: MARNE

Climb 33 metres (107 ft) up the colossal statue of Urban II, the pope from Champagne, for a view of some 22 surrounding villages (orientation table).

CHAUFFAILLES: SAÔNE-ET-LOIRE

There is a permanent motor show at 35 Rue du 8 mai. Tel: 85.84.60.30. 300 sports, luxury and collectors cars on display and for sale. Open: daily (closed: weekends July–August).

CHAUX-LES-PASSAVANT: DOUBS

Grotte de la Glacière et Maison des Minéraux. Tel: 81.60.44.26. Naturally-formed ice castles, a former ocean bed with fossils and jelly fish are among the unusual attractions to be found at these caves. Open: 1 March–31 October.

LE CREUSOT: SAÔNE-ET-LOIRE

Heavy industry is celebrated in the huge power hammer (built 1840), at the entrance to the town, which despite its size (21 metres/68 ft high and weighing 1300 tons), was accurate enough to cork a bottle without breaking it. Guided visits available. Visit too the 70-acre (28-hectare) park in the town centre and the Castle (former glass works).

DIJON: CÔTE-D'OR

Parc Récréatif de la Toison d'Or, BP 236, Rue de Colchide, 21000 Dijon. Tel: 80.74.16.16. Amusements for old and young alike, including a flume ride, a giant labryinth, and an audiovisual spectacle of the story of the Dukes of Burgundy. Open: May–September. The entrance fee also admits each person for 90 minutes to the adjoining water park, the **Aquacenter Les Cyclades** which offers a wave pool, water slides and river rapids. Closed: January.

Jardin Botanique, 1 Avenue Albert Premier. Tel: 80.43.46.39. Founded in 1771, features around 3,5000 species; plus an Arboretum which includes medicinal plants. Nearby is the **Natural History Museum** and the splendid **Jardin de l'Arquebuse**.

Cassis Lejay-Lagoute, 19 Rue Ledru-Rollin, BP 278, 21007 Dijon Cedex. Tel: 80.72.41.72. Cellars and modern plant where cassis (blackcurrant) liqueur is made, are open to the public (tastings included).

DOLANCOURT: AUBE

Nigloland leisure park. Tel: 25.27.94.52.

ETALANS: DOUBS

Gouffre de Poudrey. Tel: 81.59.22.57. The largest underground cave in France that is accessible to tourists; also has a sound and light show. Open: 1 March–11 November.

EPERNAY: MARNE

The major Champagne producers offer cellar visits, eg Moët et Chandon, Mercier and de Castellane (the latter in summer only, when they also have a Jardin des Papillons or butterflies).

FABULYS: JURA

Le Château des Automates Chaussin. Tel: 84.72.32.34. Set in the countryside near Dôle, this castle offers an enchanted world of 300 mechanical figures to fascinate adults and children alike; plus landscaped gardens.

FOUGEROLLES: HAUTE-SAÔNE

Parc Animalier de St-Valbert. Tel: 84.49.54.97. An unusual combination of a zoo (mostly deer, chamois, etc.) and a retreat park in cave and chapel. Retreat open: daily. Zoo: June–September.

GÉRARDMER: VOSGES

The largest lake in the Vosges offers plenty of leisure opportunities. See the Saut des Cuves waterfall nearby.

GIFFAUMONT: MARNE

The Maison du Lac is the information office and departure point for excursions on Europe's largest man-made lake, the Lac du Der-Chantecoq.

GUÉRIGNY: NIÈVRE

Forges Royales de la Chaussade. Tel: 86.37.31.98. Former royal blacksmiths which used to produce chains and anchors for the navy and steam engines. Open: July to mid-September, except Tuesday.

HUNAWIHR: HAUT-RHIN

Parc à Cigognes, Route du Vin. Tel: 89.73.72.62. Storks park and reintroduction centre, also otters, penguins and other animals. Open: 1 April–11 November.

KINGERSHEIM: HAUT-RHIN

Tropical Aquarium, 9 Rue du Hagelbach. Tel: 89.53.72.72. Fresh and saltwater environments; includes sharks and piranhas.

KINTZHEIM: BAS-RHIN

Volerie des Aigles, Château de Kintzheim. Tel: 88.92.84.33. Demonstrations of birds of prey in flight in the medievial courtyard of the château from 1 April–11 November.

LOUHANS: SAÔNE-ET-LOIRE

Hôtel-Dieu et Apothicairerie, the apothecary in the 17th-century former hospital boasts rare chinaware and blown glass still containing its original substances (closed: Tuesday and mornings September–June). Tel: Mr Cotte, 85.75.54.32.

Louhans itself is a very attractive town with one of the longest arcaded streets in the country; there is a Bresse poultry market on Monday.

LUXEUIL-LES-BAINS: HAUTE-SAÔNE

Conservatoire de la Dentelle, 1 Avenue des Thermes. Tel: 84.40.06.41. Watch traditional lacemakers at work. Open: Tuesday, Wednesday and Friday afternoon. The town's **Musée de la Tour des Echevins** also holds a collection of lace.

LYON: RHÔNE

Le Parc de la Tête-d'Or, spacious park laid out in English style including a botanical garden, rose garden, small zoo and children's amusements.

Domaine de Lacroix-Laval, just outside the city, a natural park of nature trails and a small farm, overlooked by an old castle.

Parc des Quatres-Rives, brand new park in the Gerland district of the city.

Magny-Cours: Nièvre

The ultra-modern motor racing circuit near Nevers is open to the public, free of charge, by appointment. Research is carried out here for the car industry. Training sessions are available on Renault or Porsche cars. For information tel: 86.21.20.74.

Ménétrux-en-Joux: Jura

Ferme de l'Aurochs Val Dessous, Vallée du Hérisson. Tel: 84.25.72.95. Follow a landscaped trail in this lovely valley and watch aurochs and other primitive species (bison, oxen, etc.) from observations towers. Open: 1 April–31 November.

Morsbronne-les-Bains: Bas-Rhin

Fantasialand, 1 Route de Gunstett. Tel: 88.09.39.36. Leisure park with amusements including a miniature train. Open: June–September.

Mulhouse: Haut-Rhin

Jardin Zoologique et Botanique, 51 Rue du Jardin-Zoologique. Tel: 89.44.17.44. Over 1,100 animals of 220 different species.

Nancy: Meurthe-et-Moselle

The Pépinière park has formal gardens alongside a small zoo and an aquarium.

Otrott: Bas Rhin

Les Naïades, 30 Route de Kingenthal. Tel: 88.95.90.32. Giant tropical aquaria displaying flora and fauna of the underwater world.

Paray-le-Monial: Saône-et-Loire

The **Diorama** in the park behind the Basilica displays painted statues in 21 settings, relating the story of Saint-Margaret-Mary and the history of the city. Open: daily Easter–October (afternoons only Easter–31 May and mid-September to 31 October). Tel: 85.88.85.80.

Passavent-la-Rochère: Haute-Saône

Verrerie de la Rochère, one of the oldest glassworks in France (established in 1475), where you can watch the glassblowers at work. Open: every afternoon from 21 April–3 October, but closed in August. Tel: 84.78.61.00.

Poligny: Jura

Maison du Comté, Avenue de la Résistance. Tel: 84.37.23.51. Find out how the delicious local Comté cheese is made. Open: daily in July and August.

Quetigny: Côte-d'Or

Parc Aquatique de Quetigny. A health centre and water park where amenities include two wave pools, three jacuzzis, river rapids and indoor amusements such as a bowling alley, billiards and squash. Hotel on the site. Open: 10am–10pm. Société Cap Vert, Rue du Cap Vert, 21800 Quetigny. Tel: 80.46.14.44.

Reims: Marne

The leading Champagne producers offer visits to their cellars, e.g. Piper-Heidseick and Taittinger, also Pommery and Mumm in summer only.

La Roche-Morey: Haute-Saône

Parc de Loisirs. Tel: 84.91.02.14. Recreational park (free entry), with "Wild West" train rides, mini-golf, dodgems, etc., and a splendid view of the Jura mountains and the Alps.

St-Amand-en-Puisaye: Yonne

The area of la Puisaye is renowned for its pottery, and there are several studios which welcome visitors; many still employ the traditional methods, which are particular to the area.

Daniel Auger, Faubourg des Poteries, 58310 Saint-Amand-en-Puisaye. Tel: 86.39.66.52.

Michel Dumont, Route de Cosne, 58310 Saint-Amande-en-Puisaye. Tel: 86.39.71.08.

Mallet Fils, Route de Cosne, 58310 Saint-Amande-en-Puisaye. Tel: 86.39.60.80.

St-Claude: Jura

Ets Vincent Genod, 13 Faubourg Marcel. Tel: 84.45.00.47. See how traditional briar pipes are made. Open: Monday–Friday.

Salins-les-Bains: Jura

Salines de Salins-les-Bains, Place des Salines. Tel: 84.73.01.34. Salt has been mined in Franch-Comté for a thousand years. Visit the underground galleries dating from the 13th century, and other aspects of the saltworks. Regular tours. Closed: December and January.

Faïencerie de Salins-les-Bains, 20 Avenue Aristide-Briand. Tel: 84.73.01.45. History of the pottery industry in an earthernware factory.

Strasbourg: Bas-Rhin

The city has plenty of open spaces, including the Citadel park, the gardens of the Orangerie and the Jardin des Contades.

Syam: Jura

Forges de Syam. Tel: 84.51.61.00. Industrial museum set up in the former ironworkers' lodgings. Open: daily (except Tuesday) in July and August, weekends in May, June and September.

Thoiria: Doubs

Fromagerie de Thoiria. Tel: 84.25.84.14. See how the local Comté cheese has been made since 1900, using traiditonal methods and wood fires. Open: Monday–Saturday afternoon in July and August.

Uchon: Saône-et-Loire

A picturesque village overlooked by unusual shaped rocks which are the stuff of local legends, called the Devil's Claw and the Tottering Stone. Splendid views of the Morvan and Arroux valley.

The **monastery** is open to visitors who can buy icons and aromatic plants there.

Ungersheim: Haut-Rhin

Ecomusée d'Alsace. Tel: 89.74.44.74. Open-air museum of traditional half-timbered houses in a village of craftsmen working in their studios. Events organised at weekends.

Vauchignon: Côte-d'Or

A remarkable natural site, with a fantastic waterfall.

Verdun: Meuse

The famous battlefields of the World War I can be toured, along with some old forts, particularly that of Douaumont where there is a museum and a memorial to the thousands of French soldiers who gave their lives. The 14–18 Historial, recreates the commune of Fleury, one of the villages destroyed, never to be rebuilt. For information tel: 29.45.18.18.

VILLARS-LES-DOMBES: AIN

Parc Départemental des Oiseaux, on the RN 83. Tel: 74.98.05.90. A bird sanctuary with some 350 species, including water birds such as pelicans and non-flying varieties like the emu. A miniature train runs from April–October.

HEART OF FRANCE

The region is full of untamed natural beauty, a land of caves, gorges and low mountains. There are many **notable cascades** (waterfalls), especially in Limousin, including the Cascades de Murel (near Argentat-sur-Dordogne), de Gimel (northwest of Tulle), the Jarreaux falls at St-Martin-le-Château and the Saut-Sali falls on the D16 near the Aigle reservoir.

ANGOULÊME: CHARENTE

Famous for its papermaking (in former times 100 mills were in operation), the 16th-century **Moulin de Fleurac** just outside the town is a living museum of the old traditions of the craft. Closed: Tuesday.

ARCACHON: GIRONDE

Parc Ornithologique, Le Teich, Bassin D'Arcachon. Tel: 56.22.80.93. Bird reserve in the Landes national park.

ARDES-SUR-COUZE: PUY-DE-DÔME

Cézallier animal park and leisure centre. Open: school holidays and 1 May–30 October; also Sundays out of season. Tel: 73.71.82.86.

AUBUSSON: CREUSE

Ets. Andraud, 2 Place M.-Dayras. Tel: 55.66.18.08. The town is famous for its production of tapestries and rugs. This workshop displays both. Closed: Sunday and Monday (but open daily 15 June–15 September).

BORDEAUX: GIRONDE

The ancient port of Bordeaux boasts the largest public square in Europe: the Esplanade des Quinquonces. Nearby on the Cours de Verdun, is the delightful Jardin Public, a former royal garden, and the Botanical Gardens, founded in 1629. The Parc Floral on the Cours Ladoumègue celebrates the towns with which Bordeaux is twinned by means of thematic gardens; it lies to the north of the city, near Bordeaux Lac, a recent development offering facilities for bathing, sailing, rowing and other activities.

BORT-LES-ORGUES: CORRÈZE

The town's name derives from the unusual natural feature of cylindrical formations of clinkstone (phonolite) along the Dordogne river, which resemble organ pipes. The tallest columns are 100 metres (325 ft) high.

LA BOURBOULE: PUY-DE-DÔME

Le Parc Fenestre. Tel: 73.65.57.71. A 30-acre (12-hectare) leisure park which features a "wild West" miniature train, cross country ski trails, footpaths and mountain bike trails. La Bourboule can be reached by cable car (in service 15 June–30 September) from the Charlannes plateau. Open: Easter–30 September.

Le Monde Merveilleux du Train et de la Miniature, Rue Voltaire. Tel: 73.65.54.61. A miniature city with 350 models and 500 vehicles, crossed by a rail network. Also slide shows.

LE BUGUE: DORDOGNE

Le Village de Bournat. Opened in 1992 this project shows living history in a village where the arts, crafts and traditions (including a working nut oil mill) of a century ago can be explored, in a park by the Vézère river. Tel: 53.08.41.99.

La Maison de la Vie Sauvage, 9 Rue de la République. Tel: 53.07.20.48. More than 1,000 stuffed birds and animals are displayed here, including many species that are now extinct.

CABRERETS: LOT

Pech-Merle caves, extensive galleries in these famous caves are decorated with prehistoric art: animals, female figures and disembodied hand. The caves were used as a hideout during the Revolution. Check locally for opening times.

CHAMPETIÈRES: PUY-DE-DÔME

Parc Zoologique du Bouy. Tel: 73.82.13.29. Zoo open during school holidays and daily 1 May–25 September.

CHÂTEAU SUR ALLIER: ALLIER

Parc Animalier de St Augustin. Tel: 70.66.42.01. Animal reserve in the grounds of an 18th-century château, which is also open to the public. Open: daily 15 July–15 September; Wednesday and weekends the rest of the year.

CLERMONT-FERRAND: PUY-DE-DÔME

Pérou de St-Alyre, calcareous springs allow the petrification of small objects. Also worth a visit are the botanical gardens (**Jardin des Plantes**) and the **Place de Jaude**, presided over by the statue of Vercingétorix, leader of the Gauls.

COGNAC: CHARENTE

The **François 1er** park originally formed the grounds of the château.

COULON: DEUX-SÈVRES

Aquarium, open Easter–15 October. Coulon is also the main departure point for excursions by flat-bottomed boat (*barque*) on the Marais Poitevin (Green Venice).

COUZE-ST-FRONT: DORDOGNE

Moulins de Couze. Tel: 53.24.36.16. Paper mills with a permanent exhibition about papermaking, and studio where hand-made paper is produced. Open: every afternoon except Wednesday 1 May–3 September; Wednesday afternoon only March–April and October–November.

DOMPIERRE-SUR-BESBRE: ALLIER

Le Pal. Tel: 70.42.01.52. Zoo and leisure park with a wide range of amusements. The amusement park is open Easter–30 September; the zoo all year except December and January.

ECHOURGNAC: DORDOGNE

Ferme du Parcot. Tel: 53.81.99.28. Exhibition showing the changing rural landscape and farmlife. Open: Saturday afternoon in May; then every afternoon June–September.

JAUNAY-CLAN: VIENNE

Parc du Futuroscope, a theme park for the future, of extraordinary architecture, with unusual amusements such as a cinema with a 600 sq. metre (6,460 sq. ft) screen, where spectators' seats are synchronised with the action. For children, a screen dramatises imaginary trips into the future. See too the enchanted lake and the digital theatre with its computerised water ballet. Information from BP 2000, 86130 Jaunay-Clan. Tel: 49.62.30.30.

LIMOGES

Dugrain-Delorge, 81-86 Avenue du Maréchal-de-Lattre-de-Tassigny. Tel: 55.30.47.41. Visit a working porcelain manufacturer, including the studio where the decoration is done. Open: Easter–31 October.

Le Pavillon de la Porcelaine, Z.I. de Magré, Route de Toulouse. Tel: 55.30.21.86. A huge complex devoted to the promotion of porcelain, one of the area's most important industries; also the **Musée de la porcelaine Haviland**. Factory sales. Open: April–October.

La Roseraie Municipale. Tel: 55.45.62.67. The town's rose gardens contain 5,300 rose trees covering 250 different varieties.

See too the picturesque Butcher's quarter, in particular, the **Maison Traditionnelle de la Boucherie**, one of 52 houses built in the 13th century, specifically for butchers – they lived upstairs and plied their trade downstairs, including slaughtering the animals; now open to the public by appointment. Tel: 55.34.46.87.

LE MONT-DORÉ: PUY-DE-DÔME

Take a ride on the Capucin funicular railway, to the Salon du Capucin, a clearing overlooking the Mont-Dore with children's play area. Shaded footpaths lead back down to the town (1-hour walk). Open: 15 May–15 October.

NONETTE: PUY-DE-DÔME

Visit the Maltrait workshop for demonstrations of traditional woodworking: clogs, bellows and lamps are among the products made here. Appointment preferred. Tel: 73.71.66.65.

OPME: PUY-DE-DÔME

The gardens of the châteaux are open to the public. Tel: 73.87.54.85.

ILE D'OLÉRON: CHARENTE-MARITIME

The island is a popular tourist resort, reached by viaduct (toll payable). Tour the island by tourist train. Visit the lighthouse, the Phare de Chassiron and the Parc Ornithologique de Maisonneuve.

ORCINES: PUY-DE-DÔME

Grotte Taillerie. Tel: 73.62.17.41. A cave at the foot of the Puy de Dôme where the public can watch demonstrations of gem cutting. Open: 28 March–30 September (afternoons only for last two weeks).

PADIRAC: LOT

Impressive caves in the Causse de Gramat, 103 metres (335 ft) underground. Visitors go by boat along the "mysterious river" to the Lac de la Pluie (Rain Lake), notable for its huge stalactite, in the immense

Great Dome cave which rises nearly 90 metres (300 ft) over the lake. Open: Easter–31 October.

POITIERS: CHARENTE

At the **Parc de Blossac** you can see parrots and monkeys; visit too the **Jardin des Plantes** at the opposite (northern end of the city).

ILE DE RÉ: CHARENTE-MARITIME

Popular holiday island, reached by ferry from La Rochelle. The Arche de Noé park at St-Clément-des-Baleines is open Easter–30 September and school holidays. The Parc de la Barbette at St Martin has a wide variety of trees. The **Baleines lighthouse** is open to the public (257 steps).

LA ROCHELLE: CHARENTE-MARITIME

Visit the **Jardin des Plantes**, Rue Albert 1er, botanical gardens. The **Tour de la Lanterne**, originally a lighthouse is open to the public (closed: Tuesday). The **Aquarium** by the Port des Minimes is one of the largest in France.

ROYAN: CHARENTE-MARITIME

The **Zoo de la Palmyre** is set in dramatic scenery. The **la Coubre lighthouse** offers stunning views, if you can make it up the 300 steps. Check locally for opening times.

ST-NECTAIRE: PUY-DE-DÔME

Grottes du Mont Cornadore, caves with Gallo-Roman remains, plus galleries, stalagmites, etc. Tel: 73.88.51.66.

La Maison du St-Nectaire, devoted to the history and production of the local cheese, plus tastings. Tel: 73.88.51.66.

It is also possible to see cheese being made on the farm of Mr Bellonte at Farges, just outside the town. Tel: 73.88.50.50.

ST-PIERRE-COLAMINE: PUY-DE-DÔME

Grottes de Jonas. Tel: 73.88.51.66. This troglodyte "city", complete with spiral staircase and a chapel, dates from the Middle Ages.

SAINTES: CHARENTE-MARITIME

The town boasts a fine stud farm (*haras*) which is open to the public in the afternoons, except 1 March–15 July. The public gardens features Roman ruins and a formal orangerie.

THIERS: PUY-DE-DÔME

Maison des Couteliers. Tel: 73.80.58.86. Working museum with fine displays of cutlery for which the town is famed, plus a demonstration studio.

TURSAC: DORDOGNE

Préhisto-parc. Tel: 53.50.73.19. An open-air museum, near the famous site at Les Eyzies, with scenes of prehistoric life using well-made models. Open: 10 March–11 November.

VICHY: ALLIER

One of the most well-known spas in France and probably the most modern in Europe, the Thermes themselves are open to the public every day. The town centre is laid out like a public park, with the springs emerging in the Hall des Sources.

La Pastillerie. Tel: 70.32.28.94. Vichy is also famous for its little pastille sweets and the factory is open for visits. See too **La Cristallière** "Les Pierres de A à Z", a museum-cum-shop, near the airport of minerals and rocks and artefacts made from them.

VILLENEUVE-SUR-ALLIER: ALLIER
Arboretum de Balaine, (access by RN7, north of the town). Tel: 70.43.30.07. This floral park boasts the largest private Arboretum in the country, with over 2,500 species of trees and shrubs.

VISCOMTAT: PUY-DE-DÔME
Cité de l'Abeille – bee city. Tel: 73.51.91.13. Guided tours. Open: every afternoon 15 June–15 September and Sunday May–October.

SOUTHWEST

AUCH: GERS
The **Maison de Gascogne** on the site of the old market square has an annual exhibition in July and August of local products and traditional crafts.

CASTELNAUDRY: AUDE
Le Moulin de Cugarel, Colline du Pech. Tel: 68.94.03.38. A 17th-century flour mill open to the public in summer and by appointment in winter.

CASTELLA: LOT-ET-GARONNE
Zoo Préhistorique. Tel: 53.40.15.29. A well laid-out park with full-size models of dinosaurs and other extinct species; also a guided tour of the caves, and a few children's amusements. Open: daily 1 June–15th September, also afternoons in Easter holidays, and Sunday in April and 16 September–15 October.

GAILLAC: TARN
Parc de Foucaud, charming terraced gardens, laid out by France's most famous landscape artist, Le Nôtre. See to the **Fontaine du Griffon**.

GAVARNIE: HAUTES-PYRÉNÉES
The Cirq de Gavarnie is famous for its views, but is accessible only by foot or horseback. See too the **great waterfall** (Grand Cascade), reputedly the highest in Europe and the Botanic Gardens nearby.

LABASTIDE-CLAIRENCE: PYRÉNÉES-ATLANTIQUES
This charming village has attracted many cratsmen and women who are happy to open their workshops to the public, they include Bernard Godignon, weaver (tel: 59.29.58.57), Bruno Touya, furniture maker (tel: 59.29.49.54), Joseph Dattas, wrought ironwork (tel: 59.29.66.92) and Jacques Pineau, enamelware and jewellery at the Grange Darrieux.

LABENNE: LANDES
La Pinède des Singes, on the RN 10. Tel: 59.45.43.66. In this park monkeys roam freely – beware they are artful pickpockets. Open: 1 May–30 September.

LÉON-MOLIETS: LANDES
Réserve naturelle du Courant d'Huchet, nature reserve on the Léon lake; can be visited by flat-bottomed boat (for reservations, tel: 58.48.75.39). Open: 1 April–30 October.

LIMOUX: AUDE
Maison Guinot, Avenue du Chemin de Ronde. Tel: 68.31.01.33. Producers of Blanquette de Limoux and crémant wines since 1875. Visit the cellars every weekday.

LUXEY: LANDES
Atelier des produits résineux. Tel: 58.08.01.39. See how resinous products are made in the Landes. Open: 29 March–1 November, all day in summer, at 10am only in April–May and October.

MONT-DE-MARSAN: LANDES
Parc de Nahuques. Tel: 58.75.94.38. Animal park where the animals roam freely. Children's amusements. Open: daily weekends afternoons only.

PERPIGNAN: PYRÉNÉES ORIENTALES
Chocolaterie Cantalou, Route de Thuir. Tel: 68.85.11.22. France's major exporter of chocolate; visit the factory Wednesday at 2.30pm or by appointment.

PISSOS: LANDES
Maison des artisans, 37 craftworkers have their studios in this restored traditional house. Open: Easter–1 November. Tel: 58.08.90.66. Opposite the house is a glass-blowing studio. Open: all year. Tel: 58.08.90.24.

RODEZ: AVEYRON
Lake Pareloup, covering some 3,000 acres (1,250 hectares) is the largest in southern France. This whole area, known as Lévezou has many lakes and many amenities for all kinds of water sports.

ROQUEFORT: LOT-ET-GARONNE
Parc Walibi. Tel: 53.96.58.32. A new leisure park with many exciting rides and other attractions. Open: 25 April–27 September, closed: Monday until June and last three weeks in September.

ROQUEFORT-SUR-SOULZON: AVEYRON
Of all the villages called Roquefort in France, this is the one that is famous for the so-called "king of cheeses". Visit the picturesque caves where gigantic chimneys and air ducts allow a slow penetration of damp air, essential for the proper production of the cheese. Check locally for opening times.

SABRES: LANDES
One of the main centres of the Landes forest is the **Ecomusée de Marquèze**, showing the Landes as it was a century ago. Reach it by tourist steam train from Sabres station. Open: 29 March–1 November (one train only March–May and October and November at 3pm; in summer trains run regularly from 10.30am). Information tel: 58.07.52.70; reservations tel: 58.07.50.47.

ST-BETRAND-DE-COMMINGES: HAUTES-PYRÉNÉES
Visit the village, then travel 8 km (5 miles) to the **Gargas Caves**, an important prehistoric site, known particularly for its paintings of mutilated hands, as well as animal engravings. Check locally for times.

ST-MARTIN D'ARBEROUE: PYRÉNÉES-ATLANTIQUES
The **Isturits** and **Oxocelhaya caves** have fantastic concretions. Open: mid-March to mid-November. Tel: 59.29.64.72.

ST-PÉE DE BIGORRE: HAUTES-PYRÉNÉES
The **Bétharram caves** are large chambers with an underground river (boat trips available). Open: in summer.

SARE: PYRÉNÉES-ATLANTIQUES

Caves with lightshow and prehistoric fables. Open: mid-March to 31 October. Tel: 59.54.26.95.

TARASCON: ARIÈGE

This pretty little mountain village and its surrounding area (Sabarthes) are famous for the number of **caves** to be found that show traces of human occupation. The Niaux caves boast some of the finest animal drawing of the Magdalenian era (14,000–10,000 BC); Lombrives cave has rich rock concretions, long galleries and sites such as Pyrene's grave and Bebryx's throne. See La Vache and the Bédeilhac caves and visit the **Catalan forge** in the village.

TOULOUSE: HAUTE-GARONNE

EDF Le Bazacle, 11 Quai St-Pierre. Tel: 61.23.23.81. A new venture created by the French Electricity company in what was the oldest hydroelectric factory in France, a 17th-century mill. Exhibitions and underground visits. Open: daily, afternoons only at the weekend.

Usine Clément-Ader. Visits are available to this, the most modern aircraft factory in Europe, where the Airbus A330 and A340 are assembled. For information contact the tourist office or Voyages FRAM, 1 Rue Lapeyrouse. Tel: 62.15.16.48.

ALPS

ALLEX: DRÔME

Aquarium. Tel: 75.62.62.11. Has tropical, seawater and freshwater species including turtles, exotic lizards and pirahnas. Open: every afternoon.

ANNECY: HAUTE-SAVOIE

The old town is criss-crossed by canals and the lakeside gardens also offer a pleasant spot to relax.

LES AVENIÈRES: ISÈRE

Parc Walibi, this new waterpark has many amusements for children and adults alike. Tel: 74.33.71.80.

LA BALME: ISÈRE

Visit the caves hidden in a curve of the Rhône, with their underground lake and petrifying waterfalls.

BOURG-EN-BRESSE: AIN

Bouvent leisure park, all kinds of leisure and sporting activities, including water sports.

LA CHAPELLE EN VERCORS: DRÔME

La Grotte de la Draye Blanche. Tel: 75.48.24.96. Caves with all kinds of concretions. Open: 1 April–31 October.

CHATTE: ISÈRE

Le Jardin Ferroviaire. Tel: 76.38.54.55. The Railway Garden boasts one of the largest miniature railway networks in Europe, with some 30 trains (some almost 100 years old) and almost 1,100 metres (3,600 ft) of track. Open: 15 March–30 November.

CHORANCHE: ISÈRE

The Coranche caves form an open-air museum, bearing witness to 70,000 years of human presence. Tel: 76.36.09.88.

DIEULEFIT: DRÔME

Dieulefit is well known for its pottery and glassworks, and some studios are open to the public,

including the Poterie Milan, on the Route de Nyons, tel: 75.46.31.22; and the Poterie des Grottes, Quai du Jabron; tel: 75.46.44.74.

MONTÉLIMAR: DRÔME

Famous for its production of nougat, several factories offer visits to the public, including **France Nougat le Sfynx**, Z.I. de Gournier, tel: 75.01.50.98. Also **Escobar**, Place Léopold Blanc is a former nougat factory open for visits and tastings. Closed: 15–30 September. Tel: 75.01.25.53.

MONTEYNARD: ISÈRE

Monteynard lake offers many amusements including windsurfing, water-skiing and a cruising restaurant. Tel: 76.30.63.43.

MONTREVEL-EN-BRESSE: AIN

La Ferme de Sougey, a large working farm, open to the public, at the heart of the Bresse poultry region. The farmhouse, with its remarkable fireplace, may also be visited. Tel: 74.25.47.12.

NYONS: DRÔME

Moulin à Huile Dozol-Autran. Tel: 75.26.02.52. Watch olive oil being produced by traditional methods. Open: daily except Sunday.

Visit too the **Jardin des Plantes Aromatiques**, Promenade de la Digue, which has over 150 plants which produce essential oils.

ST AGNAN EN VERCORS: DRÔME

La Grotte de la Luire. Tel: 75.02.05.04. An interesting geological site, these caves were used by the Resistance. Open: 1 April–30 September.

ST NAZAIRE EN ROYANS: DRÔME

La Grotte de Thaïs. Tel: 75.02.16.90. Caves with archaeological exhibits. Open: 1 April–31 October.

ST-TRIVIER-DE-COURTES: AIN

La Ferme de la Forêt, Courtes. Tel: 74.30.71.89. This beautiful 17th-century farmhouse has been well restored and now functions as a museum. Open: daily mid-June to mid-September, also every Sunday Easter–October.

SAMOËNS: HAUTE-SAVOIE

The charming **Alpine Garden** "Jaysinia" is named after its founder, a local peasant girl who went on to establish the famous Samaritaine store in Paris. It took 250 gardeners to create the terraces which display its plants to great effect.

THONON-LES-BAINS: HAUTE-SAVOIE

The pleasant **Jardin Anthoiniz** includes an English garden (on the opposite side of the Avenue du Léman. Just outside the town visit **Amphion park** built around a monument to the poet, Comtesse de Noailles.

UPIE: DRÔME

Le Jardin aux Oiseaux, more than 1,000 birds from all over the world. Picnic area and children's amusements. Tel: 75.84.45.90.

VALENCE: DRÔME

The **Verrerie d'Allex**, CIME, 471 Avenue Victor Hugo. Tel: 75.41.48.02. A glassworking studio which follows ancient traditions. The glassblowers work in front of the public Tuesday and Saturday but the studios are open every day except Sunday.

VILLARS-LES-DOMBES: AIN

Parc Départemental des Oiseaux, on the RN 83. Tel: 74.98.05.90. A bird sanctuary with some 350 species including water birds (pelicans) and non-flying varieties (emus). Children's play area and a miniature train which runs from April–October.

VOIRON: ISÈRE

Caves de Chartreuse, 10 Boulevard Edgar-Kofler. Tel: 76.05.81.77. Visit the distillery and cellars of the famous Chartreuse liqueur, made by the monks from a recipe created in 1737, incorporating over 130 plants. Open: Easter–1 November.

MEDITERRANEAN & THE SOUTHEAST

ANTIBES: ALPES-MARITIMES

Antibes Land, Route de Biot, on the RN7. Tel: 93.33.44.79. Leisure park and museum of African wildlife. Open: in summer 3pm–2am.
Marineland/Aquasplash, 306 Avenue Mozart. Tel: 93.33.49.49. Marine show, sea museum and aquaria; separate entrance fee for the water park with waterchutes, wave pool and other attractions. Aquasplash only open: June–September.
Villa Thuret, 12 acres of gardens and an arboretum with 2,000 species.

ARAMON: GARD

Central Thermique EDF, D2 Route de Beaucaire, contact Mr Tanguy. Tel: 66.57.02.66. Visit the nuclear power station producing electricity for the EDF. Open: weekdays.

BIOT: ALPES-MARITIMES

Noted for its earthenware pottery and hand-blown glass. Visit the ceramics studios dotted along the Route de la Mer; for glassworks, visit La Verrerie de Biot, Chemin des Combes. Tel: 93.65.03.00.

CANNES: ALPES-MARITIMES

Parc de la Croix des Gardes, gardens set above Le Suquet; La Roseraie de la Croisette, thousands of rose trees right on the seafront; Forêt Dominiale de l'Ile Sainte Marguerite, 420 park with herbarium and botanic trail.
Space Camp Patrick Baudry, 4 Allée des Cormorans, BP 76, 06322 Cannes-la-Boca, cedex. Tel: 93.47.68.02. Europe's first space-training centre.

CESSENON: HÉRAULT

Les Moulins de Roquebrun, ancient seed-crushing mill and oil crusher. Open: in summer except Monday. Contact Mme Auvity, tel: 67.89.64.97.

FRÉJUS: VAR

Aquatica, a waterpark on the RN98. Tel: 94.52.01.01.
Safari de l'Esterel, Le Capitou. Zoo. Tel: 94.40.70.65.

GRASSE: ALPES-MARITIMES

Many of the town's famous perfumeries offer guided tours. Try the following: **Fragonard**, Boulevard Fragonard, Route de Cannes. Tel: 93.36.44.65.
Gallimard, 73 Route de Cannes. Tel: 93.09.20.00.

HYÈRES: VAR

Magic World, leisure park with regular firework displays and *son-et-lumière* shows. Open: evenings 8pm–1am June–September.

LA LONDE LES MAURES: VAR

Tropical Bird Garden, Quartier Saint-Honoré. Tel: 94.35.02.15.

LE LAVANDOU: VAR

Parc de Loisirs, amusements for all ages.
Miagara Parc Nautique, just north of town on the D27, Route du Canadel. Tel: 94.49.58.85. Water park with a variety of amusements.

MENTON: ALPES-MARITIMES

The "Lemon Capital" boasts many **gardens**: the Palais Carnoles has some 50 varieties of citrus fruits; Les Colombières covers 6 hectares (15 acres); see too the botanical garden of the Natural History Museum and the Jardins Bioves where the International Lemon Festival is held in February.

MONACO

Parc de Fontvieille, landscaped gardens surrounding the Pricess Grace rose garden with its 150 varieties. See too the **zoological gardens** at La Condamine.

NICE: ALPES-MARITIMES

Confiserie du Vieux Nice, Quai Pacino. Tel: 93.55.43.50. Confectioners open to the public for guided tours (English spoken) and sampling. Closed: winter Sunday.
Moulin d'Alziari, 318 Boulevard de la Madeleine. Tel: 93.44.45.12. Olive mill, operational from 10 November–15 April, but open all year.
Observatoire de Calern, Centre of Geodynamic and Astronomic research offers astronomy shows May–October, tours at 3pm daily July and August. Information from 2 Passage du Petit Parc, 06000 Nice. Tel: 93.412.66.16.
Parc des Miniatures, Avenue Impératrice Eugenie. Tel: 93.97.02.02. Nice in miniature.
Zygoparc, Colline de Cremat, Saint-Isidore. Tel: 93.18.36.36. Water theme park. Open: June–September.
Nice boasts many parks and gardens including the medieval gardens of the Cimiez monastery, the Jardins d'Acropolis displaying modern sculpture and the Parc du Château.

OPIO: ALPES MARITIMES

Mouilin d'Opio, 2 Route du Chateauneuf. Tel: 93.77.23.03. 15th-century olive mill offering guided tours, November–March (not Sunday).

SAINT-CÉZAIRE: ALPES-MARTIMES

Les Grottes. Tel: 93.60.22.35. Spectacular underground caves. Open: mid-February to September.

ST-JEAN DE VEDAS: HÉRAULT

The daily regional newspaper *Midi-Libre* welcomes visitors at 2.30pm Tuesday and Friday and at 10.30pm Monday–Friday. Contact Mlle Gastou, tel: 67.07.67.07.

VALLAURIS: ALPES-MARITIMES

The haunt of many local potters; a list of studios open to the public is available from the Syndicat des Potiers, Espace Grandjean, Avenue du Stade. Tel: 93.64.17.93.

Medieval town where you can visit the **Fabrique de Nougat**, 28 Avenue Colonel Meyer.Tel: 93.58.13.28. (Guided tour of the factory in English available). Closed: Sunday afternoon.

The **Maurice Lavoillet Foundation** at the Château Notre Dame des Fleurs grows plants for the production of perfume and liqueurs, it also has a **Museum of Perfume** and a restaurant specialising in aromatic cuisine.

VERGÈZE: GARD

Source Perrier, Les Bouillens, visit the glassworks bottling the mineral waters of Perrier. Open: weekdays. Contact the Service Accueil, tel: 66.87.62.00.

LE VIGAN: GARD

La Maison des Magnans, Molières-Cavaillac. Tel: 67.81.05.06. Silkworm factory, open for visits from 15 May–15 September.

VILLENEUVE-LÈS-AVIGNON: GARD

Moulin à Huile de Chartreuse, Impasse Pouzargue. Tel: 90.25.45.59. Olive oil manufacturer. Open to the public: 15 March–15 September.

NATIONAL PARKS

France has 33 national parks (Parcs Naturels) which all come under the protection of the Fédération des Parcs Naturels de France. Covering some of the most outstanding areas of natural beauty, these parks offer a sanctuary for wildlife and a host of leisure opportunities.

The main agency concerned with promoting the parks nationally is Clés de France, who provide information regarding facilities in individual parks, as well as details about excursions and activity holidays. If you really want to discover the delights of the countryside in the Landes, the Vercors, the Vosges, the Morvan, to name but a few, contact Clés de France at 13 Rue St-Louis, 78100 St-Germain-en-Laye. Tel: (1) 30.61.23.23.

CULTURE PLUS

MUSEUMS & ART GALLERIES

Most museums charge an entrance fee; for those that are state owned expect to pay between FF10 and FF25 (half price on Sundays). Reductions are usually given for children, senior citizens and students – on production of a valid card.

In Paris a single admission ticket gives entry to 65 museums and monuments in the capital and the Ile de France for one, three or five days. Available from the main tourist office at participating museums and main métro stations. Other major cities offer a similar service; enquire at tourist offices.

The museums listed here are open every day, mornings and afternoons (opening is variable on public holidays), except where specified otherwise. As a general rule, national museums are closed on Tuesday and municipal museums on Monday. Remember, most close for a long lunch from noon or 12.30 to around 2.30pm, although major sites are often open continuously, especially during the summer months.

PARIS

Musée du Louvre, Pyramide, Cour Napoléon, 75001. Tel: 40.20.50.50. The world's largest museum, and still growing; the new Richelieu gallery is due to open in 1993 displaying the Islamic collections. The museum has five major departments; its most famous "stars" being the *Venus de Milo*, Leonardo da Vinci's *Mona Lisa* and the *Victory of Samothrace*. Closed: Tuesday. There is a separate entrance for the **Musée des Arts Decoratifs**, 107-109 Rue de Rivoli, 75001. Closed: Monday and Tuesday. Tel: 42.60.32.14.

Centre National d'Art et de Culture, Georges Pompidou, 19 Rue Beaubourg, 75004. Tel: 42.77.12.33. Huge arts centre at the heart of Paris, which holds regular exhibitions to celebrate the creativity of the 20th century. Also houses the National Museum of Modern Art, the Industrial Design Centre, the Public Information Library and the Insitute for Acoustic and Musical Research. Open: noon (weekends 10am)–10pm.

Musée d'Orsay, 1 Rue de Bellechasse, 75007. Tel: 45.49.49.49. One of the newer museums, in the former Orsay station, displaying works of art (including cinema and photographic arts) from the latter half of the 19th century to the World War I. Closed: Monday.

Musée de l'Armée, Hôtel National des Invalides, 6 Place Vauban, 75007. Tel: 45.55.37.70. Weapons, uniforms and the tomb of Napoleon I.

Cité des Sciences et de l'Industrie la Villette, 30 Avenue Corentin Cariou, 75019. Tel: 40.05.70.00. New complex, opened in 1986 including the Géode, an auditorium where the spectator feels part of the image; the Argonaute (submarine), the Inventorium and the Planetarium. Closed: Monday.

Galerie Nationale du Jeu de Paume, Place de la Concorde, Jardin des Tuileries, 20 Rue Royale, 75001. Tel: 47.03.12.50. Recently renovated, former Impressionist museum, now showing modern works of art: sculpture, photography, cinema, etc. Closed: Monday and mornings, except weekend.

Musée Marmottan, 2 Rue Louis Boilly, 75016. Tel: 42.24.07.02. Now houses the Impressionists, including 100 of Monet's works. Closed: Monday.

Musée Antoine Bourdelle, 16 Rue Antoine Bourdelle, 75015. Tel: 45.48.67.27. Recently extended, the home and workshop of sculptor Antoine Bourdelle displays most of his works. Closed: Monday.

Musée d'Art Moderne de la Ville de Paris, 11 Avenue du Président Wilson, 75016. Tel: 47.23.61.27. Features works by the Cubists and the Fauvists among others. Closed: Monday.

Musée d'Art Juif, 42 Rue des Saules, 75018. Tel: 42.57.84.15. Religious objects, models of synagogues and works by Pissaro, Chagall and Lipchitz. Closed: Friday, Saturday and Jewish holidays.

Musée des Arts de la Mode, Union des Arts Décoratifs, Pavillon de Marson, 109 Rue de Rivoli, 75001. Tel: 42.60.32.14. French fashion from the 18th century to the present day: 30,000 costumes. Closed: Monday and Tuesday.

Musée Auguste Rodin, Hôtel Biron, 77 Rue de Varenne, 75007. Tel: 47.05.01.34. Displays the works and personal collection of Rodin, including *The Gates of Hell* and the *Burghers of Calais* in the garden. Closed: Monday.

Musée Balzac, 47 Rue Raynouard, 75016. Tel: 42.24.56.38. The "Cabane de Passy", home of the writer from 1840–47. Closed: Monday.

Musée National Eugène Delacroix, 6 Rue de Furstenberg, 75006. Tel: 43.54.04.87. Paintings and memorabilia in the painter's former studio. Closed: Tuesday.

Musée Grévin, 10 Boulevard Montmartre, 75009. Tel: 47.70.85.05. Waxworks displaying 500 famous personages from French history and contemporary life. Open: daily 1–7pm (opens 10am in school holidays). See too the **Musée Grévin Forum** at Les Halles for an evocation of the *belle époque*. Tel: 40.26.28.50.

Institut du Monde Arabe, 1 Rue des Fossés St-Bernard, 75005. Tel: 40.51.38.38. Collection of riches of the Arab-Islamic world from the 7th to the 19th century in a remarkable building opened in 1987. The 9th-floor restaurant offers panoramic views of the Seine. Open: 1–8pm, closed: Monday.

Musée du Cinéma Henri Langlois, Palais de Chaillot, Aile Passy, Place du Trocadéro, 75116. Tel: 45.53.74.39. Shows the history and development of the cinema. Closed: Tuesday.

Musée de la Monnaie, 11 Quai Conti, 75006. Tel: 40.46.55.35. History of France told in its money, medals and other documents. Open: 1–6pm (9pm Wednesday, closed: Monday).

Musée National du Moyen-Age Thermes de Cluny, 6 Place Paul Painlevé, 75005. Tel: 43.25.62.00. Medieval treasures, including the "Lady and the Unicorn" tapestry, saved from ruin in the 19th century and displayed on the site of the Gallo-Roman thermal baths. Closed: Tuesday.

Musée Picasso, Hôtel du Juigné-Salé, 5 Rue de Thorigny, 75003. Tel: 42.71.25.21. Collection of over 200 paintings and other artworks, taken as death duty from the artist's estate. Closed: Tuesday.

Musée de la Sculpture en Plein Air, Quai St-Bernard, 75005. Tel: 43.26.91.90. This vast garden on the banks of the Seine displays recent sculptures from Gilioli, Zadkine, César, etc.

Musée Victor Hugo, Hôtel de Rohan Guéménée, 6 Place des Vosges, 75004. Tel: 42.72.10.16. The home of the author for 16 years; drawings, documents and memorabilia. Closed: Monday.

Musée Zadkine, 100 bis Rue d'Assas, 75006. Tel: 43.26.91.90. Renovated studio where the sculptor lived and worked until his death (1967). Closed: Monday.

Musée de la Poste, 34 Boulevard de Vaugirard, 75015. Tel: 42.79.23.00. History of the development of the French postal service. Closed: Sunday.

ILE DE FRANCE

Musée de l'Air et Espace, Aéroport du Bourget, 93350 Le Bourget. Tel: 48.35.99.99. Civil and military aircraft from 1897 to the present day. Closed: Monday.

Musée des Antiquités Nationales, Château de Saint-Germain-en-Laye, 78103 Saint-Germain-en-Laye. Tel: 34.51.53.65. Diverse collections in a former royal palace. Closed: Tuesday.

Cartier, Fondation pour l'Art Contemporain, 3 Rue de la Manufacture, 78350 Jouy-en-Josas. Tel: 39.56.46.46. Modern art in the former home of Baron Oberkampf who created the "Toile de Jouy". Open: every afternoon (closed: December).

Musée National de Céramique, Place de la Manufacture, 92310 Sèvres. Tel: 45.34.99.05. Traces the development of the pottery and porcelain industry in the Royal Sèvres factory, established in 1738. Closed: Tuesday.

Musée du Cheval de Course, Château de Maisons-Laffitte, 78600 Maisons-Laffitte. Tel: 39.62.01.49. Dedicated to horse racing. Open: 16 April–15 October.

Musée des Equipage, Domaine de Vaux-le-Vicomte, 77950 Maincy. Tel: 60.66.97.09. Carriage museum set in a splendid château.

La Grand Arche, Parvis de la Défense, 92040 Paris-La Défense. Tel: 49.07.27.57. Recent extension to the Louvre, built in 1989 to hold temporary exhibitions.

Musée de l'Ile de France, Château de Sceaux, 92339 Sceaux. Tel: 46.61.06.71. The history of the region is celebrated in a castle set in one of Le Nôtre's best gardens. Closed: Tuesday.

Musée Nationale de la Renaissance, Château d'Ecouen, 95440 Ecouen. Tel: 39.90.04.04. Collections of weapons, tapestries and objets d'art from the Renaissance, an extension of the Cluny collection in Paris. Closed: Tuesday.

LOIRE VALLEY TO THE ATLANTIC COAST

AMBOISE: INDRE-ET-LOIRE
Musée de la Poste, Hôtel Joyeuse, 6 Rue de Joyeuse. Tel: 47.57.02.21. Shows the development of the French postal service. Closed: Monday.

Manoir de Clos-Lucé. Tel: 47.57.00.73. See working models of 40 of Leonardo da Vinci's inventions at the house where he spent his last years.

ANGERS: MAINE ET LOIRE
Musée Jean Lurçat et Tapisserie Contemporaine, 4 Boulevard Arago. Tel: 41.87.41.06. Old and contemporary tapestries. Closed: Monday.

The Galerie David d'Angers, 33 bis Rue Toussaint. Tel: 41.87.21.03. Displays the art of the sculptor (1788–1856), who donated all his studio works as a gesture of gratitude to the city. Closed: Monday.

L'Espace Cointreau, Carrefour Molière, St-Barthélemy. Tel: 41.43.25.21. The producers of the famous liqueur have a museum just outside the town. Closed: Sunday.

CHÂTEAUNEUF-SUR-LOIRE: LOIRET
Musée de la Marine de Loire et du Vieux Châteauneuf, history of navigation of the great river and the people whose living depended on it. Open: weekends and mornings Monday–Friday (all day Tuesday–Sunday in July and August).

CHÂTEAU-RENAULT: INDRE-ET-LOIRE
Musée du Cuir, on RN10. Tel: 47.56.91.35. History of the leather industry in a former tannery. Open: Wednesday, Saturday and Sunday afternoons mid-May to mid-September.

CHOLET: MAINE-ET-LOIRE
Musée des Guerres de Vendée, Rue Travot. Tel: 41.62.20.78. Recounts the story of the Vendée Wars.

DESCARTES: INDRE-ET-LOIRE
Musée René Descartes et René Boylesve, 29 Rue Descartes. Tel: 47.59.79.19. Dedicated to the philosopher and the novelist, Boylesve. Closed: mornings and all day Monday.

GIEN: LOIRET
Musée de la Faïencerie, Manufacture de Gien, Place de la Victoire. Tel: 38.67.00.05. Fine pottery. Gien Château houses an International Museum of Hunting.

MONTSOREAU: MAINE-ET-LOIRE
Musée de Champignon. Tel: 41.51.70.30. Museum dedicated to one the area's most important products – the mushroom.

NANTES: LOIRE-ATLANTIQUE
Musée des Beaux-Arts, 10 Rue Georges Clemenceau. Tel: 40.74.53.24. Important collection of Western art from the 13th century to the present. Closed: Tuesday.

ORLÉANS: LOIRET
Musée Historique et Archéologique de l'Orléanais, Hôtel Cabu, Place de l'Abbée Desnoyers. Tel: 38.53.39.22. Elegant Renaissance building housing, *inter alia*, the important Gallo-Roman bronzes from Neuvy-en-Sullias. Closed: Tuesday.

Maison de Jeanne d'Arc, Place du Gén. de Gaulle. Tel: 38.42.25.45. Dedicated to Saint Joan. Open: mornings (not Monday), also afternoons May–October.

Musée des Beaux-Arts, Place Ste-Croix. Tel: 38.53.39.22. Arts museum with good collections of 17th and 18th French and European paintings and decorative arts section. Closed: Tuesday.

POITIERS: VIENNE
Musée Sainte-Croix, 61 Rue Saint-Simplicien. Tel: 49.41.07.53. Houses two main collections, one displaying the history of the Poitous region, the other paintings and *objets d'art* including a collection of medallions. Closed: Tuesday.

ROMORANTIN: LOIR-ET-CHER
Musée Municipal de la Course Automobile, 29-32 Faubourg d'Orléans. Tel: 54.76.07.06. Racing car museum. Open: mid-March to 31 October (not Monday or Sunday morning).

LES SABLES-D'OLONNE: VENDÉE
Musée de l'Abbaye Sainte-Croix, Rue de Verdun. Tel: 51.32.01.16. A former Benedictine convent housing the work of Gaston Chaissac and other modern artists. Closed: Monday November to mid-June.

SACHÉ: INDRE-ET-LOIRE
Musée de Balzac, housed in the château where the writer spent 10 years. Closed: Wednesday November to mid-March.

SCUILLY: INDRE-ET-LOIRE
Maison Natale de Rabelais, La Devinière, 37500 Chinon. Tel: 47.95.91.18. Museum in the writer's birthplace. Closed: Wednesday February to mid-March and October–November.

TOURS: INDRE-ET-LOIRE
Musée des Beaux Arts, 18 Place François Sicard. Tel: 47.05.68.73. One of France's best provincial arts museums. Closed: Tuesday.

TRÉLAZE: MAINE-ET-LOIRE
Musée de l'Ardoise, 32 Rue de la Maraîchère. Tel: 41.69.04.71. Traces the history of slate mining in the region. Open: March–30 November Tuesday–Sunday afternoons; demonstrations at 3pm.

BRITTANY, NORMANDY & THE NORTH

ALENÇON: ORNE

Musée des Beaux-Arts et de la Dentelle, near Place Foch. Tel: 33.32.40.07. Important collections on lacemaking for which the area is famous; closed: Monday.

Musée de la Dentelle au Point d'Alençon, 33 Rue du Pont-Neuf. Tel: 33.26.27.27. The national gallery for this particular craft; closed: Sunday.

AMIENS: SOMME

Musée de Picardie, 48 Rue de la République. Tel: 22.91.36.44. Decorated in remarkable Napoleon III style, the museum houses archaeological collections and more recent objets d'art and paintings. Closed: Monday.

Maison à la Tour, 2 Rue Charles Dubois. Tel: 22.45.37.84. A vast collection of documentation on the life of Jules Verne in the house where the writer lived and worked.

BAGNOLES-DE-L'ORNE: ORNE

Musée des Sapeurs Pompiers, 16 Boulevard Albert-Christophe. Tel: 33.38.10.34. Houses the biggest collection of horse-drawn fire appliances. Open: 1 April–30 October, closed: Wednesday.

BALLEROY: CALVADOS

Musée des Ballons, in the château. Tel: 31.21.60.61. The world of hot-air balloons from the Montgolfier brothers onwards. Open: 15 April–31 October, closed: Wednesday.

BAYEUX: CALVADOS

Musée de la Tapisserie, Centre Guillaume le Conquérant, Rue de Nesmond. Tel: 31.92.05.48. Displays the whole of the historic Bayeux Tapestry depicting the story of the conquest of England by William the Conqueror. To see it "in the flesh" is quite breathtaking.

BEAUVAIS: OISE

Galerie Nationale de la Tapisserie et d'Art Textile. Tel: 44.05.14.28. Modern gallery housing national collections of tapestries and textiles spanning five centuries. Closed: Monday.

BLÉRANCOURT: AISNE

Musée National de la Coopération Franco-américaine. Tel: 23.39.60.16. In 1917 two Americans set up the American voluntary ambulance service in this 17th-century château. To commemorate this, it became in 1929 a museum of Franco-American cooperation. Closed: Tuesday.

BREST: FINISTÈRE

Musée des Beaux Arts, 22 Rue Emile-Zola. Tel: 98.44.66.27. Collection 16th–18th century French and Italian paintings, Pont-Aven school and 19th–20th century Breton paintings. Open: daily except Tuesday and Sunday mornings.

Musée Naval, naval museum in the castle.

BUIRONFOSSE: AISNE

Musée du Sabot. Tel: 23.97.24.28. See how traditional clogs are made in the working museum. Closed: Sunday.

CAEN: CALVADOS

Musée des Beaux Arts, in the château. Tel: 31.85.28.63. The former home of William the Conqueror. Collections include faïence and 16th to 18th-century paintings. Closed: Tuesday.

CHÂTEAU-THIERRY: AISNE

Musée Jean de la Fontaine. Tel: 23.69.05.60. Museum of the fabled author in his birthplace. Open: daily, except Tuesday (afternoons only 1 October–31 March).

CONCARNEAU: FINISTÈRE

Musée de la Pêche. Tel: 98.97.10.20. Fishing museum in the walled town.

See too the **Marinarium**. Tel: 98.97.06.59.

DINAN: CÔTES D'ARMOR

Musée du Château. Tel: 96.39.45.20. Breton costumes and local history in Duchess Anne's castle. Open: daily (afternoons only November–February; closed: Tuesday afternoon except in summer).

Musée de l'Oiseau. Tel: 96.39.22.43. Stuffed birds, aviary and gardens. Open: daily (afternoons only November–February; closed: Tuesday afternoon except in summer).

DINARD: ILLE-ET-VILAINE

Musée de la Mer, 17 Avenue Georges V. Tel: 99.46.13.90. Devoted to the sea. Open: Whitsun to mid-September.

DOUAI: NORD

Musée de la Chartreuse, 130 Rue des Chartreux. Tel: 27.87.26.63. A former Carthusian convent housing superb collections of paintings, faïence and other objets d'art. Closed: Tuesday.

DOUARNENEZ: FINISTÈRE

Musée du Bateau, Place d'Enfer. Tel: 98.92.65.20. Fascinating collection, all about boats, housed in a former cannery.

FARGNIERS: AISNE

Musée Départemental de la Résistance et de la Déportation en Picardie, Place Carnégie. Tel: 23.57.93.77. Presents documents and other materials relating to the resistance movement, particularly in Aisne. Open: Wednesday–Sunday afternoon.

FÉCAMP: SEINE-MARITIME

Musée de la Bénédictine, 110 Rue Alexandre-le-Grand. Tel: 35.28.00.06. Find out all about the production of this famous liqueur and the abbey where its production started.

FOUGÈRES: FINISTÈRE

Musée de la Chaussure, in the castle. Tel: 99.99.18.98. Dedicated to footwear. Open: daily except January.

Musée de la Villéon, 51 Rue Nationale. Tel: 99.99.18.98. Works of the Impressionist painter Emmanuel de Villéon. Open: daily Easter–September, otherwise weekends and school holidays.

JOSSELIN: MORBIHAN

Musée des Poupées, 3 Rue des Trente. Tel: 97.22.36.45. Doll museum.

LAMBALLE: CÔTES D'ARMOR

Musée Mathurin Méheut, Place du Martray. Major collection of works by Breton artists. Open: 1 June–15 September (not Sunday).

LILLE: NORD
Musée des Beaux-Arts, Place de la République. Tel: 20.57.01.84. Outstanding collections from all schools of painting – Flemish, Dutch, French, Spanish, etc. Closed: Tuesday.

LORIENT: MORBIHAN
Galerie Espace l'Orient, 13 Rue Beauvais. Tel: 97.21.78.73. Modern art. Open: Monday–Saturday afternoon.
Musée de la Mer, Maison de la Mer, Quai Rohan. Tel: 97.84.87.37. Sea museum. Closed: Tuesday.

LE MANS: SARTHE
Musée de Tessé, 2 Avenue de Paderborn. Tel: 43.47.38.51. Paintings and objets d'art displayed in former diocesan buildings in the Jacobin quarter.

MONTFORT-SUR-MEU: FINISTÈRE
Eco-Musée d'Art et Traditions Populaire. Rural arts, costumes and traditions. Closed: Monday and Sunday morning (also Saturday October–May).

NOGENT L'ARTAUD: AISNE
Centre de l'Automobile Ancienne, 10 Square de Labédoyère. Tel: 23.70.11.10. Working museum where vintage cars are lovingly restored. Closed: Tuesday.

PAIMPOL: CÔTES D'ARMOR
Musée de la Mer. Tel: 96.20.80.15. The sea – its history and evolution. Open: April to mid-September.

PLEDELIAC: CÔTES D'ARMOR
Ferme de St Esprit des Bois. Tel: 96.31.14.67. Reconstruction of an early 20th-century Breton farm. Open: every afternoon 1 July–30 September and Sunday afternoon Easter–1 November.

PONT-AVEN: FINISTÈRE
Musée des Beaux-Arts. Tel: 98.06.14.43. Twenty galleries including works of the Pont-Aven school initiated by Gauguin.

PONT-L'ABBÉ: FINISTÈRE
Musée Bigouden. Tel: 98.87.24.44. Local costumes. Guided visits June–September; closed: Sunday.

PONT-L'EVÊQUE: CALVADOS
Musée du Calvados et des Métiers Anciens. Tel: 31.64.12.87. Dedicated to the production of Calvados and old trades of the region.
Musée "La Belle Epoque de l'Automobile", Château de Betteville. Tel: 31.65.05.02. Displays 100 vehicles produced between 1898 and 1950. Open: Easter–11 November.

PORT-LOUIS: MORBIHAN
Musée de la Citadelle. Tel: 97.82.19.13. Encompasses two museums, one of naval weaponry, one dedicated to the Compagnie des Indes. Closed: Tuesday and 1 November–15 December.

QUEBRIAC: FINISTÈRE
Musée Internationale de la Faune, Les Brulons. Tel: 99.68.10.22. Three hundred stuffed animals in "naturalistic" settings. Open: Easter–31 October.

QUIMPER: FINISTÈRE
Musée des Beaux-Arts, 40 Place Saint-Corentin. Tel: 98.95.45.20. This museum was founded in 1864 to house the collections bequeathed by Jean de Silguy; one gallery is devoted to the Pont-Aven group. Closed: Tuesday.

Musée de la Faïence, Route de Bénodet. Tel: 98.90.09.36. Pottery museum.

RENNES: FINISTÈRE
Musée des Beaux Arts, 20 Quai Emile-Zola. Tel: 99.79.44.16. Fine arts from 15th to 20th century. Closed: Tuesday.
Musée de Bretagne, on the same site as above. Tel: 99.28.55.84. For costumes and an insight into Celtic life.

ROUEN: SEINE-MARITIME
Musée Le Secq des Tournelles, Eglise Saint-Laurent, Rue Jacques-Villon. Tel: 35.71.28.40. Named after the donator of the most important collection of antique wrought-ironwork in the world. Exhibits date from the Roman period to the present day. Closed: Tuesday and Wednesday morning.

Rouen has several other museums, including Fine Arts, Pottery and the Musée Corneille, dedicated to the poet.

ST-MALO: FINISTÈRE
Musée d'Histoire de la Ville, in the castle. Tel: 99.56.41.36. The town's history from the slave trade to the Nazi occupation. Closed: Tuesday.
Musée Quic-en-Groigne, also in the castle. Tel: 99.40.80.26. Waxworks. Open: April–September.

ST-MARCEL: MORBIHAN
Musée Régional d'Histoire de l'Occupation et de Résistance en Bretagne. Tel: 97.75.17.41. Recalls wartime occupation and resistance.

ST-OMER: PAS-DE-CALAIS
Musée de l'Hôtel Sandelin, 14 Rue Carnot. Tel: 21.38.00.94. This 1776 mansion displays precious objects and furniture that graced 18th-century life, including 750 Delft pieces. Closed: Monday, Tuesday.

ST-QUENTIN: AISNE
Musée Antoine Lecuyer, 28 Rue Antoine Lecuyer. Tel: 23.64.06.66. Pastels by De la Tour; also drawings by other artists and faïence. Closed: Tuesday and Sunday morning.

TREGASTEL: CÔTES D'ARMOR
Aquarium de la Côte de Granit Rose. Tel: 96.23.88.67. Breton fauna and exotic fish set amongst the rocks. Open: May weekends, afternoons in June, September and October, all day July and August.

VALOGNES: MANCHE
Musée Regional du Cidre. Tel: 33.40.22.73. In a 15th-century house, discover the history of the production of cider in the region over the past 500 years, plus old costumes and furniture. Open: 1 June–30 September (not Sunday morning or Wednesday).

VANNES: MORBIHAN
Musée des Beaux Arts, Rue des Halles. Tel: 97.42.59.56. Works by local and internationally renowned artists (Corot, Goya, Delacroix).
Musée Préhistorique, Château Gaillard, Rue Noë. Tel: 97.42.59.80.

VILLEDIEU-LES-POÊLES: MANCHE
Maison de la Dentellière et Musée du Cuivre Ancien. Tel: 33.90.20.92. Lacemaking and

copperworking in a working museum. Open: Easter–11 November except Tuesday morning. See too **Atelier du Cuivre** and the **Maison de l'Etain**, for demonstrations of working with copper and tin.

VILLENEUVE-D'ASCQ: NORD

Musée d'Art Moderne, 1 Allée du Musée. Tel: 20.05.42.46. Museum built in 1983 to house the collections bequeathed by the Masurels, including works of Braque, Moro and Picasso. Closed: Tuesday.

VILLERS-COTTERETS: AISNE

Musée Alexandre Dumas. Tel: 23.96.23.30. A museum dedicated to the writer in his home town. Open: every afternoon except Tuesday.

VIMOUTIERS: ORNE

Musée du Camembert. Tel: 33.39.30.29. Reconstruction of a farm producing the famous local cheese. Open: 1 March–31 December (closed: Monday morning 1 May–31 October, plus Saturday afternoon and Sunday morning in March, April, November and December).

War Museums and the **Normandy Landing Beaches**: There are roughly 20 war museums in Normandy, including the Pegasus Bridge museum at Benouville, The Battle of Normandy Museum at Bayeux, the Utah Beach Museum at Ste-Marie-du-Mont and the Peace Museum at Caen's war memorial which includes the new Galerie of the Nobel Peace Prize. 1994 is the 50th anniversary of the Normandy landings and will be marked by ceremonies and remembrance services throughout the summer. For more information, contact the Normandy tourist office (see *Useful Addresses*).

EASTERN FRANCE & BURGUNDY

AINVELLE: HAUTE-SAÔNE

Musée du Chat, Rue de l'Eglise. Tel: 84.49.89.19. For cat lovers: paintings, sculptures, etc. Open: Wednesday–Sunday afternoon Easter–30 September, weekends only 1 October–31 December.

AMPLEPUIS: RHÔNE

Musée Barthélémy-Thimonier. Tel: 74.89.08.90. Unusual museum displaying the complete history of the sewing-machine, with some unique examples. Open: afternoons Wednesday and Friday–Sunday.

ANCY-LE-FRANC: YONNE

Musée de l'Automobile et de l'Hippomobile. Tel: 86.75.12.41. Cars and horse-drawn carriages in the grounds of the Renaissance château. Open: April–November. Information: M de Menton, Château d'Ancy-le-Franc, 89160 Ancy-le-Franc.

ARBOIS: JURA

Musée de la Maison Paternelle de Pasteur, 83 Rue des Courcelles. Rooms kept as they were at the time of the scientist's death, in his family home. For information about visits contact M Rémy, tel: 84.66.11.72.

AUTUN: SAÔNE-ET-LOIRE

Musée Lapidaire, 10 Rue Saint Nicolas. Tel: 85.52.35.71. Gallo-Roman architecture. Open: daily mid April–September; otherwise closed on Tuesday and all of February.

Musée Rolin, 3 Rue des Bancs. Tel: 85.52.09.76. Collections include Roman mosaics, 12th-century sculpture of Eve and 19th-century paintings. Closed: Tuesday.

Musée Verger Tarin, 7 Rue Sous-Chantre. Tel: 85.52.09.76. Shows the interior of a Burgundian house exactly as it would have been in 1845. Closed: Tuesday, Sunday mornings and October.

AUXERRE: YONNE

Musée Leblanc-Duvernoy, 3 Place du Coche-d'Eau. Tel: 86.51.09.74. Important collections of regional porcelain and Puisaye earthenware; also Beauvais tapestries and furniture all set in a grand 18th-century house. Open: every afternoon, except Tuesday. Ticket includes entry to the crypts of Saint-Germain Abbey.

Nearby is the **Musée du Coche-d'Eau**, Place du Coche-d'Eau. Tel: 86.51.09.74. In a beautiful 16th-century house, it specialises in temporary exhibitions on different themes: archaeology, porcelain, popular art etc. Open: every afternoon, except Tuesday. Free entry.

BEAUCOURT: TERRITOIRE DE BELFORT

Musée Européen de l'Industrie Horlogorie et Mécanique, 16 Rue F-Japy. Tel: 84.56.57.52. The Japy factory has been transformed into a museum dedicated to clockmaking. Open: Wednesday–Sunday afternoon.

BEAUNE: CÔTE-D'OR

Musée du Vin de Bourgogne, Rue d'Enfer. At the heart of the wine-making region, in the splendid former mansion of the Dukes of Burgundy; 12 rooms devoted to viticulture and Bacchanalian art, including a tapestry by Lurçat. Closed: Tuesday from November–April.

Maison des Confréries, 20 Rue du Faubourg Madeleine. Tel: 80.24.05.05. Museum of the European Brotherhoods of wine also offers wine-tastings, shops and banqueting suites.

BELFORT: TERRITOIRE DE BELFORT

Musée d'Art et d'Histoire, in the château. Tel: 84.28.52.96. History of the city as well as displays of paintings (including Courbet and Durer), military paraphernalia, numismatics and a growing collection of modern sculpture. Closed: Tuesday.

BESANÇON: DOUBS

Musée des Beaux-Arts et d'Archéologie, 1 Place de la Révolution, one of the first municipal collections to be gathered in France, housed in a former granary.

Musée Populaire Comtois, in the Citadel. Tel: 81.82.16.22. Rich collections relating to the history and the people of the region of Franche-Comté. Closed: Tuesday.

Musée de la Résistance et de la Déportation, also in the Citadel. Tel: 81.83.37.14. History museum dealing with World War II, including artworks created by prisoners of concentration camps. Closed: Tuesday.

BRIENNE-LE-CHÂTEAU: AUBE
Napoleon attended the military academy in the town from the age of nine and there is a small museum dedicated to him. Closed: Monday.

CHALON-SUR-SAÔNE: SAÔNE-ET-LOIRE
Musée Denon, Place de l'Hôtel de Ville. Tel: 85.48.01.70. ext. 4237. Diverse collections ranging from archaeological exhibits, an important Bronze Age collection and transport on the waterways. Closed: Tuesday.

Musée Nicéphore Niepce, 28 Quai des Messageries. Tel: 85.48.41.98. Named after the father of photography, it claims to be the best photographic museum in Europe, with an outstanding collection of cameras, the first colour photos every taken and contemporary exhibitions. Closed: Tuesday.

CHARLEVILLE-MÉZIÈRES: ARDENNES
The **Vieux Moulin** (not in fact a mill, but a town house decorated with monumental ionic columns), houses the **Ardenne Museum** and the **Rimbaud Museum**, dedicated to the 19th-century poet who was a native of the town. Check locally for times.

CHÂTEAU-CHINON: NIÈVRE
Musée du Septennat, 6 Rue du Château. Tel: 86.57.80.90, ext: 418. Unusual museum, showing the collection of gifts received by President Mitterrand, since 1981. Open: daily May–September.

CHATILLON-SUR-CHALARONNE: AIN
Apothicairerie de l'Ancien Hospice, Place Saint-Vincent-de-Paul. Tel: 74.55.02.27. Former pharmacy, established in 1731 with a remarkable collection of 120 pots made from local faïence. Open: every afternoon (closed: Sunday, except June to mid-September).

CHÂTEAU-LAMBERT: HAUTE-SAÔNE
Musée de la Montagne, Le Haut du Them. Tel: 84.20.43.09. An evocation of life in the Vosges mountains. Closed: Tuesday.

CHATILLON-SUR-SEINE: CÔTE-D'OR
Musée Archéologique, 7 Rue du Bourg. Tel: 80.91.24.67 (town hall). A fine 16th-century building housing one of the most important collections in the region, including the Vix treasure (remarkable 1.64-metre high urn). Closed: Monday, except from mid-June to mid-September.

COLOMBEY-LES-DEUX-EGLISES: HAUTE-MARNE
La Boisserie was De Gaulle's country home, where he spent his final year (he is buried in the little churchyard). Popular with French tourists. Closed: Tuesday. Outside the village stands the imposing memorial to the General, the Cross of Lorraine.

COLMAR: HAUT-RHIN
Musée d'Unterlinden, Place d'Unterlinden. Tel: 89.41.89.23. Varied collections, particularly Late Medieval and Renaissance art from the Rhinelands, housed in an old Dominican convent. Closed: Tuesday. See too the **Bartholdi Museum** in the sculptor's birthplace.

DICY: SAÔNE-ET-LOIRE
La Fabuloserie. Tel: 86.63.64.21. An museum where Alain Bourbonnais exhibits the works of modern fringe artists, and stages spontaneous happenings. Open: daily July and August; other times at weekends and public holidays only.

DIJON: CÔTE-D'OR
All museums closed: Tuesday. Buy a museums pass from The Dijon tourist office.

Musée des Beaux Arts, Place de la Sainte-Chapelle. Tel: 80.74.52.70. The region's most important museum is housed in the former Ducal Palace. Collections include the tombs of Philip the Bold and John the Fearless; sculptures, ceramics, medieval weaponry and European paintings. The Philippe le Bon tower itself offers panoramic views over the city.

Musée d'Art Sacré, 15 Rue Sainte Anne. Tel: 80.30.06.44. Collections of liturgical objects (12th to 19th centuries) from France and other countries, plus 19th-century chasubles, copes etc.

Musée Grévin de Bourgogne, 13 Avenue Albert 1er. Tel: 80.42.03.03. The city's newest museum (opened June 1990), depicting the region's history by means of 17 waxwork tableaux, starting with the 6th century BC.

Musée de la Vie Bourguignonne Perrin de Puycousin, 17 Rue Sainte-Anne. Tel: 80.30.65.91. Scenes from everyday life in old Burgundy; reconstructed 19th-century shops and workshops; collections of ethnographical items and costumes.

See too the **Musée Archéologique**, 5 Rue du Docteur Maret, for the Blanot Treasture and the **Musée d'Histoire Naturelle**, 1 Avenue Albert 1er (in the Arquebuse gardens).

DÔLE: JURA
Musée de la Maison Natale de Pasteur, 43 Rue Pasteur. Tel: 84.72.20.61. Museum concerned with the history of science, in Pasteur's birthplace. Open: July and August.

DOMRÉMY-LA-PUCELLE: VOSGES
There is a little museum dedicated to Joan of Arc in the cottage where she was born. Check locally for opening times.

DOUZY: ARDENNES
Musée des Débuts de l'Aviation. The exploits of early aviators are the subject of this airfield museum. Open: every afternoon, except Monday May–September (plus mornings June–August); weekends in April and October.

EPERNAY: MARNE
Musée des Pressoirs. Champagne Mercier, the vineyard's own museum.

Musée du Vin de Champagne et d'Archéologie. Closed: Tuesday.

GRAY: HAUTE-SAÔNE
Musée Baron Martin, Château de Gray, Rue Pigalle. Tel: 84.64.83.46. Arts museum covering the 15th to 20th century. Closed: Tuesday.

Visit too the **National Esperanto Museum** in the town. Tel: 84.65.11.73. Open: Wednesday and Saturday afternoons.

EPINAL: VOSGES
The town is well known for its prints and engravings, a good collection of which is on view in the museum. The Imagerie Pellerin still produces these cartoons and can be visited. Check locally for opening times.

KAYSERSBERG: HAUT-RHIN
Albert Schweitzer, the Nobel prizewinner, was born here and his birthplace now houses a small museum dedicated to him. Check locally for opening hours.

LADUZ: YONNE
Musée Rural des Arts Populaires. Vast collection of tools, plus local crafts and toys of the 19th and 20th century. Open: daily June to end-September; weekends only Easter–May and October. Tel: 86.73.70.08.

LANGRES: HAUTE-MARNE
The home of Diderot to whom a room is dedicated in the Musée de l'Hôtel du Breuil de St-Germain. Also paintings, furniture and ceramics. Closed: Tuesday.

Lons-le-Saunier – Musée Municipal d'Archéologie, 25 Rue Richebourg. Tel: 84.47.12.13. Important regional archaeological collections. Closed: Tuesday and mornings at the weekend. The town also has a Fine Arts museum and a mini military museum.

LURE: HAUTE-SAÔNE
Musée du Boomerang. Tel: 84.30.06.56. Quirky little museum devote to the art and science of the boomerang. Open: 28 May–15 October, except Tuesday.

LYON: RHÔNE
Lyon has many museums, here is a selection:
Musée des Beaux-Arts, Palais St-Pierre, Place des Terreaux. Tel: 78.28.07.66. In a former 17th-century convent, the most important arts museum after the Louvre; newly restored. Closed: Monday and Tuesday. Also houses the St-Pierre museum of Contemporary Art. Closed: Tuesday. Tel: 78.30.50.66.
Musée de la Civilisation Gallo-Romaine, 17 Rue Cléberg. Tel: 78.25.94.68. Rich collections from the period when France was ruled from Rome. Closed: Monday and Tuesday.
Musée Historique des Tissus, 34 Rue de la Charité. Tel: 78.37.15.05. Wide-ranging collections on the history of textiles, including silk manufacture in Lyon. Closed: Monday.
Musée de la Marionette, Place du Petit-Collège. Tel: 78.42.03.61. Features the puppets of Laurent Mourguet, creator of the Guignol, plus other puppets from around the world. Closed: Tuesday.

LA MACHINE: NIÈVRE
Musée de la Mine, 1 Avenue de la République. Tel: 86.50.91.08. Reconstruction of the mines, galleries, engine rooms etc. Open: mid-June to mid-September, except Tuesday; Sunday afternoons in October and April–May.

MACON: SAÔNE-ET-LOIRE
Musée Lamartine, Hôtel Sennecé, Rue Sigorgne. Tel: 85.38.96.19. Documents concerning the life and work of the poet Lamartine, plus furniture, tapestries, paintings and other objets d'art. Closed: Tuesday and Sunday mornings, also January and February.
Musée des Ursulines, 5 Rue des Ursulines. Tel: 85.38.18.84. Collections from prehistoric and Gallo-Roman times, also medieval art, furniture and popular arts. Closed: Tuesday and Sunday mornings.

MERSAULT: CÔTE D'OR
Archéodrome, Aire de Beaune-Tailly on the A6. Tel: 80.21.48.25. Presents lifesize reconstructions of monuments and sites found in the great periods of history, including a Gallic farm.

METZ: MOSELLE
Musée d'Art et d'Histoire, 2 Rue du Haut-Poirier. Tel: 87.75.10.18. Three museums in one: exhibits of Gallo-Roman life are displayed around the ruined Roman Baths; the Architecture Museum is organised around the 15th-century Attic of Chèvremont; the Fine Arts Museum includes weapons and uniforms, mostly from the First Empire. Closed: Tuesday.

MOIRANS-EN-MONTAGNE: JURA
Maison du Jouet, 4 Rue Murgin. The town declares itself the French capital for toy manufacture and this museum explores the development of the industry since the beginning of the 19th century. Closed: Monday, also Saturday and Sunday morning from 1 November–30 April. Tel: 84.42.38.64.

MULHOUSE: HAUT-RHIN
Musée National de l'Automobile Collection Schlumpf. Tel: 89.42.29.17. Famous collection of over 500 vehicles, particularly notable for its Bugattis. Closed: Tuesday, except June–September.
Musée du Chemin de Fer, 2 Rue Alfred-de-Glehn. Tel: 89.42.25.67. Displays 100 engines and railway wagons of all kinds.

NANCY: MEURTHE-ET-MOSELLE
Musée de l'Ecole de Nancy, 36-38 Rue du Sergent-Blandan. Tel: 83.40.14.86. This old mansion is dedicated to the decorative arts, particularly under the influence of Emile Gallé of Nancy (1846–1904). Closed: Tuesday. Also worth a visit is the Museum devoted to the history of the Lorraine in the Ducal Palace.

NOGENT: HAUTE-MARNE
The town is noted for its decorative cutlery which can be admired in the Espace Pelletier, open Wednesday–Sunday afternoon, and the Musée du Patrimoine Coutelier, open every afternoon except Monday.

NOYERS-SUR-SEREIN: YONNE
Donation Yankel. Museum of naive art, including modern collections. Open: weekends Easter–November, daily from June–September in the afternoons. Information from the town hall: tel: 86.55.83.72.

ORNANS: DOUBS
Musée de la Maison Natale de Gustave Courbet, Place Robert Fernier. Tel: 81.62.23.30. Museum in the birthplace of the Impressionist painter. Closed: Tuesday and 1 November–31 March.
Maison Nationale de l'Eau et de la Pêche, 36 Rue St-Laurent. Tel: 81.57.14.49. Devoted to fishing and freshwater habitats. Closed: weekends.

PARAY-LE-MONIAL: SAÔNE-ET-LOIRE

Musée d'Art Sacrée, "Le Hiéron", 28 Rue de la Paix. Tel: 85.88.85.80. Major collection of religious works, including the 12th-century tympanum from the priory of Anzy-le-Duc.

Musée de la Faïence Charolaise, Prieuré Bénédictin, Avenue Jean-Paul II. Tel: 85.88.83.07. A fine collection of porcelain dating from 1836 to the present day. Also exhibition of moulds and tools. Open: 20 March–20 October daily, except Tuesday.

Musée de l'Insigne et de la Médaille, 7 Rue Billet. Tel: 85.88.83.08. Private collection of military insignia, heraldry, civil, religious and military medals. Open: March to end-December, except Monday.

PIERRE-DE-BRESSE: SAÔNE-ET-LOIRE

Ecomusée de la Bresse Bourguignonne, Château de Pierre. Tel: 85.76.27.16. The main departments of the ecomuseum are in the château and its remarkable ensemble of 17th-century buildings, others are scattered around the region. Exhibits on the natural environment, archaeology and history of the region. In the grounds are works of the British sculptor, David Nash. Open: every afternoon.

PIREY: DOUBS

Musée des Automates, Centre Commercial, Rue du Collège. Tel: 81.59.04.62. Exhibits 130 mechanical figures. Open: every afternoon except Monday.

PRÉMANON: JURA

Centre Paul-Emile-Victor, France's first museum dedicated to polar exploration and the life of Paul-Emile-Victor. Open: afternoons, closed: Monday–Wednesday in May and June.

REIMS: MARNE

Musée Saint-Rémi, 53 Rue Simon. Tel: 26.85.23.36. Regional history and archaeology housed in the former Benedictine Abbey of Saint-Rémi of Reims. Open: every afternoon.

There are several other museums in the city, including the **Museum of Old Reims** and the **Beaux-Arts Museum**.

RIQUEWIHR: HAUT-RHIN

The former château houses a regional postal museum, while other local history can be discovered in the museum in the Porte Dolder. Check locally for opening times.

ST-BRISSON: NIÈVRE

Musée de la Résistance en Morvan, Maison du Parc Naturel Régional du Morvan. Tel: 86.78.70.16. Dedicated to the local activities of the maquis, the resistance movement of the World War II. Open: every afternoon July to mid-September.

SAVIGNY-LES-BEAUNE: CÔTE D'OR

Part of the castle has been made into a motor-bike museum, with 200 models from 1903–1960; see too the showroom of 15 Abarth cars and an Aircraft Museum, with the French Mirage III jet. Closed: 15–31st December. Tel: 80.21.55.03.

SCEY-SUR-SAÔNE: HAUTE-SAÔNE

Musée de l'Histoire du Costume. Tel: 84.68.81.77. Open: weekends from 13 April–12 November, every day in July and August except Tuesday.

SENS: YONNE

Musée, Place de la Cathédrale (entrance via the Palais Synodal). Tel: 86.64.15.27 (curator). In the former Archbishop's Palace, houses all the major local collections. Next door is the treasure house (Le Trésor) which is one of the richest in France Open: daily, except Tuesday; closed: Monday, Thursday and Friday mornings from October–May. Free entry on Wednesday.

SOCHAUX: DOUBS

Musée Peugeot, Carrefour de l'Europe. Tel: 81.94.48.21. Display of Peugeot products: cycles, motorbikes, cars and tools.

STRASBOURG: BAS-RHIN

Musée des Beaux-Arts, Palais Rohan, 2 Place du Château. Tel: 88.32.48.95. Fine collections housed in the former residence of the prince-bishops. Closed: Tuesday. Visit too the nearby **Musée de l'Oeuvre Notre Dame**. Tel: 88.32.48.95. Showing medieval sculpture and stained glass. Closed: Tuesday.

TOURNUS: SAÔNE-ET-LOIRE

Musée Bourguignonne de Perrin de Puycousin. Reconstructed interiors and scenes from traditional Burgundian life; plus Napoleonic souvenirs of the Tournus soldier, Jean-Marie Putigny. Open: daily, except Tuesday, April–November.

Musée Greuze. Paintings and drawings by Greuze, plus regional archaeology and sculpture. Open: Monday–Saturday April–October.

TROYES: AUBE

Musée d'Art Moderne, houses the collection of Pierre and Denise Levy. Closed: Tuesday.

The unusually named **Maison de l'Outil et de la Pensée Ouvrière** at the Hôtel de Mauroy is literally the House of tools and working class thinking. See too the **Pharmacy Museum**.

HEART OF FRANCE

AMBERT: PUY-DE-DÔME

Moulin Richard-de-Bas. Tel: 73.82.03.11. Museum tracing the history of papermaking and studios where paper is made by hand.

Musée de la Fourme d'Ambert et des Fromages, 29 Rue des Chazeaux. Tel: 73.82.49.23. In a 13th-century house, visitors can follow the processes of making the local cheese, ending with a tasting. Closed: Monday and 15–30 January.

ANGOULÊME: CHARENTE

The **Musée Municipal** is housed in the former Bishop's Palace and offers a variety of collections including the art of the *bande déssinée* (BD or comic). Closed: Monday. See too the **Archaeological museum**.

ARLANC: PUY-DE-DÔME

Musée Municipal de la Dentelle. Tel: 73.95.00.03. Lace museum. Open: afternoons 15 April–15 October (also mornings 1 July–16 September).

AUBUSSON: CREUSE

Musée Départemental de la Tapisserie. Tel: 55.66.33.06. Tapestries ancient and modern. Closed:

Tuesday morning. See too the **Maison du Vieux Tapissier**, a 15th-century house with a reconstructed tapestry worker's studio. Open: 15 June–15 September. Tel: 55.66.32.12.

BERGERAC: DORDOGNE

Musée du Tabac, Maison Peyrarède, Place du Feu. Tel: 53.63.04.13. Interesting museum about tobacco manufacture in the district. Closed: Monday.

There are also museums in the town devoted to Wine and Religious Art.

BORDEAUX: GIRONDE

Musée des Arts Decoratifs, Hôtel de Lalande, 39 Rue Bouffard. Tel: 56.90.91.60. Decorative arts displayed in a fine Louis XVI mansion. Closed: Tuesday.

Goya à Bordeaux, 57 Cours de l'Intendance. Tel: 56.52.79.37. Goya died in exile in 1828 and his last home in Bordeaux is a memorial to the artist. Open: weekday afternoons (apartment closed on Thursday). Also of interest, among Bordeaux's many museums, is the **Musée des Douanes** (customs museum) and the **Musée des Beaux Arts**.

LE BUGUE: DORDOGNE

Musée de Paléontologie. Tel: 53.04.24.34. Concerns local discoveries. Open: daily (until midnight in July and August). Visit too the village of Bournat "La vie d'un village périgourdin au siècle dernier", showing village life (farming, local crafts) as it was a century ago. Tel: 53.04.24.34.

CLERMONT-FERRAND: PUY-DE-DÔME

Musée du Ranquet, 34 Rue des Gras. Tel: 73.91.93.78. Just one of the several museums in the town, this one keeps medieval treasures and other artefacts from the 18th and 19th centuries. Closed: Sunday morning and Monday.

COGNAC: CHARENTE

Musée du Cognac, Hôtel Dupuy d'Angeac, regional museum, with the basement devoted to the history and production of the brandy. Check locally for opening times. Several producers, e.g. Martell and Hennessy, are open to visitors; Hennessy has its own Musée de la Tonnellerie.

DOMAINE DE CUZALS

Musée de Plein Air du Quercy, Sauliac-sur-Celé. Tel: 65.22.58.63. Open-air museum based around two reconstructed farms from the 18th and 19th centuries. Open: June–September (not Saturday).

LES EYZIES-DE-TAYAC: DORDOGNE

Musée National de Préhistoire. Tel: 53.06.97.03. In the former castle of the Barons of Beynac displaying some of the oldest works of art in the world – paleolithic artefacts carved from limestone blocks from 35,000 BC. Closed: Tuesday.

FIGEAC: LOT

Musée Champollion, the birthplace, in 1790 of Jean-François Champollion, the Egyptologist who decyphered the Rosetta Stone (the stone itself is in the British museum, but there is a copy here).

The 13th-century former mint, the **Hôtel du Monnaie**, is now a local history museum. Check locally for opening times.

GANNAT: ALLIER

Musée des Ducs de Bourbon. Tel: 70.90.23.78. Collections of religious art as well as horse-drawn vehicles. Open: every afternoon, except Tuesday, June–October.

ILE D'OLÉRON: CHARENTE-MARITIME

Musée Oléronais Aliénor-d'Aquitaine at St-Pierre-d'Oléron is devoted to the history and traditions of the island. Check locally for opening times.

LIMOGES: HAUTE-VIENNE

Musée National Adrien-Dubouchée, Place Winston Churchill. Tel: 55.77.45.58. Named after its patron who donated much of his superb collection of porcelain to the museum. It houses one of the finest exhibitions of Limoges porcelain (over 10,000 pieces), as well as 400 glass objects. Closed: Tuesday.

Musée de l'Evêché. Tel: 55.45.60.00. Concentrates on the other aspect of Limoges art: enamelling. Also a picture gallery (including works by Renoir and Suzanne Valadon), and other departments. Closed: Tuesday, except July–September.

MENAT: PUY-DE-DÔME

Musée de Paléontologie, at "Le Gîte à Fossiles". Tel: 73.85.50.29. A former abbey (12th century) now houses a notable collection of fossils. Open: daily, except Tuesday, June–September; also weekends in April–May.

MONTLUÇON: ALLIER

Musée du Vieux Château. Tel: 70.05.00.16. The former Bourbon castle (15th century) offers an insight into local history and a delightful collection of hurdy gurdies. Closed: Tuesday, also in the morning from 16 October–14 March.

MOULINS: ALLIER

Musé d'Art et d'Archéologie, 3 Place du Colonel-Laussedat. Tel: 70.20.48.47. Collections include important Bourbon sculptures, weapons and faïence. Closed: Tuesday.

Also worth a visit are the **Musée du Folklore** and the **Bourbon museum**.

NONTRON: DORDOGNE

Musée Départemental des Poupées et Jouets d'Antan. Tel: 53.56.20.80. Dolls and toys of yesteryear. Open: 1 February–15 December, closed: Tuesday except July and August.

POITIERS: VIENNE

Musée-Ste-Croix, the town's most important museum is housed in a modern building with local ethnological and archeological collections as well as paintings from various international schools. Check locally for opening times.

LE-PUY-EN-VELAY: HAUTE-LOIRE

Le Musée Crozatier, situated in the Vinay gardens, this museum has a fine collection of lace, for which the town is famous.

ILE DE RÉ: CHARENTE-MARITIME

Musée Naval et Ernest Cognacq, at St-Martin, is on two levels, comprising a maritime museum and collections of ceramics and other artefacts including Louis XIII furniture. Check locally for opening times.

ROCHEFORT: CHARENTE-MARITIME

The **Maison de Loti** is in fact two houses, the birthplace of the writer Pierre Loti and the house next door which he acquired later. It has a splendid collection of foreign artefacts, particularly from Turkey and Arabia; also some Gobelin tapestries. Check locally for opening times. See too the **Musée de la Marine** for the history of the town's arsenal.

LA ROCHELLE: CHARENTE-MARITIME

Musée des Automates, at Ville-en-Bois is a small museum with a collection of 300 *automates* – mechanical toys. See too the **Musée de Peinture** (art museum) and the **Musée d'Orbigny** (local artefacts and ceramics). Check locally for opening times.

ST-CÉRÉ: LOT

Les Tours de St-Laurent, the former home (1945–66) of the famous tapestry designer Jean Lurçat, with many examples of his splendid works; also his ceramics. Check locally for opening times.

ST-ETIENNE: LOIRE

Musée d'Art Moderne, La Terrasse. Tel: 77.93.59.58. This museum (1987) has a permanent collection of 20th-century art (Kandinsky, Dubuffet, Soulages, etc), plus temporary exhibitions. Closed: Tuesday.

ST-JEAN-D'ANGÉLY: CHARENTE-MARITIME

The town's museum in the beautiful 18th-century Hôtel d'Hausens, has varied collections including souvenirs of early expeditions by automobile, in particular the first crossing of the Sahara in 1922. Check locally for opening times.

ST-LÉONARD: HAUTE-VIENNE

Musée Gay-Lussac. Tel: 55.56.25.06. Science museum named after the man who gave his name to the measurement of alcohol. Closed: Monday.

ST-YRIEIX-LA-PERCHE: HAUTE-VIENNE

Musée de la Porcelaine "Les Palloux". Tel: 55.75.10.38. It was here in 1766 that the first kaolin was discovered in France, to form the basis of all hard porcelain. Closed: Sunday and Monday.

SAINTES: CHARENTE-MARITIME

The **Musée Archéologique** is in a former pottery next to the Arc de Germanicus; several Roman remains can be seen in the surrounding park.
See too the traditional costumes and other local artefacts in the **Musée Dupuy-Mestreau** in the former home of the Marquis de Monconseil. Also worth a visit is the **Fine Arts museum**. Check locally for opening times.

SARLAT: DORDOGNE

This delightful town boasts several museums including a collection of sacred art in the **Chapel of the White Penitents** (open: Easter–11 November, except Tuesday and Sunday morning, tel: 53.31.53.31.) and a museum of **prehistory and palaeontology** (open: 19 April–15 September, closed: Monday except July and August). Tel: 53.31.29.92.

SAULIAC: LOT

Musée du Quercy, open-air museum of the old province of Quercy. Check locally for opening times.

VOLVIC: PUY-DE-DÔME

Musée Marcel-Sahut. Tel: 73.33.57.33. Arts museum housing works by Guaguin, Manet, Braque, Daumier among others, also Chinese porcelain and Japanese prints.

SOUTHWEST

ALBI: TARN

Musée Toulouse Lautrec, Palais de la Berbie. Tel: 63.54.14.09. The former Archbishops' Palace now houses Lautrec's most important works, the largest single collection of his paintings, along with other modern art, e.g. Utrillo, Bonnard and Vuillard. Closed: Tuesday.

AMÉLIE LES BAINS: PYRÉNÉES ORIENTALES

Musée Départemental de la Poste, Centre Médiéval de Palalda. Tel: 68.39.34.90. Postal museum. Open: every afternoon.

AUCH: GERS

The **Musée des Jacobins** boasts one of the largest public collections of pre-Columbian art in France. Check locally for opening times.

BAGES: PYRÉNÉES ORIENTALES

Le Palais des Naïfs, 9 Avenue de la Méditerranée. Tel: 68.21.71.33. Naive art from all over the world. Closed: Tuesday in winter.

BASCONS: LANDES

Musée et Chapelle de la Course Landaise. Tel: 58.52.91.76. Devoted to the traditonal bull runs of the region. Open: every afternoon 15 May–15 October.

BAYONNE: PYRÉNÉES-ATLANTIQUES

Musée Bonnat, 5 Rue Jacques-Lafitte. Tel: 59.59.08.52. Works collected by Léon Bonnat from 1870–1900, and the municipal collection which includes some Impressionist works. Closed: Tuesday. **Musée Basque**, 1 Rue Marengo. Tel: 59.59.08.98. Shows the history of the port of Bayonne and Basque traditions, including a reconstructed Basque home. Check for opening times.

BISCAROSSE: LANDES

Musée Historique de l'Hydraviation, 332 Avenue Louis Bréguet. Tel: 58.78.00.65. The history of aquaplanes from their invention in 1910 to the present day. Open: every afternoon (also mornings in July and August).

BRASSEMPOUY: LANDES

Musée de la Préhistoire. Tel: 58.89.02.47. Archaelogical museum, known for the Lady of Brassempouy, the earliest known sculpture of a woman, dating from 23,000 BC. Open: every afternoon July and August, weekends in June and September.

BOUTENAC: AUDE

Musée de la Faune. Tel: 68.27.57.02. Animals and insects.

CANET EN ROUSSILLON: PYRÉNÉES ORIENTALES

Musée du Jouet, Place Méditerranée. Tel: 68.73.20.29. Toys ancient and modern. Open: daily in summer and every afternoon except Tuesday in winter.

Musée de l'Auto de Jadis, Front de Mer. Tel: 68.73.22.56. Cars from 1895 to the present day. Hours as toy museum.

Musée du Bateau, Front de Mer. Tel: 68.73.12.43. Boats from Roman times to the Titanic. Hours as toy museum.

CAPBRETON: LANDES

Ecomusée de la Pê et de la Mer. Tel: 58.72.40.50. All about the sea and fishing in the region.

CARCASSONNE: AUDE

Musée des Beaux Arts, Rue de Verdun. Tel: 68.77.73.70. Painting and porcelain mostly. Closed: Monday and Tuesday in summer, Sunday and Monday winter. See too the museum in the château.

CASTRES: TARN

Musée Goya, Hôtel de Ville. Tel: 63.59.62.63. Specialising in Spanish painting, this museum is housed in former episcopal buildings with gardens designed by Le Nôtre. Closed: Monday.

DOUZENS: AUDE

Musée des Oiseaux. Tel: 68.79.09.27. 2,500 species of birds, plus insects, shells and butterflies, plus tableaux of the Fables of La Fontaine. Open: weekend afternoons 16 March–30 November, plus every day 1 June–15 September.

ILLE SUR TÊT: PYRÉNÉES ORIENTALES

Centre d'Art Sacré et de l'Hospice, 10 Rue de l'Hôpital. Tel: 68.84.83.96. Religious objets d'art. Closed: Tuesday in winter.

LABÈGE: HAUTE-GARONNE

Centre Régional d'Art Contemporain Midi-Pyrénées, Labège Innopole, just outside Toulouse. Tel: 61.39.29.29. A centre for local contemporary artists. Open: Wednesday–Sunday afternoon.

LECTOURE: GERS

Classified as a "city of art", Lectoure possesses one of the oldes museums in France, in the cellars of the former Bishop's Palace. It has a unique collection of objects used in sacrificing bulls. Check locally for opening hours.

LEZIGNAN-CORBIÈRES: AUDE

Musée de la Vigne et du Vin, Rue Turgot. Tel: 68.27.07.57. The complete guide to viticulture.

LIT-ET-MIXE: LANDES

Musée "Vielles Landes". Tel: 58.42.79.54. The life and traditions of people of the Landes from 1850–1950. Open: every morning.

LOURDES: HAUTES-PYRÉNÉES

The castle above the town (accessible by lift) is now the **Musée des Pyrénées**, dedicated to the customs, craft and folkore of the central region of the range. Good views. See too the **wax museum** nearby, a branch of the Grévin Museum in Paris. Check locally for opening times.

MAS D'AZIL: ARIÈGE

The caves here are an important prehistoric site and many of its treasures (tools, decorated pebbles and finely carved harpoons) can be seen in the **Musée de la Grotte**. Also in the village museum is a beautiful work of art *Le Faon aux Oiseaux* (Fawn with Birds). Check locally for opening times.

MAURINIÉ: TARN

Le Musée d'Icônes, N. Grechny, collection of icons in this museum near Marsal in the Tarn valley. Check locally for opening times.

MIRANDE: GERS

The town's museum is one of the most important in Gascony, with collections of 17th to 19th-century paintings and decorative faïence. Check locally for opening times.

MONT-DE-MARSAN: LANDES

Musée Despiau-Wlérick, 6 Place Marguerite de Navarre. Tel: 58.75.00.45. The only museum in France devoted exclusively to modern figurative sculpture. Closed: Tuesday.

MONTAUBAN: TARN-ET-GARONNE

Musée Ingres, 19 Rue de l'Hôtel-de-Ville. Tel: 63.63.18.04. Former Bishops' Palace displaying a collection of paintings by Ingres and others, including Bourdelle and Desnoyers. Closed: Monday and Sunday morning in winter.

NARBONNE: AUDE

Musée de l'Horreum, Rue Rouget de l'Isle, all kinds of Roman ware. Tel: 68.90.30.30. Narbonne's other museums include archaeology and culture, the latter in the Archbishops' Palace.

NIAUX: ARIÈGE

The **Musée Paysan** gives a fascinating insight into rural life. Check locally for opening times.

PERPIGNAN: PYRÉNÉES-ORIENTALES

Musée Hyacinthe Rigaud, 16 Rue de l'Ange. Tel: 68.35.66.30. Housed in a fine 17th-century mansion, the museum displays works of art from the 13th-century to the present day, including notable Hispano Mauresque ceramics and Early Catalan paintings. Closed: Tuesday.

ST-ANTONIN-NOBLE-VAL: TARN-ET-GARONNE

The Town Hall, built 1125 is reputedly the oldest in France and is now a museum housing an impressive collection of local prehistoric finds. Check locally for opening times.

ST-CYPRIEN: PYRÉNÉES-ORIENTALES

Musée des Artistes Catalans, Rue Jules Romains. Tel: 68.21.32.07. Display the work of Catalan artists. Open: every afternoon except Tuesday.

ST-JEAN-DE-LUZ: PYRÉNÉES-ATLANTIQUES

Ecomusée, Ferme Berain on the RN 10 to Guéthary. Tel: 59.51.06.06. Living museum of Basque textiles.

SIGEAN: GARD

Musée des Corbières, Place de la Libération. Tel: 68.48.14.81. Arts and traditions of the region, plus archaeology. Open: 1 June–15 September.

SOLFÉRINO: LANDES

Musée Napoléon, the village was founded by Napoleon in 1863 and the museum contains objects owned by himself and the Empress. Open: 15 June–15 September. Tel: 58.07.24.92.

TARBES: HAUTES-PYRÉNÉES

The birthplace of Maréchal Foch is now a small museum devoted to the Hussars. See too the museum in the delightful Jardins de Massey. Check locally for opening times.

TOULOUSE: HAUTE-GARONNE

Musée des Augustins, 21 Rue de Metz. Tel: 61.23.55.07. Created during the Revolution and house in the former Augustinian convent, it has a large collection of paintings and shows the importance of Toulouse as an artistic centre. Also Romanesque and Gothic sculptures. Closed: Tuesday.

Galerie Municipale du Château d'Eau, Place Laganne. Tel: 61.42.61.72. One of the first and most popular photographic galleries in France. Open: every afternoon except Tuesday.

Centre Municipal de l'Affiche, de la Carte Postale et de l'Art Graphique, 58 Allées Charles-de-Fitte. Tel: 61.59.24.64. Highly regarded collections of posters, postcards and other examples of graphic art. Open: weekdays.

Musée d'Art Moderne, Refectoire des Jacobins, 69 Rue Pargaminières. Tel: 61.55.26.24. Modern art gallery with regular exhibitions. Closed: Tuesday.

TOURNAY: HAUTES-PYRÉNÉES

Le Musée de l'Arctique. Devoted to the landscape and exploration of the Arctic. Check locally for opening times.

ALPS

AIX-LES-BAINS: SAVOIE

Musée du Docteur-Faure. Art museum housing, among other works a collection of Impressionist paintings (including Sisley, Renoir, Pissaro). Check locally for opening times.

ANNECY: HAUTE-SAVOIE

The **Bell Museum** is housed in one of the last surviving bell foundries. Among the 40,000 bells that have been cast here, the most famous is in the Sacré Coeur, Paris. Check locally for opening times.

ASSIEU: ISÈRE

Musée d'Instruments Anciens. Old musical instruments. Tel: 74.84.45.37.

LA BATIE-MONTGASCON: ISÈRE

La Maison du Tisserand. Tel: 74.88.81.80. Weaving museum with working exhibits. Open: May–September Saturday–Sunday afternoon, Sunday only in October.

BOURG-EN-BRESSE: AIN

Musée de Brou, 63 Boulevard de Brou. Tel: 74.22.22.31. Installed in a former monastery dating from the 16th century, and unique in France for its three cloisters. Good collection of Dutch, Flemish, French and Italian paintings from the 16th to 20th century, plus sculpture, pottery and old furniture. The Church of Brou is a major sight in its own right.

BOURG-D'OISANS: ISÈRE

Musée Municipal des Mineraux et de la Faune des Alpes, Place de l'Eglise, wildlife and minerals found in the Alps, and information centre for the Parc des Ecrins. Open: every afternoon (closed: Tuesday except school holidays); also open mornings from 15 June–15 September. Tel: 76.80.27.54.

CERDON: AIN

Musexpo du Cuivre. Tel: 74.39.96.44. Dedicated to copper and those who work with it, including old tools and working studios which have been in use since 1854.

CHAMBÉRY: SAVOIE

Musée Savoisien. A former Franciscan convent, then the Bishop's Palace, this building now houses collections relating to local art and traditions and the House of Savoy. Closed: Tuesday.
See too the **Fine Arts museum** with a good collection of Italian paintings. Closed: Tuesday.

CHAMONIX: HAUTE-SAVOIE

Musée Alpin. Interesting museum dedicated to the Alps and its people, in one of the first Alpine resorts. Open: every afternoon, June–September and school holidays.

CHATILLON-SUR-CHALARONNE: AIN

Apothicairerie de l'Ancien Hospice, Place St-Vincent-de-Paul. Tel: 74.55.02.27. Former pharmacy (1731), with a remarkable collection of 120 pots of local faïence and other objects. Open: every afternoon, closed: Sunday (except June to mid-September).

LA COMBE DE LANCEY: ISÈRE

Musée Rural d'Arts et Traditions Populaire, Foyer Dupanloup, Château de la Combe. Tel: 76.71.48.09. Displays tools, arts and crafts from bygone days and shows how people lived in the mountain villages. Open: Saturday afternoon Easter–1 November.

LA CÔTE-ST ANDRÉ: ISÈRE

Musée Hector Berlioz, 69 Rue de la République. Tel: 74.20.24.88. Museum in a beautiful 18th-century house, the birthplace of the composer. Closed: in January.

GRENOBLE: ISÈRE

Musée Dauphinois, 30 Rue Maurice-Gignoux. Tel: 76.87.66.77. Regional ethnographical museum in a 17th-century convent, plus exhibits on the Alps and alpine life. Closed: Tuesday.

Musée de Peinture et de Sculpture, Place de Verdun. Tel: 76.54.09.82. Good collections, particularly the Impressionists. Closed: Tuesday.

GRIGNAN: DRÔME

Centre Vivant d'Art Contemporain. Tel: 75.46.56.75. Stages regular exhibitions of all forms of modern art.

LACOUX: AIN

Centre d'Art Contemporain. Tel: 74.35.25.61. Modern art gallery with different exhibitions each summer. Open: every afternoon in July and August.

LANS-EN-VERCORS: ISÈRE

Musée "La Magie des Automates". Tel: 76.95.40.14. Over 200 mechanical toys.

LORIOL: DRÔME

Musée de l'Insolite. Tel: 75.61.63.88. This museum "of the unusual" has an eclectic collection, including an erotic gallery (adults only). Open: every afternoon except Tuesday 15 June–15 September; weekends only the rest of the year.

MONTGUERS: DRÔME

Écomusée de la Lavande, Maison des Arômes. Tel: 75.28.08.67. Lavender and all kinds of aromatic and medicinal plants are displayed here; also distilleries. Open: weekdays (plus weekends 15 June–15 September).

MONTREVEL-EN-BRESSE: AIN

Musée Océanien et de St-Pierre Chanel, Cuet. Tel: 74.30.86.94. Local art and the life story of St-Pierre Chanel. Open: every afternoon 25 April–1 September.

NANTUA: AIN

Musée de la Résistance et de la Déportation, Montée de l'Abbaye. Tel: 74.75.07.50. Souvenirs of the local resistance movement. Open: 1 May–30 September except Monday.

NYONS: DRÔME

Musée de l'Olivier. Tel: 75.26.12.12. Learn about the cultivation of olive trees and the production of olive oil in the last century. Open: Thursday–Saturday July and August; Saturday only out of season.

PÉROUGES: AIN

Musée du Vieux Pérouges. Tel: 74.61.00.88. Local arts and traditions; also Aubusson tapestries, weapons and temporary art exhibitions. Closed: Wednesday out of season.

ROMANS: DRÔME

Musée de la Chaussure et d'Ethnographie Régionale, Rue Ste Marie. Shoe museum of international repute with examples from ancient times to the present day. Closed: Sunday and Monday morning and Tuesday.

ST-MARCELLIN: ISÈRE

Musée du Fromage, 2 Avenue du Collège. Tel: 76.38.53.85. How the local cheese is made now, and in the past. Closed: Sunday and Monday morning.

ST PAUL-TROIS-CHÂTEAUX: DRÔME

Maison de la Truffe et du Tricastin. Tel: 75.96.61.29. Dedicated to truffle hunting and the local wine. Closed: Monday morning.

ST-PIERRE-DE-CHARTREUSE: ISÈRE

Musée de la Correrie. Tel: 76.88.60.45. Gives a vivid insight into the life of the Chartreuse monks, whose monastery nearby (but closed: to the public for reasons of solitude). Open: Easter–1 November.

THONON-LES-BAINS: HAUTE-SAVOIE

Musée du Chablais. Regional folklore museum, installed in the Château de Sonnaz. Open: 1 July–15 September, except Sunday.

VALENCE: DRÔME

Musée Municipal. Tel: 75.43.04.88. Contains some interesting Gallo-Roman artefacts, including a collection of mosaics; also drawings by Hubert Robert.

VIENNE: ISÈRE

Musée Lapidaire St-Pierre, Place St-Pierre. Tel: 74.85.20.35. Fine lapidary collections, including mosaics and Gallo-Roman objects in a former church. Closed: Tuesday (also Monday and Sunday morning 16 October–31 March).

See too the **Fine Arts Museum**, Place de Miremont. Tel: 74.85.50.42. Closed: Tuesday (also Monday and Sunday morning 16 October–31 March).

VIZILLE: ISÈRE

Musée de la Révolution Française, Place de la Libération. Tel: 76.68.07.35. Situated in a magnificent 17th-century castle, it houses many treasures related to the museum, some of which have recently been deposited there by the Louvre and the Château of Versailles. Also delightful grounds. Closed: Tuesday (also Monday October–March).

VOIRON: ISÈRE

Musée Lucien Mainssieux, Rue Bance de Cour. Tel: 76.65.67.17. Paintings donated to the town by Mainssieux of his own and other artists' works. Open: every afternoon except Monday.

Visit too the silk museum (**Espace de la Soie**, 5 Boulevard Edgar-Kofler, tel: 76.65.68.28). Closed: Thursday morning.

VONNAS: AIN

Musée des Attelages, de la Carosserie et du Charronnage, Rue du Moulin. Tel: 74.50.09.74. Collection of 40 vehicles from the 19th and 20th centuries. Closed: January and Tuesday.

MEDITERRANEAN & PROVENCE

AGDE: HÉRAULT

Musée d'Archéologie Sous-marine et Subaquatique, Cap d'Agde. Tel: 67.26.81.00. Devoted to underwater archeology. Closed: Tuesday October–May.

ALÈS: GARD

Mine Témoin, Chemin Cité, Rochebelle. Tel: 66.30.45.15. History of mining presented in almost 600 metres (2,000 ft) of galleries.

ANTIBES: ALPES-MARITIMES

Musée Picasso, Château Grimaldi, Place Mariejol. Tel: 93.34.91.91. Picasso once used part of the château (already by then a museum) as a studio and left almost all 180 works he created there, to the museum. Closed: Tuesday.

ARLES: BOUCHES-DU-RHÔNE

Musée Camarguais, Mas du Pont de Rousty. Tel: 90.97.10.82. Part of the Regional Park of Camargue, this modern museum is housed in all old sheep barn of a Provençal farm, displaying objects donated by the Camargue people. Closed: Tuesday October to 30 March.

ARPAILLARGUES: GARD

Musée 1900, Moulin de Charlier. Tel: 66.22.58.64. Old vehicles, farm machinery and other objects in a former olive oil mill. Closed: Monday except July and August.

AVIGNON: VAUCLUSE

Musée du Petit Palais, Place du Palais des Papes. Tel: 90.86.44.58. Former papal palace, now displaying a collection of medieval Italian painting, including 400 panels from the Campana collection. Closed: Tuesday.

Le Musée Vouland. Tel: 90.86.03.79. A superb collection of French furniture from the 17th and 18th centuries as well as ceramics. Closed: Sunday and Monday.

BIOT: ALPES-MARITIMES

Musée National Fernand Léger, Place de la Chapelle, known as the "Cathedral of Modern Art", including stained glass and ceramics. Closed: Tuesday.

CAGNES-SUR-MER: ALPES-MARITIMES

La Maison de Renoir, Les Collettes. Tel: 93.20.61.07. Where Renoir spent his last years, displaying 10 of his best paintings, plus drawings and sculpture. Nice gardens. Closed: Thursday and mid-October to mid-November.

LA CANORGUE: LOZÈRE

Centre Archéologique Charles Morel, Rue du Maillan, Banassac. Tel: 66.32.82.10. Artefacts from Gallo-Roman workshops. Closed: Saturday afternoon and Sunday.

CHANAC: LOZÈRE

Domaine Mediéval des Champs, Le Villard. Tel: 66.48.25.00. Reconstruction of a medieval farm. Open: weekends Easter–1 November (daily 1 July–9 September).

COUSTELLET: VAUCLUSE

Musée de la Lavande. Tel: 90.76.91.23. Devoted to lavender, an important local product. Open: Easter–31 October; closed: Monday.

FONTVIEILLE: BOUCHES-DU-RHÔNE

The windmill which featured in the writer Daudet's famous *Lettres de mon Moulin* is now a museum. Tel: 90.54.60.78. Closed: in January.

FRÉJUS: VAR

Fondation Templon, ZI du Capitou. Tel: 94.40.76.30. Advertises itself as one of the best collections of modern art in Europe, principally showing works under 30 years old.

GRASSE: ALPES-MARITIMES

Musée International de la Parfumerie, 8 Place du Cours. Tel: 93.36.80.20. One of only three museums of its kind in the world. Closed: Monday, Tuesday and November. See too the **Villa-Musée Fragonard**, 23 Boulevard Fragonard. Tel: 93.36.01.61. Where the artist took shelter during the Revolution. Closed: weekends and November.

LE GRAU DU ROI: GARD

Musée de la Mer, Port Camargue. Tel: 66.51.57.57. Museum about the sea and aquaria. Closed: Monday morning.

MARSEILLE: BOUCHES-DU-RHÔNE

Musée d'Histoire de Marseille, Centre Bourse. Tel: 87.75.10.18. Displays Marseille's history from 600 BC to the end of the Roman period. Closed: Tuesday.

MENTON: ALPES-MARITIMES

Musée Jean Cocteau, Vieux Port. Tel: 93.36.01.61. Devoted to the life and works of Cocteau. Closed: Monday and Tuesday.

MIALET: GARD

Musée du Desert, Le Mas Soubeyran. Tel: 66.85.02.72. The development of Protestantism. Open: March–30 November.

MONACO TOWN

Musée Océanographie, Avenue Saint-Martin. Tel: 93.15.36.00. Very popular museum of marine technology and a superb aquarium.

MONTE-CARLO

Musée National, 17 Avenue Princesse Grace. Tel: 93.30.91.26. Housed in a fine 19th-century villa, surrounded by the Princess Grace rose garden, it houses a good collection of antique dolls and working automats.

MONTPELLIER: HÉRAULT

The town boasts several museums, including the **Musée Fabre**, displaying works of art from the 16th century to the present. Tel: 67.66.06.34. Closed: Monday. Also worth a visit are the **Musée de l'Infanterie**, the **Musée Atger** (Italian School) and the **Archeological museum**.

NICE: ALPES-MARITIMES

Musée d'Art Moderne et Contemporain, Promenade des Arts. Tel: 93.62.61.62. A new complex housing very modern art (post-1960) and sculptures in the surrounding gardens.

Musée International d'Art Naïf Anatole Jakovsky, Château Ste-Hélène, Avenue Val-Marie. Tel: 93.71.78.33. Villa owned by the founder of Monte-Carlo's casino housing the gift of the Jakovskys of 600 works, plus other naive art from around the world. Closed: Tuesday.

Musée Matisse, 164 Avenue des Arènes. Tel: 91.53.17.70. Housing the personal collection of the artist who died in Nice in 1954.

Musée National Message Biblique Marc Chagall, Avenue du Docteur-Ménard. Tel: 93.81.75.75. Built to house Chagall's works inspired by the Bible; the most important collection of his art in all its forms. Closed: Tuesday.

NÎMES: GARD

Musée du Vieux Nîmes, Place aux Herbes. Tel: 66.36.00.64. Local history and art collections, particularly textiles. Nîmes has several other museums including Fine Arts, Archeology and one dedicated to bullfighting, for which the town is something of a regional centre.

LE PONT DE MONTVERT: LOZÈRE

Ecomusée du Mont-Lozère. Tel: 66.45.01.75. The main branch of the museum is here, but there are other branches elsewhere in the region. Dedicated to the geographical and human development of the immediate vicinity.

ST-JEAN CAP FERRAT: ALPES-MARITIMES

Musée Ephrussi de Rothschild. Tel: 93.01.33.09. Italianate villa designed by Baroness de Rothschild to house her sumptuous collection of artistic treasures and bequeathed to the nation. See too the ornamental gardens. Closed: Sunday and Monday mornings and November.

ST-PAUL-DE-VENCE: ALPES-MARITIMES

Fondation Maeght. Tel: 93.32.81.63. In an impressive modern building overlooking the town, this museum of modern art was established in 1964 by art dealer Aimé Maeght; includes works by Chagall, Braque, Bonard, Kandinsky, Matisse, etc. many interestingly placed in the landscaped garden.

ST-TROPEZ: VAR

Musée de l'Annonçiade, Rue de l'Annonçiade. Tel: 94.97.04.01. Housed in a 16th-century chapel to pay homage to the 20th-century painters that were drawn to the town under the influence of Paul Signac, including Matisse, Bonnard, Utrillo, etc. Closed: Tuesday and November.

STES MARIES DE LA MER: BOUCHE-DU-RHÔNE

Musée Camarguais. Tel: 90.97.10.82. Dedicated to the natural environment and people of the Camargue.

SALON-DE-PROVENCE: BOUCHES DU RHÔNE

The birthplace of the 16th century astrologer, **Nostradamus** is now a museum.

SÈTE: HÉRAULT

Espace Brassens, 67 Boulevard Camille Blanc. Tel: 67.53.32.77. Dedicated to the life and work of popular musician Georges Brassens. Closed: Monday.

VALLAURIS: ALPES-MARITIME

Musée National Picasso, Place de la Libération. Tel: 93.64.18.05. Entirely devoted to the life and works of the artist, in particular, his work *La Guerre et la Paix* (War and Peace). Closed: Tuesday.

LIVE ARTS

There is a huge variety of live entertainment in France. In the summer, many major cities (and even small towns) present a programme of events, including music and drama festivals (often including street theatre and other outdoor performances). An annual programme listing all the major festivals and fêtes throughout the country is published each year and is available from the French Government Tourist Offices around the world.

Son-et-lumière displays are now a popular way of presenting historical events; these started at the châteaux in the Loire Valley and have spread to historic monuments all around the country. Performances are normally at around 9 or 10pm, with often several shows a night in July and August. For information and reservation contact the local tourist offices; a national guide of historical shows is published annually and is available from the Fédération Nationale des Fêtes et Spectacles Historiques, Hôtel de Ville, 60000 Beauvais. Tel: 44.79.40.09.

DIARY OF EVENTS

Listed here are brief details of the main annual events. For more specific information, contact the local tourist offices.

February: Paris Fashion Shows; Menton Lemon Festival; Nice Carnival.

March: Monte Carlo festival of contemporary film music.

May: Cannes Film Festival; Grasse international rose show; Mâcon wine fair; Nice Art Jonction International.

June: Strasbourg Music Festival; Touraine Music Festival and Tours international choral music competition.

July: Aix-en-Provence Festival; Anjou Festival; Antibes Jazz Festival; Avignon Festival; Bastille Day – celebrated throughout France on the 14th; Nice Jazz Festival Quimper – Fêtes de Cornouailles.

August: Antibes International fireworks festival; Lorient Celtic Festival; Marciac Jazz Festival; Menton International chamber music festival.

October: Dijon International Gastronomy fair; Paris Motor Show; Paris Jazz Festival.

November: Beaujolais Nouveau celebrations; Beaune Wine Auction.

December: Paris Boat Show.

NIGHTLIFE

Paris, of course, offers the best in nightlife, with a huge choice of venues and entertainment; in the provinces you need to be in the major towns. Many towns now organise festivals which run through the summer for the local people and tourists; also popular are *son-et-lumière* displays which started in the châteaux country of the Loire Valley but which are now performed at suitable sites all over France. Many performances are not only given in French but also in English and German. If you intend to take young children to such displays, note that they often start quite late, around 10 pm.

If you are staying on a farm or in a country area, you may be invited to join in local festivities. Almost every town and village has its own fête during the summer; these can range from a simple *boules* competition finished off with a dance, hosted by an enthusiastic (and sometimes excruciating) band, playing traditional music (or, if you're unlucky, ancient pop songs), to a full-blown carnival with street theatre, fireworks and sophisticated entertainment.

Information about nightclubs, cinemas and other entertainment in the provinces is available from the tourist offices, or at your hotel. Listed below are some of the most famous and popular nightspots in Paris.

CABARETS

The Crazy Horse, 12 Avenue George V. Tel: 47.23.32.32. Famous music hall, with two or three shows nightly.

Paradis Latin, 28 Rue du Cardinal Lemoine. Tel: 43.25.28.28. Built in 1889 by Eiffel, and reopened as a theatre in 1977.

La Nouvelle Eve, 25 Rue de La Fontaine, 75009 Paris. Tel: 48.78.37.96. Offers genuine Pigalle music hall, but without the vulgarity. It has a good dinner menu; show starts at 10.30pm.

NIGHT CLUBS

Régine's, 9 Rue de Ponthier, 75008 Paris. Tel: 43.59.21.13. The most famous night club in Paris, frequented by the rich and famous, and hard to get into (membership usually necessary). The disco is open 11.30pm until dawn; also a restaurant.

Les Bains, 7 Rue du Bourg-l'Abbé, 75003 Paris. Tel: 48.87.01.80. Trendy venue, converted from an old public baths. Disco from midnight until dawn, plus a restaurant.

Folies Pigalle, 11 Place Pigalle, 75018 Paris. Tel: 48.78.25.56. Fashionable disco in a district alive at night.

Le Balajo, 9 Rue de Lappe, 75011 Paris. Tel: 47.00.07.87. Old-fashioned hall attracting a chic crowd, near the Bastille.

JAZZ CLUBS

Caveau de la Huchette, 5 Rue de la Huchette, 75006 Paris. Tel: 43.26.65.05. Opens at 9.30pm.

New Morning, 7-9 Rue des Petites Ecuries, 75010 Paris. Tel: 45.23.51.41. Concerts generally start at around 9pm.

Le Montana, 28 Rue St Benoit, 75006 Paris. Tel: 45.48.93.08. Has performances every night; first drink costs FF110.

Le Sunset, 60 Rue des Lombards, 75001 Paris.Tel: 40.26.46.60. Dine in the ground-floor restaurant, then descend to the basement for the jazz at 10.30pm. Closed: Sunday.

CINEMA

Cinema programmes in Paris change every Wednesday. Films marked V.O. are screened in the original version (not dubbed into French). The following cinemas frequently show films in English.

Les Forums Cinemas Orient Express, Rue de l'Orient-Express, 75001 Paris. Tel: 42.33.42.26.

Gaumont Champs-Elysées, 66 Avenue des Champs-Elysées, 75008 Paris. Tel: 43.59.04.67.

Le Grand Rex, 1 Boulevard Poissonnière, 75002 Paris. Tel: 42.36.83.93. A single theatre with the largest screen in Paris.

UGC Biarritz, 79 Avenue des Champs-Elysées, 75008 Paris. Tel: 45.62.20.40.

THEATRE & OPERA

The Comédie Française and the Opéra Garnier are most famous for their classical productions, but there is a good choice of theatre, concerts, opera and ballet for all tastes to be enjoyed in the capital. Some of the major venues are listed below:

Comédie Française, 2 Rue Richelieu, 75001 Paris. Tel: 40.15.00.15.

Opéra Garnier, 8 Rue Scribe, 75009 Paris. Tel: 47.42.53.71.

Opéra Bastille, 2bis Place de la Bastille, 75012 Paris. Tel: 44.73.13.00.

Théâtre du Châtelet, 75001 Paris. Tel: 40.28.28.40.

Théâtre Madeleine, 19 Rue de Surène, 75008 Paris. Tel: 42.65.07.09.

Théâtre Palais Royal, 38 Rue Montpensier, 75001 Paris. Tel: 42.97.59.81.

SHOPPING

Over the past couple of decades, most major towns in France have made the sensible decision to keep town centres for small boutiques and individual shops. Many of these areas are pedestrianised and very attractive (although beware – some cars ignore the *voie piétonnée* signs). The large supermarkets, hypermarkets, furniture stores and do-it-yourself outlets are grouped on the outskirts of the town, mostly designated as a Centre Commercial.

These centres, although aesthetically quite unappealing, are fine for bulk shopping for self-catering or for finding a selection of wine to take home at reasonable prices. But for gifts and general window-shopping the town centres are far more interesting. It is here that you will find the individual souvenirs with a particularly local flavour, alongside the beautifully dressed windows of delicatessens and *patisseries*.

The heart of every French town is its market; they mostly start early in the morning and close at midday, although some bigger ones are open in the afternoon too. The French themselves usually visit early to get the best of the produce. Markets are a riot of colour and bustle; the best have all kinds of stalls from flowers to domestic animals (do not be deceived – these are for the pot). Local cheeses, honey, wine, pâté and other specialities are oftened offered for tasting to encourage browsers to buy.

There are more and more antique or second-hand (*brocante*) markets springing up around the provinces, as well as flea markets (*marchés aux puces*), which are also fun to look around – you may find a genuine bargain antique amongst all the old junk. The most famous of these, indeed the biggest flea market in the world, is Les Puces de St-Ouen at Porte de Clignancourt in Paris, it is open Saturday, Sunday and Monday from 6am to 7.30pm.

Look out for special fairs held all over the country at various times throughout the year, such as harvest times. Some of the most important are listed in the Diary of Events section (*see Culture Plus*); for others, check with the local tourist office for details.

The different regions of France are famous for particular products for example Breton lace, Limoges porcelain, Provençal fabrics, perfume from Grasse, to name but a few. Paris, naturally, has a fascinating range of shops from the fashion houses in the 8th arrondissement, particularly around the Faubourg St-Honoré, to the more affordable, but still chic department stores such as the famous Galeries Lafayette and Le Printemps (which boasts the largest perfume department in the world) both on the Boulevard Haussman, 75009 Paris.

The newest shopping arcade in Paris is Les Trois Quartiers at the Madeleine in the 8th arrondissement. Also worth a visit is the Forum des Halles, 75001 Paris, for a diverse selection of stores.

BUYING DIRECT

Around the country, you may be tempted by all the signs you see along the road for *dégustations* (tastings). Many wine producers and farmers will invite you to try their wines and other produce with an eye to selling you a case, or maybe, a few jars of pâté. This is a good way to try before you buy and can sometimes include a visit to a wine cellar. Sometimes farm produce is more expensive to buy this way than in the supermarkets – do not forget that it is home-produced and not factory-processed.

PRACTICAL INFORMATION

Food shops, especially bakers, tend to open early; boutiques and department stores open from 9am, but sometimes not until 10am. In most town centres, just about everything closes from noon until 2.30 or 3pm but in Paris and other major tourist areas, stores and some other shops stay open. Most shops close in the evening at 7pm. Out of town, the hypermarkets are usually open all day until 8 or even 9pm.

Most shops are closed Monday mornings and many all day. If you want to buy a picnic lunch, remember to buy everything you need before midday. Good delicatessens (*charcuterie*) have a selection of delicious ready-prepared dishes, which make picnicking a delight.

On most purchases, the price includes TVA (VAT or valued added tax). The base rate is currently 18.6 percent, but can be as high as 33 percent on luxury items. Foreign visitors can claim back TVA; worth doing if you spend more than FF2,400 (FF1,200 for non-EC residents) in one place. Some large stores and hypermarkets have information bureaux or welcome desks where you can obtain a refund form. This must be completed to show (with the goods purchased) to customs officers on leaving the country (pack the items separately for ease of access). Then mail the form back to the retailer who will refund the TVA in a month or two. Certain items purchased (e.g. antiques) may need special customs clearance.

If you have a complaint about any purchase, return it in the first place to the shop as soon as possible. In the case of any serious dispute, contact the Direction Départementale de la Concurrence et de la Consommation et de la Répression des Fraudes (see telephone directory for number).

CLOTHING

Most shops are happy to let you try clothes on (*essayer*) before buying. Children's clothes sizes, in particular, tend to be small compared with British and US age ranges. Hypermarkets are good for children's clothes at reasonable prices.

SPORTS

Sports facilities are first-rate throughout France. Most towns have swimming-pools and even small villages often have a tennis court, but you may have to become a temporary member to use it – enquire at the local tourist office or *mairie* (town hall) which will also provide details of all other local sporting activities.

It seems to be a quirk of the French tourist industry that they do not always take full advantage of their facilities. Even though there may be good weather in early summer and autumn, open-air swimming-pools and other venues often limit their seasons to the period of the school holidays.

Many companies offer sporting and activity holiday in France; these are often orgnaised too by the tourist offices in individual *départements*; write to the Services Loisirs Accueil at the destination of your choice (*see Useful Addresses*).

WATER SPORTS

All over France water sports can be enjoyed at a Base de Loisirs. These centres, found not just on the coast, but inland on lakes and quiet river stretches, offer various leisure activities – not just water sports. They usually have a café or bar, maybe even a restaurant, as well as picnic areas.

Many such centres offer tuition in the various sports available – canoeing, wind-surfing etc; fees are usually charged at an hourly or half-hourly rate. Where boating and windsurfing is permitted, equipment is often available for hire, or you may take your own.

The following addresses are the central offices of the various water sports organisations in France; they will supply addresses of regional members and clubs.

Canoeing: Canoë-Kayak de France, 47 Quai Ferber, 94360 Bry-sur-Marne. Tel: (1) 48.81.54.26.

Sailing: Fédération Française de Voile, 55 Avenue Kléber, 75784 Paris Cedex 16. Tel: (1) 45.53.68.00.

Rowing: Fédération Française des Sociétés d'Aviron, 7 Rue Lafayette, 75009 Paris. Tel: (1) 48.74.43.77.

Swimming: Fédération Française de Natation, 148 Avenue Gambetta, 75020 Paris. Tel: (1) 40.31.17.70.

White-water swimming: Fédération Française de Nage en Eau Vive, 229 Avenue Jean-Jaurès, 92140 Clamart. Tel: (1) 40.95.03.49.

Rafting: Société AN Rafting, 15 Rue Charles-et-René-Auffray, 92110 Clichy. Tel: (1) 47.37.08.77.

Water skiing: Fédération Française de Ski Nautique, 16 Rue Clément-Marot, 75008 Paris. Tel: (1) 47.20.05.00.

Underwater sports: Fédération Française d'Etudes et de Sports Sous-Marins, 24 Quai de Rive-Neuve, 13007 Marseille. Tel: 91.33.99.31.

ANGLING

With its wealth of waterways and lakes, fishing is a popular activity in France. It is possible to book fishing holidays (a weekend or longer) with accommodation, try the Loisirs Accueil services (*see Useful Addresses*). A permit (*permis*) is usually required for coarse fishing; enquire at local tourist offices. Sea fishing trips are widely available on the coast – look out for sign boards advertising trips on the quayside.

The following are the national organisations which promote all kinds of fishing:

Angling: Fédération Française de Pêche au Coup, 20 Rue Emile-Zola, 93120 La Courneuve. Tel: (1) 48.34.45.01.

Sea Fishing: Fédération Française des Pêcheurs en Mer, 8 Rue de la Constellation, 40520 Biscarosse Plage. Tel: 58.78.20.96.

Sport Fishing: Fédération Française des Groupements de Pecheurs Sportifs, 5 Rue Jules-Verne, 69740 Genas. Tel: 72.36.30.33.

CYCLING

To take your own *vélo* to France is easy – they are carried free on most ferries and trains – or you can rent cycles for a reasonable cost; main railway stations usually have them for hire and you can often arrange to pick up at one station and leave the bike at a distant one. Alternatively, try bicycle retailers/repairers or ask at the local tourist office.

Some youth hostels rent cycles and also arrange tours with accommodation in hostels or under canvas. For more information, contact the YHA (*see Where to Stay*). French Routes, 1 Mill Green Cottages, Newbridge, Yarmouth, Isle of Wight, PO41 0TZ, UK, tel: 0983-78392, offers a route planning service for individual tourists and will also arrange bicycle hire and accommodation.

Cycling holidays are offered by various organisations; with campsite or hotel accommodation with the advantage that your luggage is often transported for you to your next destination. Some operators are listed below:

Fédération Française de Cyclotourisme, 8 Rue Jean-Narie-Jégo, 75013 Paris. Tel: (1) 45.80.30.21. More than 60 guided tours offered each year, all over France, 60–100 km (40–60 miles) per day. Bring your own bike.

Fédération Française de Cyclisme, Bâtiment Jean-Monnet, 5 Rue de Rome, 95561 Rosny-Sous-Bois. Tel: (1) 49.35.69.00.

Bicyclub SA, 8 Place de la Porte-Champerret, 75017 Paris. Tel: (1) 47.66.55.92.

Vélo-Relais/Hexaclub, 38 Rue du Mesnil, 78730 St-Arnoult-en-Yvelines. Tel: (1) 30.59.34.09.

Cresta Holidays, 32 Victoria Street, Altrincham, Cheshire WA14 1ET. Tel: 061-927 7000.

Cyclists Touring Club, Cotterell House, 69 Meadrow, Godalming, Surrey GU7 3HS. Tel: 0483-417217.

Headwater Holidays, 146 London Road, Northwich CS9 5HH. Tel: 0606-48699. Hotel accommodation, and your luggage transported.

Susi Madron's Cycling for Softies, Lloyds House, 22 Lloyd Street, Manchester M2 5WA. Tel: 061 834 6800. Well-established company with a good reputation offering holidays with good hotel accommodation in many parts of France.

It is advisable to take out insurance before you go. Obviously the normal rules of the road apply to cyclists (*see Getting Around*). Advice and information can be obtained from The Touring Department of the Cyclists Touring Club (*address above*). Their service to members includes competitive cycle and travel insurance, free detailed touring itineraries and general information sheets about France. The club's French counterpart, Fédération Française de Cyclotourisme (*see above*) offers a similar service. Rob Hunter's book *Cycle Touring in France* is also useful as a handbook.

Such is the French passion for cycling that local clubs organise many trips lasting a day or more and visitors are often more than welcome to join in. Weekend or longer tours are organised by the national Bicyclub (*address above*). Lists of clubs and events are also organised by local members of the Fédération Française de Cyclotourisme (*address above*), write to them for regional or departmental offices. They also produce leaflets giving suggested cycle tours for independent travellers, ranging from easy terrain to very hard going for the more experienced cyclist, with details of accommodation, cycle repairers and other facilities en route.

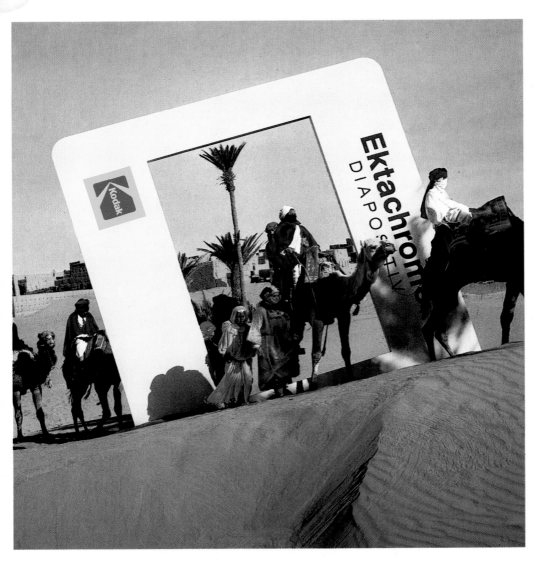

THE COLOUR OF LIFE.

A holiday may last just a week or so, but the memories of those happy, colourful days will last forever, because together you and Kodak Ektachrome films will capture, as large as life, the wondrous sights, the breathtaking scenery and the magical moments. For you to relive over and over again.

The Kodak Ektachrome range of slide films offers a choice of light source, speed and colour rendition and features extremely fine grain, very high sharpness and high resolving power.

Take home the real colour of life with Kodak Ektachrome films.

LIKE THIS?

OR LIKE THIS?

A KODAK FUN PANORAMIC CAMERA BROADENS YOUR VIEW

The holiday you and your camera have been looking forward to all year; and a stunning panoramic view appears. "Fabulous", you think to yourself, "must take that one".

Unfortunately, your lens is just not wide enough. And three-in-a-row is a poor substitute.

That's when you take out your pocket-size, 'single use' Kodak Fun Panoramic Camera. A film and a camera, all in one, and it works miracles. You won't need to focus, you don't need special lenses. Just aim, click and... it's all yours. The total picture.

You take twelve panoramic pictures with one Kodak Fun Panoramic Camera. Then put the camera in for developing and printing.

Each print is 25 by 9 centimetres. Excellent depth of field. True Kodak Gold colours.

The Kodak Fun Panoramic Camera itself goes back to the factory, to be recycled. So that others too can capture one of those spectacular phoooooooooootooooooooooos.

MOUNTAIN BIKING

This sport has really taken off in recent years, particularly among the French, many of whom are already dedicated cyclists. Many of the organisations listed under *Cycling* offer mountain bike holidays, or contact the Association Française de Mountain Bike, 3 Villa des Sablons, 92200 Neuilly-sur-Seine. Tel: (1) 46.24.48.53.

Mountain bikes (known in French as VTT – *Vélo Tout Terrain*) and protective gear can be hired locally, try the local tourist office, or cycle shops/repairers.

HORSE RIDING

All riding holidays in France come under the umbrella of the Délégation Nationale au Tourimse Equestre de la Fédération Française d'Equitation (ANTE) based at Ile Saint-Germain, 170 Quai de Stalingrad, 92130 Issy-les-Moulineaux. Tel: (1) 40.93.52.88. This organisation embraces 1,200 specialist riding centres; contact them for regional or local branches who can also provide information about marked bridleways, maps, riding centres and insurance.

Treks lasting a day or more and also longer holidays on horseback can be organised locally. Information can be obtained from the organisations mentioned above, from tourist offices and from the Loisirs Accueil services of the individual *départements* (*see Useful Addresses*).

Local tourist offices will provide details of stables, if you simply wish to hire a horse by the hour or day. Expect to pay about FF75 per hour/FF350 per day.

GOLF

In recent years, golf has caught on in a big way in France and the Regional Tourist Boards have joined forces with the French Golf Federation in an effort to promote it better and set standards. The resulting organisation, France Golf International, embraces over 100 golf courses around the country which must provide a certain standard of facilities available to all. They require courses to have weekend reservation systems, and have multilingual staff on hand.

Information can be obtained from the individual Comité Régional au Tourisme (*see Useful Addresses*). Expect to pay around FF180 for a day's play.

WINTER & MOUNTAIN SPORTS

From the famous resorts, such as La Clusaz and Chamonix, founded early this century, to the state of the art facilities provided for the 1992 Olympics at Albertville, France offers plenty of scope for skiers of all abilities and all ages. The newest resorts at Valmorel and Valfréjus make an effort to keep the activity as environmentally-friendly as possible.

Ski France is the major winter sports body in France, grouping over 100 resorts and providing accommodation reservations. They also offer a 24-hour telephone ski bulletin from mid-December to mid-April, tel: 42.66.64.28. For information, contact them at 61 Boulevard Haussman, 76008 Paris. Another organisation represents 15 of France's most prestigious ski resorts, which are especially equipped to offer a wide range of holidays to an international clientele. France Ski International (FSI) is based at 2 Rue Esnault-Pelterie, Aérogare des Invalides, 75007 Paris, tel: (1) 43.23.94.96.

Other useful addresses are the Fédération Française de Ski, 50 Rue des Marquistas, 74000 Annecy, tel: 50.51.40.34; and Ecoles de Ski Français, 6 Allée des Mitaillères, 38240 Meylan, tel: 76.90.67.36 for information about skiing lessons and courses.

The most famous and popular ski resorts are to be found in the Alps, but the sport is also available in the Pyrenees and the Massif Central. The peak period for winter sports is February, although in some resorts it is still possible to ski in May. There are now several variations on traditional skiing, which are practised at many resorts. Cross-country skiing has been popular for some years now and marked trails are checked every day. Monoskiing was started in Chamonix and has quickly spread to other resorts, while snowsurfing is a relatively new sport, particularly attractive to inexperienced skiers.

Other activities which are becoming increasingly popular are snowshoe walking, which requires no particular skills, climbing frozen waterfalls (which does), and dog-sleigh driving, which is now recognised as a competitive sport. More information on these are available from tourist offices.

Mountain climbing, caving and potholing are all practised in France, and organisations exist for the promotion of the sports and dissemination of information to enthusiasts:

Mountain climbing: Fédération Française de la Montagne et de l'Escalade, 20 bis Rue de la Boétie, 75008 Paris. Tel: (1) 47.42.39.80.

Sherpa Expeditions, 131a Heston Road, Hounslow, Middlesex TW5 0RD, tel: 081-577 2717 are specialists in mountain walking holidays. They also have agents abroad:

US: Himalayan Travel, 112 Prospect Street, 2nd Floor, Stamford CT 06901, tel: 800-225 2380.
Australia: Outdoor Travel PTY Ltd, 1st Floor, 55 Hardware Street, Melbourne, Victoria 3000, tel: 03-670 7252
New Zealand: Venture Treks, PO Box 37610, 164 Parnell Road, Auckland, tel: 09-799 855.
Potholing: Fédération Française de Spéléologie, 130 Rue St-Mur, 75011 Paris. Tel: (1) 43.57.56.54.

Details of sporting events can be obtained from the nearest tourist office, or from national organisers of events. Some of the better known competitive events are the Tour de France, a 22-day, 2,500-mile (4,000-km) bicycle race in July; the 24-hour car race at Le Mans in June; the Monaco Grand Prix in May and the Monte Carlo Motor Rally in January. May in Paris sees the International Tennis Championships and the Prix de Diane Hermès the French Derby, is held at Chantilly in June.

SPECIAL INFORMATION

DOING BUSINESS

Business travel now accounts for roughly a third of French tourism revenue. This important market has lead to the creation of a special Conference and Incentive Department in the French Government Tourist Office in both London and New York (*see Useful Addresses*) to deal solely with business travel enquiries. They will help organise hotels, conference centres and incentive deals for any group, large or small.

Paris is a world leader for conferences, exhibitions and trade fairs and the capital's facilities are impressive; many châteaux now offer luxurious accommodation for smaller gatherings – and you can even organise a congress at Euro Disney.

For anyone wishing to put on a major business event in Paris, the first line of contact is the **Bureau des Congrès de Paris**, Office du Tourisme, 127 Champs-Elysées, 75008 Paris. Tel: (1) 47.20.60.20.

There are several tour operators who specialise in conference organisation. For example:
Convergences, 120 Avenue Gambetta, 75020 Paris. Tel: (1) 43.64.77.77, fax: (1) 40.31.01.65.
SOCFI, 14 Rue Mandar, 75002 Paris. Tel: (1) 42.33.89.94, fax: (1) 40.26.04.44.
Voyages Hamelin, 31 Rue Bergère, 75009 Paris. Tel: (1) 48.01.86.00, fax: 40.22.94.12.
Wagons Lits Tourisme, 40 Rue Kléber, BP 244, 92307 Levallois Perret. Tel: 47.59.47.43.

For general information about business travel and facilities around the country contact the regional tourist offices (*see Useful Addresses*). Another good source of business information and local assistance, are the Chambres de Commerce et d'Industrie in the individual *départements*. Here you can obtain details about local companies, assistance with the technicalities of export and import, interpretation/translation agencies and conference centres – indeed, most chambers of commerce have conference facilities of some kind themselves.

There is also a French Chamber of Commerce in London (tel: 071-225 5250) which exists to promote business between the two countries, and at the same address is French Trade Exhibitions: 2nd floor, Knightsbridge House, 197 Knightsbridge, London SW7 1RB. Tel: 071-225 5566.

A calendar of trade fairs all over France is published every year and this is available in August, for the following year, from the Chambre de Commerce et d'Industrie de Paris, 16 Rue Chateaubriand, 75008 Paris.

GAYS

The best source of information for Gays is the national *Gai Pied Guide* (published in French, sold in the UK). If you need urgent help or information, try the Paris-based gay switchboard (SOS Homosexualité), tel: (1) 46.27.49.36, where there are English-speakers; note, however, that this service is only active Wednesday and Friday from 6pm until midnight.

TRAVELLERS WITH SPECIAL NEEDS

Most less able travellers will be keen to book accommodation in advance rather than arriving "on spec". Most of the official list of hotels (available from the FGTO or the regional tourist office – *see Useful Addresses*) include a symbol to denote wheelchair access, but it is always advisable to check directly with the chosen hotel as to exactly what facilities are available.

Balladins is a chain of newly-built, budget-priced hotels throughout France which all have at least one room designed for disabled guests and restaurants and all other public areas are accessible. For a complete list contact Hotels Balladins, 20 Rue du Pont des Halles, 94656 Rungis Cedex. Tel: 49.78.24.00, fax: 46.86.41.44.

A guide, *Où Ferons Nous Etape?* (published 1990 in French only), lists accommodation throughout France suitable for the disabled, including wheelchair users, but again if you have specific needs you would need to double-check when booking. It is available (for FF40 by post) from the **Association des Paralysés de France**, Service Information, 17 boulevard August Blanqui, 75013 Paris. Tel: (1) 45.80.82.40. This organisation may also be able to deal direct with specific enquiries and can provide addresses of their branches throughout France.

The **Royal Association for Disability and Rehabilitation** (RADAR), 25 Mortimer Street, London WIN 8AB, tel: 071-637 5400, has some useful information for tourists, including a guide book, *Holidays and Travel Abroad* (£3 including postage).

This is a general country by country guide and provides information about France as a whole, including hotel chains offering suitable accommodation, and tour operators offering specialist holidays. In particular, try Village Vacances Famille, Tour Maine Montparnasse, 33 Avenue du Maine, 75755 Paris Cedex 15, tel: 45.38.28.28, and Renouveau, 2 Rue Trésorie, 73023 Chambéry cedex, tel: 79.75.75.39, who both run holiday villages especially adapted to visitors with special needs.

France's sister organisation to RADAR, the **Comité National Français de Liaison pour la Réadaption des Handicapés** (CNFLRH), is based at 38 Boulevard Raspail, 75007 Paris. Tel: (1) 45.48.90.13. They offer a good information service for visitors with special needs to France and publish a useful free guide in French/English entitled *Touristes Quand Même* which gives information about access at airports, stations, tourist sites, restaurants, etc. as well as where to hire wheelchairs and other aids.

Specifically for young people, the **Centre d'Information et de Documentation Jeunesse**, 101 quai Branly, 75740 Paris Cedex 15 provides information on services for young less able travellers. It publishes *Vacances pour Personnes Handicapées* and annual leaflets on acitivity and sports holidays for young disabled people.

The **Comité de Liaison pour le transport des personnes handicapées**, Conseil National des Transports, 34 Avenue Marceau, 75009 Paris publishes a booklet called *Guide des Transport à l'usage des Personnes à Mobilité Réduite*. This gives brief information on the accessibility and arrangements for less able passengers on all forms of public transport and contacts for special transport schemes throughout France.

From the UK, **Brittany Ferries** offers free passage for cars of registered disabled travellers on all their routes (except Plymouth–Santander). More information about air and sea travel is also available in a guide entitled *Door-to-Door*. For a free copy write to Department of Transport, Door-to-Door Guide, Freepost, Victoria Road, South Ruislip, Middlesex HA4 0NZ who can also provide copies on cassette for the vision-impaired.

In the US, the following organisations offer services to disabled travellers:
Travel Information Service, Moss Rehabilitation Hospital, 1200 West Tabor Rd., Philadelphia, PA 19141-3099, tel: (215) 329 5715 ext: 2233 – has general information for would-be travellers.
Society for the Advancement of Travel for the Handicapped (SATH). 26 Court Street, Brooklyn, New York 11242, tel: (718) 858 5483 – offers advice and assistance in travel matters.
Evergreen Travel Service, 19505 44th Avenue West, Lynnwood, WA 98036, tel: (206) 776 1184 – private company with over 30 years experience of organising holidays for the disabled.
Accessible Journeys, 412 South 45th Street, Philadelphia, PA 19104, tel: (215) 747 0171 – offers tours using wheelchair accessible transport in Europe.
Flying Wheels Travel Inc, PO Box 383, 143 West Bridge Street, Owatonna MN 55060, tel: (507) 451 5005 – has been organising worldwide travel for over 20 years.

In Canada, the following organisations may be of help:
Canadian Rehabilitation Council for the Disabled, 45 Sheppard Avenue E, Toronto, Ontario, M2N 5W9, tel: (416) 250 7490 – national organisation producing some material relating to travel.
Association for Specialised Services Involving Special Travellers, c/o ACTA, Suite 1106, 75 Albert Street, Ottawa, Ontario K1P 5E7. Tel: (613) 238 1361.

CHILDREN

In France generally, children are treated as people, not just nuisances. It is pleasant to be able to take them into restaurants (even in the evening) without heads being turned in horror at the invasion. It has to be said, however, that French children, being accustomed to eating out from an early age, are on the whole well behaved in restaurants, so it helps if one's own offspring are able to understand that they can't run wild.

Many restaurants offer a children's menu; if not they will often split a *prix-fixe* menu between two children. If travelling with very young children, you may find it practical to order nothing specific at all for them but just to request an extra plate and give them tasty morsels to try from your own dish. It is a good introduction to foreign food for them, without too much waste. French meals are generally generous enough (*nouvelle cuisine* excepted) to allow you to do this without going hungry yourself, and you are unlikely to encounter any hostility from *le patron* (or *la patronne*). Another option is to order a single simple, inexpensive dish from the *à la carte* menu, such as an omelette, which most childen will happily eat.

Most hotels have family rooms so children do not have to be separated from parents and a cot (*lit bébé*) can often be provided for a small supplement, although it is a good idea to check availability if booking in advance.

Many of the activities listed in the Things to Do section are suitable for, or aimed specifically at children. It is also possible to organise activities for unaccompanied children, including stays in *gîtes d'enfants* or on farms, or activity holidays. Naturally, children would only be happy to be left if they have a reasonable command of French, but it is quite common in France, as in the United States, for children to spend at least a part of their summer vacation at a holiday centre.

For more information, contact the Loisirs Accueil service in individual *départements* (*see Useful Addresses*). Loisirs de France Jeunes is a national organisation which offers good-value activity holidays (including winter sports) for young people. Contact them at 30 Rue Godot de Mauroy, 75009 Paris. Tel: (1) 47.42.51.81.

STUDENTS & YOUNG PEOPLE

Students and young people under the age of 26 can benefit from cut-price travel to France and rail cards for getting around the country – for details see *Getting There*.

If you wish to have a prolonged stay in the region, it may be worth finding out about an exchange visit or study holiday. Several organisations exist to provide information or arrange such visits.

In the UK, the **Central Bureau for Educational Visits and Exchanges**, Seymour Mews House, Seymour Mews, London WlH 9PE, tel: 071-486 5101, produces three books; *Working Holidays* (opportunities in France are limited; the grape harvest is still a big draw for young people and employment opportunities are listed here); *Home from Home* (a wealth of useful information about staying with a French family) and *Study Holidays* (details of language courses). Another option, for those with decent French is to approach one of the UK-based camping holiday operators who often employ students as site courriers during the vacation (see *Where to Stay* for companies).

Organisations in the US include:
Council on International Educational Exchange (CIEE), 205 E. 42nd Street, New York, NY 10017, tel: (212) 661 1414 – a wide range of services, including travel.
American Council for International Studies Inc., 19 Bay State Road, Bost, Mass. 02215. Tel: (617) 236 2051.
Youth for Understanding International Exchange, 3501 Newark Street, NW, Washington DC 20016. Tel: (202) 966 6800.

Volunteers are welcome at the workcamps organised on several on the archeological and cultural sites in Burgundy (mainly during the summer). For information contact the Direction Régionale des Affaires Culturelles, 39 Rue Vannerie, 21000 Dijon. Tel: 80.67.22.23. Although unpaid, this is a good way of meeting other young people of all nationalities and an opportunity to learn the language.

There many several French tour operators which organise study tours and language courses, some of the more reputable are listed here:
Accueil des Jeunes en France, 12 Rue des Barres, 75004 Paris. Tel: (1) 42.72.72.09. Offers French study programmes, inexpensive accommodation (or with a family), and tours for individuals or groups.
Centre des Echanges Internationaux, 104 Rue de Vaugirard, 75006 Paris. Tel: (1) 45.49.26.25. Sporting and cultural holidays and educational tours for 15 to 30-year-olds. Non-profit making organisation.

Séjours Internationaux Linguistiques et Culturels (SILC), 32 Remparts-de l'Est, 16002 Angoulême. Tel: 45.95.83.56.
Union National des Organisations de Séjours Linguistiques (UNOSEL), 293/295 Rue de Vaugirard, 75015 Paris. Tel: (1) 42.50.44.99.

A complete list of private language schools is obtainable from regional tourist offices (*see Useful Addresses*). **Souffle** is an organisation created in 1991 which embraces 11 centres which specialise in teaching French as a foreign language, and have all signed a quality charter. Contact Souffle at 43 Rue Cécille-Dunant, 92140 Clamart. Tel: (1) 46.45.90.40.

Once in France, students will find a valid student identity card is useful in obtaining discounts on all sorts of activities. including admission to museums and galleries, cinema, theatre, etc. If you do not happen to have your ID card with you reductions may sometimes be allowed by proving your status with a passport.

The **Centre d'Information et Documentation de Jeunesse** (CIDJ), based at 101 Quai Branly, 75740 Paris, tel: (1) 45.67.35.85, is a national organisation which disseminates information pertaining to youth and student activities. The noticeboard in the Paris office is a mine of useful information regarding accommodation and events.

For individual holidays, the cheapest way to stay is generally under canvas, or in a hostel (expect to pay around FF55 a night without meals).

LANGUAGE

French, the native language of more than 90 million people and the acquired language of another 180 million, is one of the romance languages, descended from the Vulgar (popular) Latin spoken by the Roman conquerors of the Celtic Gaul. It still carries the reputation of being the cultured language of the world and, for what it's worth, the most beautiful. People often tell stories about the impatience of the French toward foreigners not blessed with fluency in their language. In general, however, if you try to communicate, they will too.

Since much of the vocabulary of English is related to French, thanks to the Norman Conquest of 1066, travellers will recognise many helpful cognates. You should be aware, however, of "false friends", as misleading cognates are termed. There are more false friends than true, it often seems.

Everyone in France can speak French, but

THE KODAK GOLD GUIDE TO BETTER PICTURES.

Good photography is not difficult. Use these practical hints and Kodak Gold II Film: then notice the improvement.

Move in close. Get close enough to capture only the important elements.

Frame your Pictures. Look out for natural frames such as archways or tree branches to add an interesting foreground. Frames help create a sensation of depth and direct attention into the picture.

One centre of interest. Ensure you have one focus of interest and avoid distracting features that can confuse the viewer.

Use leading lines. Leading lines direct attention to your subject i.e. – a stream, a fence, a pathway; or the less obvious such as light beams or shadows.

Maintain activity. Pictures are more appealing if the subject is involved in some natural action.

Keep within the flash range. Ensure subject is within flash range for your camera (generally 4 metres). With groups make sure everyone is the same distance from the camera to receive the same amount of light.

Check the light direction. People tend to squint in bright direct light. Light from the side creates highlights and shadows that reveal texture and help to show the shapes of the subject. If shooting into direct sunlight fill-in flash can be effective to light the subject from the front.

CHOOSING YOUR KODAK GOLD II FILM.

Choosing the correct speed of colour print film for the type of photographs you will be taking is essential to achieve the best colourful results.

Basically the more intricate your needs in terms of capturing speed or low-light situations the higher speed film you require.

Kodak Gold II 100. Use in bright outdoor light or indoors with electronic flash. Fine grain, ideal for enlargements and close-ups. Ideal for beaches, snow scenes and posed shots.

Kodak Gold II 200. A multipurpose film for general lighting conditions and slow to moderate action. Recommended for automatic 35mm cameras. Ideal for walks, bike rides and parties.

Kodak Gold II 400. Provides the best colour accuracy as well as the richest, most saturated colours of any 400 speed film. Outstanding flash-taking capabilities for low-light and fast-action situations; excellent exposure latitude. Ideal for outdoor or well-lit indoor sports, stage shows or sunsets.

INSIGHT GUIDES

COLORSET NUMBERS

You'll find the colorset number on the spine of each Insight Guide.

regional languages still exist in Brittany (Breton), Alsace (Alsatian), the western Pyrénées (Basque), and the eastern Pyrénées (Catalan). The three former tongues are not Romance languages; you will hear strains of both Spanish and French in the later.

A list of helpful terms follows.

GENERAL

hello	bonjour, bonsoir
thank you	merci
you're welcome	de rien
please	s'il vous plaît
good-bye	au revoir
the airport	l'aéroport
the bank	la banque
customs	la douane
the police station	la gendarmerie
the bathroom	la salle de bains/les toilettes
the train station	la gare
the metro stop	la station de métro
the post office	le bureau de poste
the embassy	l' ambassade
Help!	Au secours!
Where is, are…?	Où est, sont…?
What is it?	Qu'est-ce que c'est?
When?	Quand?
How much is it?	C'est combien?
Do you have?	Avez-vous..?
What time is it?	Quelle heure est-il?
the hospital	l'hôpital
the doctor	le médecin
the nurse	l'infirmière
I am sick	Je suis malade
medicine	les médicaments
to dial a number	composer un numéro
to call collect	téléphoner en P.C.V.
to make a person-to-person call	
	téléphoner avec préavis

EATING OUT

breakfast	le petit déjeuner
lunch	le déjeuner
dinner	le dîner
a cup	une tasse
a glass	un verre
a plate	une assiette
a napkin	une serviette
a fork	une fourchette
a knife	un couteau
a spoon	une cuillère
the bill	l'addition
the waiter	le garçon
the waitress	la serveuse

DRINKS

drinks	les boissons
coffee	du café
coffee with milk	du café au lait
tea	du thé
beer	une bière
wine	du vin
mineral water	de l'eau minérale
juice	du jus

FRUIT, NUT

fruit and nuts	les fruits et les noix
pineapple	ananas
cherries	cerises
strawberries	fraises
raspberries	framboises
chestnuts	marrons
hazel nuts	noisettes
grapefruit	pamplemousse
grapes	raisins

MEAT

meat	viande
lamb	agneau
steak	bifteck
beef	boeuf
pork cold cuts	charcuterie
rump steak	châteaubriand
chop	côte
rib steak	entrecôte
leg of lamb	gigot d'agneau
wild game	gibier
ham	jambon
rabbit	lapin
bacon	lard
mutton	mouton
pork	porc
roast beef	rosbif
sausages	saucisse
veal	veau
goose	oie
guinea hen	pintade
chicken	coq
pheasant	faisan
duck	canard
duckling	caneton
young cock	poulet
eel	anguille
mackerel	maquereau
cod	morue
bass	perche
salmon	saumon
trout	truite
shrimp	crevettes
crawfish	écrevisses
snails	escargots
mixed shellfish	fruits de mer
frogs' legs	grenouilles
lobster	homard
oysters	huîtres
spiny rock lobster	langouste
mussels	moules

clams	*palourdes*
brains	*cervelles*
liver	*foie*
tongue	*langue*
kidney	*rognon*

VEGETABLES

vegetables	*légumes*
mushrooms	*champignons*
cabbage	*chou*
cauliflower	*chou-fleur*
green beans	*haricots verts*
turnip	*navet*
potato	*pomme de terre*

DAIRY PRODUCTS, DESSERTS

dairy products	*produits laitiers*
butter	*beurre*
cheese	*fromage*
egg	*oeuf*
fritters	*beignets*
cake	*gâteau*
ice cream	*glace*
pie	*tarte*

USEFUL ADDRESSES

IN FRANCE

Air France, 119 Champs Elysées, 75384 Cedex 08, tel: 1-43.23.81.81; Central Reservation: tel: 1-45.35.61.61.

Maison de la France, 8 Avenue de l'Opéra, 75001 Paris. Tel: 1-42.96.10.23.

Office National des Forêts (Forestry Commission), 217 Rue Grande, 77300 Fontainebleau. Tel: (1) 64.22.18.07.

Ligue Française pour la protection des Oiseaux (bird protection league), La Corderie Royale, BP 263, 17305 Rochefort.

REGIONAL TOURIST OFFICES

These are listed as CRT (Comité Regional du Tourisme) which is the most common title, and give the individual départements for which information may be obtained.

CRT d'Ile-de-France, 73-75 Rue Cambronne, 75015 Paris. Tel: (1) 45.67.89.41. For the départements of Seine-et-Marne, Yvelines, Essone, Hauts-de-Seine, Seine-St-Denis, Val-de-Marne and Val-d'Oise.

CRT Centre-Val de Loire, Conseil Régional, 9 Rue St-Pierre-Lentin, 45041 Orléans Cedex. Tel: 38.54.95.42. For Cher, Eure-et-Loir, Indre, Indre-et-Loire, Loir-et-Cher and Loiret.

CRT des Pays de la Loire, 2 Rue de la Loire, 44200 Nantes. Tel: 40.48.24.20. For Loire-Atlantique, Maine-et-Loire, Mayenne, Sarthe and Vendée.

CRT Poitou-Charentes, 2 Rue Sainte-Opportune, BP 56, 86002 Poitiers Cedex. Tel: 49.88.38.94; **Maison Poitou-Charentes**, 68-70 Rue du Cherche-Midi, 75006 Paris. Tel: (1) 42.22.83.74. For Charente, Charente-Maritime, Deux-Sèvres and Vienne.

CRT de Picardie, BP 2616, 8006 Amiens Cedex. Tel: 22.91.10.15. For Somme, Aisne and Oise.

CRT du Nord/Pas-de-Calais, 26 Place Rihour, 59800 Lille. Tel: 20.57.40.04. For Nord and Pas-de-Calais

CRT de Bretagne, 74 B Rue de Paris, 35069 Rennes Cedex. Tel: 99.28.44.30; **Maison de la Bretagne**, Centre Commercial Maine-Montparnasse, 17 Rue de l'Arrivée, 75737 Paris Cedex 14. Tel: (1) 42.79.07.07. For Côtes d'Armor (formerly Côtes du Nord), Finistère, Ille-et-Vilaine and Morbihan.

CRT de Normandie, 14 Rue Charles-Corbeau, 27000 Evreux. Tel: 32.33.79.00. For Calvados, Eure, Manche, Orne and Seine-Maritime.

CRT de Champagne-Ardenne, 5 Rue de Jéricho, 51037 Châlons-sur-Marne cedex. Tel: 26.64.35.92. For Ardennes, Aube, Marne and Haute-Marne

CRT de Lorraine, 1 Place Gabriel-Hocquard, BP 1004, 57036 Metz Cedex 1. Tel: 87.33.60.00. For Meurthe-et-Moselle, Moselle, Meuse and Vosges.

CRT d'Alsace, 35 Avenue de la Paix, 67000 Strasbourg. Tel: 88.25.68.67. For Bas-Rhin and Haut-Rhin.

CRT de Franche-Comté, 9 Rue de Pontarlier, 25000 Besançon. Tel: 81.83.50.47. For Doubs, Jura, Haute-Saône and Territoire-de-Belfort.

CRT de Bourgogne, Conseil Régional, 21035 Dijon Cedex. Tel: 80.50.10.20. For Côte-d'Or, Nièvre, Saône-et-Loire and Yonne.

CRT d'Auvergne, 43 Avenue Juline, BP 395, 63011 Clermont-Ferrand Cedex. Tel: 73.93.04.03. For Allier, Cantal, Haute-Loire and Puy-de-Dôme.

CRT du Limousin, Ensemble Administratif Régional, 27 Boulevard de la Corderie, 87031 Limoges Cedex. Tel: 55.45.18.80; **Maison du Limousin**, 30 Rue Caumartin, 75009 Paris. Tel: (1) 40.07.04.67. For Corrèze, Haute-Vienne and Creuse.

CRT Vallée du Rhône, 2 Place des Cordeliers, 69002 Lyon. Tel: 78.92.90.34. For Ain, Ardèche, Drôme, Loire and Rhône.

CRT Dauphiné Alpes Française, 14 Rue de la République, BP 227, 38019 Grenoble Cedex. Tel: 76.54.34.36. For Isère.

CRT Alpes Savoie Mont-Blanc, 9 Boulevard Wilson, 73100 Aix-les-Bains. Tel: 79.88.23.41. For Savoie and Haute-Savoie.

CRT Provence Alpes Côte-d'Azur, Immeuble CMCI, 2 Rue Henri-Barbusse, 13241 Marseille Cedex 01. Tel: 91.39.38.00. For Alpes de Haute Provence, Hautes Alpes, Bouches du Rhône, Var and Vaucluse.
CRT de Riviera/Côte d'Azur, 55 Promenade des Anglais, 06000 Nice. Tel: 93.44.50.59. For Alpes-Maritimes
CRT du Languedoc-Roussillon, 27 Rue de l'Aiguillerie, 34000 Montpellier. Tel: 67.22.81.00. For Aude, Gard, Hérault, Lozère and Pyrénées-Orientales.
CRT Midi-Pyrénées, 54 Boulevard de l'Embouchure, BP 2166, 31022 Toulouse Cedex. Tel: 61.13.55.55. For Ariège, Aveyron, Haute-Garonne, Gers, Lot, Hautes-Pyrénées, Tarn and Tarn-et-Garonne.
CRT Aquitaine, 21-23 Rue de Grassi, 33000 Bordeaux. Tel: 56.44.48.02. For Dordogne, Gironde, Landes, Lot-et-Garonne and Pyrénées-Atlantiques.

SERVICES RESERVATION LOISIRS ACCUEIL

Many *départements* now offer a central booking facility for accommodation (sometimes including *gîtes*) and for activity holidays and other services. Addresses are given below:

ILE-DE-FRANCE
Seine-et-Marne, 170 Avenue Henri-Barbusse, 77190 Dammarie-les-Lys. Tel: (1) 64.37.19.36.
Val d'Oise, TAVO, Hôtel du Département, 2 le Campus, 95032 Cergy-pontoise Cedex. Tel: (1) 34.25.32.52.

CENTRE – VAL-DE-LOIRE
Cher, 5 Rue de Séraucourt, 18000 Bourges. Tel: 48.67.01.38.
Eure-et-Loir, 19 Place des Epars, BP 67, 28002 Chartres Cedex. Tel: 37.21.37.22.
Indre-et-Loire, 38 Rue Augustin-Fresnel, BP 139, 37171 Chambray-les-Tours Cedex. Tel: 47.48.37.27.
Loir-et-Cher, 11 Place du Château, 41000 Blois. Tel: 54.78.55.50.
Loiret, 8 Rue d'Escures, 45000 Orléans. Tel: 38.62.04.88.

PAYS DE LA LOIRE
Loire-Atlantique, Maison du Tourisme, Place du Commerce, 44000 Nantes. Tel: 40.89.50.77.
Mayenne, 84 Avenue Robert-Buron, BP 343, 53018 Laval Cedex. Tel: 43.49.35.40.
Vendée, 8 Place Napoléon, 85000 La Roche-sur-Yon. Tel: 51.62.65.27.

POITOU-CHARENTES
Charente, Place Bouillaud, 16021 Angoulême. Tel: 45.69.79.19.
Vienne, 15 Rue Carno, BP 287, 86007 Poitiers Cedex. Tel: 49.88.89.79.

PICARDIE
Aisne, 1 Rue St-Martin, BP 116, 02005 Laon Cedex. Tel: 23.20.45.54.
Oise, 19 Rue Pierre Jacoby, BP 822, 60008 Beauvais Cedex. Tel: 44.45.82.12.

Somme, 21 Rue Ernest Cauvin, 80000 Amiens. Tel: 22.92.36.39.

NORD/PAS-DE-CALAIS
Nord, 15-17 Rue du Nouve-au Siècle, 59027 Lille Cedex. Tel: 20.57.00.61.
Pas-de-Calais, Antenne Départementale, Rue Désillé, 62200 Boulogne-sur-Mer. Tel: 21.83.32.59.

BRETAGNE
Côtes d'Armor (formerly Côtes du Nord), 29 Rue des Promenades, 22000 St-Brieuc. Tel: 96.62.72.15.
Ille-et-Vilaine, 1 Rue Martenot, BP 5093, 35061 Rennes Cedex. Tel: 99.02.97.41.
Morbihan, Hôtel du Département, BP 400, 56009 Vannes Cedex. Tel: 97.42.61.60.

CHAMPAGNE-ARDENNE
Ardennes, 18 Avenue Georges Corneau, 08000 Charleville-Mezières. Tel: 24.56.00.63.
Haute-Marne, BP 509, 52011 Chaumont. Tel: 25.32.87.70.

LORRAINE
Moselle, Hôtel du Département, BP 1096, 57036 Metz. Tel: 87.37.57.63.

ALSACE
Haut-Rhin, BP 371, 68007 Colmar Cedex. Tel: 89.20.10.62.

FRANCHE-COMTÉ
Doubs, 15 Avenue Edouard Droz, 25000 Besançon. Tel: 81.80.38.18.
L.A. Jura, Hôtel du Département, BP 652, 39021 Lons-le-Saunier. Tel: 84.24.57.70.
Haute-Saône/Belfort, 6 Rue des Bains, BP 117, 70002 Vesoul. Tel: 84.75.43.66.

BURGUNDY
Nièvre, 3 Rue du Sort, 58000 Nevers. Tel: 86.59.14.22, fax: 86.36.36.63.
Yonne, 1-2 Quai de la République, 89000 Auxerre Tel: 86.51.12.05.

AUVERGNE
Allier, 35 Rue de Bellecroix, BP 50, 03402 Yzeure Cedex. Tel: 70.46.00.11.
Cantal, 2 Place de la Préfecture, BP 75, 15017 Aurillac Cedex. Tel: 71.48.84.84.
Haute-Loire, 12 Boulevard Philippe Jourde, 43000 Le Puy-en-Velay. Tel: 71.09.26.05.

LIMOUSIN
Corrèze, Maison du Tourisme, Quai Baluze, 19000 Tulle. tel: 55.26.39.99.
Creuse, 43 Place Bonnyaud, 23000 Guéret. Tel: 55.52.87.50.
Haute-Vienne, 4 Place Denis Dussoubs, 87000 Limoges. Tel: 55.79.04.04.

RHÔNE-ALPES
Ardèche, 4 Cours du Palais, 07002 Privas Cedex. Tel: 75.64.04.66.
Loire-Forez, 5 Place Jean-Jaurès, 42021 St-Etienne Cedex 1. Tel: 77.33.15.39.
Savoie, 24 Boulevard de la Colonne, 73000 Chambéry. Tel: 79.85.01.09.

PROVENCE-ALPES-CÔTE-D'AZUR
Bouches-du-Rhône, Domaine du Vergon, 13370 Mallemort. Tel: 90.59.18.05.

Aude, 39 Boulevard Barbès, 11000 Carcassonne. tel: 68.47.09.06.

Lozère, 14 Rue Henri Bourrillon, BP 4, 48002 Mende Cedex. Tel: 66.65.60.01.

Pyrénées-Orientales, Quai de Lattre-de-Tassigny, 66000 Perpignan. Tel: 68.34.55.06.

MIDI-PYRÉNÉES

Ariège, BP 143, 09003 Foix. Tel: 61.02.73.29.

Aveyron, APATAR, Carrefour de l'Agriculture, 12026 Rodez Cedex 9. Tel: 65.73.77.33.

Haute-Garonne, 70 Boulevard Koenigs, 31300 Toulouse. Tel: 61.31.95.15.

Gers, Maison des Agriculteurs, Route de Tarbes, 32003 Auch Cedex. Tel: 62.63.16.55.

Lot, 53 Rue Bourseul, BP 162, 46003 Cahors Cedex. Tel: 65.22.19.20.

Hautes-Pyrénées, 6 Rue Eugène Tenot, 65000 Tarbes. Tel: 62.93.03.30.

Tarn, Hôtel du Département, 81014 Albi Cedex. Tel: 63.60.33.83.

Tarn-et-Garonne, Place du Maréchal Foch, 82000 Montauban. Tel: 63.63.31.40.

AQUITAINE

Dordogne-Périgord, 16 Rue Wilson, 24009 Périgueux Cedex. Tel: 53.53.44.35.

Gironde, 21 Cours de l'Intendance, 33000 Bordeaux. Tel: 56.52.61.40.

Lot-et-Garonne, 4 Rue André Chénier BP 304, 47008 Agen. Tel: 53.66.14.14.

IN THE UK & IRELAND

French Government Tourist Office, 178 Piccadilly, London W1V 0AL. Tel: 071-491 7622, fax: 071-493 6594.

Air France, 158 New Bond Street, London W1Y 0AY. Tel: 071-499 9511; 29-30 Dawson Street, Dublin 2. Tel: 77-8272 (reservations: tel: 77 8899).

Consulat Général de France, 21 Cromwell Road, London SW7 2DQ. Tel: 971-581 5292. Visa section: 6a Cromwell Place, London SW7. Tel: 071-823 9555.

Consulat Général de France, 11 Randolph Crescent, Edinburgh EH3 7TT. Tel: 031-225 7954.

French Embassy, 58 Knightsbridge, London SW1X 7JT. Tel: 071-201 1000. Commercial department: 21-24 Grosvenor Place, London SW1X 7HU. Tel: 071-235 7080. Cultural department: 23 Cromwell Road, London SW7. Tel: 071-581 5292.

Western Loire Tourist Office, 306 Upper Richmond Road West, London SW14 7JG. Tel: 081-392 1580.

Monaco Government Tourist and Convention Office, 3-18 Chelsea Garden Market, Chelsea Harbour, London SW10 0XE.

IN THE US & CANADA

Air France, 666, Fifth Avenue, New York, NY 10019, tel: 212-315 1122 (toll-free reservations: 1-800-237 2747); 8501 Wilshire Boulevard, Beverly Hills, Los Angeles, CA 90211, tel: 213-688 9220; 979 Ouest Boulevard de Maisonneuve, Montreal, Quebec H3A 1M4, tel: 514-284 2825; 151 Bloor Street West, Suite 600, Toronto, Ontario M5S 1S4, tel: 416-922 3344.

French Government Tourist Office, 610 Fifth Avenue, Suite 222, New York, NY 10020-2452, tel: 212-757 1125, fax: 212-247 6468; 9454 Wilshire Boulevard, Beverley Hills, Los Angeles, CA 90212-2967, tel: 213-272 2661; 645 North Michigan Avenue, Suite 630, Chicago, Illinois 60611-2836, tel: 312-337 6301; Cedar Maple Plaza, 2305 Cedar Springs Road, Suite 205, Dallas, Texas 75201, tel: 214-720 4010, fax: 214-702 0250.

Business Travel Division, 610 Fifth Avenue, Suite 222, New York, NY 10020-2452, tel: 212-757 1125, fax: 212-247 6464.

French Government Tourist Office, 1981 McGill College, Tour Esso, Suite 490, Montreal H3A 2W9, Quebec, tel: 514-288 4264, fax: 514-845 4868; 30 St Patrick Street, Suite 700, Toronto, M5T 3A3 Ontario, tel: 416-593 6427.

CONSULATES

In most cases, the nearest consular services are in Paris.

American Consulate, 2 Rue St-Florentin, 75001 Paris. Tel: (1) 42.96.14.88.

Australian Embassy, 4 Rue Jean-Rey, 75015 Paris. Tel: (1) 45.75.62.00.

British Consulate, 9 Avenue Hoche, 75008 Paris. Tel: (1) 42.66.91.42.

Canadian Consulate, 35 Avenue Montaigne, 75008 Paris. Tel: (1) 47.23.01.

Irish Embassy, 12 Avenue Foch, 75116 Paris. Tel: (1) 45.00.20.87.

German Consulate, 34 Avenue d'Ilena, 75016 paris. Tel: (1) 42.99.78.00.

Further Reading

ARTS & ARCHITECTURE

Art & Architecture in Medieval France, Whitney Stoddard. New York: Harper & Row, 1972.

Change. New Haven: Yale University Press, 1979. An illustrated architectural history of Paris.

France: A History in Art, by Bradley Smith. New York: Doubleday & Company, Inc. 1984. The history of France as seen through the eyes of artists who have portrayed it in their work.

The Cathedral Builders, by Jean Gimpel. New York: Harper & Row, 1984. First published in French, this work tells the story of the hands and minds behind the cathedrals of France.

HISTORY & SOCIAL COMMENTARY

A Concise History of France, by Douglas Johnson. New York: The Viking Press, 1971.

A Holiday History of France, by Ronald Hamilton. London: The Hogarth Press, 1985. An illustrated guide to history and architecture designed to be taken along on a trip.

A Traveller's History of France, by Robert Cole. London: The Windrush Press. Slim volume for background reading.

A Women's Life in the Court of the Sun King, by Duchesse d'Orléans. Introduction and translation by Elborg Forster. Baltimore: Johns Hopkins University Press, 1984. The Duchesse d'Orléans' letters reveal about the court-life of the 17th century.

France Today, by John Ardagh. London: Secker and Warburg. Up-to-date, hefty tome on modern France.

France Today, J.E. Flower (ed). New York: Methuen & Co., Ltd, 1983. Essays on contemporary France.

The French, by François Nourissier. New York: Alfred A Knopf, 1968. A witty treatment of his compatriots, translated from the French.

The French, by Theodore Zeldin. New York: Random House, 1983. A witty and insightful treatment of how the French live today.

The Identity of France, by Fernand Braudel. London: Fontana Press.

The Illustrated History of Paris and the Parisians, by Robert Laffont. New York: Doubleday & Co., 1958.

BELLES LETTRES

A Little Tour in France, by Henry James. New York: Farrar, Straus and Giroux, 1983. James originally published this account of his travels through France in 1885.

A Moveable Feast, by Ernest Hemingway. New York: Scribner, 1964. The life of the artist in Paris.

Mont-Saint-Michel and *Chartres*, by Henry Adams. New York: Doubleday and Co., Inc., 1959. Privately printed in 1905 and published in 1913, the book is an examination of architecture, literature and spirit.

Satori in Paris, by Jack Kerouac. New York: Grove Press, 1966. *Satori* is the Japanese word for sudden illumination. These are 10 days of travel à la Kerouac as he searches for the name Jean Louis Lebris de Kérouac in France.

Two Towns in Provence, by M.F.K. Fisher. New York: Vintage Books, 1983. A tribute to Aix-en-Provence and Marseille.

Village in the Vaucluse, by Laurence Wylie. 3rd ed. New York: Harper & Row, 1974. Country life in southern France.

FRENCH LITERATURE

Manuel des Etudes Litéraires Françaises, by P.G. Castex and P. Surer. 4 vol. Paris: Hachette, 1967.

The Oxford Companion to French Literature, by Sir Paul Harvey and J.E. Heseltine. Oxford: Oxford University Press, 1959.

Suggested classic works in order of publication:
La Chanson de Roland, c.1100.
Rabelais, *Gargantua and Pantagruel*, 1532–64.
Molière, *Tartuffe*, 1669.
Racine, *Phèdre*, 1677.
Voltaire, *Candide*, 1759.
Hugo, *Nôtre-Dame de Paris*, 1831.
Balzac, *Eugénie Gramdet*, 1833.
Flaubert, *Madame Bovary*, 1857.
Zola, *Germinal*, 1885.
Proust, *Du Côté de chez Swann*, 1913.
Camus, *La Peste*, 1957.

FOOD & WINE

The Food Lover's Guide to France, by Patricia Wells. London: Methuen. The best restaurants, food shops and markets in France, plus regional recipes.

French Regional Cooking, by Anne Willan. New York: William Morrow & Co., Inc., 1981. The founder of La Varenne's cooking school travels through the regions of France via her recipes. Both weights and measures are given for each recipe.

Mastering the Art of French Cooking, by Simone Beck and Julia Child. New York: Alfred A. Knopf, 1983.

The New Larousse Gastronomique, by Prosper

Montagné. New York: Crown Publishers, Inc, 1977.
Translated from the French; a complete encyclopedia of the food, cooking techniques and dishes of the world, especially of France.

Wine Atlas of France, by Hugh Johnson and Hubrecht Duijker. London: Mitchell Beazley. Well illustrated atlas, concentrating on wine and vineyards, but also supplementary information on history, architecture and culture.

The Wines and Winelands of France, Charles Pomerol (ed). London: Robertson McCarta. Guide to the wine regions of France, paying particular attention to the geology and science of the subject, plus itineraries and history.

OTHER INSIGHT GUIDES

Several other *Insight Guides* and *Insight Pocket Guides* highlight destinations in France:

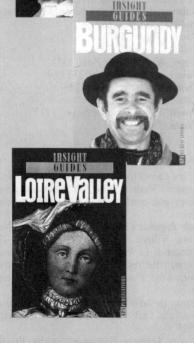
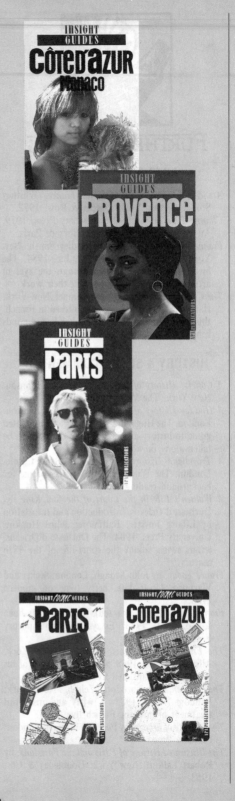

ART/PHOTO CREDITS

INDEX

A
B
C
E
G
H
I
J
a
b
c
d
e
f
g
h
i
j
k